COURT POETRY IN LATE MEDIEVAL ENGLAND AND SCOTLAND

This book explores the anxious and unstable relationship between court poetry and various forms of authority, political and cultural, in England and Scotland at the beginning of the sixteenth century. Through poems by Skelton, Dunbar, Douglas, Hawes, Lyndsay and Barclay, it examines the paths by which court poetry and its narrators seek multiple forms of legitimation: from royal and institutional sources, but also in the media of script and print. The book is the first for some time to treat English and Scottish material of its period together, and responds to European literary contexts, the dialogue between vernacular and Latin matter, and current critical theory. In so doing it claims that public and occasional writing evokes a counter-discourse in the secrecies and subversions of medieval love-fictions. The result is a poetry that queries and at times cancels the very authority to speak that it so proudly promotes.

ANTONY J. HASLER is Associate Professor in the Department of English, Saint Louis University.

CAMBRIDGE STUDIES IN MEDIEVAL LITERATURE

General editor
Alastair Minnis, *Yale University*

Editorial board
Zygmunt G. Barański, *University of Cambridge*
Christopher C. Baswell, *University of California, Los Angeles*
John Burrow, *University of Bristol*
Mary Carruthers, *New York University*
Rita Copeland, *University of Pennsylvania*
Simon Gaunt, *King's College, London*
Steven Kruger, *City University of New York*
Nigel Palmer, *University of Oxford*
Winthrop Wetherbee, *Cornell University*
Jocelyn Wogan-Browne, *Fordham University*

This series of critical books seeks to cover the whole area of literature written in the major medieval languages – the main European vernaculars, and medieval Latin and Greek – during the period *c.* 1100–1500. Its chief aim is to publish and stimulate fresh scholarship and criticism on medieval literature, special emphasis being placed on understanding major works of poetry, prose, and drama in relation to the contemporary culture and learning which fostered them.

Recent titles in the series
Andrew Cole *Literature and Heresy in the Age of Chaucer*
Suzanne M. Yeager *Jerusalem in Medieval Narrative*
Nicole R. Rice *Lay Piety and Religious Discipline in Middle English Literature*
D. H. Green *Women and Marriage in German Medieval Romance*
Peter Godman *Paradoxes of Conscience in the High Middle Ages: Abelard, Heloise and the Archpoet*
Edwin D. Craun *Ethics and Power in Medieval English Reformist Writing*
David Matthews *Writing to the King: Nation, Kingship, and Literature in England, 1250–1350*
Mary Carruthers (ed.) *Rhetoric Beyond Words: Delight and Persuasion in the Arts of the Middle Ages*
Katharine Breen *Imagining an English Reading Public, 1150–1400*
Antony J. Hasler *Court Poetry in Late Medieval England and Scotland: Allegories of Authority*

A complete list of titles in the series can be found at the end of the volume.

COURT POETRY IN LATE MEDIEVAL ENGLAND AND SCOTLAND

Allegories of Authority

ANTONY J. HASLER

CAMBRIDGE
UNIVERSITY PRESS

CAMBRIDGE UNIVERSITY PRESS
Cambridge, New York, Melbourne, Madrid, Cape Town,
Singapore, São Paulo, Delhi, Tokyo, Mexico City

Cambridge University Press
The Edinburgh Building, Cambridge CB2 8RU, UK

Published in the United States of America by Cambridge University Press, New York

www.cambridge.org
Information on this title: www.cambridge.org/9780521809573

© Antony J. Hasler 2011

This publication is in copyright. Subject to statutory exception
and to the provisions of relevant collective licensing agreements,
no reproduction of any part may take place without the written
permission of Cambridge University Press.

First published 2011

Printed in the United Kingdom at the University Press, Cambridge

A catalogue record for this publication is available from the British Library

Library of Congress Cataloguing in Publication data
Hasler, Antony.
Court poetry in late medieval England and Scotland : allegories of authority / Antony J. Hasler.
p.   cm. – (Cambridge studies in medieval literature)
Includes bibliographical references and index.
ISBN 978-0-521-80957-3 (hardback)
1. English poetry – Early modern, 1500–1700 – History and criticism.   2. Political poetry, English –
History and criticism.   3. Politics and literature – England – History – 16th century.   4. Politics and
literature – Scotland – History – 16th century.   5. Authority in literature.
I. Title.
PR525.H5H37   2010
821'.3093581–dc22
                                    2010030520

ISBN 978-0-521-80957-3 Hardback

Cambridge University Press has no responsibility for the persistence or
accuracy of URLs for external or third-party Internet websites referred to
in this publication, and does not guarantee that any content on such
websites is, or will remain, accurate or appropriate.

For Joan, Jack, Loie and Maud

Contents

Acknowledgements		*page* viii
Abbreviations		x
	Introduction	1
1	Beginnings: André's *Vita Henrici Septimi* and Dunbar's aureate allegories	19
2	*The Bowge of Courte* and the birth of the paranoid subject	43
3	"My panefull purs so priclis me": the rhetoric of the self in Dunbar's petitionary poems	63
4	Translative senses: Alexander Barclay's *Eclogues* and Gavin Douglas's *Palice of Honour*	87
5	*Mémoires d'outre-tombe*: love, rhetoric and the poems of Stephen Hawes	108
6	Mapping Skelton: "Esebon, Marybon, Wheston next Barnet"	145
	Conclusion	168
Notes		174
Bibliography		217
Index		243

Acknowledgements

This book has come together over many years, but I am inclined to think of it as framed between two groups. At the University of Cambridge, where it began all too long ago as a doctoral thesis, the Cambridge "alternative" medieval seminar provided a model of interchange rarely encountered since. Ardis Butterfield, the late Ruth Bagnall, Mark Chinca, Elizabeth Edwards, Simon Gaunt, Jane Gilbert and Gabrielle Lyons are all owed much. Sarah Kay and Nicolette Zeeman, both also members of the group, were generous enough to take on the additional task of reading early versions of the material, as were Richard Axton and Rita Copeland. More recently those early days have been recalled in the St. Louis Lacan reading group, and here I would like particularly to thank Guinn Batten, Jessica Rosenfeld and Jon Todd Dean, who provided wonderful dialogue and feedback when parts of Chapters 2 and 5 were presented as part of a panel at the Lacanian Affiliated Psychoanalytic Workgroups conference in Philadelphia in March 2008.

To individuals now, more and less formally. My interest in the material began with an undergraduate dissertation directed by A. C. Spearing, who also supervised the initial stages of the subsequent doctoral dissertation. Richard Beadle took over the latter stages, and I'm grateful for the wisdom, acumen and steady support of both. As doctoral examiner, John Scattergood deployed his immense Skeltonian knowledge with light-handed bounty. Linda Bree and Elizabeth Hanlon have been more than reasonably forbearing with an author who must have seemed professionally infirm.

I could not imagine more careful or thoughtful readers of the original typescript than James Simpson and R. James Goldstein, both of whom have been positive influences in a host of other ways. Nor can I begin to reckon the immense personal and intellectual generosity of Paul Strohm, who at one stage took time out from a busy summer to read an earlier version of the work, and who has sustained my thinking across the years. Ad Putter has been a lively and perceptive source of dialogue on everything whenever dialogue has been possible. All of them inhabit a strange profession in a fashion I can only describe as exemplary.

When parts of the first and sixth chapters were read at Columbia University's early modern graduate seminar in 2004, Patricia Dailey and David Scott Kastan were terrific interlocutors. During a one-year visiting lecturership at Indiana University, Sheila Lindenbaum's alertness was invaluable, as were talks with Kim Keller, Joan Pong Linton and Richard Nash. Remarks by Ellen Carol Jones and Nancy Bradley Warren made important points flip into place, and I also owe thanks to Kathy Lavezzo, David Carlson and Greg Walker. Priscilla Bawcutt, Steven Gunn, Lotte Hellinga, Mervyn James and Sally Mapstone responded most helpfully to written queries. Thanks too to others who have been tolerant from the fringes: Mary Garrison, David Guthrie, Andrew Lovett, Melissa Lane, Jeffrey Farb, Leo Human.

The College of Arts and Sciences at Saint Louis University has assisted me with a number of Mellon Grants over the years, and I would like to thank too Liz Gordon and the wonderful staff at Westcott House. I want to record my deep appreciation of Clarence Miller's kindness and vigilance in keeping my Latin on track. I've also been very lucky in the graduate students with whom I have been able to work: Tom Dieckmann, Lea Luecking Frost, Jossalyn Larson, Jennifer Culver and Lauren Coker-Durso have all contributed something to this book. I have been fortunate indeed in my chairs of department. Sara van den Berg was appropriately tough and tender by turns, and in the end stellar. I can only hope the book will be an adequate memorial to my late colleague and former chair Tom Moisan, whose wit, intelligence and compassion were a privilege to be around.

Circumstances made it impossible for my mother Joan Catherine Hasler and my late father Jack Hasler, to attend university. Thanks to their love of learning they gave up much so that their son could, and I am profoundly grateful.

Five people are left, in an area which makes dedicatory rhetoric look a little fatuous. Beth Human helped in the final stages of this book's preparation with a selflessness it would be futile to try to calculate. More to the point, her tireless, alert, knowledgeable and challenging input has constantly impelled me to refine and rethink. My children, with surefire intelligence, have carved the book up between them; Jack Hasler has taught me all I know about rhetoric and violence, in the most good-humoured and genial of ways, Loie Hasler about the politics of mediation, and Maud Hasler about style and modelling (and juggling). Joan Hart-Hasler's contribution covers all of the above, and everything. It is to Joan, Jack, Loie and Maud that this book is dedicated.

Abbreviations

BL	British Library, London
CCSL	Corpus Christianorum Series Latina
EETS	Early English Texts Society
EHR	English Historical Review
ELH	English Literary History
JEGP	Journal of English and Germanic Philology
JMEMS	Journal of Medieval and Early Modern Studies
MLN	Modern Language Notes
MLR	Modern Language Review
PL	Patrologia Latina
PMLA	Proceedings of the Modern Language Association
SAC	Studies in the Age of Chaucer
SATF	Société des Anciens Textes Français
SSL	Studies in Scottish Literature
STC	*A Short-Title Catalogue of Books Printed in England, Scotland and Ireland & of English Books Printed Abroad, 1475–1640*, 2nd rev. edn, 3 vols. (London: Bibliographical Society, 1976–91)
STS	Scottish Text Society

Introduction

The woodcut on the cover of this book stands as frontispiece to the earliest surviving print of John Skelton's *The Bowge of Courte* (*c.* 1499). This may not be its first association with courtly duplicity, since it was likely attached around 1495 to a Wynkyn de Worde edition of Caxton's *Historye of Reynart the Foxe*.[1] Bruyn the bear is delivering to the elusive Reynart a summons to the court of Noble the lion. The bear's jaws are clenched in a grin that we are not quite sure how to read. Slavering sycophancy? The *Schadenfreude* of the messenger bearing bad news, or his repressed anger at a thankless and doomed task? Predatory instinct, servile resentment or sadistic enjoyment? Meanwhile, Reynart sits above and aloof, amid the "hooles" and "secrete chaumbres" of his lair of Maleperduys.[2] Perhaps he is relishing his iconographic resemblance to the monarch in a scene of poet-to-patron dedication, but his closed bodily surface (no bared teeth) still harbors a certain inscrutability. At the center is the sealed royal summons tendered by Bruyn, an executive document whose effects are deflected, not least across the textual tradition itself.[3] Renart pleads delay with the fiction that he hungers for (in the original) or has surfeited on (Caxton and his Dutch source) honey. Bruyn, of course, cannot resist the bait, with disastrous consequences. This scene, in which a sealed royal and official text shifts appetite, object and consequence along a chain of identities, provides an apt threshold both to Skelton's poem and to this book.[4]

The poets who figure in these pages all spent some part of their lives writing at the royal courts of England and Scotland between 1485, when Henry VII ascended the English throne, and 1528, when the minority of James V came to an end in Scotland. In addition to Skelton, they include Stephen Hawes, Alexander Barclay and Bernard André to the south of the border, and Gavin Douglas and William Dunbar to its north.[5] Both the courts and the poets have elicited lively attention, particularly with regard to the larger narratives that look back across the historiographically familiar divide of 1485. This has allowed me to focus more narrowly on my subject here: the forms of poetic identity generated in a cluster of works, in response to the multiple sources of authority[6] that surround these authors. Such sources include monarchs and courts, and genres and texts, both vernacular and classical. I also take it as axiomatic that "authority" and "court" are unstable categories answered by unstable texts, which means that we glimpse the selves enunciated in these poems in – or as – their own unmaking. The poet's position in history and culture is visible as displaced, other (*allos*) – as, we might say, always allegorized. It offers itself to our reading through genre, or rather through a mixture of genres, some of them the expressions of that capacious discourse, the writing of *fin amour*. In such cases the discursively stable is recurrently disturbed, and versions of narratorial identity are exposed to especial risk.[7]

THE COURTLY FIGURE

The term *court* offers, as historians are quick to point out, some epistemological problems of its own. Walter Map, comically baffled at his inability to define it, notoriously has recourse to Augustine's words on human alienation in time:

"In time I exist, and of time I speak," said Augustine: and added, "What time is I know not." In a like spirit of perplexity I may say that in the court I exist and of the court I speak, and what the court is, God knows, I know not. I do know however that the court is not time; but temporal it is, changeable and various, space-bound and wandering, never continuing in one state.[8]

Over eight centuries later, Map's words still seem to exert a shaping force on the medieval court's literary-historical reception. For historians of England, attempts to place the court in time have unsurprisingly raised questions of identity and origin. Can the court be restricted to "the spatial confines of ... royal palaces," and if so, how does it relate to proximate worlds?[9] If the court as royal household is itinerant, what to make of its claims to place? At what historical point can we properly situate the emergence of a royal court,[10] or an ideology of courtierly behavior or court service?[11] For students of literature, the main issue is highlighted by Map's observation that the court "is not time; but temporal" ["non est tempus; temporalis quidem est"]. Is the court noun or adjective, a political institution with a firm location in history or a term describing a loose collection of attitudes and values hard to confine to a specific epoch? How can we really define the connections between historical courts and "courtly" culture?[12] As the very existence of such questions indicates, the court of our imagining is inescapably multiple: political institution, symbolic focus, literary trope.[13]

Several of the poems discussed here (Skelton's *Bowge of Courte*, *Speke Parott* and *The Garlande of Laurell*, Dunbar's *The Thrissill and the Rois* and *The Goldyn Targe*, Douglas's *The Palice of Honour*) have in critical response caught up the label of allegory, largely because of their reliance on personification. All foreground elaborate degrees of formalization, or indeed formal breakdown. André's *Vita Henrici Septimi*, with its poetic elements, and Barclay's *Eclogues* bring the estranging effects of unfamiliar classicizing paradigms. Dunbar's petitionary poems, often regarded as his most "personal," are in some ways, as I shall aim to show, his most figurative. These poets work within a political structure dominated by the monarch: a "real" historical being, but one surrounded by a vast symbolic panoply that extends and alters being. They are also situated in a network of forces that at once sustains and exceeds the specific pressures of court politics, and which is registered in their poems through the entitlement to discursive authority asserted by certain literary genres.[14] This authority is in turn disseminated by differing technologies, since the notion of "the court" at this juncture does not restrict literary production to scribal practice or to a narrow coterie of readers within a royal household; most of the poets I have named were associated with the medium of print and its reconfigurations of readership.[15]

My own intervention aims to highlight the necessary obliquity that allegory introduces into self-presentation. Nearly three decades ago now, Stephen Greenblatt memorably recreated the "self-fashioning" of three figures, More, Tyndale and Wyatt, whose lives overlapped with those of the poets I discuss here. The richness of Greenblatt's depictions of his subjects, in which lives and writings alike participate in the status of "theatre," stems in large part from the documentary evidence left by their highly public careers.[16] With the exception of Douglas, little is known of the lives of the poets discussed here. Moreover, their poems use highly conventional modes – if often in explosively eclectic combinations – and as a result resist decoding for topical and biographical reference, working hard to refuse history a way in. The catchphrase that language speaks the subject, not the subject language, becomes for the reader of these texts a matter of practical fact; they represent a relation between text and history that is less a theatrical than a secretive one.

Medievalists have long been familiar with Medvedev and Bakhtin's contention that the world beyond a text is not directly "reflected" in it, but enters it by way of "refraction" through an ideological environment, in a passage characterized by indirection. Less attention, perhaps, has been paid to their supporting claim that a crucial contributor to this refraction is genre: "Every significant genre is a complex system of means and methods for the conscious control and finalization of reality."[17] In an aside – that most revealing of rhetorical gestures – they suggest that genre is a psychological rather than an exclusively literary category, a medium in operation before the word ever appears on the page: "human consciousness possesses a series of inner genres for seeing and conceptualizing reality."[18] Genre, then, both "refracts" the real and becomes the scene on which it is displayed. This suggests another paradigm of psychic functioning that also entails a connection running along crooked and tortuous routes, the Freudian notion of *Verschiebung* or displacement. The term denotes in Freud's earlier writings the process by which "ideas which originally had only a weak charge of intensity take over the charge from ideas which were originally intensely cathected" – that is, charged with psychic energy – "and at last attain enough strength to enable them to force an entry into consciousness."[19]

The idea, present both in Bakhtin and Medvedev and in Freud, that an energy at once psychic, semantic and ideological is displaced from a secret site to an open one – for Freud, of course, the unconscious is "ein anderer Schauplatz" or "other (or different) scene (or stage)"[20] – immediately suggests a correspondence with the figure of allegory. Indeed, it is the indirection traditionally ascribed to allegory that seems to lie behind Puttenham's description of "the Courtly figure *Allegoria*, which is when we speake one thing and thinke another, and that our wordes and our meanings meete not." Puttenham's allegory is a figure "which for his duplicitie we call the figure of Fals Semblant or Dissimulation,"[21] and the allusion to the *Roman de la Rose* at first suggests an ethical critique of allegory's dissembling. But Puttenham's portrayal of the figure becomes itself increasingly shifting and elusive: "But properly & in his principall vertue Allegoria is when we do speake in sence translatiue and wrested from the owne signification, neuerthelesse applied to another not altogether contrary, but hauing much conueniencie with it."[22] The rhetoric of this passage resonates markedly with Freud's theory of displacement. Just as the obscure roads from one idea to another, apparently impassable, are nevertheless smoothed in Freudian displacement by a chain of associations, so the violence of "wresting" occurs side by side with a basic congruency, a "conueniencie" between meanings "not altogether contrary."[23]

These terminological considerations will return in the course of the book as a whole, but my aim in this introduction is to bring them into the necessary historical frame. The patterns I describe are most readily visible in depictions of late-medieval literary patronage, and accordingly I first examine several such depictions from the period between 1390 and 1485, attending in particular to the psychosocial dimension of patronage, but embedding it in national-cultural difference and institutional location.[24] In contrast to the noble and especially the royal patron, on whom the "symbolics of blood"[25] confers an *a priori* sublimity, the poet's body is subjected to age and decay – even as he is also possessed of a slippery, changeful being that negates all claim to a secure and stable self. The subject is thus rather a flow, or a lack, than a fixed essence – "non est tempus; temporalis quidem est" – and it finds a virtual, if alienated, coherence in the figure of the patron.[26] What emerges is a pattern of identification, in which the poetic subject seeks to model itself on "authorities," in particular, but not exclusively, those furnished by patron and literary precursor. Its endeavors to do so are attached to a repertoire of fleeting mediations, ranging from the textual and rhetorical (style, allusion, representation of person) to the social and cultural (status, gender).[27] While the workings of identification are readily recognizable from a psychoanalytic perspective, I also suggest that identification here receives its own late-medieval theorization in the literature of counsel, particularly royal counsel. My reading of the fashion in which this occurs complements current critical perspectives on fifteenth- and early sixteenth-century poetry, but with a difference. I finally outline the elaborations of monarchic style and material medium that towards the end of the century alter literary practice.

PATRONS AND PATTERNS

The most perceptive critics of fifteenth-century poetry have found a variety of deep divisions at its heart. For A. C. Spearing, referring to Harold Bloom's "anxiety of influence," Chaucer's followers are troubled by their relation to a poetic father whose cultural dominance is all too closely matched by his elusiveness within his own text.[28] David Lawton finds in their self-professed "dullness" before literary forebears and powerful patrons a multivalent rhetorical tactic: the extravagant modesty *topoi* of the period become at once an ethical stance which privileges sound morality over poetic craft, a promotion of political truthtelling, and an endeavor, in a politically turbulent century, to construct a form of public discourse grounded in a stable and homogeneous body of values.[29]

Our understanding of the social and historical contexts of this poetry, and its renditions of selfhood, has increased immeasurably in the last two decades.[30] At the same time, the very studies that have furthered our awareness the most have often become locked in an energetic agon about the question of intent, which has swirled in particular around the figures of Hoccleve and Lydgate, the repeatedly twinned poets of a Lancastrian dynasty. Some of the most compelling work on these poets' historical place – on Lydgate's monastic allegiance, or Hoccleve's bureaucratic identity – has gone hand in hand with assertions that these figures are covert but unmistakable dissenters from a proposed Lancastrian *status quo*.[31] Not all commentary has taken this line.[32] Paul Strohm argues for a poetry which assumes its dullness "with respect to the affective trajectories of its own desire," a trajectory thwarted by the contradictory mandates imposed by its sponsors.[33] In Robert Meyer-Lee's recent narrative of poetry and power, the conditions of post-Lancastrian patronage compel the poet to negotiate a tightrope between the roles of "laureate" and "beggar" embodied in Lydgate and Hoccleve.[34] My own account emphasizes the inevitable breakdown written into even the most adroit fifteenth-century poet's performance of identity, a staging cast by the poet's own figurative language.

In Gower's *Confessio Amantis*, the revelation of the lover-narrator Amans's advanced age has justly been described as the poem's "dramatic masterstroke."[35] In the first recension's epilogue, that same aging body then enters an explicitly encomiastic register, as it is drawn into the sphere of the royal figure of Richard II, who has the undiminishing power of his badge, the sun:

> The Sonne is evere briht and fair,
> Withinne himself and noght empeired:
> Althogh the weder be despeired
> The hed planete is not to wite.   (VIII, 3010*–13*)[36]

The body of the subject Gower, by contrast, shows the depredations of time:

> As I which in subjeccioun
> Stonde under the proteccioun,
> And mai miselven not bewelde,
> What for seknesse and what for elde,
> Which I receyve of goddes grace.   (VIII, 3039*–43*)

This body, of course, has already been attached by Venus to Gower's own name (VIII, 2908), and the "feble and old" poet still summons up the courage to dedicate his book "to the worschipe of mi king" (VIII, 3070*–71*). We may ask how far Gower's authorship of "a bok for king Richardes sake" (Prologue, 24*) answered a genuine royal request; we may skeptically compare his professions of Ricardian allegiance to Richard II with his subsequent dedicatory shift to Henry IV; we may assume the passage to be a veridical representation of the relative ages of young king and old poet.[37] Literal considerations alone, however, cannot account for the regularity and the degree of detail with which this scene is repeated throughout the fifteenth century in England. The subject's body, feeble or old or indigent, is counterpoised to the glorified body of a patron who is beyond such constraints. In the Gower instance, the idealization of the patron withdraws a particularity that is left clinging to the poet in the text by a signature and by enclosure within a wasting natural body. The rhetorically exalted patron, however, is also commutable. Richard II and Henry Bolingbroke are constructed as interchangeable patrons, and it is the elevation of the patron that frees the poem as commodity.

After Chaucer's death, powerful patrons share such scenes with the evocation of authoritative literary ancestors. In *The Regement of Princes*, in 1410, a Hoccleve worried by money and passing years is caught between two figures of considerable discursive weight, Henry, Prince of Wales and Geoffrey Chaucer. The dead Chaucer figures as personal friend to the poet, but also as culturally powerful symbolic father, whose authority underwrites a Lancastrian dynasty of questionable legitimacy, a royal policy directed against heresy, and a literary and political privileging of the vernacular with strong nationalist overtones.[38] Lydgate's numerous prologues and envoys similarly convey a debility in the face both of mighty patrons and of Chaucer. In *The Fall of Princes*, the powerless author oscillates between the "prynce ful myhti off puissaunce" (I, 373) Humphrey, Duke of Gloucester, and Chaucer, the "cheeff poete off Breteyne" (I, 247).[39] The beginning of Book III presents a Lydgate old ("in stal crokid age," 65), poor and bereft of "witt" (58), helped to continue on his "pilgrimage" of translation by "Mi lordis fredam and bounteuous largesse" (74). In Book II, the dead Chaucer halts the translator about to tackle the story of Lucrece in his tracks: "it were but veyn / Thyng seid be hym to write it newe ageyn" (1000–1). However, the living patron urges him onward: "my lord bad I sholde abide, / By good auys at leiser to translate / The doolful processe off hir pitous fate" (1006–8). Here, the patron's word is shown to endow a hesitant poet, evidently afraid to emulate Chaucer, with the desire to proceed. The inclusion of this staged vacillation dramatizes the multiple authorities that speak through and across the text. The "chapitle of þe gouernance of Poetis" (III, 3837–871) begs the "welle of fredam" Gloucester to help a poet "Oppressid with pouert" (3865, 3869). Whatever the level of literal truth here, the recurrence of such statements suggests that the real economy at work is once again a representational one; the poet's age and poverty point contrastively to patronal magnificence, and the subject's voice flags and is lost where it is not one with the patron's. Lydgate's addresses to Gloucester through the 1430s are not only functional interventions in his translation of Laurent de

Premierfait, but integral to the poem. Similarly, John Shirley's jokes about Lydgate's poverty do not comment on the poet's actual situation so much as recognize a subject-position adopted in his work and wittily set it in further circulation, where it may become part of Lydgate's commercial reputation.[40] In *The Fall*, this ceaseless succession of images, of presences that take on body and then recede, inform a poetic subject constantly unstable and identifications that fail to hold their place.

In John Walton's translation of Boethius's *Consolation of Philosophy*, evidently written before 1410, such fluctuations begin with violence.[41] Here, the translator's modesty, his "Insuffishaunce of cunnyng" and "Defaut of language and of eloquence," are an inertia forcibly interrupted by the Countess of Berkeley's command that he translate: "ʒoure heste haþ done me violence" (1). Female patronal violence, too, is compounded by an avowed inability to match the labors of Gower or Chaucer ("I to þeym in makyng am vnmete," 5).[42] This sets the stage for a brief and muted contest between Walton and one of his renowned predecessors, who takes on the danger of the figured patroness. If Chaucer as a model is inimitable, he is also immoral; the prospect of translating Boethius evidently recalls *Troilus and Criseyde*, to whose classicizing and amatory agenda Walton is resistant. He has no desire to engage with "þese olde poysees derk" (6) or "Towhette now le dartes of cupide" (7), and will pray to God rather than to Tisiphone, Allecto or Megara (8) for success in his enterprise. Yet this insertion of a clerical, anti-Chaucerian frame – a reclamation, we might say, of the *Consolation* from its more ambiguous presence in the *Troilus* – has by the end of Walton's prologue changed obedience to a patron's peremptory command into a religious "obseruance," performed, he now tells the Countess, "in reuerence of youre worthinesse . . . In wil to do ʒour seruice and plesance" (9). In this rhetoric of transcendence, the literary precursor is left behind for identification with a higher authority and a patroness's "violent" bidding is transformed into reverent and willing service.

In several instances, the miniature narratives implied in such addresses to patrons extend across a larger canvas, as the flawed subject is moved into a position of imaginary stability and coherence through encounters with a patronal surrogate, or the sudden intervention, in some form, of an author or authoritative text. This is the case in the entire prologue of Hoccleve's *Regement of Princes*; in a progress akin to that of Walton's prologue, the poet's dialogue with an old almsman, in some ways figuring a patron, leads by way of a strategically placed allusion to Chaucer to Hoccleve's remaking as a subject ready to signify on behalf of his lord. The dialogue in Book VIII of Lydgate's *Fall of Princes* between Boccaccio, by this stage clearly a stand-in for the exhausted poet Lydgate ("My lymys feeble, crokid & feynt for age, / Cast in a dreed, for dulnesse of corage," VIII, 18–19) and a spectral Petrarch ("the laureat poete," VIII, 61) who emboldens him anew, repeats the same process.

We find a similar scene in the *Secrees of Old Filisoffres*, begun by Lydgate and completed after the latter's death (*c*. 1449) by Benet Burgh. Derek Pearsall has suggested that Burgh, Lydgate's admirer, reorganized the Lydgate text bequeathed him towards a mortal conclusion, with Lydgate's own comparison of the four seasons to the life of man ("To our foure Ages / the sesouns wel applyed; / deth al consumyth / which may nat be denyed," 1490–91).[43] After this "morallite" (1485), the rubricator, perhaps Burgh, continues: "Here dyed this translator and nobil poete: and the yonge folowere gan his prologe on this wise." Lydgate is caught at the very moment of his translation into an *auctor*, as death borders on resurrection.

The "yonge folowere" then begins his endeavors to occupy the space left by his dead precursor with a spectacular profession of modesty, which certainly gives ample occasion for talk of anxiety of influence. Fourteen stanzas address a patron, possibly Henry VI, at whose command the translation was completed,

> The dulnesse of my penne / yow besechyng tenlumyne
> Which am nat / aqueynted / with the musys nyne   (1497–98)

The latter half-line supplies a refrain for the stanzas, which ultimately turn to Lydgate, who of course was so "aqueynted" (1585).

The poet's estimate of his own powers, as represented in the text, would appear to be at a low ebb at this point; his body here is grotesque, diminished, infantilized. He is the dwarf of chivalric romance, entering the lists where the knight should fight (1499–500);[44] a mere child (1532), terrified by royal splendor:

> of the persone / the magnificence Royal,
> To whom I wryte / in-to tremlyng cause me fal;
> Of dirk ignoraunce / feryng the Engyne ...   (1558–60)

However, the tone suddenly changes as he once more addresses his patron, this time with a proverbial claim that "Ech tale is endyd / as it hath favour" (1585). He cannot continue without the word of his patron; if he can bring his tale to an end, it will be through another's "favour," not his own labors. The request for favor, however, involves the use of a proverb, and such sententious material is after all the stock-in-trade of counsel. The revision of Lydgate's text enacts multiple forms of identification; it at once enables a gesture of homage to a patron and inscribes Lydgate's death into a moral schema that authenticates that gesture generically.

Jean Laplanche and Jean-Bertrand Pontalis define identification as the psychological process "whereby the subject assimilates an aspect, property or attribute of the other and is transformed, wholly or partially, after the model the other provides." It is, they add, "by means of a series of identifications that the personality is constituted and specified."[45] My account above suggests that the poet is, in his rhetorical statements, "constituted and specified" through his differential relationship to patron and predecessor.[46] Such performances of humility among fifteenth-century poets tend at present to be regarded as stalking-horses for a previously formed selfhood which then stages its own representations. We might rather say, however, that convention here is culturally constitutive and productive, providing positions from which subjects speak, and thus upholding certain relations of power. The poet's postures of humility mark a double subjection, as he emerges as a twofold absence – a space where Chaucer (or Gower, or Lydgate) should be but is not, a potential conduit of the patron's desire rather than a being possessed of desire.[47]

Two points will serve as a coda to this discussion. First, while poet may palpably fail to coincide with patron and precursor, such failures also appear at the most integral levels of language and style, and are adumbrated in Chaucer's own work. In the prologue to Chaucer's *Clerk's Tale*, Harry Bailly urges the Clerk to

> Tele us som murie thyng of aventures.
> Youre termes, youre colours, and youre figures,
> Keepe hem in stoor til so be ye endite
> Heigh style, as whan that men to kynges write.   (E, 15–18)[48]

His famous definition of the *artes dictaminis* reminds us that when fashioned to the ear of an imagined auditor high in the scale of social relations, the author's discourse is itself elevated.[49] Harry Bailly's "heigh style" addressed to kings and governors was to become the dominant formal poetic model for Lydgate and his successors; in addressing a text to a powerful recipient, the poet's words acquire what Bourdieu has called "symbolic capital."[50]

The modest fifteenth-century poet's version of such capital is a contradictory one. The amplitude of his syntax – and, as the century advanced, his elaborate aureate diction, derived chiefly from Lydgate – bespeak a symbolic capital that embodies the reflected glory of patron and poetic ancestor.[51] However, his most reliable means of accruing interest on it is to declare himself bankrupt as often as possible. For his tropes of bodily self-humiliation constitute "symbolic capital" in their very denial of power and prestige; as we have seen, his identity enters a series of transactions between author and patron, to circulate as the "fallen second term" which points up by contrast the "authentic, originary perfection" of idealized prince or noble.[52] This is the ultimate disruption of identification; the poet does not, indeed cannot, coincide with his own elevated language.

Secondly, I wish finally to offer, by way of contrast, an instance from a different genre and nation. At the end of Hary's *Wallace* (*c.* 1476–78), that generic hybrid which offers the most powerful of fifteenth-century Scottish historiographies, there is a moment that throws into sharp relief the shape of literary patronage in one quarter of the Scottish polity. The *Wallace*, as has long been recognized, responds to its looming predecessor, John Barbour's *Bruce*, by promoting the figure of Sir William Wallace, who led resistance against English occupation while Robert Bruce was fighting on the opposing side. As R. James Goldstein has described in detail, Hary inherits from his source, Walter Bower's *Scotichronicon*, an ideological double bind: "Bruce represents the legitimate right [to the Scottish throne] but suffers from effeminate idleness, while Wallace must presume on another's right in order to free his homeland by using his manly courage."[53] The poem has to negotiate this dilemma, in part by inventing a scene in which Wallace does strategically adopt the crown for a day. At its very end, however, its complications are put into playful, if not quite untroubled, suspension. Hary has flatly denied the receipt of any remuneration ("For my laubour na man hecht me reward. / Na charge I had off king nor othir lord," XII, 1432–33), insisting that his motives for writing are purely patriotism and the wish that Wallace's name and memory not be "smord" (1434).[54] Now, however, the poet draws accomplices into the fiction:

> Bot in a poynt I grant I said amys.
> Thir twa knychtis suld blamyt be for this:
> The knycht Wallas, of Cragge rychtwys lord,
> And Liddaill als, gert me mak wrang record.
> On Allyrtoun mur the croun he [Wallace] tuk a day
> To get battaill, as myn autour will say.
> Thir twa gert me say that ane othir wys;
> Till mayster Blayr we did sumpart off dispys. (1441–48)

"Mayster Blayr" is Hary's Lollius, and Hary's imaginary fault against his "autour" emphasizes the multiplicity of the authorities on which Hary's poem builds and to whom it answers. The "twa knychtis" are Sir William Wallace of Craigie in Ayrshire, and Sir James Liddale of Halkerton, both associated with those members of the southern Scottish nobility opposed to James III's pursuit of closer ties with England and the attendant loss of profitable border raids. (Liddale was steward to one of the most prominent among them, the king's brother Alexander Stewart, Duke of Albany.[55])

Whatever the role of Wallace of Craigie and Halkerton in the production of Hary's work, their cooption in the fiction supplies a suggestive imaginary template of a political structure. It has been argued by Sally Mapstone that James III's reign did not see the "court culture" that was to emerge with James IV; the Scottish polity at this stage was dependent on a cluster of regional interdependencies between and among crown and magnates.[56] "Patronage" here is complicated in a style that suggests – in manner if not in content – a coconspiratorial, quasi-Chaucerian audience rather than the defining relationships of fifteenth-century England.[57] The *Wallace* hints at a distinct patronal economy, just as the work of Douglas, Dunbar and Lyndsay will suggest in their own ways a sudden and even vertiginous centralizing of this wider compass.

CANCELLED COUNSEL

Fifteenth-century poetry supplies its own theorization of the poetic subject and identification. One of the *sententiae* translated in George Ashby's version of the *Dicta philosophorum* puts the relationship between subject and noble into peculiarly clear relief, also exposing its underlying social constraints:

> A seruaunt shold nat be euen equal
>   To his lorde, but in thre thinges trewly,
> That is, in feithe, wytte, & pacience al,
>   Not in estate nor clothinges richely,
>   Ner in other delites excessely;
>   But iche man knowe hym self and his degre,
>   Non excedyng for possibilite.[58]

The "seruaunt" may model himself inwardly and ethically after "his lorde," aspiring to the virtues of "feithe, wytte, & pacience al" – the merits which, according to innumerable advisory texts of the period, accompanied aristocratic magnanimity. He must not, on the other hand, lay claim to the outward splendor by which the noble body differentiates itself from that of the commoner: such imitation in a servant would amount to excess, of the kind that sumptuary laws were expressly passed to prohibit.[59] The "sentence" uncannily prefigures Freud's formulation, in "The Ego and the Id," of the ego-ideal's or super-ego's workings: the super-ego's "relation to the ego is not exhausted by the precept: 'You ought to be like this (like your father).' It also comprises the prohibition: 'You may not be like this (like your father) – that is, you may not do all that he does; some things are his prerogative.'"[60] The desire to identify must remain secret, disavowed.

It is almost unnecessary at this late stage to indicate how deeply the distance of lordship described by Ashby participates in certain medieval doctrines of monarchy. As Louise O. Fradenburg puts it, in her superb explication of the imaginative purchase of the legal fiction of the monarch's dual corporeality, "the king is an effect of paradox. He is the most representative of people, but this makes him unique."[61] In his body politic, the king represents his subjects because he is different from them: symbolizing the realm, it is an eternal *corpus mysticum*, transcending mortality and death. In his body natural, the king represents his subjects because he is like them: his own human body, subject to mortality and death, links him to the least of his subjects and can be used to engender an affect of community, of "common cause" shared by subject and sovereign.[62]

The king's symbolically representative function is succinctly summarized once again by Ashby: "Suche as the kynge is, suche bene al other" (*Dicta*, 393).[63] Texts of advice literature such as Ashby's inscribe subject and sovereign in a relationship of identification; the figure of the prince embodies the human potentialities of all his subjects – "toutes les possibilités humaines,"[64] in Daniel Poirion's words – and a fault in the king means a defective commonwealth. As Aristotle advises Alexander the Great in Sir Gilbert Hay's *Buik of King Alexander*, the people are the mirror of any flaws in their ruler; Alexander is told to

> gar inquire quhat all men sayis of þe,
> Quhidder ill or gud, or quhat-sum-euer it be –
> Thare may þow se ane face in ane myrroure,
> Baith lak and lois, wourschip and dishonoure;
> Than may Þow vesche þi face and put away,
> Giff ony filth apoun þi wissage lay ...   (10536–41)[65]

Hay's, of course, is a narrative rendition of the scene which underlies the very tradition of the *Secretum secretorum*, whose structural division incarnates the relation between state and self-government.[66] The *Secretum*, Aristotle's purported advice to his pupil Alexander, counterbalances counsel to the king on how to govern his natural body with advice on the good government of the state. Hay's Aristotle furthermore argues that

> nocht forthi that of kingis speke we,
> All kynd of men to king may liknyt be

> That governis him bot lak to God and man –
> He is worth be king that governe him sa can;
> Suppois he be nocht lord of toure na toun,
> He micht richt wele for wourschip bere the croun –
> Giff he luffis law, vertew and veretie,
> He is owdir king, or kingis fere suld be. (9815–22)⁶⁷

The logic by which king and subject were able to identify was thus made available in the tradition of the *Secretum*. In his body natural, the king shared the subject's imperfections but was also invited to correct them through a programme of discipline to which the subject too could aspire. However, the king also partook of an ideality that made him radically different from the rest of humanity, for his body politic was unsusceptible to "the thousand natural shocks / That flesh is heir to."⁶⁸

The language of the *speculum principis* is, I think, poised to conduct its own intervention in the debates that have shaped the study of fifteenth-century poetry. Texts of counsel, and other advisory texts, intimate that the poetic subject's gestures towards identification with the image of power take place under the mask of – are, indeed, finally inseparable from – an explicit, perhaps inevitable, failure to identify. Many late-medieval poems in English narrate a progress from troubled beginnings to a closure underwritten by an authoritative text, the invocation of a patron or the intervention of a powerful precursor or patronal surrogate – a closure that marks the adoption of the right to speak. Yet that progress is devious and covert, for it takes place under the sacrificial sign of an explicit recognition and internalization of deficiency, the mimesis of a willed embrace of frailty and defect. Once again, Hoccleve's *Regement* provides an exemplary case; failure of identification is rewritten in order that it may culminate in a scene of self-recognition and the subject's "sincerity" finally emerge as the measure of lack, a being-for a royal other ("Myne inward wil that thristith the welfare / Of your persone").⁶⁹ Considerable debate was at one stage focused on the supposed inability of New Historicist critics to imagine the emergence of a fully formed interiority in literature prior to the sixteenth century.⁷⁰ The evidence of much fifteenth-century poetry suggests that inwardness is born – and repeatedly reborn – in the self-scrutinizing address of poetic subject to patron, while the subject's introspection becomes the source of a patron's entertainment.⁷¹

The process of modeling behavior and conduct assumes on the part of the model an ontological priority over the subject seeking to model itself. The model is there first, and is "real" in a way that the subject is not, but desires to be. The desire of the late-medieval poetic subject consequently passes through the substance ascribed to the sovereign. We might compare Mikkel Borch-Jacobsen's account of the mimetic ego. Borch-Jacobsen notes that "Though the *ego* is everywhere in the dream . . . we still have to recognize that it is nowhere properly itself, given that it never avoids yielding to an identification and always confuses itself in some way with another (an alter ego – but one that is neither other or self)." The ego's finding of its own pleasure requires "a detour, one that causes its own pleasure to pass through that of another. And this detour is identification (*mimesis*), resemblance (*homoïosis*). One only enjoys, in fantasy, as another: tell me whom you are miming, and I'll tell you who you are, what you desire, and how you enjoy."[72]

A fifteenth-century English version of Alain Chartier's *Dialogus familiaris amici et sodalis* repeats the usual commonplaces about exemplary kingship, warning the ruler against vice. In so doing, it makes the ruler's role as pattern of conduct especially clear:

yt ys a scorneful thynge and a foule spectacle to the comon wele yf men pollute wyth vyces sytte yn hyghe offyces or estate as though thyr vyces schulde opynly be schewed and / brought forthe yn syght of the peple. The freel and mevable comonte lyuen by ensample and folowen the maneres and fortvne of myghty men, but they put not theyre soules, lawes and ordenaunces made by commaundement so ryghtfully and wyth so grete reme[m]braunce as they emprynte by ensample the lyuenge of theyr governour . . . The lest man [th]at synneth synneth to hymself, but they whos lyuenge ought to be as ymage and ensample to othyr men, whan they synne they synne to alle men.[73]

The "freel and mevable comonte" live indifferently; they "emprynte by ensample the lyuenge of theyr governour," replicating the image "opynly . . . schewed and / brought forthe yn syght of the peple."

Such figures suggest that in later medieval poetry written around courts, critique is as likely to emerge in the poem's own structures and textures as in the aware and programmatic resistances of historical agents. Richard Firth Green points to the anomalies of the court poet's social and economic position ("some kind of ill-defined no-man's-land somewhere between a job and a hobby"), which meant that in general "the lot of English court authors in the late middle ages was not a very happy one."[74] A long prior critical history, much of it antedating the current interest in fifteenth-century English poetics and some of it based in the study of other European vernacular literatures, had already broached the matter of the court poet's desire and its relation to power, working from psychosocial and often avowedly psychoanalytic paradigms. For Daniel Poirion, nonnoble poets responding to an alien aristocratic ideal display a "conscience morose du labeur" ["a morose consciousness of labour"] in which we hear "le grincement d'insurmontables contradictions" ["the creaking of insurmountable contradictions"].[75] Most immediately relevant to the late fifteenth and early sixteenth centuries, Paul Zumthor's *grands rhétoriqueurs*, their bodies and words signs of the prince's *gloire*, can take refuge from the vulnerabilities of patronage only in punning, equivocal subversion of the verbal sign itself.[76] In 1985, Fradenburg provided an anticipatory check to overly sanguine voluntarisms, reminding us that the presentation of the court poem as gift rather than as paid labor "goes over and above the actual meanings of the poem to designate these meanings as *for* the master."[77] She also points out that "The desire of the patronized poet of the later Middle Ages does not … exist solely in opposition to the 'exigencies of the political'; the desire of the poet is intertwined with the political demand, defining it, defined by it as well as by resistance to it, seized of its weapons and seized by them."[78] We may recall that Lacan's model of the ego's formation links identification with the mirror image with a fundamental alienation from the image, misrecognition of an imaginary coherence with aggressiveness.[79] It need not surprise us that in courtly writing, too, identification with images and languages of power interweave with traces of a muted, stifled resentment and with a sense that the subject speaking these texts does not inhabit them with complete assurance or certainty.

Our discussion has moved between identification with the monarch, with the authoritative voices of literary style and genre, and with specific authors, all functioning, often simultaneously, as modes of self-authentication. It should not, then, surprise us that political obedience could itself be seen as a form of literary *imitatio*, as Chartier once again illustrates:

For looke wher a prince is withow(t) wisedom there be the people withowte discipline, for and a booke be falsly wretyn it shall make the reders for to erre, and he that wrytith aftir that booke ioyneth false vpon false. So thanne the kynge is the booke of the people wherein thei shulde lerne to lyve and amende their maners. But and the originall be corrupt / thanne by the copyes vntrewely wretyn. For the corrupcion that descendith from the hede chavefith the lyvir, chargith the harte and filith the stomacke; it stoppith thentrailes and alterith all the body.[80]

Here, the prince is truly the origin and ground of his subjects' being: his physiological status as "hede" makes him an exemplar both textual and moral, even as he shares the same body with "the people." Like Freud, Chartier draws on the language of book production to describe the process of identification. Where poetry is concerned, the presence of "corrupt originals" points to others whose desires, imputed or illegible, may not map securely on to the poet's desire.

I have tried to sketch some aspects of a fifteenth-century writing inherited by the authors I describe at the beginning of the sixteenth century, and these will be explored in the chapters that follow. Three significant conditions remain to be outlined. First, while specifics and antecedents have been endlessly debated, there has been little serious challenge to the view that the period was marked, in both Scotland and England, by the increasingly elaborated political strategies of an incipient centralized power. More than one historian has seen in James IV's reign a steadily increasing movement towards absolutism,[81] on the part of a king "bent ... on the political hegemony of the kingdom."[82] This drive to hegemony was manifested in the "pacification" of the Highlands and the imposition of effective control on the lordship of the Isles and the powerful earldoms of Ross and Mar. The king's marriage to Margaret Tudor in 1503 "had for the moment quelled the restless Anglophobia of some of his border magnates," while the range of his control was also extending to the Scottish church.[83] This expansion and elaboration of royal sway was – as has frequently been noted – reflected in a court culture that accentuated in ways unprecedented in Scotland the projection of royal magnificence. The early Tudor polity, of course, has also been associated by historians with an increasing concentration of power and patronage,[84] though opinion has varied as to how innovative the new dynasty in fact was, or how far Henry VIII's assumption of the Royal Supremacy in 1534 was the outcome of a long-term program.[85] The chapters below will consider several aspects of this phenomenon, in particular the changing linguistic politics of Henry VII's reign and the emergence of the Privy Chamber.

Secondly, the new conditions of power inform a context in which the genealogies of English vernacular poetry are not disrupted so much as consolidated at an unprecedented rate. A strong case has been made by William Kuskin that the culture of print is integral to this process. In Kuskin's account, print reinforces, in a mode internal to culture, the links between literary production and social authority.[86] Such recent work may usefully be read against Harry Berger Jnr.'s earlier meditation on the intersections between the order of the text and the order of the body. For Berger, the forms of medieval graphic culture "give back to its readers an image of themselves transformed by chirographic artifice."[87] Berger notes the means by which writing "progressively abstracts the means of production from the control of the body and thus alienates the production of meaning,"[88] a tendency which is built into scribal culture and which reaches its culmination in print. "The typographic revolution," Berger writes, "is at once the consequence, the catalyst, and the symbol of the general rift between the order of the body and the order of texts that characterizes early modern culture." For the poets I discuss below, who work in both script and print, such rifts and their consequences are writ especially large.

My third and final point here might best be described as a corollary of the first two. All the poems I discuss here concern themselves with identificatory desire and with power, and most figure that desire through popular amatory modes: romance, lyric, dialogue, complaint. The statutory tropes of *fin amour*, guarantees of that secrecy which is the traditional reflex of aristocratic privilege, move in printed works into a wider cultural domain, to become the open secrets of secret subjects. Such amatory matter constantly moves into abrasive contact with other genres, as the texts reach in different discursive directions in order to close the sense of loss generated by failed identification. Their narrators are traumatized by abrupt and uncanny shifts of register and genre, vividly fantasized episodes of paranoia, appeals to genres with all-inclusive truth claims and truth-effects. In particular, we find gestures towards moments of unusually violent closure: narrators contemplate or enact their own deaths, or threaten apocalyptic vengeance. In this very violence, and between the differing generic commitments of these poems – the most accurate registers of what was once called an age of "transition" – a residue of disquiet evades articulation and exerts its silent pressure on language.

CHAPTER I

Beginnings: André's Vita Henrici Septimi *and Dunbar's aureate allegories*

Narratives of origin, in particular dynastic or regnal origin, may not bear very much looking into. Henry of Richmond's's accession to the English throne was based in a tenuous claim and military violence. The marriage of James IV with Henry's eldest daughter Margaret Tudor sealed the misnamed Treaty of Perpetual Peace between England and Scotland of 1502, but in the event marked only a brief cessation in a history of hostility that had included James's clash with his own royal father James III at Sauchieburn in 1488. Both Bernard André's *Vita Henrici Septimi*, along with the writings of his fellow Latinists at Henry VII's court, and William Dunbar's *The Thrissill and the Rois* represent these crucial scenes as matters of sight, with André's self-projection as blind *vates*, and his role as humanist historiographer, mirrored by Dunbar's investment in stylized image and heraldic display. Both texts, while revealing of their contrasted court cultures, seek authority in blindness, absence and the unnamed spaces *between* figurations of presence, and find it a precarious formation indeed.

"UT CAECUS IN TENEBRIS": BERNARD ANDRÉ AND THE BLINDNESS OF ORIGINS

Between 1489 and 1490 some important Anglo-French negotiations took place in London. The subject was the control of Brittany, laid open by a Breton ducal minority to the marital designs of the French king, Charles VIII, and the diplomatic standing of the new English regime was highly visible. Henry VII, who had spent much of his exile in Brittany, sought to keep it independent, both to maintain an asylum for sympathetic refugees from the French court and to limit French hegemony along the Channel seaboard. The French ambassador and noted humanist[1] Robert Gaguin, incensed by what looked like diplomatic dilatoriness, wrote a bad-tempered epigram, published in Paris, which attacked the English and their king. This stirred up a quick response at the English court, where rhetoricians both defended Henry and attacked the conventional "doubleness" of the French.² The fullest contemporary account of the matter, in Bernard André's *Vita Henrici Septimi*, gives some idea of the diversity of the group involved in this coincidence of Tudor political ambition with the long fifteenth-century record of humanist speculation in English patronage.³ Giovanni Gigli ("vir profecto divinarum humanarumque rerum peritissimus" ["a man very expert indeed in divine and human affairs"]), born around 1434, had received ecclesiastical preferment from Edward IV, and would do so again under Henry VII. Pietro Carmeliano, "orator et poeta clarissimus" ["a most renowned poet and orator"], and Cornelio Vitelli, "facundissim[us] orator" ["an orator most eloquent"], were more recent arrivals; Carmeliano had capitalized on his humanist training and skills to become a royal secretary after a fallow period under Richard III, Vitelli was one of the first humanists to teach at Oxford.⁴ André, however, is – on his showing – the outstanding figure here:

Et nos quoque, qui de grege poetarum sumus, non paucos ut illi, sed pene ducentos in illum debacchati sumus, quippe nil audacius est malo poeta. Primum igitur heroicis fere quinquaginta, quorum initium:
"Phoebe pater, jam, Phoebe, veni: fas antra movere Delia."
Post, elegis:
"Nestoris annosi," etc.
Item aliis sic initientibus:
"Puppis ad Oenopiam," etc.
Iterum aliis hendecasyllabis, "Cum tot sustineas"; quorum finem hic apposui propter memoriam, seu majus jactantiam:
"Miles gaudet equis, colonus agris
Venator canibus, poeta musis;
Sic urit sua quemlibet voluptas." (57)

[And we too, who belong to this flock of poets, raged madly against [Gaguin], not with a few verses, as did the others, but with nearly two hundred – for no one is bolder than a bad poet: first in almost fifty hexameters, which began with "Father Apollo, now, Apollo, come: there is cause to rouse the Delian oracle"; next, in elegiacs: "Of aged Nestor"; again, in others beginning thus: "The ship to Oenopia," etc.; again in others, hendecasyllabics: "Since you suffer so much," the end of which I set here to call them to mind, or rather to boast about them: "The knight takes joy in horses, the farmer in fields, the hunter in hounds, the poet in the muses; thus does his own pleasure fire each man."]

While André and his peers compete for favor from a royal English patron who bestows on them actual and potential subsidy, this vertical model is offset by a contest among rival-doubles for the prestige conferred by success in a transnational rhetorical market where proficient Latinity, and the dexterous wielding of classical metre and allusion, are major commodities.

As we shall see in later chapters, this new development subjects the textual self-imagining of poets writing in English near the center of power after 1485 to imaginary dislocation, contestation and interference. The relations of identification on which cultural identity had been founded – identification with monarch and nation, with the English language and with a post-Chaucerian literary past – encounter a competing model. The reign of Henry VII witnessed the emergence – intermittent and compromised, but present nonetheless – of a Latin humanist poetics at court, which, as we shall see, answered the problem of Tudor legitimacy by fusing the originary moment of the new dynasty with tropes of humanist *renovatio*. They thus effected a break both with the immediate political past of dynastic strife, and with its vernacular literary equivalent. Like their English counterparts, they celebrated the images of monarch and nation, but articulated these components of cultural identity with a different and in certain domains more prestigious language, and with literary and dynastic lineages in which the fifteenth-century poetic and political genealogies of their English counterparts, closely bound to the Lancastrian moment and its troubled aftermath, did not figure. Their incipient literary professionalism linked them to the economic register in a style that distinguished them sharply from their English forebears and contemporaries. In short, this new rhetoric was grounded in material and immaterial considerations – a Latin language according its practitioners quasiprofessional status and accompanied by its own authenticating narratives – alien to the temporal categories and imaginary structures in which English public poetry was based. In his position at this conjuncture, André was a professional poet in a sense hardly true of earlier native authors, in whose vernacular work a temporality based in erratic, *ad hoc* payment had revealed itself in the markings of an edgy petitionary inwardness.

Hawes ponders an explicit opposition between native public poetry in the Lydgatean mould and the new language of political panegyric when, at the beginning of *The Comfort of Lovers*, he submits himself to his readers' "grete gentylnes" as one who is

> none hystoryagraffe / nor poete laureate
> But gladly wolde folowe / the makynge of Lydgate[5]

The allusion is almost certainly to Bernard André, one of the first recorded poets laureate in England[6] and holder of the title of historiographer royal: a distinct innovation at the English court, and one emblematic of the new conjunction of revisionist dynastic history, Latinity and professionalism.[7]

The arrival of the *grex poetarum* marked a significant moment in the history of relations between Latin and a vernacular which, for all the political and ideological weight it had gathered in the course of the fifteenth century, could not easily aspire to Latin's cultural title.[8] André came to England shortly after Richard III's defeat at Bosworth Field, and quickly began to serve as the new regime's unofficial propagandist. By November 1486 he had entered the records as "poeta laureatus" and was receiving an annuity, and he is the recorded recipient of many payments to "Master Bernard the blynde poete."[9] The Gaguin episode, of course, is as much about André's professional self-promotion as about his solidarity with a professional clique. As a member of the *grex* he is quite egregious, firing off four poems in a dizzying variety of meters (and his experimentation with classical meters does in fact mark him off from his contemporaries in England),[10] whereas Carmeliano, Gigli and Vitelli, admittedly on his evidence, modestly make do with one each. He further quotes the opening lines of the other poems in order to "frame" their authors, illustrating, in the most casual fashion, the greater density of classical allusion in his own *incipits* (55–56). Bourdieu's notion of a "profit of distinction" does double duty here:[11] if the Latinists are purveying a commodity distinct enough to put them in unusual demand, André offers the distinction of distinction.

André's lines, however, offer other seductions. His wild cumulation of metrical possibilities displays a craftsman in charge of his matter, but also comes very close to suggesting the opposite: a delirious yielding, a self-dispersal into these (in England at least) exotic patterns. We return to his own conclusion: what are the pleasures that "fire" his poetry? On the reading of David Carlson, who has done more than anyone to make these poets visible, they would hardly be legible, for the *grex* are nothing but signs. "We cannot know" Carlson writes, "whether Bernard André was without sight," since the figure of the blind *vates* "ha[s] no existence except as [a] functional location ... in a system of cultural-political relations in place in England at the time."[12] Several other essays by Carlson have shown what this system entailed. These authors from outside England initiate, as I have already noted, a very direct break in genre and allusion with prevalent English fifteenth-century models of "public" poetic discourse. In the cluster of birthday poems written to Prince Arthur in 1486, Arthur's advent comes in the trappings of Virgilian and Horatian messianism, Henry is a "triumphator," and London becomes ancient Rome, its plebs celebrating the new order with cries of "yo Paean" while its bards strum with their plectra. Discontinuity, as Carlson notes, is the order of the day; the reign of the Tudors will be the new age of gold, the *imperium*, liberation from a past of political strife.¹³ If this can sound unintentionally comic, we should nonetheless not ignore these poets' fascination with the transfiguring power of language. Their poems can, to be sure, be read as rehearsals of an exhausted political syncretism; but they are also exercises in risk, their enjoyment deeply vested in the precariousness of a rhetoric that allusively splits and reduplicates the present moment in acts of memory and anticipation. Such writing itself serves an imperial desire to engulf time and subordinate it to local meaning. The very strenuousness of these Roman identifications, and the poets' identification with regal *potestas* through so culturally unfamiliar a medium, produce some startling libidinal narratives, in which the erotics of patronage takes unexpected paths. These turn on the symbolic weight the poet has to bear as the speaker of a genealogy that must both fulfill and break with the past. I address here two particular instances. One involves a characteristic act of invocation, in which a poet's word takes on a problematic relationship to the body of the queen in the poems on Arthur's birth. The other suggests the tensions that arise when such atemporal moments of hortatory and panegyric address are forced, in André's *Vita*, to adjust to the requirements of historical narrative.

Giovanni Gigli wrote three poems for Prince Arthur's birth, two epigrams and a longer *Genethliacon*. The *Epigramma in natalem principis* begins as follows:

> Henricûm suboles, dudum promissa Britannis,
>   E celo veniens, nascere, magne puer;
> Tolle moras; tenere vexas cur membra parentis?   (1–3)

[Offspring of Henries, for a long time now promised to the Britons, coming from heaven, be born, great youth; have done with delays; why do you tenderly trouble your mother's body?]

The "tenere" (mildly, gently) has an unsettling ambiguity. Does Gigli suggest that the yet unborn Arthur's courteous "gentleness" demands to be realized in his historical person? Or that Arthur is "troubling" the mother's body *too* gently, and should subject it to the active violence ("vexas") of birth? The queen's body is a familiar site of danger, of transition and becoming,¹⁴ and Elizabeth of York, who holds the desired end of a divided past, bears an especially fraught real and symbolic burden. Gigli's response is to endow his own word with begetting force, a disciplined frenzy of symbolic mediation; passing through her body to call forth a son in a formal annunciation, it eliminates the time of waiting ("Tolle moras"). "Be born, great youth!" is followed a few lines later by a kletic "Ecce ades" ["Behold, you are here!"] (11).

In Carmeliano's *Suasoria Laeticiae*, the peace-bringing dynastic union is subtended by a more private eroticism authorized by classical precedent:

> Quae Cassandra sibi, vel quae Lucretia, vel quae
>   Penelope similis, aut Galathea fuit?
> Quamvis ille prius speciem formamque futurae
>   Coniugis audierat pictaque mente foret,
> Ante oculos tamen illa suos magis urget amantem
>   Vicinoque magis fomite crescit amor.
> Nec minus ipsa suum spectans dominumque maritum
>   Ardet amore sui regia virgo viri;
> Ambobus pariter sunt vincla iugalia curae,
>   Et damnant taciti tempora longa nimis:
> Obstabat tantum sacrae reverentia legis,
>   Nam fuerat quarto iunctus uterque gradu.   (239–50)

[What Cassandra, or what Lucretia, or what Penelope or Galatea was like to her [Elizabeth]? Although he had heard before of the face and form of his future bride, and she was pictured in his mind, before his eyes she stirred the lover yet more, and with such tinder nearby his love increased. No less did the royal virgin herself burn with love for her husband as she looked on her lord and spouse; both alike are eager for the bonds of matrimony and silently they curse a wait too long: but there stood in the way a reverence for holy law, for they were related to one another in the fourth degree.]

Carmeliano's poem attempts to serve two masters; its overt impulse is to idealize the love that will produce erotic and political union, but poetic fervor – translated here into his subjects' "burning" desire – cannot allow the royal couple to anticipate dispensation and infringe the "sacrae reverentia legis" and its gradations.[15]

Gigli employs similar tropes in the *Genethliacon*, which reflects on the *Epigram* (they appear together in the same presentation manuscript, BL MS Harley 336):

> O quantum superis, Britanne, debes;
> O quantum pariter parenti utrique,
> Lux per quos micuit tibi salutis,
> Pignus perpetue datum quietis.   (32–35)

[O, how much, Britain, you owe to the gods, how much to each parent alike, through whom the light of your safety shone forth, a pledge of perpetual peace.]

This figure, in which Arthur breaks through the parental bodies like the sun, also reads Gigli's other exegesis of the maternal body. From the perspective of the *Genethliacon*, that body becomes an opaque, clouded history from which the future must be released, just as the commanding word of Gigli's Latin supersedes the mother tongue. The queen's body, scene of political risk, calls into being an answering risk, as Gigli's word warily assumes the generative powers of an idealized male royalty.

For André, desire and identification are intertwined in more oblique ways, which turn on the status of his blindness. It is revealed in the *Vita*, as, about to tackle the strife between Edward IV and Henry VI, he introduces it with an open digression:

Qua in parte lectores rogatos velim ut me excusatum habeant, si illorum temporum procellas per gestorum seriem non exequar. Nam illis ego temporibus non aderam, neque antea quicquam de his auribus acceperam ... Certe dum haec scriberem relatorem sive recensorem quempiam non habebam, qui mihi, ut principio optaveram, dicendorum materiam mihi proponeret. Quare ut caecus in tenebris ambulans sine ductore, nihil praeter auditum habeo. Ad haec accedit hebes tantarum rerum et obtusa malis mens atque memoria. Quas ob res si parum ordinate singula carptimque non attigero, ignoscant mihi precor humillime qui nostra legent. (19)

[I would here ask my readers to hold me excused if I do not describe the troubles of those times in the order in which events occurred. For I was not present in those times, nor have I hitherto heard anything about them directly ... Certainly while writing this I have had no oral informant or storyteller, who might offer me, as I had originally hoped, the subject matter I was bound to treat. And so, like a blind man walking in darkness without a guide, I have no information besides what I have heard. And moreover my mind and memory are dull in so many matters, and blunted by hardships. I therefore most humbly beg my readers to pardon me if I touch on details in a piecemeal and somewhat disorderly fashion.]

Whether or not André really was blind, by the time he arrives at these lines the darkness ("tenebris") in which his blind man walks is already tropological. André writes: "si quid forte mansurum scripsero, his potissimum inscribam, quorum gloriae quadam velut participatione clarescere tenebrisque resistere valeam, quas mihi temporum fusca profunditas et nominum consumptrix illustrium obliviosa posteritas intentat" ["If by chance I shall have written anything that will endure, let me ascribe it chiefly to those through whose glory I may, as if by a kind of participation, have power to shine and to fight that darkness with which I am menaced by the gloomy depths of the ages and forgetful posterity, eater of illustrious names"] (3). André's blindness signifies.[16] He looks on a darkness brought by devouring time, which can only be dispelled by participation in the light of patronal, here royal, glory. This afflicted body is also the place where political and cultural registers cross, since darkness is now, on André's own showing, an alibi for a range of interventions and mediations. Caught in a historical twilight, seemingly compelled to speak of *res gestas* without reliable informant, he must have recourse, decorously or not, to matter which is "boldly" added from his own invention ("audaciae potius quam negligentiae abs te accusatum iri potevolui" ["I would rather you held me accused of rashness than of negligence"], 4), and to the replacement of a historical *ordo naturalis* with his own, quite aggressively artificial one, ironically named here as fragmentation. The supplementary additional matter, as it happens, is in fact central, for on the speeches, poems and digressions derived from classical precedent rests André's purpose of defining the Tudor present anew. As he does so, he accrues cultural capital, becoming the vatic bearer of a new kind of *translatio*, and a new understanding of *imperium*. What is striking is that instead of in any way concealing turbulent dynastic origins and questionable legitimacy, André's blindness hides them in plain sight.[17]

On a chronological and biographical level, André's life mirrors that of his ruler. The *Vita* surveys the monarch's reign and achievements up to the surrender of the pretender Perkin Warbeck in 1498, but also uses this narrative to frame a series of occasional poems in which André ceremonializes major events. The manuscript thus advertises itself as a work in progress for a dynastic foundation in process.[18] Large gaps are frequently left, usually introduced by a claim that André will write more on the topic at hand once he is better informed. The effect of this "retrospective collection," as Carlson calls it, is to maintain a double focus on poet and prince, on the narrative moment of lineal origin but also on the qualities of the historiographic and lyric fictions in which it is couched.[19] As a character in his work André bears a special relationship to what we might call occasional timing, as each new event of royal politics is accompanied by André's appearance within the frame, writing or singing a poem.

But when we look to the dynasty's founding moment at Bosworth, André is not all there:

Hoc ego bellum quamvis auribus acceperim, tamen hac in parte certior aure arbiter est oculus. Diem, igitur, locum, ac belli ordinem, quia ut dixi sum privatus hac luce oculorum, ne quid temerarie affirmem, supersedeo. Et pro tam bellico campo, donec plenius instructus fuero, campum quoque latum hoc in albo relinquo. (32)

[Though I heard of this battle with my ears, yet in this matter the eye is a surer judge than the ear. I therefore omit the day, the place and the order of battle (since as I have said I did not see it with my own eyes) lest I make any rash assertions. And so until I am more fully instructed, I leave a wide space in my book for such a warlike field.]

There is then a gap of a page and a half in the manuscript, to be filled in, André says, once he knows more. Readers have been quick to presume tactful evasion, and certainly if any historical event could defy representation in the ethical terms mandated by André's ancient model Sallust, it would be Bosworth, with its numerous equivocations and last-minute shifts of allegiance.[20] There is, however, more at stake here. We may recall that Ned Lukacher has read Freud's concept of the primal scene – where the child supposedly beholds its parents in intercourse, an act that analysis must then construct or reconstruct – in terms possessed of a historical significance that goes beyond the family romance. "Rather than signifying the child's observation of sexual intercourse," Lukacher writes, "the primal scene comes to signify an ontologically undecidable intertextual event that is situated in the differential space between historical memory and imaginative construction." Deployed for different medieval moments by Fradenburg and Paul Strohm, the notion suggests a confrontation with the radical contingency of historical origins. In this sense, the treacheries of Bosworth are indeed the Tudor primal scene.[21] My translation, for fluency's sake, blurs André's pun on *campum*, at once the battlefield and the gap in the manuscript. In a series of substitutions, André faces this "warlike" space of masculine action from what Patricia Parker has called the "ambiguous" position of men of letters,[22] repeated and displaced in succession by his sightless eyes and a blank space in a text. He thus points to his narrative's inability to sustain a point of origin, which instead starts to look suspiciously like an unnameable trauma.[23]

But this blindness is, as soon becomes apparent, rather constitutive of dynasty. For the heavily signposted absence that is Bosworth ("X doesn't mark the spot") acquires meaning as it were *nachträglich*, in a new metaphoric substitution in which André's poetry is profoundly implicated. Henry of Richmond's post-Bosworth entry into London receives striking preparation in André's text. Up to this point, all we have heard of André's own metrical proficiency is a brief Sapphic stanza, as Henry addresses the clergy after his victory:

> Praesules sacri celebres ministri,
> Prima sunt vobis quibus Ille primo
> Visus est olim recubare foeno
>   Gaudia certe. (34)

> [O holy bishops, numberless ministers,
> you, certainly, were the first to have
> the joy of seeing Him lie upon straw
>   long ago.]

The stanza form is visible in Gairdner's edition; in the manuscript it is entirely buried, written as continuous with the surrounding prose.[24] In the *Vita*, in other words, the first poet we hear – the foundation, indeed, of poetry – is the king himself describing the incarnate Christ, but the material source occludes this kingly making. Henry is figured as the hidden progenitor of André's classicizing art, an art inseparable from the *anima* breathed into this new monarchy. When Henry enters London, the art becomes explicit:

Rex ipse Richemundiae comes Saturni luce, quo etiam die de hostibus triumpharat, urbem Londinum magna procerum comitante caterva laetanter ingressus est. Ad cujus adventum ego, etsi oculis captus, amore jampridem sui ac desiderio inflammatus astiti, laetusque poetico furore afflatus palam hoc carmen cecini:

> De Prima Regis Victoria Carmen Sapphicum
>
> Musa, praeclaros age dic triumphos,
> Regis Henrici decus ac trophaeum
> Septimi, lentis fidibus canora
> Dic age, Clio.   (34–35)

[On Saturday – the same day of the week on which he had defeated his foes – the king himself, the earl of Richmond, joyfully entered the city of London, accompanied by a great retinue of nobles. Though I did not see his arrival with my eyes, I was present at it because inflamed by my desire and my long-standing love for him; and full of joy and inspired by poetic frenzy I publicly sang these verses:

> Sapphic Ode on the King's First Victory
>
> Muse, sing of illustrious triumphs,
> of the glory and trophies of King Henry
> the Seventh, sing songs, Clio, with
>   your pliant strings.]

"Cecini" is, I think, to be understood in its fullest vocal sense here; André bursts into song. If Bosworth was lost among the lacunae of text, the blind bard can now recapture origin through pure voice. It is not, of course, unmodulated; as the *vates* seized with divine frenzy, André is also heard in the Sapphic meter that signifies his own humanist competence. Lack is rewritten as plenitude; in a move presented both as spontaneous and as multiply determined – not least by the homoerotics of patronage ("desiderio") – André's blindness ("oculis captus") enables him to "see" the event, kindled by bardic *furor* and by sovereign love.²⁵ Poetry comes from the desire for Henry, who has himself already been figured as poetry.

This ode inaugurates the series of occasional poems noted earlier: a poem on Arthur's birth, one on the death of the Earl of Northumberland in a 1489 tax riot (48–49; a topic of course also treated by Skelton), one on Henry's return to London after the battle at Stoke (52–54), one addressed to the Papal Legate, and two "gratulationes" on the king's return from the brief and unglamorous French campaign, along with addresses to the city of London on the same occasion (61–64). These are typical of André's Roman style; the city is commanded to twine its brows with laurel at its king's return, and Henry himself is raised to the stature of a veritable sun king: "quod, si privatus Apollo / Paverit Admeti rursus et ipse boves, / Principis hic nostri vultus Jovialis abunde / Lumina, crede mihi, Phoebe recede, dabit" ["if Apollo, god no more, should return to pasture the herds of Admetus, then trust me, even with Phoebus gone, the Jove-like countenance of our king would shed light in plenty "] (62). In all these instances, André includes himself in the terms described, only once stepping back to suggest coyly that his vocal effusion comes from "quidam" – a certain person (39).

In such verse, André and his confrères body forth their ruler's interests. Their very allusiveness, however, gravitates to areas of danger even as they sustain the order that produces the danger. When Henry is about to set sail for England to claim the throne, André characterizes the episode through extensive allusions to Lucan's *Pharsalia*, in particular those passages in Book One where Caesar, having crossed the Rubicon, is coming within sight of Rome, and his first centurion ("primipilus") Laelius speaks on behalf of the army. When Henry/Caesar has addressed his forces, justifying his claim to the crown, the earl of Oxford replies:

Quare vetustissimi instituti consuetudo sane laudabilis est, ut bellorum imperatores commilitones suos ad fortiter pugnandum admoneant, non quod de illorum fide dubitent, sed ut ad rem gerendam avidius excitentur. Sic ille diligentissimus ac victoriosissimus Julius Caesar ante Pharsalicam expeditionem, sic Pompeius Magnus, sic Lucius Catilina, sic quicunque perlegitur optimus dux fecit ... Ignosce mihi precor, optime princeps, si hanc respondendi provinciam ante alios omnes susceperim. Nam postquam me primipilum primaeque aciei ductorem ordinasti, ut Laelius ille Caesari, sic ego excellentiae tuae verbis illius respondere iubeor in hunc modum Britanni ô vere successor et haeres imperii, veras exprimere voces ubi jubes, quod tam lenta tua tenuit patientia vires, conquerimur. Deeratne tibi fiducia nostri? (27–28)

[And so we should highly praise that custom established far in antiquity, according to which commanders exhort their fellow soldiers to fight boldly, not because they doubt their loyalty, but so that they may be more eagerly aroused to the task in hand. The most conscientious and victorious Julius Caesar did so before the campaign of Pharsalus; so did Pompey the Great, so did Lucius Catiline, so did every great general of whom we read ... Forgive me, best of princes, I ask, if I take on the office of this reply before all others. For since you ordained me first centurion and chief of the battle-line, as Laelius was to Caesar, so I am constrained to reply to your excellence in this way, in his words. O true successor and heir to the empire of Britain, since you ask us to speak the truth, we complain that your patience has restrained your powers for so long. Did you not trust us?"]

Oxford's speech here leans on a source highly ambivalent in its view of imperial power. André rehearses the key scenes in his models, Lucan and Sallust, and Oxford's "jubeor" ["I am constrained"] trembles with a larger compulsion, as if Oxford is ordered into action by Lucan's source text, and is driven into the role of Lucan's fictional Laelius by a kind of intertextual pressure. At first glance, André's text seems to follow earlier examples in which Lucan's critique of Caesar is assimilated to a Virgilian framework and so partially neutralized.[26] Though Oxford is allowed to retain Laelius's defense of civil war, the Tudor Caesar is no Lucanian force of nature or avenging destroyer, but an evidently honorable commander moved solely by the plight of his tyrannized and suffering land; he later orders his soldiers on no account to plunder the civilian population, a decree which, along with its accompanying threat of punishment, they cheerfully accept. Later, however, just before the battle of Stoke, the same episode is about to repeat itself, but is truncated when the king intervenes. Henry has again encouraged his army: "Finierat cum jam respondere parato ut ante comiti Oxoniensi rex quia tempus urgebat silentium indicit ac temporis angustiae consulendum imperavit" ["When he had finished the earl of Oxford was ready to reply as before, but the king cut him off because time was pressing, and ordered that the limited time be taken into account"] (51). This is remarkable for a narrative that has been so far given to creating expansive, and fictional, rhetorical spaces. The king calls for silence, as if the real peril to be avoided is repetition itself. And at the end of the narrative, which breaks off abruptly with Henry's harangue to the Cornish rebels, silence, in one way, is what we are left with, as if the darkness from which Henry's blind poet seeks to recall history has closed in once more.

Such disquiet speaks even louder if we consider what the work's reception, if any, may have been. Recent accounts of André's role in the new poetic economy have often, on limited evidence, pictured a "literary system" in which he measured the terms of possible success for Skelton and others, and important distinctions between vernacular and Latin poetic practice have often been collapsed. It might be altogether more accurate, however, to imagine the period's poetic energies as raging around a kind of black hole. There has been an inevitable tendency to think of the work of the *grex poetarum*, largely encomiastic and spectacularly overt politically and ideologically, as "public" poetry. Lately, however, in an essay whose title provocatively refers to the "humanist anti-literature" of early Tudor England, Carlson suggests that their writings were, quite programmatically, written not to be read. A number of them exist in presentation manuscripts only, and as such, they are expensive commodities, reified before – if ever – they are read, and destined for inert, unopened life in a royal library to which they add nothing but dead and ornate bulk. The poems do not circulate beyond these manuscripts, "nor" – Carlson's words – "were they recopied by others or put directly into print. But no matter: the short-term success André enjoyed highlights the importance of the singular audience for whom he worked, who would rarely if ever have put much effort into studying André's copious output: the English king." Pure surplus, useless magnificence, conspicuous consumption at its most extreme: this is the purpose of "the deluxe presentation copy that would not circulate, of poetry that could not be read." "This" Carlson writes, "is not literature. It is a quasi-dramatic, ritualized public manifestation of anti-social waste, involving lavish expenditure of training, time, and materials, for no other end."[27] Public poetry, then, destined for the crypt. Yet this is one crypt whose contents we should not underestimate. When the *Ancien Régime* collapsed in 1789, Walter Benjamin notes, the signifiers of the Roman polity returned with a vengeance, signaling a utopian break with the past by rewriting the calendar of the new Republic.[28] The classicizing of Henry's rhetoricians carries a related charge, with the crucial and unsettling difference that what it intuits is the absolutist moment whose undoing Benjamin describes. In this chiastic history, what speaks to these Tudor poets is not the Roman republic but the *imperium* that replaced it. And imperial destiny here becomes a peculiar bondage: intimate commerce with a possibly unresponsive monarch, within pages perhaps unread.

MISSING COURT

The marriage of James IV of Scotland and Henry VII's eldest daughter Margaret Tudor at Holyrood Palace on 8 August 1503 solicited a rhetoric of "new beginnings" with some urgency. James's own accession to the Scottish throne, as noted earlier, had been sufficiently turbulent; Lyndsay notoriously describes it as a full-blown oedipal drama:

> The civyll weir, the battell intestine;
> How that the sonne, with baner braid displayit,
> Agane the fader in battell come arrayit.[29]

The subsequent years had been marked by multiple cross-border invasions in both directions, including James's support of Warbeck in 1496 and the siege of Norham in 1497, undertaken while English forces were preoccupied with the Cornish rebellion on which André's *Vita* fades out. The marriage was, ironically, a sequel to the unpopular policy of alliance with England formerly pursued by James III, not least matrimonially. It was also intended to consolidate the Peace of Glasgow, itself a fragile alliance. The treaty had been urged by the English to deflect the dangers posed by Scotland's French ally, though the sudden deaths of Prince Arthur and Henry's queen Elizabeth brought into play the real risk that the English succession might pass to a Scottish heir. Hostility was acute on both sides; as Norman Macdougall remarks, "the councillors of Henry VII who had advised against the Scottish match can hardly have enjoyed the pageantry of Margaret Tudor's progress north."[30]

The Thrissill and the Rois,[31] in which Dunbar anticipates the union, has echoed such divided apprehensions in its modern critical reception. Division is inescapable in the poem itself. The marriage is foretold through a dazzling landscape of heraldic allegory, expansively rendered; it is in turn framed by a dreamer who can trace a clear ancestry to *The Parliament of Fowls* and French love-*dit*. At the poem's end, in five abrupt lines, the imaginary court vanishes, and the dreamer awakens in something like terror to write the poem down. Critic have asked how far the poem might be understood as a critique of the royal language it inhabits. Spearing offers the fullest compromise position, suggesting that *The Thrissill* "genuinely celebrates an ideal, while at the same time admitting, with poise and toughness, that reality often diverges from it."[32] I argue here that Dunbar's poem echoes André's work in its concerns – with the transfiguring power of language, with the visibility of figures, and with the imagining of imperial temporality – but to very different ends. *The Thrissill* is haunted by anxieties that embrace Dunbar's own style and its relation to the herald's twinned properties of ekphrasis and memory. The outcome is a poem to whose representations the poet himself is finally alien. Royal desire plays through the poem as a series of prohibitions that in the end are not easily deciphered. To illuminate this aspect of the poem, I draw on Dunbar's *The Goldyn Targe*, often viewed as a companion piece to *The Thrissill*, and imbued with its ceremonial and spectacular allegorical quality.

The openings of both *The Thrissill* and the *Targe* evoke the *Roman de la Rose*, which the *Targe* abbreviates with delightful insouciance ("I raise and by a rosere did me rest," B59, 3).³³ *The Thrissill* moves through comparable layers of allusion, and as it does so it dissolves the punctuality of beginning into a series of leave-takings. May begins its rule, impelling "the birdis to begyn thair houris" (B52, 5), because March "wes with variand windis past" (1) and April has "Tane leif at Nature" (3). The spring landscape is outside, but in the dreamer's chamber it is repeated, acted out by personifications. Aurora looks in at his window with an attendant lark who exhorts lovers to celebrate the "lusty morrow" (14), while May, "In weid depaynt of many diuers hew" (16) and "flouris forgit new" (18), is still more pressing:

> "Slugird," scho said, "Awalk annone for schame,   *sluggard awake*
> And in my honour sum thing thow go wryt.
> The lork hes done the mirry day proclame,
> To rais vp luvaris with confort and delyt,
> ʒit nocht incresis thy curage to indyt,
> Quhois hairt sum tyme hes glaid and blisfull bene,
> Sangis to mak vndir the levis grene."   (22–28)

This poet, however, sullenly refuses to fit in with the generic frame imposed. The birds "haif moir caus to weip and plane thair sorrow" (31); the air outside is "nocht holsum nor benyng" (32) and "Lord Eolus" (33) is still master in this season. This narrator has come to resemble the obstreperous nightingale of *The Kingis Quair*, a dysfunctional stage property who remains silent when he should sing.³⁴

May's response is to encourage the dreamer again, this time alluding to a prior promise not represented within the poem:

> Thow did promyt, in Mayis lusty quhyle
> For to discryve the ros of most plesance.   (38–39)

Fradenburg observes that this requires the poet-dreamer to rewrite a desire which without the sovereign demand has fallen into lassitude: "once desire coincided with expectation, devotion, with 'honoring' the sovereign," but now it is disconnected from fulfillment, floating in empty space (135). At this point, however, political codings are in abeyance. The "variand windis" may well hint at past political instabilities, just as the "ros of most plesance" may "be" Margaret Tudor, but these figures are not about to disclose their meaning yet. May's invitation rather directs this crabbed lover towards two other objects. One is an already eroticized garden where – to recall David Hult's description of the *Roman de la Rose* – "the relationship between the entire allegorical *paysage* and the woman's bodily representation" is ambiguous, and an "ultimately unlocalizable, ineffable body" produces "a mental *utopia*, literally a no-place in which vague notions circulate but in which no representation of a governing, responsible center is to be found."³⁵ The dreamer, Guillaume-de-Lorris-style, follows this seductive lure, suddenly "full fresche and weill besene / In serk and mantill" (45–46) like his French forebear. The other incentive offered, however, may be more startling:

> Go se the birdis how thay sing and dance,
> Illumynit our with orient skyis brycht,
> Annamyllit richely with new asur lycht. (40–42)

It is on this note that May performs her final farewell ("Quhen this was said departit scho, this quene," 43), concluding the poem's opening movements away from origin; the shifts through allusion and reflexion, thematized as departures, elude occasion even for this poem that will reveal itself as "occasional." Terms such as "Illumynit" and "Annamyllit," and the Latinate "orient," raise the real possibility that Dunbar's poet is beckoned into the garden by the image of his own style at its richest, allured by the distinctive signifiers he has used elsewhere.

Given the uncertainties of Dunbar's chronology, the claim that three words would instantly announce a "signature" requires some caution. There can, however, be little doubt that Dunbar's poem shares distinctive stylistic features – "aureate" Latinized diction, the metaphors of artifice, a fascination with the textural play of color and light – both with his other extended allegory *The Goldyn Targe*, and with Gavin Douglas's *The Palice of Honour*, to be discussed later.³⁶ R. J. Lyall has interestingly suggested a chronology on internal grounds: Douglas's poem (datable to 1501) highlights the sensuous elements in this style, while Dunbar responds with a critique of such excess in *The Goldyn Targe* and then provides a ceremonial compromise in the "authentically" transfiguring language of *The Thrissill*, which honours a meeting between sensory nature and the supranatural order in a royal union.³⁷ I will have cause to return to the question of chronology; it is enough to note here the real possibility that the "depaynt" May draws a dreamer clearly identified as a poet into this vision through a captivating version of his own "Dunbarian" poetics. At the outset, poet and poem, dreamer and garden suggest a desire circling through the other of verbal artifice and body/garden to return to the subject, through the transferred and improper to the proper, a movement established both by the distant evocation of the *Roman de la Rose* and perhaps by a self-citation.

As he enters this illumined "lusty gairding gent" (44), the dreamer accordingly becomes part of its optics, and it is useful at this point to glance at *The Goldyn Targe*. This poem has regularly been assigned to the periphery of courtly ceremonial, with Pamela King offering the judicious perspective that it is a script for an imaginary pageant.[38] The beginning offers a notoriously virtuoso rendition of an aureate landscape, with Dunbar's Latinate diction at its most elevated:

> Wp sprang the goldyn candill matutyne,   *of the morning*
> With clere depurit bemes cristallyne,   *purified*
> Glading the mery foulis in thair nest.   *delighting*
> . . .
> Anamalit was the felde wyth all colouris.   *Enameled*
> The perly droppis schuke in silvir schouris,
> Quhill all in balme did branch and leuis flete.   *fragrance; flow*
> . . .
>   The rosy garth, depaynt and redolent,
>   With purpur, azure, gold and goulis gent,
>   Arayed was by dame Flora, the quene,
>   So nobily that ioy was for to sene
>   The roch agayn the riwir resplendent,
>   As low enlumynit all the leues schene.   *flame; brightly*
>   (B59, 4–6, 13–15, 40–45)

This is a landscape where discourse is, to borrow Lacan's phrase, "aligned along the several staves of a musical score."[39] The landscape that May promises to speak into existence in *The Thrissill* is here a poetic *fait accompli*. Previous scholarship has done much to elaborate the sources and resources of Dunbar's diction: his periphrastic techniques, the metaphors which in the *artes rhetoricae* lend form and body to words, lapidary, biblical, liturgical and doctrinal symbolism, various forms of artisanal labor.[40] Nature is conceived in terms of artifice, and a repertory of verbs – "Apparalit," "Anamalit" (12–13), "Ourgilt" (27). The narrator here is, like the figure in the *Thrissill*'s long central section, little more than a "pair of eyes" mediating text to reader, and as the colors of line 41 hint, one element in the picture these ekphrastic eyes observe is heraldic.[41]

This poem too is a dream vision. The narrator falls asleep on "Florais mantill" (48) and a form of semantic slippage begins. If the poem's prologue began "Ryght as the stern of day begouth to schyne" (1), the dream starts with the approach of "A saill als quhite as blossum vpon spray, / Wyth merse [*top-castle*] of gold brycht as the stern of day" (51–52). As Spearing has noted, these lines seem to enact an entirely programmatic reversal; while the garden *topos* at the beginning of the poem rendered the natural world through a lexis of artifacts, the emblematic ship that suddenly arrives on the scene presents human making in the terms of nature.⁴² The erotic allure of those terms becomes unmistakable when the ship's passengers disembark:

> quharfro anon thare landis
> Ane hundreth ladyes, lusty in to wedis,
> Als fresch as flouris that in May vp spredis,
> In kirtillis grene, withoutyn kell or bandis,　　　　*cap*
> Thair brycht hairis hang gleting on the strandis,
> In tressis clere wyppit wyth goldyn thredis,　　　*bound about*
> With pappis quhite and mydlis small as wandis.　　*breasts*
> (57–63)

Style is decomposed into a series of metaphoric shifts that are also courtly "guisings," and the narrator remains a cipher, a moving eye ("There saw I," 73, 82, 87). When, their number swollen as if in some glossator's mythographic delirium by a company of gods and goddesses, they begin to dance, the narrator

> Crap . . . throu the levis and drew nere,
> Quhare that I was rycht sudnynly affrayt,
> All throw a luke, quhilk I have boucht full dere.
> (133–35)

The rest of the poem unleashes the force of what has hitherto been a seemingly redundant "look," as if to demonstrate the terrifying potentialities that might lie within ekphrasis itself. Venus spots the voyeur and sends in her "archearis kene" (137):

> Than ladyes fair lete fall thair mantillis gren,
> With bowis big in tressit hairis schene
> All sudaynly thay had a felde arayit.
> And yit rycht gretly was I noucht affrayit,
> The party was so plesand for to sene.
> A wonder lusty bikkir me assayit.　　　　　*assault; beset*
> (139–44)

Interiority emerges in the gap between the menace presented by this erotic artillery and the narrator's (largely) unperturbed response; the "wonder lusty bikkir" introduces the playful irony of love-*dit*, conspicuous till now by its absence. Yet erotic arousal still belongs chiefly to the landscape, released from within its verbal and corporeal folds. These ladies expose themselves and deploy their amorous and bodily armory; the ladies' hair, a standard fetish of *amour courtois* (compare Chrétien de Troyes's *Chevalier de la Charrette*)⁴³ now becomes a weapon. The lover-narrator's desire is fully alienated in spectacle; indeed, he himself is on the side of the spectacle, defended by Reason "with schelde of gold so clere" (151). He is assaulted by a steady wave of personifications – beginning with "dame Beautee" (146), followed by figures of the stages of a woman's life ("tender Youth," 154; "Grene Innocence," 155; "Suete Womanhede" 160) – and his defense collapses only in the face of "Perilouse Presence" (196). After a love affair, which evidently lasts "quhill men mycht go a myle" (221), the lover is deserted, and Eolus blows his "bugill" (230):

> And sudaynly in the space of a luke
> All was hyne went, thare was bot wildernes,
> Thare was no more bot birdis, bank and bruke. (232–34)

Allegorical representation fails when "Presence" – the point at which one might indeed expect figures to fail – "kest a pulder" (203) in Reason's eyes.[44] This is accompanied, too, by a stripping down of the landscape – all properties and ladies vanish, and "the space of a luke" becomes conterminous, as it always was, with lack and evanescence.

Christopher Pye speaks of the "specular conceit" that "lends the irrecoverable moment of the subject's entry into the symbolic order its recursive form, casting it as an instance of loss endlessly returning upon the self."[45] Such recursiveness, I think, marks the bond in the poem between the demolition of the garden *topos* and the note of loss on which the poem closes. The ship, like one of the elaborate structures of courtly revel, departs with a deafening cannonade that awakens the dreamer: "Wyth spirit affrayde apon my fete I sprent" (242). He returns to the garden of the opening, but it is of course a world of artifice, whose relations with the erotic body remain obvious: "In quhite and rede was all the felde besene, / Throu Naturis nobil fresch anamalyng" (250–51). There is, however, a final transformation in store. Poetic fathers are absorbed into the landscape, or rather, perhaps, their presence is revealed. Chaucer is apostrophized as "rose of rethoris all," "ane flour imperiall," and "all the lycht" of "oure Inglisch" (253–54, 59), who "This mater coud illumynit haue full brycht" (258). The poem then hails the two other members of the fifteenth-century English triumvirate:

> O morall Gower and Ludgate laureate,
> Your sugurit lippis and tongis aureate
> Bene to oure eris cause of grete delyte.
> Your angel mouthis most mellifluate
> Oure rude langage has clere illumynate
> And fair ourgilt oure spech, that imperfyte
> Stude or your goldyn pennis schupe to write.
> This ile before was bare and desolate
> Off rethorike or lusty fresch endyte. (262–70)

The fathers are evoked in a mobile terminology that moves between speech and writing, transferring the metaphoric "sun" to Chaucer and making him the "flour" of English, but also linking the "desolate" (in Scots "left without a king")[46] "ile" to the "wildernes" that is "the space of a luke" between figures, and to the death as well as the – literal – *floreat* of makars. The topology of Dunbar's pageant language, too, is caught within iteration. Rereading the poem enacts a fall, since the reader knows that the language of the paradisal opening will unavoidably enter a region of unlikeness, begin to differ from itself.[47] Readerly desire, like that of Dunbar's voyeur, is wedded to style in a strange and finally disrupted intimacy. This aggressively visual poem is finally located in a "could have," and a paradoxical injunction to draw itself "out of sicht" (277), with a hint that its evidently seamless flamboyance is in fact "disteynit, bare and rent" (278), perhaps because it is made up of the languages of others.

The Goldyn Targe begins by drastically reducing its cast of characters to ekphrastic eye and style as object, and goes on to take as its very subject the dissolution of boundaries drawn between ekphrasis and the erotic I/eye. A reified language, detached from the vocal register of praise in which aureate diction thrives, arouses visual idolatry, and even those words most densely bound to the most irreproachably doctrinal meanings are haunted by the danger of expropriation, or of sliding back into a form of fetishism. In *The Thrissill and the Rois*, Dunbar's strategy of leave-takings – displacing the poem steadily from some imagined point – purposefully strives to evade such risks, just as it seeks to withdraw from a treacherous history. The notion that this poem might find its own object in its style and be narcissistically lost is here allowed to fall away abruptly. This garden is introduced with a relative minimum of Latinisms, and Aurora's earlier prosopopeic appearance is recast in the form of the rising "purpour" sun

> Throw goldin skyis putting vp his heid,
> Quhois gilt tressis schone so wondir cleir.
> That all the world tuke confort, fer and neir,
> To luke vpone his fresche and blisfull face,
> Doing all sable fro the hevynnis chace.   (52–56)

This solar "fresche and blisfull face" ushers in a language of dazzlingly irradiated surfaces, which, as Fradenburg observes, transfigures the garden and transcends history. The ekphrastic "I" gives place entirely to the vivid landscape, just as narration cedes to the attraction to figure to which it is invariably prone.[48] After restraining potentially disturbing forces, such as "Eolus the bawld" (65), Nature summons birds, beasts and flowers, her power to compel obedience magically asserted in the "twynkling of ane e" (85). Chief among them are the three figures of Jamesian royalty: "the Lyone, gretast of degre" (87), "the Egle king of fowlis" (120), and "the awful Thrissill" (129). Royal plurality of being appears as three symbolic creatures; history depends not on Bernard André's occluded "fields," but on the highly visible fields of heraldry (the Lion stands "On feild of gold . . . full mychtely," 97). The heraldic, elsewhere a strand in Dunbar's diction, is crucial here, and the bejeweled ground of *The Goldyn Targe* is consolidated into real property. The Lion, appointed king of beasts, is endowed with a "dyademe full deir, / Off radyous stonis most ryall for to se" (101–02). On the Rose herself, characteristically, is bestowed "A coistly croun with clarefeid stonis brycht . . . Quhill all the land illumynit of the licht" (155, 157).

Beginnings are not so decisively past in Nature's gift of a crown to the Thrissill. As Nature surveys "all flouris that grew on feild" (127) she sees the thistle

> kepit with a busche of speiris.
> Concedring him so able for the weiris,
> A radius croun of rubeis scho him gaif
> And said, "In feild go furth and fend the laif" (130–33)

The Thistle's qualification for kingship, then, is his strength in arms, an oblique reference, perhaps, to earlier history, but one which realizes usurping as defensive violence.[49] If the poem presents "three symbols of James IV, the royal lion (justice), the eagle (liberality), and the thistle (strength)," the only symbol given a justification for its coronation – and, indeed, a mate – is the one whose emblematic attributes can compel coronation.[50]

Fradenburg's superb account of *The Thrissill* conceives of its heraldic symbolism as direct revision of Chaucer's *Parliament of Fowls*. Unlike Chaucer's tercel eagles, whose competitive and endlessly self-replicating language of aristocratic complaint can only be locked in the gap between body and figure – to speak of dying for love and to die are not the same – "Dunbar's triplication of sovereignty . . . tries to assert a fullness of being in and through the very 'irreality' of the monarch, his entitlement to a surplus figuration, a richness of imagination."[51] There may, however, be something disquieting in this very fullness. Dunbar's dreamer must, as herald, enter a field which already abounds with other desires – not only the sovereign's, but the multiple desires attending on the metaphors and registers on which the poem draws – and which is therefore finally inscrutable.

Certainly some interdictions are more recognizable than others. The heraldic sign is necessarily conflicted, and in ways that suit this particular royal referent well. As D. Vance Smith observes, that sign's genealogical dimension necessarily points to the death of fathers, while asserting the public rights of the living to use the sign. Dependent both "on proximity to the ancestors and on their absence" for its legitimacy, the symbolic law of heraldry thus becomes identical to the law of the father and its accompanying interdiction "not to become too much like the father, not to undermine by making real the symbolicity of the paternal metaphor."[52] And if this signified monarch combines the roles of parricide and royal regicide, he is transgressive in other respects too. Critics of Middle Scots writing have been almost romantically swift to remind us of James's IV's attentions to successive royal mistresses in the years before 1503; however relevant this may be, *The Thrissill* is certainly a work of counsel to princes advocating the disciplining of sexual appetite.[53] From this point of view, the ruler's unpredictable desires make him not only the son who usurps, but the father (*pater patriae*) who enjoys. Nature must domesticate him, posing with the royal lion as if, once again, on a field:

> This lady liftit vp his cluvis cleir   *paws (lit. cloven hooves)*
> And leit him listly lene vpone hir kne
>
> (99–100)

Violent hierarchies are subsumed ("Do law elyk to aipis and vnicornis," 109). The lion's wrath is revealed through the power of restraint; the eagle, with its feathers sharpened "as steill dertis" (121), and the thistle with its "busche of speiris" (130) become icons of self-control.

The focal point of this advice is the Rose herself, a body that must, literally, not be adulterated. Distinction pertains; the king is enjoined not to allow the "nettill vyle" (137) or "wyld weid" (139) to mingle or compare with "the gudly flour delyce" (138). In this scene's profusion of figures, the rose's perfection excludes comparison; small wonder that, in the poem's most notoriously advisory section, the "king" is admonished

> Nor hald non vdir flour in sic denty
> As the fresche Ros of cullour reid and quhyt,
> For gife thow dois, hurt is thy honesty   (141–43)

The erotic body of the *Roman de la Rose* has become the kingdom's body, as the ensuing ceremonious hymn to the Rose confirms. Dunbar is constructing a myth in the strict Barthesian sense: the "Rois both reid and whyt" (171) is already a sign of the union of York and Lancaster, but is here caught up in a discourse where she becomes the signified of another sign, the union of the Stewart "Fyancells."[54]

These, however, are only the accessible shapes of a desire that lies just out of the elaborately rendered "light" of heraldry – enigmatic, self-involved, not fully available.[55] The appeal laid out by the love-garden, with its lover who appears only to be sent into the heraldic wallpaper, becomes an unanswered question, an unsettling surplus in a vision akin to Lacan's "ambiguity of the jewel."[56] In contrast to the modesty *topos* which belatedly replaces the garden of *The Goldyn Targe* with "this ile," the end of *The Thrissill*, like that of André's *Vita*, hints at the subtraction of the object of vision from memory:

> Than all the birdis song with sic a schout
> That I annone awoilk quhair that I lay,
> And with a braid I turnyt me about   start
> To se this court, bot all wer went away.
> Than vp I lenyt halflingis in affrey,   half
> And thus I wret, as ʒe haif hard toforrow,
> Off lusty May vpone the nynt morrow.
>   (183–89)

For Fradenburg, the birds' "schout" is sovereign authority which becomes all too loud: "the univocity deafens; the poem is silenced by its own phonic power."[57] Yet in this poem that has been concerned with pointing to origins beyond origins, the final stanza returns us to the beginning, giving us another origin, another explanation for the poet's activity. The poem is pushed into existence not by the birds' sudden chorus ("Go se the birdis how thay sing and dance" [40] has been replaced by "sic a schout") but by the vanishing of the court. May demanded that the poet return to his former state, and produce a "hairt ... glaid and blissful ... Sangis to mak undir the levis grene" (27–28), but now it is the very absence of the court, the lack framed by the "space of a luke," that requires the poet to produce court poetry.

The Thrissill's attempt to establish a "natural" basis for the Anglo-Scottish marriage, like André's contemplation of Henry VII's progress to the throne, evolves into a subtle meditation on oblivion. Here Smith is once again instructive in his exploration of heraldry's memorial workings. While it commemorates, he suggests, it is also bound in the end to an antiquity beyond reach; it is a mortuary practice resting on the dead that cannot be memorialized, a time "dont memoire de home ne courte." The "very potency of the heraldic depends upon something unknowable, ungraspable at its very heart," a "failure of technologies of registration to account for something that will always be a remainder."[58] Absorbed in its own enjoyment, "this court" that the dreamer so desperately tries to "see" goes away because, as the double story told by the dream structure makes clear, it was never there and cannot look back. In the end, *The Thrissill* presents two accounts of its genesis, one which styles it a response to a command, and one which creates a demand in order to fill an absence. It cannot sustain, therefore, a subject to whom it was always blind. Dunbar's poetic language, insofar as it partakes of the visual spectacle of the court, cannot see its author, and retains alterity. In John Skelton's *The Bowge of Courte*, the subject of our next chapter, the problematic center of the court poet's authority will be the focus of further scrutiny.

CHAPTER 2

The Bowge of Courte *and the birth of the paranoid subject*

We have seen that André's *Vita Henrici Septimi* is a remarkably miscellaneous compilation. Biography, autobiography, chronicle, ode, elegy, panegyric, set speech based on classical precedent, are all narratively juxtaposed. In a comparable fashion, the early career of John Skelton – royal tutor to Prince Henry, as until 1500 was André to Arthur, Prince of Wales – also knots together various strands, which recent scholarship has done much to unpick. Skelton's position at this juncture is made up of several contradictory elements, which can only be sketched here, but which ask precisely the question of what a "court" poetry might be. His entry into royal service was marked by a highly personal system of chronology,[1] connecting him to the ruler but also asserting an idiosyncratic difference. The attention given to his self-definition as "Skelton laureate" has proved laureation itself to be a remarkably fissile trope. As translator in 1488 of Diodorus Siculus's universal history, the *Bibliotheca historica*, from Poggio Bracciolini's fifteenth-century Latin version, he confirmed a Latinate *auctoritas*, already recognized by Oxford's laureation, which would be repeated at Louvain and Cambridge. He is also "Skelton laureatus" at the head of his first English poem, *Upon the Dolorous Dethe of the Erle of Northumberlande*. Recent studies have further shown laureate authority to be rooted in material and in immaterial considerations – political sanction, court standing, the steady economic support enjoyed by André, imagined roles, more noumenal forms of "inspiration" – which rarely sit well together.[2]

All these ambiguities cluster when William Caxton, prefacing his *Eneydos* in 1490, invites "Mayster John Skelton, late created poete laureate in the Unyversite of Oxenforde, to oversee and correct this sayd booke."[3] The gesture is clearly a complex one. For Daniel Wakelin, the mention of Skelton actually goes with disenfranchisement from the "humanist inheritance";[4] Caxton, desired by "som honest and grete clerkes … to wryte the most curyous termes that I could fynde," is rather interested in a wider audience. William Kuskin argues compellingly for a multifaceted agenda on

Caxton's part. Since Skelton translates "into Englysshe, not in rude and olde langage but in polysshed and ornate termes craftely," he is also a vernacular *auctor*. This is of a piece with Caxton's wider, layered project, which gestures towards academic and aristocratic readers while fashioning a different material product for a "broader audience" conceived as the community of the state. Skelton's *Upon the Dolorous Dethe*, on Kuskin's showing, locates itself similarly. Extant in one presentation manuscript, the poem adheres to the authority of vernacular high style and aristocratic allegiance in its modesty topos:

> Mi wordis unpullysht be nakide and playne,
> Of aureat poems they want ellumynynge;
> Bot by them to knouledge ye may attayne
> Of this lordis dethe and of his murdrynge.   (127–30)[5]

Ultimately, however, it estranges both sources of authority, in the heavily classicizing agenda presumably noted by Caxton and in the uneasy, fatalistic suggestion of possible treachery in Northumberland's death. The ground of power it eventually outlines is an imagined community, tacitly centered on the monarch. Thus Skelton's identity, both poetic and political, is defined less through feudal tradition than through "a juxtaposition of entrepreneurial autonomy and allegiance to centralized power."[6] In *The Bowge of Courte* Skelton, household servant and laureate, writes a poem for print dissemination, at a point (*c.* 1499) when Wynkyn de Worde's interest in promoting contemporary English poetry is especially visible,[7] and addresses the distinct, as yet partly symbolic, community that the medium endeavors to define.

Writing on Skelton and laureation has largely been preoccupied with Petrarch's 1341 coronation by Robert of Sicily, and for the most part has accordingly neglected the laurel crown's Ovidian aetiology in erotic pursuit, metamorphosis and loss.[8] Skelton himself is not unmindful of the scene, as *The Garlande of Laurell* will show. His poetry of the 1490s, however, discloses a more vernacular eroticism. The Lydgatean formality of *Upon the Dolorous Dethe* has a low-style double in *Manerly Margery Milk and Ale*, and the shorter poems later collected in *Agaynst a Comely Coystrowne* and *Dyvers Balettys and Dyties Solacyous*. Alongside aristocratic elegy and a vernacular laden with classical reference there appears, as I have pointed out elsewhere, a very different vernacular, one fascinated by "the female body as figure of verbal excess,"[9] the dominant role of what Roland Greene calls "the material patterns of sound,"[10] and an abrasive, disjunctive relation between genres. The construction of "the sexual Skelton" – to borrow A. W. Barnes's evocative phrase – is the author's own project before it is that of a post-Reformation interest in associating Catholicism with the stigma of sodomy.[11]

PRIVY SPACES

The Bowge of Courte, printed in 1499,[12] brings together these different versions of Skelton, embracing the royal household and print. Its readers have admired the artifice by which it translates the standard *topoi* of anticourt satire into the subjective mode of dream vision.[13] They have also, however, detected within the artifice an authentically autobiographical fear and disgust.[14] While the poem shows all too convincingly the terrors that presumably did beset medieval and Renaissance court men, we perhaps do well to remind ourselves, obvious though the point may be, that the poem's effect of terror is the measure of a poet-rhetorician's mastery and resourcefulness as well as of a real and vicious court world. Its self-reflexive removal of ground from beneath the reader's feet seems aimed, not solely to document the courtier's "real" paranoia, but to participate in the discursive production of paranoia – rather, in fact, as if paranoia were itself some form of commodity. I shall argue here that *The Bowge* promotes not a critique of secret royal power, but its very replication.

Having rejected the more lurid tints in Bacon's picture of an avaricious monarchic spymaster and his "new men,"[15] and looked rather to continuities with Yorkist and earlier government, the recent historiography of Henry VII's reign has nevertheless perceived a distinctive style of rule. In the 1490s the monarch was shaken by the perceived betrayal of his lord chamberlain Sir William Stanley, in a household conspiracy that itself appears at least in part to have been fabricated by the informers of whom the understandably insecure new king was making extensive use.[16] David Starkey, in one of the major early Tudor historiographic shifts of the last decades, has argued that as a result the Privy Chamber was sequestered from the rest of the household, and Henry retreated there attended by men "too humble to play politics."[17] While the magnificence of Henry VII's court is not in question, there are grounds for diagnosing a perceptible split between the monarch's position as head of the *domus magnificenciae*, and some displacement of power into less visible and more privy areas, centered, in the most literal of ways, on the royal body natural (from these years dates the post of Groom of the Stool). An act passed after the victory at Stoke also reveals much about the temper of the household. It decreed that "when compassyng of the deth of such as were of the Kynges trewe Subgiettis was hadd, the destruccyon of the prynce was ymagyned therby," authorized a jury of the household to determine whether any of its lesser members had conspired to murder the king or one of several prominent officials, and made any such offence a felony even in the absence of "actuell dedis." Intended to nip in the bud any such "confyderses compassynges Consperaces [and] ymagynacyons," the act illustrates, as J. R. Lander points out, "how terrified Henry VII had become of the very centre of power, the royal household itself."[18]

This response to the long-standing problem of household security had implications for patronage, which earlier curial satire had often grasped as a personal relation (the lord's or sovereign's neglect breeds injured merit and righteous outrage). The reign's deployment of money as an instrument of control was unprecedented, and while this is most familiar from the elaborate system of bonds and recognizances that were imposed on the nobility and many others as pledges of good behavior, especially after 1502,[19] the king's manipulation of finance also intervened in the body politic in ways which, while less draconian, were no less far-reaching. Edward IV had replaced the complicated system by which the Exchequer formerly managed the crown lands with the mechanics of chamber finance, by which revenues were sent directly, via so-called "receivers," to the financial office of the court and household, the royal Chamber. In Henry VII's reign this continued: the yield of the crown lands, indeed, was higher, since Henry held many of the relevant territories in his possession, making few grants either to the relatively scarce surviving members of his family or to the nobility.[20] This rechanneling of revenue also sustained royal independence, and Henry's personal involvement in the examination of the Chamber accounts was consistent.[21] Margaret Condon points out that

> Henry's great extension of chamber finance [was] important because of the disturbing influence which it enabled the King to exert upon all ruling groups ... Chamber finance, in conjunction with conciliar control, radically changed the channels of patronage for certain matters of grace, as the whole transaction was reduced to a financial one ... The need to pay and outbid became a pressing necessity.[22]

The emergence of the Privy Chamber itself was in part the result of the Chamber's transformation from household department to national treasury: the Privy Chamber took over the more intimate, less public and formal elements of the king's life, and by the end of the reign other officials looked after the elements of household finance that now fell outside the Treasurer of the Chamber's purview.[23]

My general point is that there may be a more specific context for Skelton's poem than we often assume. A bifurcation is at work; while the monarch figures as spectacle and source of conspicuous consumption, he is also associated with private spaces within the court, secrecy and surveillance, and the money that usurped the pathways of grace and favor.[24] These redistributions of authority overlap in *The Bowge* with print's emergent consolidation, in piecemeal and locally determined fashion, of English vernacular poetic traditions, and the fact that various European works of court satire – *L'Abuzé en cour*, Chartier's *Curial* – had already circulated in script and print for some time, providing templates to apply to the English court.[25] Skelton's printed poem shows an author for whom formal poetic authority turns into erotic submission. It is, like the court it serves, at once open and secret; it veils behind its moral pretensions its own complicity in a world of paranoid pragmatism, to issue finally in the narrator's turning of a chillingly interrogatory gaze on the reader into whose hands the printed poem may happen to fall.

PROLOGUE

The louring opening chronographia is established with several brushstrokes: autumn (the perfect time for the "wandering" dreams called *insomnia*), fickle moon, baleful Mars, an uneasy balance of unstable opposites. The narrator appears, only to disappear again:

> I, callynge to mynde the great auctoryte
> Of poetes olde, whyche, full craftely,
> Under as coverte termes as coude be,
> Can touche a troughte and cloke it subtylly
> Wyth fresshe utteraunce full sentencyously;
> Dyverse in style, some spared not vyce to wrythe,
> Some of moralyte nobly dyde endyte;
>
> Wherby I rede theyr renome and theyr fame
> Maye never dye, bute evermore endure.   (8–16)

In Stephen Dickey's claim that the "I" of the eighth line is left "naked, alone and insubordinate" by the unfolding hypotaxis, a nice pun hides a slightly inaccurate point.[26] The speaker is rather lifted into suspension on a surge of present participles, clauses and parentheses that clearly evoke Lydgate's version of Chaucer's high style, and its transformations of Chaucer's complex syntax into absolute constructions.[27] The poet's aspirations, however, are abruptly punctured as a dissuading female Ignorance cuts in: "For to illumyne, she sayde, I was to dulle" (20). Ignorance here targets the poetic terminology of vernacular "heigh style," with catastrophic effect. This author would no doubt like to adopt Lydgate's stylistic mantle – suggested by a term which sparks a chain of associations back to Petrarch's "enlumynyng" labors in the prologue to the *Clerk's Tale*, and which we have seen in Dunbar – but Lydgatean "dullness" stops short here of establishing rhetorical and moral authority. On the contrary, it is all too authentic, leaving the speaker genuinely grounded. Such an aspirant writer, stalled even before he has begun, clearly could not stretch to the gargantuan outpourings of a *Troy Book* or a *Fall of Princes*. The very invocation of "auctoryte" brings a clausal ramification that carries enunciation out of reach; the "great auctoryte / Of poetes olde" is no sooner mentioned than it leaves the narrator's own to vanish, dispersed into a *diminutio* pushed to its logical extreme. Far from being magnificently assertive, this narrator struggles in the voluminous coils of an invertebrate Lydgatean syntax.

This is not all, for the poet's self-enunciation at this point is divided. Between the lines of this hyperextended fifteenth-century poetics, there is much interest in what its language might cover. Poets are poets, it transpires, because they can, under "coverte termes," "touche a troughte and cloke it subtylly." Commonplace though these sentiments might be, we should nevertheless pause. They suggest a clerical hermeneutics deriving from exegesis, which is always a practice of reading before it is a practice of writing. That hermeneutics is not entirely without precedent in Lydgate – who in *The Fall of Princes* asserts of poets that "Ther cheeff labour is vicis to repreve / With a maner couert symylitude" (III, 3830–31)[28] – but it remains true that the trope is rare in his work when compared to the lexis of illumination and aureation. We have, then, a narrator split between different poetic models, and a tantalizing suggestion that within fifteenth-century public discourse there may lie a privy kernel of secrecy, a poetics of obscuring hidden within the language of "illumyning." This division will be played and replayed within the narrative of Skelton's poem, to lethal effect. For *The Bowge* discloses a violence *within* the fifteenth-century modesty *topos*, replaying its thematics of authority as a scene of aggressive looking and ignominious humiliation, in which mastery is inseparable from masochism.

That the ship which enters harbor is called *The Bowge of Courte* might surprise no one, given the poet-dreamer's predicament. In Chartier's *Curial* – whose English version by Caxton was published in 1484 – the speaker notes that "whan thou enforcest the to entre [the court] / thenne begynnest thou to lese the seygnorye of thy self" (13).[29] The court "maketh a man to leue hys propre maners / And to applye hym self to the maners of other" (7); eating, sleeping, outward deportment and the most basic of bodily functions are modeled after the courtier's environment, in particular the prince on whose word he hangs, and desire is alienated in imitation. Here too, the narrator's desire seems not to be his own – rather, he is afflicted with the desire to desire.

> But than I thoughte I wolde not dwell behynde;
> Amonge all other I put myselfe in prece.   (43–44)

The unanchored "I" is now dropped into a mercantile milieu of objects and exchanges. Their value is defined in the language and register of *fin amour*, as the throng of lover-merchants converge on the figure of a lady called Dame Sans-Pere:

> Than sholde ye see there pressynge in a pace
>
> Of one and other that wolde his lady see,
> Whiche sat behynde a traves of sylke fyne,
> Of golde of tessew the fynest that myghte be,
> In a trone whiche fer clerer dyde shyne
> Than Phebus in his spere celestyne,
> Whoos beaute, honoure, goodly porte,
> I have to lytyll connynge to reporte.   (56–63)

The lady's "traves of sylke fyne" resembles the *integumentum* of allegory,[30] so returning us to the prologue's talk of "clokynge." Such figures evoke the multiple readings of allegorical interpretation of Scripture and of classical writings. Augustine had lastingly influenced such interpretation with his formulation of the dual-level reading of Scripture in the *De doctrina christiana*, which relegates to the condition of "carnal" slavery those who enjoy the seductive pleasures of the sign without recognizing that it should be "used" to spiritual ends.[31] The trope had found its way into curial satire, where Chartier had identified courtiers as collective nominalists: "allewaye emonge vs courtyours enfayned / we folowe more the names of thoffyces / than the droytes and ryghtes / we be verbal / or ful of wordes / and desyre more the wordes than the thynges" (10). In *L'Abuzé en court* the deluded hero's predicament is caused by a failure to read rhetorical figures correctly. His false guide Abuz personifies Time for him,[32] and as a result he fails to notice the passage of real time until it is too late. The Court finally tells l'Abuzé that those ruined by court life are left with the mere image of what they desired to gain from it, which they can retain as a warning ("Du bien de quoy sont desserviz / La figure ont pour defiance").

Other commentaries are still more equivocal about what might lie behind the allegorical veil. The Roman philosopher and grammarian Macrobius recounts an anecdote in which his Greek forerunner Numenius proves that to interpret the Eleusinian mysteries is to divulge them. Since the verb *vulgare* (to spread abroad, divulge) can also mean "to prostitute," Numenius then has a dream in which the Eleusinian goddesses appear to him standing before an open brothel, dressed as courtesans. "When in his astonishment he asked the reason for this shocking conduct," reports Macrobius, "they replied that he had driven them from their sanctuary of modesty and had prostituted them to every passer-by."[33] The goddesses have been undressed and expelled, their mysteries revealed; in Macrobius's anecdote, however, the unveiling gives place to a reveiling, for the goddesses are not stripped naked, but "habitu meretriciae." The eroticized narrative suggests, in Hult's words, that truth "is *never* perceived without its figurative covering";[34] the "numina" have no bodies. As R. Howard Bloch too has noted, Macrobius phrases "a potent paradigm of representation," which is "bodiless, empty, less capable of expressing a reality exterior to it than of covering up an absence that is also, finally, scandalous."[35]

The same scandal arises in Skelton's poem. Like Chartier's courtiers, Skelton's eager merchants are readers enslaved to a sign, which here takes the form of an image beyond description. Their onrush gives place to a moment of unknowable commerce, as the *domina*'s radiance defeats the "connynge" of the poet who, pre-oneirically, was already overwhelmed by past authorities. The moment is impenetrable to our reading. Does the speaker see the lady but find her beauty indescribable? Does he see her at all through the concealing "traves"? Either way, she is no sooner mentioned than she gives place to a series of signs. Once again recalling the lady of the *Roman de la Rose*, Dame Sans-Pere, having eluded the narrator's "connynge," is nowhere definitely present, but is rather incarnated in two figures, one daunting, the other more enticing. As the dreamer is left deciphering a sinisterly ambiguous motto on the lady's throne, he is accosted by Daunger – not Guillaume de Lorris's churl with a club, but a waiting-woman:

> Than asked she me, "Syr, so God the spede,
> What is thy name?" and I sayde it was Drede. (76–77)

The dreamer's name is a startling revelation, not least because its content is a prosopopeic identity by which he is already circumscribed. Having failed in the prologue to enter an anterior order of poets, he is now exposed as a figure in an order of personification, as Drede. Daunger's fellow "gentylwoman," Desyre, offers new advice:

> What though our chaffer be never so dere,
> Yet I avyse you to speke, for ony drede:
> Who spareth to speke, in fayth, he spareth to spede. (89–91)

"For ony drede": Drede is invited to differ from his own inscription in the allegory through ambitious speech. If this is one of the lures that power offers, Desyre follows it with another. Drede fears that he will fail in this new world; he has no advocate who will be his "medyatoure and mene," and "but smale substaunce" (93–94). In response, Desyre offers Drede something suspiciously resembling a fetish,[36] a "precyous jewell" called *Bone aventure* (98) that will assuage his anxieties. He must befriend the ship's highly capricious steerswoman, one Fortune. Drede is dismayed:

> "Alas," quod I, "how myghte I have her sure?"
> "In fayth," quod she, "by *Bone aventure*." (118–19)

The tautologous ironies unleashed by this unmasking of the fetish – Paul D. Psilos aptly comments that the line denotes no more than "a good-luck handshake"[37] – confirm all too clearly Drede's subordination to the letter of the allegorical signifier, to an order by which he is already spoken.

This entry into love-allegory has not gone entirely unprepared, since the prologue has already set poetic aspiration against *doubles entendres* derived from Skelton's own work. Ignorance cuts short the poet's syntactically precarious strivings with blunt advice his "penne away to pulle / And not to wrythe" (21–22). This deflating imperative undercuts the endeavor to imitate literary fathers, and the dreamer, denied access to authority through an act of creation *interruptus*, falls asleep. It is not surprising that this should occur "In myne hostes house called Powers Keye" (35), for here Skelton writes over the slyly dialogic antifeminism of his earlier lyrics; in "Womanhod, wanton, ye want!" (in *Agaynst a Comely Coystrowne*) "key" punningly refers both to the name of a house and to the clitoris.[38] The secrets of figural cloaking whispered in the prologue are, it seems, informed by a carnality bound up with the vernacular polysemy of Skelton's own low style.

Now, as the beauty of the lady shades off into an indescribability *topos*, the limitations of the poet's "connynge" are once again to the fore; the earlier failure to measure up to poetic fathers is here refigured as the dazzled lover's inability to "reporte" his lady's beauty. The relentless particularity of the fantasy she represents – we hear of "one and other that wolde his lady see" (57) – has already pointed to a world where isolation is the rule ("Than there coude I none aquentaunce fynde," 45), and where the lady of romance is brusquely revealed as every solipsist's personal vision, in a group of figures struggling for gain.[39] Her presence, or absence, therefore, is intimately bound up with this dreamer's "connynge" to describe her; and since, as we know from the prologue, he has no such "connynge," she can only figure as the projection of what he lacks – as the absence implied by Macrobius. Brought to the "traves of sylke fyne" that hides the invisible object of desire – the very door of the privy chamber, the veil which conceals the lady of allegorical courtly entertainment – the narrator falls victim to a catastrophic failure of identification with the image of power, the failure of an ambition at once sexual and political.[40]

Some light, I think, is thrown on the progress of the poem so far by Lacan, whose *Seminar VII* specifically explores courtly love. Skelton's Dame Sans-Pere (Lady Peerless) is a characteristic instance of the woman as Lacan's "terrifying ... inhuman partner" (150). She is placed behind a veil, an enigmatic intermediary, "introduced through the door of privation or of inaccessibility" (149), and functioning both as woman and as "secret" (151). Lacan's phrases here are part of an extended examination of the woman as Thing – at once, as Sarah Kay puts it, "the point on the horizon of the symbolic where the pressure of the real is sensed" and "the hole or vortex which the real opens at the heart of our systems of representation." The Thing "is simultaneously a nothing, the gap within or beyond representation, and a powerful something, an irreducible kernel where the pressure of the real is condensed."[41] The dreamer's encounter with the unrepresented (unrepresentable) Lady results in incapacity: he cannot "reporte" the beauty of the mysterious *domina*. It is language's function, according to Lacan, to regulate, under the dominion of the pleasure principle, the subject's distance from the inscrutable and terrifying – because inaccessible – Thing. "The distance between the subject and *das Ding*," Lacan observes, "is precisely the condition of speech" (69).[42]

Such a logic defines the movement of Skelton's narrative. The alternation of Daunger and Desyre plunges Drede into a world marked by an atmosphere of "vain incantation and fruitless connection" (56), in which speech only offers hallucinated satisfaction and thwarted gratification. His feckless bid for satisfaction has drawn him into an economy of *prosopopeia*; he is now enclosed in a signifier, as if in response to the absent Thing's straitening mandates, and in the face of Desire's tautologies he fades to an empty letter ("Dread"), dependent on other empty letters for consistency.[43] This predicament looms even larger when Skelton's grotesque and sinister Vices arrive on the scene. As the dream proceeds, speech will further entail neurotic reenactment of the absent object's terrifying inscrutabilities in the form of imagined intrigues, confrontations in which the narrator is terrorized, but also – as he is increasingly identified substitutively with the figure of authority he aims to be – inspires terror ("Drede") himself. The result is a knowledge that can only be described as paranoid.

SYMBOLIC CURRENCY

Lacan tells us that the Thing marks the place of a loss beyond representation, figured in psychoanalysis as the loss of the mother's body, and that the space of fantasy is tenanted by the objects of imaginary identification, at once interchangeable and rivalrous. *The Bowge*'s very beginning is emulous; a narrator struck by poetic ambition is troubled by a desire to rival "the great auctoryte / Of poetes olde." The poem never leaves, but rather revolves around this scene of failed identification. As the dream begins, a ship arrives in port called *The Bowge of Courte*, which already posits a fluid relationship between pleasure and objects; it is "fraghted with pleasure to what ye coude devyse" (42). When the ship enters harbor an anonymous voice subjects it to an act of naming as initially arbitrary as that of Drede himself ("'the shyp that ye here see, / The Bowge of Courte it hyghte for certeynte,'" 48–49) and after the introduction of Dame Sans-Pere the merchandise it carries is termed "Favore-to-stonde-in-her-good-grace" (55). The words of Fortune, the steerswoman, are themselves suggestive:

> Of Bowge of Court she [Fortune] asketh what we wold have,
> And we asked favoure, and favour she us gave. (125–26)

Just as Dame Sans-Pere is a projection of individual desire, so Fortune's proclamation confirms that "Bowge of Court" is fashioned to appetite – it is a shifting signifier with no clear identity of its own, existing at an interface between desire and signification.

Lacan observes that *Vorstellungen* or ideas "operate exchanges and are modulated according to ... the fundamental laws of the signifying chain" (62). The pleasure principle's inertia is guaranteed by the valorization or substitution of one sign over or for another, and a concomitant transferral of affective charge. It is no accident that Skelton's poem features a metaphorics of traffic and commerce; the word is object, often a distorted kind of gift, and personifications themselves are no exception. The phrase "bouge of courte" derives from the Old French phrase, "bouche [mouth] à court," and denotes "an allowance of food and drink granted by a king or nobleman to a member of his household or of the retinue of a guest."[44] Like all wages to the royal *familia*, it was a payment in kind, and had the advantages and limitations of all such payments. A source of immediate sustenance to the royal servant, it nonetheless afforded him no lasting security; as *L'Abuzé en court* succinctly puts it, "Brouet de Court n'est heritaige!" ["Court-broth is no inheritance!"].[45] It thus had the quality of a credit voucher:[46] an entitlement to eat at royal expense without enduring substance or content, which could be arbitrarily revoked. This renders it an appropriate center for the symbolic economy of Skelton's poem, where it takes on a bewildering variety of forms.

The first of the Vices, Favell or Flattery, sets the tone with Drede's "Than Favell gan wyth fayre speche me to fede" (147). Words become food; in effect, "Bowge of Courte." The flatterer's language functions as a medium of courtly exchange, becoming identical with court rations of a more alimentary kind. The "banquet of rhetoric" is a familiar trope in the twelfth-century *artes poeticae*. Geoffrey of Vinsauf exhorts the reader to take delight in apostrophe, "[w]ithout which the food would be sufficiently abundant, but whose presence swells dishes of an outstanding feast ... this food for the ear, when it arrives savory, fragrant and costly, lets us feast our ears for a longer time on its greater riches and variety."[47] Favell's unseemly behavior, however, transfigures such expansive diction into the grotesque body of rhetorical carnival: "Me thoughte, of wordes that he had full a poke; / His stomak stuffed ofte tymes dyde reboke" (179–80).[48] Dissimulation approaches Drede wielding further culinary and iconographic stage properties:

> And in his other sleve, me thought I sawe
> A spone of golde, full of hony swete,
> To fede a fole, and for to preye a dawe. (435–37)

An associated play on words may even be implied in Dissimulation's weirdly recondite reference to his knife as the "stoppynge oyster" in his "poke" (477). Dissimulation's "poke" points to a further semantic extension of the title, for a "bowge" is also "a leather bag,"[49] pouch, purse or – another usage we find in the poem – the "male"[50] that Hervy Hafter is out to "picke" (138). Riot combines the characteristic *topoi* of petitionary poetry and descriptions of fictional gallants;[51] his purse, empty enough to imperil his soul ("The devyll myght daunce therin for ony crowche," 364), contains nothing but a "buckell" (397).

On one level, this extends a common topos of curial satire. The courtier's own commodification – his too is a value to be negotiated – is explicitly stated in Skelton's poem: Favell tells Drede that to the mysterious lady who presides over the court he is "worth a thousande pounde" (157). Chartier, too, depicts the court as a marketplace in which the subject's sole value resides in the favor shown him by the sovereign. "For emonge vs of the courte," he writes, "we be meschant and newfangle / that we bye the other peple / And sommtyme for theyr money we selle to them our humanyte precyous / we bye other / And other bye vs" (13).[52] More important, however, is the part played by "bowge of court" in the poem's figuration. A blank space in itself, it becomes the medium by which words acquire a more evident materiality. As one of the possible meanings of the word *bowge* is converted into another, it becomes the center of a figurative currency: an agent of endless commutation, symbolic money.[53] Words are coin, devoid of universal value, or food, reducing the relation between truth and figural garment to a body whose contents spill unpredictably, and which is always visible, as if turned inside out. This, Skelton's poem suggests, is the nature of a court body where the currency of relations is monetary. The body of rhetoric becomes the object of vision: the knowledge produced by a subject who "sees." It is to this subject that we shall now turn.

SUBSTANTIAL WORDS

In its remorseless, literalizing techniques of embodiment, *The Bowge of Courte* points to a traditional problem in the rhetorical construction of subjectivity: the difficulty of assessing the sincerity behind the rhetorician's mask, the perennial anxiety as to whether adept speech necessarily betokens moral worth. Thus Petrarch points out that the arts which make a good rhetorician – mimetic skills, the ability to use the colors of rhetoric well – become immoral when translated into conduct, and indeed generate a kind of alienation from the self. "What is advantageously taught in the art of oratory, the art, that is, of speaking with propriety and elegance," he writes, "has ... been mischievously applied to the art of wicked and disgraceful living ... no one is of a clear mind as to his costume, his speech, his thought – in short, as to what sort of man he would like to be, and therefore every man is unlike himself."[54] Petrarch's emphasis is not new; rhetorical texts, classical and postclassical, warn against seduction through persuasive rhetorical artifice by troping rhetoric itself as a body either diseased or overdressed, whose defects may not readily meet the eye. Quintilian fears lest stylistic excess, through overdressing and cosmetic adornment, render the body of rhetoric "effeminate"; to the author of the *Ad Herennium*, inflated language may seem impressive to the novice ear, just as a tumor may be indistinguishable from a "healthy condition of the body"; in an especially violent figuration, Alberic of Monte Cassino depicts the introduction of abrupt transitions into the calm flow of a work as at once a grafting of deformed members on to the rhetorical stock and a form of violation.[55] In a suggestive discussion, Rita Copeland has argued that such figures emerge from the desire to control rhetoric's inherent delinquency. Rhetoric, she argues, "repeatedly – almost ritually – re-enacts and enforces its self-discipline by exposing its continual struggle with its wayward body."[56] In Skelton's poem, this disciplinary dimension is explicitly evoked as the Vices' rhetorical artifice shapes speech and is realized in both dress and physical appearance. The Vices are first and foremost embodied tropes, and through them rhetoric is imaged not merely as ethically deplorable, but as manically out of control.

The dangers that supposedly lay in wait for the courtier on all sides, including his fear of the watching eyes of others, had long been documented by the 1490s.[57] Chartier speaks of the court as "the nourysshe of peple / whyche by fraude and franchyse / studye for to drawe from one and other suche wordes / by whyche they may persecute them."[58] Previous accounts of the poem have emphasized the terror instilled in Drede by those who watch him, but that terror cuts both ways; as the poem's personified vices "studye for to drawe … wordes" from Drede, they expend a great many themselves. Suspycyon claims that "The soveraynst thynge that ony man maye have / Is lytyll to saye, and moche to here and see" (211–12). Yet the "Full subtyll persones in nombre foure and thre" (133) in fact talk a great deal, testing both their adversary's defences and their own. Fish, who speaks of the Vices' "baseless sureness,"[59] misses the point of the psychomachia of the dream, which turns on the double sense of the line "They sayde they hated for to dele with Drede" (146). Skelton's Vices are conspicuously lacking in "sureness," and their attitude to a character who embodies a word as multiple in meaning as "drede" is an index of their fears. In Skelton's morality *Magnyfycence*, Crafty Conveyaunce says

> many tymes moche kyndnesse is denyed
> For drede, that we dare not ofte, lest we be spyed.   (1338–39)

The poem here is well inside the genre of curial satire, and the arts of courtiership that were to develop in the course of the sixteenth century. In such a psychological context, "drede" is at once despised and desperately seized when occasion demands. It indicates the furtive watchfulness, exemplified in Suspycyon's lines, through which the courtier avoids exposure and assesses the opposition. But as hesitation, it can also be lethal; any suggestion of diffidence spells disaster in the competition suggested, at the beginning of the dream, by the merchants' unthinking scramble to board the ship.[60] When the courtier's mentality is broken down into the Vices composing a psychomachia – by dramatizing it, Skelton seems to analyze it – they flee Drede's presence, and yet must speak to him. On one level, they cannot bear even to acknowledge his presence; on another, they are compelled to do so.

In his study of espionage in Renaissance literature, John Michael Archer has suggested that the courtly subject of early modern culture is essentially paranoid in structure.[61] Drede's encounters with his adversaries, as I suggested above, confirm this by troping anew the encounter with Dame Sans-Pere, this time in a panicked rivalry of courtierly male "authorship" where revulsion and attraction are intertwined. Fearful himself, Drede has taken on some of her fearful inscrutability on this terrain of wavering identities. The Vices are at once irresistibly attracted to him and terrorized by him, and Drede is as deeply implicated in this mutual observation as any of them. His complicity with his interlocutors is explicitly revealed in his colloquy with Suspycyon, after which the poem looks back at a reader caught out in inquisitiveness:

> Soo he departed. There he wolde be come,
> I dare not speke; I promysed to be dome.   (228–29)

On many occasions Drede, observing the seemingly arbitrary encounters that go on around him, moves in to listen: "And I drewe nere to harke what they two sayde" (296). Drede, it would seem, is as alert as the most devious among his interlocutors; he is apparently shocked by what he hears:

> What sholde I tell more of his rebaudrye?
> I was ashamed so to here hym prate.
> He had no pleasure but in harlotrye.   (372–74)

But he has heard it, and like an adept informer reported it, so that the reader is given "all the pleasures of surveillance" that might on another day be found in the confessional.[62]

The exchanges between Drede and his enemies mesh with the poem's concern with figurative language. They endlessly and anxiously strive to read and gloss him; simultaneously, they impose themselves on his vision in almost excessive iconographic detail

> Than, in his hode, I sawe there faces tweyne … (428)
>
> Thenne I behelde how he dygysed was … (351)
>
> I saw a knyfe hyd in his one sleve … (433)

or merrily sing songs like "Sythe I am no thynge playne" (236). As Ad Putter observes, these characters are "instantly 'readable' to anyone but Drede himself."[63] Their vicious self-advertisement, however, also marks a surplus that intimates the doubleness of Drede's clerical "connynge." While not immune to the Vices' menaces, he can in a sense read them, tabulating the details of their verbal opacity, with its hints and gaps, in the equally obscure fiction he himself inhabits. They repeatedly assimilate him to the stereotype of the terrified cleric at court, while the poem that "authors" him, and for which he stands, quietly exhibits the very "connynge" with which they mock him,[64] weaving them into its text. There can be few dream allegories in which the words "me thoughte" acquire quite the weight of meaning they do here. As we have seen, *The Bowge of Courte* is a poem marked by disclaimers and disavowals, which seem to be the only means by which this subject can register his desire. He first acknowledges his ambition with a half-hearted "But than I thoughte I wolde not dwell behynde"; now, the standard formula of dream vision functions as an alibi. Drede spies on others, while denying that he does so. His unresisting eye is constantly producing knowledge, in the shape of figurative Vices covered in legible signs; but that knowledge itself, in Skelton's poem, rests on an unstable, mirroring ascription of attributes, in which author, narrator and characters are all implicated. Meanwhile, the speeches of Drede's adversaries, building a menacing, deathly reality of which he evidently knows nothing, are creating epistemological panic.

THE UNCANNY RHETORICIAN

The climax of the Vices' persecution also brings to a head Skelton's linking of literalization and paranoia. Having alluded casually to yet another conversation going on just out of earshot, Dissimulation suddenly points to a new character:

> Naye, see where yonder stondeth the teder man!
> A flaterynge knave and false he is, God wote.
> The drevyll stondeth to herken, and he can.
> It were more thryft he boughte him a newe cote;
> It wyll not be, his purs is not on-flote.
> All that he wereth, it is borowed ware;
> His wytte is thynne, his hode is threde-bare. (484–90)

As Anna Torti has pointed out, this mysterious and evidently disreputable figure seems to sum up the Vices we have so far seen. The portrait's specifics recall Favell ("A flaterynge knave and false"), the meager garments of Riot ("his hode is threde-bare"), and the obsessional eavesdropping of everyone, including Drede. The moment, however, has also a near Gothic quality, for in Dissimulation's speech there suddenly arises the uncanny double of the aspiring rhetorician who narrated the prologue: deficient in "connynge" ("his wytte is thynne"); in need of "a newe cote" as his original wished to "cloke" truth like his poetic forebears; short of resources (488); laboring under the epigone's nagging anxiety that there is no poetic garment not already used ("All that he wereth, it is borowed ware").[65] In this dismal virtual reality, Drede glimpses his waking avatar ingloriously revealed. The poet-dreamer's emulous desire to write stands exposed as a crude desire to acquire power through listening ("The drevyll stondeth to herken, and he can"), and ambitions to adopt the public voice of Lydgate have shrunk to this poem of esoteric, paranoid exchanges. Drede has now become the object of his own anxious look.

This "teder man" is a nightmare vision of the other that haunts rhetorical discourse, the *homo rhetoricus* described by Richard Lanham[66] – a figure (in every sense) who is solely a collection of patches from the rhetorical garments of others. At the end of this long tunnel, the rhetorician has encountered a simulacrum of himself; he has become the object of his own vision and his own knowledge, although that knowledge is – aptly enough – filtered through the words of Dissimulation, as if to imply that it will always be the product of a pervasive, unlocatable deceit and misrecognition. As the dream's frame breaks and the prologue intrudes, Drede's look gives him access to an ascendancy that is indistinguishable from the most degrading exposure.

Another frame now cracks, for the threat this uncanny being prefigures is soon made clear. As the last and deadliest Vice comes at him from behind, a frightened Drede reacts:

> I lyked no thynge his playe,
> For yf I had not quyckely fledde the touche,
> He had plucte oute the nobles of my pouche. (502–04)

A sinisterly "privy" overture ("behynde me he sayde 'Bo!'," 500) is swiftly transformed into a threat of castration.[67] The Wedo in Dunbar's *Tretis of the Tua Mariit Wemen and the Wedo* uses the same analogy:

> Quhen I that grome geldit had of gudis and of natur,
> Me thoght him gracelese one to goif, sa me God help. (B3, 393–94)

The impotence – the symbolic castration, indeed – that frames the poem once again breaks in as it did with the introduction of Dame Sans-Pere. Disceyte also returns us to the breakdown of language, which, as we saw, was so conspicuous in that scene. The speech he produces communicates most fully the "cruel emptiness" of the Thing, here "unveiled with a cruel and insistent power";[68] it is that of an unrepresentable absolutist Other, menacing, arbitrary and incomprehensible:

> Parde, remembre whan ye were there,
> There I wynked on you – wote ye not where?

> In A *loco*, I mene *juxta* B:
> Woo is hym that is blynde and maye not see! (515–18)

Such alienated speech plays along the border of the signified, effectively abolishing language's ceaselessly shifting relation throughout the poem to some supposed allegorical interior. The narrator's response in the face of Dame Sans-Pere's lady Desyre was, we recall, to announce himself as the "letter" Drede. Now, Drede in turn bestows literal substance on an imaginary conspiracy:

> And as he rounded thus in myne ere
> Of false collusyon confetryd by assente,
> Me thoughte I see lewde felawes here and there
> Came for to slee me of mortall entente. (526–29)

The "lewde felawes" are themselves corporeal, if shadowy, figurings of the moral generalities of "false collusyon confetryd by assente" (the very line could furnish the plot of a miniature morality play). Drede narrowly deflects castration by hallucinating a plot, for we cannot know how far the "collusyon" and "assente" are part of others' conspiracies against him, and how far they are his own. The dreamer who began with a wish to write moral poetry has finally acquired authority through having "authored" a conspiracy, and at the end of the dream he is poised to leap from the ship – an ironic reduction to the letter indeed of his initial desire to join the company of dead poets.[69]

Historians of curial satire have remarked on its highly conventional nature. Rooted by origin in the experiences of clerics at early courts,[70] it is less remarkable for concrete social criticism than for its translation of the nuances of political circumstance into a hypostatized literary mode, marked by the repetition of topoi that change very little.[71] With its elite range of literary reference, it offers to a knowing clerisy its own most flattering mirror, producing an apparently limitless self-consciousness that is a matter of always *knowing better* than the courtierly dupes whose sole preoccupation is with secular ambition and polity.[72] *The Bowge*'s innovations, as critics have agreed, are generic and formal; the introduction of dream vision produces a new chronotope. Historical specificity may be glimpsed in the imaginary topography of the poem's action. It is initially organized around a chimerical Dame Sans-Pere, who, as the "awnner" (50) of the ship *The Bowge of Courte*, is analogous to the monarch, and whose dazzling defiance of representation, which precipitates the dreamer's imaginary crisis, mirrors a "kingship of distance"[73] in which the monarchic body is ambivalently divided between its spectacular political function and the invisibility of the

Privy Chamber. Similarly, the strangely labile figure of "bowge of courte" disrupts personification allegory, mirroring the royal association of money with the inner reaches of power and the disturbance of prior structures of patronage. Such historical considerations, as we have seen, enter Skelton's text through rhetorical strategies that literalize – that execute, in other words, the due processes of a punitive law. And *The Bowge of Courte* does indeed fulfill the law, in no uncertain terms. At the end, Drede, panicked by the conspiracy he imagines, prepares to leap overboard. This gesture has been interpreted as one either of despair (the poet is forced out of his own poem by courtierly evils)[74] or of a qualified creative optimism (the stalled poet of the prologue has at least overcome writer's block).[75] However, I would submit that Drede, in evoking these terrors, also coopts them in the interests of self-promotion, for he is merely fulfilling the terms of a statute with which the poem finally reveals itself to be identical. "Me thoughte I see lewde felawes here and there / Came for to slee me of mortall entente": Drede has detected a homicidal conspiracy, compassed and "ymagyned" in the absence of "actuell dedis."

And with this initial work of "ymagyning" done, *The Bowge of Courte* is finally sent forth to conduct its enigmatic work of surveillance among the unsuspecting readers of the printed book, setting paranoid selfconsciousness in circulation as a condition of participation in that readership. The paratext, indeed, underscores this: the 1499 edition is published anonymously, and the figure of the author and the act of writing are both elided, the last lines of the poem's first-person narrative moving straight into an explicit and colophon ("Enprynted at westmynster By me wynkyn the worde"). The anxieties so subtly harnessed by Skelton in *The Bowge* speak to a court increasingly structured around the monarchal seclusion of the Privy Chamber, but also to a press whose instrumentality in imagining national inclusivity and obedience has not by 1499 gone untested.[76] Drede is a vanishing mediator, moving at once inward and outward into a printed text that will conduct its own disembodied, reified scrutiny of political subjects. The terrified Drede is invited to supply his own meanings to the Vices' menacing indirection, filling in what their words leave out:

> Iwys I coude tell – but humlery, home,
> I dare not speke, we be so layde awayte   (467–68)

But, of course, the terrifying dream supplies him with the "mater of to wryte" he lacks at the outset, and he is left imitating the "poetes olde" whom in the Prologue he felt unable to follow, writing "this litel boke."[77] Yet the rhythm of the lines that communicate this intent – glib, insinuating, confiding, self-qualifying – by now sounds grimly familiar:

> I wolde therwith no man were myscontente;
> Besechynge you that shall it see or rede,
> In every poynte to be indyfferente,
> Syth all in substaunce of slumbrynge doth procede.
> I wyll not saye it is mater in dede,
> But yet oftyme suche dremes be founde trewe.
> Now construe ye what is the resydewe.   (533–39)

The Vices, too, terrified Drede by implying, then denying, that a conspiracy was forming against him (173–74; 493–94). Now Drede, the eighth courtly vice, ensnares the reader in the same anxiety, implying that to have followed and understood this tale of moral corruption so far is by definition to be privy to its world, to be one of the damned. And the poem, having, like the monarch it serves, constituted its own secretive inner spaces, now turns finally on the reader, and peremptorily demands further self-scrutiny: "Now construe ye what is the resydewe" (539).

CHAPTER 3

"My panefull purs so priclis me": the rhetoric of the self in Dunbar's petitionary poems

>Je ne plains riens que ma paine et despens:
>A vous en est; plus ne les poursuira
>Mon las de corps, qui a servi long temps
>A vo plaisir[1]
>
>[I only lament my pain and my losses: it's up to you now; my peasant of a body, which has served your pleasure for so long, will pursue them no more.]

The first documented notice of William Dunbar's royal pension, dated August 15, 1500, grants him £10 "to be pait to him of soverane lordis cofferis, be the thesaurare, for al the dais of his life or quhil he be promovit be oure soverane lord to a benefice of xl. lib. or abone."[2] By 1507 the pension had been raised to £20,[3] and in 1510 it reached £80.[4] Dunbar appears to have survived the death of his "soverane lord" James IV at Flodden in 1513, but his name disappears from the records shortly afterwards, leading to speculation that he may at last have received his benefice. Whatever the truth of the matter, there is a certain aptness both in the story the documents tell, and in their silences. Perhaps by sheer chance, they imply a reciprocal relationship between poet and king; in the written record the one does not long outlive the other. More importantly, they inscribe Dunbar in the position of gratification constantly deferred which dominates his petitionary poems – as if his unsatisfied desire for a benefice were itself a service to be rewarded, his self-representation as supplicant part of an economy. That self-representation, and the discursive conditions it suggests, will be the subject of the following chapter.

None of the petitionary poems appear in manuscript or print witnesses dating from Dunbar's lifetime. Most are collected in the Maitland Folio (Cambridge, Pepys Library, 2553, Magdalene College), and the Reidpeth Manuscript (Cambridge University Library, Ll. 5. 10), evidently copied from the Maitland Folio when the latter was in an earlier and more complete form. The folio appears to have been compiled between 1570 and 1586, and is associated with the family of Maitland, in particular with Sir Richard Maitland of Lethington (1496–1586). While knowledge of its composition and origins is still limited, Priscilla Bawcutt has suggested that in his youth Sir Richard "could well have known Dunbar," and that the folio's grouping of his poems suggests circulation within a small court coterie.[5] The possibility that the petitions were a form of intimate address, written to amuse an audience to whom the poet was familiar, is borne out by their shifts of tone and alert notation of the pleader's psychology, which seem to evoke the very presence of a speaking voice. "Here, if anywhere," Bawcutt writes, "is the core of Dunbar's poetry, and that 'unifying consciousness' that some critics would deny him."[6] The petitions, indeed, have been shaped into a hypothetical autobiography, their changing moods read as a linear move from earlier discontent to satisfaction in 1507, when Dunbar's pension was doubled.[7]

The begging-poem as such has courted various interpretations. Bawcutt argues that while poetic petitioners may have written within a tradition, any genre the literary petition might constitute "is remarkably flexible, partaking both of the epigram and the verse epistle, and determined more by function than by literary form."[8] For Christine Scollen-Jimack, conversely, "the pathetico-comic begging-poem constitutes a well-worn literary set-piece" of a definite kind.[9] I wish to argue, however, that both these positions overlook the culturally and politically productive function of literary convention. Throughout I draw parallels between Dunbar's petitionary self-projection and those of his contemporaries and predecessors[10] to substantiate my claim that the begging-poem is not reducible either to convention or to function, but rather represents with remarkable consistency certain relations of power between subject and sovereign. Since James IV was much concerned with visibility, the identity Dunbar must perform is that of his king's spectacular obverse – fluid, "complex" and multiple, at times rather a point of disappearance than a self.[11] If Dunbar's petitionary poems may at first appear difficult to situate in his biography and his historical environment, they nevertheless richly illuminate the relationship between poet and sovereign at one late medieval court, and the symbolic negotiations of which that bond is woven.

AUTONOMY AND RIVALRY

In "Complane I wald, wist I quhome till" (B9), the speaker begins in the mode of generalized complaint,[12] aligning himself both with "nobillis" who endure "vrangis and … gryt iniuris" (9–10) and "men off wertew and cuning, / Off wit, and vysdome in gydding" (11–12). The prizes in the incessant contest of court life are carried off not by such deserving cases, but by

fowll, iow-iowrdane-hedit ievellis,	*foul jew-chamberpot-headed rascals*
Cowkin kenseis and culroun kewellis;	*beggarly/shitty (?) base knaves*
Stuffettis, strekouris and stafische strummellis …	*grooms, hounds, stubborn farm animals*

(15–17)

and so forth. This tirade, which can stand for a number of similar passages in Dunbar's petitionary poems, sets in train a process of disfigurement – of making monstrous – that becomes increasingly embodied and specific. The poem surveys several types of ecclesiastical ambition before fixing on one, "Ane pykthank [*sycophant*] in a prelottis clais" (53), whose dubious corporeal characteristics fit him more for manual labor than for his present occupation. This unworthy figure, as he advances, despises "Nobles off bluid" and "helpis for to hald thame downe / That thay rys neuer to his renowne" (64–66). The speaker casts himself by contrast as a "lerit sone off erle or lord" (41), who is also "maister natiwe borne / And all his eldaris him beforne" (45–46). Bawcutt acutely observes that this figure is "presumably an impoverished younger son" and that it is "through his eyes that we see the 'odious ignorance' of this upstart."[13] Nature, nurture and craft are conflated, as the virtues of blood, lineage and nation merge with the acquired attributes of the poet-rhetorician, "maistrye" and "cuning." On the other hand, social ambition, inadmissibly exceeding the bounds laid down by rank and birth, is figured as a grotesque, excessive and aberrant body – the proper referent, indeed, of that quintessentially agonistic genre, the flyting.[14] Whilst the aim may be to valorize the standpoint of the "lerit sone off erll or lord," the strategy only serves to press home the extent to which the perspective Dunbar articulates is defined rivalrously. It is formed around its imagining of the disfigured abomination of the parvenu, whose shape is a scandal to genealogy and the perfect aristocratic body. Complaint and flyting are two sides of the same coin.

A similar dissolution of difference is enacted in "Schir, ʒit remember as befoir" (B68). The poem again begins with formal complaint, and here the natural hierarchy of the bestiary is affirmed by "gentill" heraldic allegory. These are the sources of a rhetoric which urges the speaker's merits against the upstarts – the birds of ravine – who snatch away the benefices he desires, and culminates in an appeal to the king, here, as in the heraldic *Thrissill and the Rois*, the "gentill egill" (26; cf. B52, 120–26). This mode, however, is soon dropped, as Dunbar inaugurates an alternative representational strategy.

He lays ironic claim to rights of a more egalitarian kind; he, too, is "cum of Adame and Eve / And fane wald leif as vtheris dois" (38–39). He thus associates himself both with the famed "poor men" of romance and ballad – "Raf Colȝearis kynd and Iohnne the Reif" (33) – and lowborn clerics, who are the objects of his subsequent attack. The speaker abandons the pretensions to status of his opening plaint in order wishfully to associate himself with the attention-getting boors he has hitherto deplored, tactically taking a cargo of defects on board.

The resulting poem is aptly summed up by its refrain, "Exces of thocht dois me mischeiff." "Thocht" (Hoccleve's main affliction at the opening of the *Regement of Princes*)[15] is in fact all that holds together the poem's unsteady shuttling between traditional topoi, self-canceling pleas for favor, and faintly blasphemous hyperbole (81–85), and "Exces" is the chief characteristic of its unpredictable shifts of tone.[16] The poem enacts the gradual dispersal of its initial hierarchical assurance and injured merit into rivalrous identifications. It finally presents not an approximation to the poet's "personality," but a "comédie du *Moi*" whose "moi" is a representational excess.[17]

Dunbar's represented court is shaped by mimetic desire; "[t]o imitate the desires of someone else is to turn this someone else into a rival as well as a model."[18] When the victims of Dunbar's satire are themselves frauds and tricksters, the maker of fictions becomes indistinguishable from his enemies. Dunbar's most memorable attacks are leveled at John Damian, the notorious "Fenȝeit Freir of Tungland,"[19] and royal kept alchemist, because Damian is Dunbar's mirror image. As one of James IV's "ingynouris joly, / That far can multiplie in folie" (B67, 55–56), Damian's shape-shifting reflects Dunbar's own metamorphoses of persona across his poems, just as his alchemy mirrors Dunbar's own attempt to transform a rude vernacular into aureate "gold." In "Lucina schyning in silence of the nycht" (B29), Dunbar will only receive his benefice (22), and spiritual peace (21), "quhill ane abbot flew abone the mone" (50). Damian's absurd plunge from the walls of Stirling Castle corresponds to each of Dunbar's petitionary poems in its trajectory of ambition and failure. Benefice and abbot's flight belong in the category of *impossibilia*, both signs of impending apocalypse.[20]

If "Lucina schyning" provides a wittily ironic gloss on the rivalrous structures of courtly desire, as the courtier ends by being indistinguishable from the rival model, then fantasized vengeance elsewhere presents the same dialectic in darker tones. Damian's mobbing by the birds of the air[21] is merely the most extreme of Dunbar's punitive visions. The king is begged to have the mysterious "refing [*thieving*] sonne off rakyng [*roaming*] Muris" (B64, 2), who has in some way "magellit [*mangled*]" (3) Dunbar's writing, dressed as a fool "That ladis may bait him lyk a buill" (27). The Queen's "wardraipper" James Doig is humiliated through both plays on his name and a fabricated reputation as henpecked husband. His wife in turn is verbally punished for contemplating his cuckolding, though it is of course Dunbar himself, setting this slanderous suggestion in circulation, who becomes the fickle *fabliau* wife (B72; B73, 17–19). Dunbar's competitors are threatened with the "Tolbuyth" (B67, 60), and those who snatch his beloved benefices even incur heavenly punishment (B43, 29–30).

Readers have found in Dunbar's short poetic forms evidence of a lack of poetic integrity, an inability to achieve wholeness in a "decevabill" court, or a psychological "splitting" caused by the pressures of court existence.[22] Such fragmentation is starkly illuminated by the petitionary poems, as they at once recoil from and flirt with identification with the rival of courtly competition. This combination of desire and disgust, hinging on a loss of identity at once dreaded and courted, reaches visibility in images of bodily splintering and metamorphosis. Dunbar projects this condition on to rivals in the courtly scramble for preferment; the grotesques who populate his crowded royal anterooms are an extraordinary, expressionistic assemblage of deformed and apparently disconnected body parts.

"OFF QUHILK MY VRYTTING VITNES BERIS"

Poets and alchemists may both be frauds. Yet when Dunbar mentions his own writing in these poems, it is often to attest to his plainness, his incapacity to feign. When a bevy of grotesques preempts the royal attention, it is "vrytting" that becomes the final "vitnes" to Dunbar's claim to consideration (B9, 73). In one standard posture, such hints that the poet's gifts count for nothing in this world can be loudly ironic: "Allace, I can bot ballattis breif. / Sic barnheid [*childishness*] leidis my brydill reynʒe" (B68, 48–49). The poet becomes the sincere truth-teller adrift in a corrupt court, who

> all his tyme neuir flatter couthe nor faine,
> Bot humblie into ballat wyse complaine
> And patientlie indure his tormenting.   (B75, 68–70)

In such statements, mention of Dunbar's poetic reputation and work allies itself with the plain speech that sometimes resembles direct affront: "I say not, schir, ʒow to repreiff, / Bot doutles I go rycht neirhand it" (B68, 78–79).

Critics have long noted the element of calculation in such outspoken professions of honest anger and moral discernment among poets close to power.[23] In Dunbar's work, too, bluntness is not without its own equivocations, and they have a long history. Jacqueline Cerquiglini has drawn attention to a well-attested tradition in which the sight of the poet-*clerc* is defective or deviant sight; he squints or is blind in one eye, or stands concealed in a corner or behind a wall. The resulting perspective is oblique and furtive.[24] In *Le Champion des dames* by Martin le Franc, the *acteur* watches "le hault prince d'Amours" ["the high prince of love"] and his court from a corner ("ung canton"), "Vergongneux et remply de honte, / Tout ainsy que l'en fait, quant on / Scet bien que l'en n'est point du compte" ["ashamed and abashed, just as you do when you know that you are of no account"].[25] In *Li Regret Guillaume Comte de Hainaut*,[26] Jean de la Mote hears cries, wailing and sighs coming from a strange castle – the lamentations, he is to discover, of ladies mourning for the deceased Count of Hainault (179–89, 338–44). One of the ladies, Débonnaireté, turns him back at the entry (236–40), but permits him to look into the dark chamber ("Une cambre ù mout fist obscur," 310) where "Les vaillans dames" (314) are gathered through a hole in the wall – made, as it happens, long before ("de pieça," 312), no doubt because integral to the poetic architecture. Such scenes, Cerquiglini writes, are not seen "in the eye of God ... an omniscient observer," but rather aslant from the perspective "of a humble subject." Of this "frustrated spectator," she contends, "is born a reward: the act of writing as the art of deviation; in short, the mediated vision objectified."[27] Writing, the literate cleric's distinguishing technology, always offers a "mediated vision," at one remove from experience and so from direct access to power. This indirect vision, though, offers perverse compensations; necessarily sidelong, it purports in its obliquity to guarantee the *clerc*'s truth and honesty, even as it satisfies his desire to expose and reveal.

Dunbar pushes "the act of writing as the art of deviation" to its limits. "In secreit place this hyndir nycht" (B25) and of course *The Tretis of the Tua Mariit Wemen and the Wedo* (B3) owe their existence to such a perspective, in which salacious pleasures are voyeuristically evoked so that they can be safely ascribed either to women's secret gossip or to the ludicrous endearments of *bürgerlich* lovers. Such deviation is never far away in the petitionary works. Standing "fastand in a nwke [nook]" (B43, 7), like Martin le Franc's "canton," Dunbar deals in the pleasures of "exposure," by means of the pen, of upstarts the poem itself has constructed, and at the same time of his own duplicity.

"Wrytting" doubles the figure of the poet. "Be diuers wyis and operatiounes" (B5) sets the speaker's "sempillnes" (21) against another catalogue of rapacious court types, one of whom is a figure who "musand be the waw / Luikis as he mycht nocht do with aw" (11–12). "Luikis as": Dunbar briefly exposes the curial satirist's detachment and contempt for the throng as itself a pretence.[28] The text incorporates a split between ostensible simplicity and actual deviousness, the latter weirdly embodied in a skewed narrative self-positioning midway through the poem. A more complex version of such doubling appears in "This hinder nycht, halff sleiping as I lay" (B75). The dreamer – once again the plain speaker doomed to fail at a deceitful court – becomes the prone, passive scene of a debate among personifications. One of these is "Inoportunitie" (Importunity), who presents his suit at unseasonable moments, yet has an enviable record of success. His apparent blundering is both calculated and profitable:

> ʒe sall not all gar him speid without me,
>   For I stand ay befoir the kingis face.
>   I sall him deiff or ellis my self mak hace,   *deafen, hoarse*
> Bot gif that I befoir him seruit be.
> Ane besy askar soonner sall he speid
> Na sall twa besy servandis, out of dreid …   *Than*
>   (77–82)

The two "befoirs" produce ambiguity; does the second simply echo the first (so that both mean "in the king's presence") or is Inoportunitie pressing to be served before (ahead of) the dreamer of whom he is also a personified facet? The hesitation between these alternatives wryly implies that "Inoportunitie" is a figure for the subject of these petitionary texts, one simultaneously indulged and disavowed. Their Dunbar is the ultimate, and yet the most insidious, "besy askar."

    Overt simplicity, covert duplicity and the writing that comprehends both of them shape "Schir, ʒe haue mony seruitouris" (B67). It opens with a catalogue of those who at court work legitimately for rightful reward, ending with the poet's claim for the enduring value of his own "making." Although, he says with mock humility, he may be unworthy compared to "the laif" [*the rest*],

> Als lang in mynd my work sall hald,
> Als haill in everie circumstance,   *whole, respect*
> In forme, in mater and substance,
> But wering or consumptioun,   *without*
> Roust, canker or corruptioun,
> As ony of thair werkis all,
> Suppois that my rewarde be small.   *Although*
>   (28–34)

Dunbar's words may appear a more forceful, less compromised apology for poetry than others in his canon.[29] But heavy irony ("ʒe sa gracious ar and meik, / That on ʒour hienes follwis eik / Ane vthir sort," 35–37) introduces another long list of court parasites – a bravura display piece comparable in spirit and in verbal invention to that in "Complane I wald, wist I quhome till" (B9). And as payoff, the speaker advertises a readiness to join the self-seekers. If he were given reward,

> It wald me sumthing satisfie
> And les of my malancolie,
> And gar me mony falt ourse   *cause; overlook*
> That now is brayd befoir myn e.   *broad (evident)*
> (B67, 73–78)

Dunbar's all-seeing, ruthlessly honest "e" can be bought.

We are by now familiar with the rivalrous basis of such arguments. This speaker, openly unfaithful to his professed word, is as duplicitous as his opponents – one with the "Fantastik fulis, bayth fals and gredy, / Off toung vntrew" (57–58). And since the poem invests its fiercest energies in finding new names for the mobile, evasive beings of its second catalogue, it becomes a covert celebration of the inauthenticity it purports to describe. The claim that Dunbar's "werk" will transcend time is offset by its inventive coinage of the ephemeral and recondite terms of abuse that have invariably vexed his editors, and which turn the poet into a dealer in perishable goods. The king is finally presented with two alternatives; he can either reward the poet or have a singularly virulent "flyter" on his hands. Spearing, who associates Dunbar's earlier claim for the poet's nobility with Renaissance ideals, notes that Dunbar has become "one of the 'Thrimlaris and thristaris' who are at court only for what they can get."[30] Spearing's fine account bears extension in one crucial respect. The poem's manifest insincerity is not in some way unforeseen or accidental, but rather so pervasive in Dunbar's begging-poems as to be already implicit in the patronal structure in which the poem participates – a structure that locates the subject-poet in a predetermined insufficiency. This subject is not so much open as positively exhibitionistic about his duplicity. Dunbar's writing does not after all authenticate his honesty, and when he elsewhere attacks a lowborn benefice-seeker

> Iok that wes wont to keip the stirkis   *bullocks*
> Can now draw him ane cleik of kirkis,   *number; churches*
> With ane fals cairt in to his sleif,   *card; sleeve*
> Worthe all my ballattis vnder the byrkis ...   *ballads; birches*
> (B68, 66–69)

we may suspect more to this commensurability of his "ballattis" and a concealed "fals cairt" than meets the eye.

Dunbar observes others in a rivalrous struggle; like Skelton in *The Bowge of Courte*, he seems chiefly concerned to bestow a disfiguring visibility on the competitors his poem so vividly embodies. His own performance is filled with doublings and disappearances, and yet these are conspicuous enough to be themselves a spectacle. There is, however, a rhetorical constant in this shadow-play, to which we now turn.

THE PETITIONER'S BODY

One possible approach to the self-contradictory Dunbar of the petitionary poems is to assimilate him to a penitential vision of the self as variable and fickle, beyond the rule of reason and constantly slipping back into sin because it is outflanked by an unpredictable corporeality. This penitential emphasis on human unpredictability and its roots in the body – Rutebeuf regrets that "J'ai fait au cors sa volontei" ["I've given my body its head"][31] – for some readers lends the petitionary poem a striking verisimilitude. In J. A. Burrow's sensitive appraisal, the genre becomes the locus of a "discovery of the individual" in English poetry; as poets try to amuse potentially generous patrons by entertainingly recounting the hard-luck stories of their lives, they discover autobiography.[32] While Burrow's account raises some questions that I will address below, it well describes the sophistication of many begging-poems from the Middle Ages. The twelfth-century Archpoet confronts his audience with "Vitam meum vobis enucleo, / paupertatem meam non taceo" ["I'll lay bare my life to you, and not hide my poverty"].[33] Deschamps breaks off his tale of the miseries of being horseless to ask a laughing audience, "Est ce beaus gieux que dolens vous raconte?" ["Can this be a good joke if I suffer as I tell it to you?"].[34] The French *rhétoriqueur* Guillaume Crétin, as far as we can judge Dunbar's direct contemporary, says at the outset of one verse epistle that he can tell of his troubles without "grande solemnité." The humor, however, soon takes on a more sombre tone:

> Quant a part moy je pense et me souvient
> Du temps passé, et de celluy qui vient,
> Que j'ay vescu, et qu'il fault que je vive,
> Et que le sort sur moy si mal advient,
> A peine scay que tout mon sens devient,
> Craignant de veoir que paovreté s'ensuyve ...[35]

[When I consider and remember times past and to come, that I have lived and yet must live through, and that fate treats me so poorly, I hardly know what will become of my sanity, fearing as I do to see poverty follow ...]

The petitioner is often conspicuously subject to old age, a factor that Dunbar's poems handle variously. In "This waverand warldis wretchidnes" (B79), Dunbar, weary of "The lang availl [*service*] on humill [*humble*] wyse"(14), is a knowing *exemplum* of the mutability "Off this fals failʒeand [*failing*] warld" (94).[36] From this position, however, he opens up a gap between the institutional weight of complaint and the apparent pettiness of his own grievances: as we shall see shortly, the poem's movement is one of gradual diminution, the complaint's pretensions to universality slowly draining away. At the opposite extreme of generality falls an unusual instance of the anecdotal vignette more popular with other petitionary poets, as Dunbar harks back to a time when he "wes ... on nwreice kne / Cald dandillie, bischop, dandillie" (B68, 61–62) and ironically reflects that age has not fulfilled the narcissistic predictions of baby talk. He thus inscribes himself within the poem as boy-bishop, protagonist in a disorderly carnival of "thocht."

The petitioner more than once cites time lost as evidence of "liell seruice" (B79, 13), telling his king "How that my ʒowthe is done forloir / In ʒour seruice with pane and greiff" (B68, 2–3). Retrospect is testament; called to witness, the past figures in a moral balance sheet used to underwrite the petitioner's request for notice.[37] Time and court service are quite differently related in a poem to a different courtly subculture, "My lordis of chalker [*exchequer*], pleis ʒow to heir" (B36), which once again turns on a witty contrast of scale. Penitential hindsight is replaced by its analogue in the records of the court concerned with royal revenues, where time figures as "rekkyning" (6). In this small-scale local judgement day, the "lordis" have no need to waste ink "In the ressaueing of my soumes" (10); Dunbar's money is gone, and he does not know how:

> I cannot tell ʒow how it is spendit,
> Bot weill I waitt that it is endit;
> And that me think ane coumpt our sair. *account; sore*
> (13–15)

If other petitions depend on a conscious testamentary retrospect over time past, Dunbar here is comically in the dark as to how his losses have come about. Time's predatory workings are inaccessible to the speaker – mysteriously "out of his hands" – and can only be registered by appeal to another witness, his purse "Quhilk wald not lie and it war luikit [*examined*]" (20). The purse's unheard voice becomes part of a bureaucratic audit, and biography is measured by income and expenditure.[38]

In B79, time is hyperbolically mapped on to the space of precolonial marvel. Dunbar waits for a benefice for so long that

> It micht haue cuming in schortar quhyll
> Fra Calʒecot and the New Fund Yle, *Calcutta*
> The partis of transmeridiane.
> (61–63)

or from such wondrous regions as "the desertis of Ynde" (66), "the orient partis" (70) and "the ylis of Aphrycane" (71).[39] The universal "pane" of the refrain, however, finally becomes corporeal; Dunbar's anguished anticipation "breikis my hairt and birstis my brane" (83). In other poems, too, the body is both confined and confining, its boundaries imprisoning the aging or impoverished speaker and isolating him from community. This self-enclosed misery recalls the "thocht" named elsewhere, and here too a penitential dimension, sometimes spun to parodic ends, may be noted. In "Sanct saluatour, send siluer sorrow!" (B61), poverty "grevis" Dunbar

>   both evin and morrow,
> Chasing fra me all cheritie.
> It makis me all blythnes to borrow ... (2–4)

Charity's participatory integration in the social world[40] is unavailable to the speaker, and it strikes too at the roots of his courtly "makyng": "Quhen I wald blythlie ballattis breif / Langour thairto givis me no leif" (6–7). Like the Archpoet's, this poet's verse is dependent on material considerations. Like the Archpoet's, too, the performance it enacts has a penitential edge, since as Chaucer's Parson notes, "langour" is associated with a branch of the sin of sloth: "Thanne comth undevocioun, thurgh which a man is so blent ... and hath swich langour in soule that he may neither rede ne singe in hooly chirche, ne heere ne thynke of no devocioun, ne travaille with his handes in no good werk, that it nys hym unsavory and al apalled" (I, 723). It broods over the petitioner even as he dreams, playing excruciating music:

>   Langour satt wp at my beddis heid
> With instrument full lamentable and deid
>   Scho playit sangis, so duilfull to heir,
>   Me thocht ane houre seimeit ay ane ʒeir. (B75, 21–24)

"My heid did ʒak ʒester nicht" (B35), however, takes melancholic languor to its limit. A migraine "Perseing my brow as ony ganʒie [*arrow*]" (4) cuts the speaker off from social pastime and writing (6–10). As Burrow acutely notes, "the tone of complaint suggests an unspoken petition."[41] The poem's petitionary force is indeed reliant on its muteness. There is no generic or theological frame to which bodily pain can be assimilated, and no overt cause, only an irreducible, inaccessible anguish at the heart of petition.

Physical sickness bulks large in the petitionary poem, and ailments may even be a poetic signature. The most famous instance, of course, is the cough that interrupts the Archpoet's inscriptions:

>   Continuam tussim pacior, tanquam tisicus si ....m.
>   Sencio per pulsum, quod non a morte procul su....... m.
>   Esse probant inopes nos corpore cum reliquo pe..... s.[42]

[I cough endlessly, as if I were consumptive. My pulse tells me death is not far off. My feet prove I'm helpless, as does the rest of my body.]

Machaut and Molinet both display in their poems the single eye we have noted in connection with the petitionary poet's vision.[43] For Crétin, the physical miseries of serving the prince are writ deliriously large:

> Le jeu me fuyt, malheureté m'aterre
> Pour entonner goutte, fiebvre, catharre,
> Froid, chault, faim, soif, pulces, pulnaises et poulz,
> Boutz, mal de dents, rongne, entrac, morve, toux,
> Viennent souvent ...

[Pastime flies from me, misery knocks me down to pour gout into me, fever, catarrh, cold, heat, hunger, thirst, fleas, bedbugs and lice, toothaches, scabies, carbuncles, snot, coughs visit me often ...]

Organic growth is a thing brutishly apart from the fluctuating desires and disappointments of royal service: "Espoir me paist de promesses et veux, / Et ne me croist que la barbe et cheveulx" ["Hope feeds me with promises and oaths, and all that grows is my beard and hair"].[44]

In Dunbar, as in Hoccleve ("My body and purs been at oones seeke"),[45] the ailing body merges with that characteristic stage property of petitionary poetry, the disordered and unregulated purse that cannot hold its contents. The trope's lineage is a long one. Walter of Châtillon laments that "in deserto mundi huius / nemo floret, nisi cuius / bursa nondum vomuit" ["in the desert of this world no one flourishes, unless his purse never vomits"].[46] In one notable contrary instance, Deschamps reads the "retention" of his salary as constipation:

> au partir le flux du ventre avoye,
> Or ne l'aray des mois ne des sepmaine;
> Qu'entre les gens mon seigneur de Touraine
> N'a homme nul qui ait esté restraint,
> Fors Eustace qui de ce se complaint,
> A qui on a .xx. jours serré le ventre
> Sans croix avoir; pour ce doubte et se craint
> Qu'il ne puisse jamaiz aler a chambre.[47]

[When we left I had the flux of the belly, but now I won't have it for months or weeks; no one among my lord of Touraine's people has been blocked, apart from Eustache who is lamenting about it; for his belly has been stopped without a cross for twenty days, so that he cannot go to the privy.]

Lydgate's letter to Gloucester mixes purse and body in a dazzling series of metaphorical reversals, in which inside and outside, poet and purse, cannot be told apart:

> my purs was falle in gret rerage,
> Lynyng outward, his guttys wer out shake,
> Oonly for lak of plate and of coignage.
>
> Botme of his stomak was tournyd vp-so-doun,
> A laxatif did hym so gret outrage,
> Made hym slendre by a consumpcioun …

The disorderly body promotes natural disorder, as the ship imprinted on the gold noble expands into an image of the poet's fortunes, impeded by "wynd froward" and "lowh ground-ebbe."[48] For Dunbar, the device on the coin's face is the image of a similarly troubling meditation: "My purs is maid of sic ane skyn, / Thair will na cors byd it within" (B61, 21–22). As in other begging-poems, poverty is an open invitation to the devil; the old almsman of Hoccleve's *Regement* reminds us that "Þe feend, men seyn, may hoppen in a pouche / Whan þat no croys þere-innë may a-pere,"[49] while one of Deschamps's poems has the refrain "Le crucefis et je n'ont que .II. crois" ["The crucified and I have only two crosses between us"].[50]

"Sanct saluatour, send siluer sorrow" (B61) draws other meanings from the beggar's purse. Its refrain, "My panefull purs so priclis me," has suggested to some readers a punning reference to the scrotum.[51] Bawcutt is skeptical: "The relevance to the poem of such a sexual innuendo is unclear, and has never been demonstrated."[52] Dunbar's allusion, however, shares with other court poets of the period a figurative link between poverty, emasculation and clerical status. Molinet's indigence connotes old age and loss of virility:

> D'argent je suis et de jonnesse vuit,
> Viellesse approche et gaires ne me duit;
> J'ay perdus voix et sy ay perdu nom,
> Chanter ne puis le Credo in unum
> Et mon pouvre v. i. t. ay perdu aux
> Deduis d'amours …[53]

[I'm void of money and youth alike, old age comes on and gives me little delight; I've lost my voice and I've lost my name, I can't sing the Credo, and I've lost my poor prick to the delights of love …]

For him, indeed, impotence is a major concern: "je dis / Que mon engin rude et rond comme ung oeuf / Le jeu Sainct Pry ne puist faire tout neuf"

["I tell you that St. Pry's game can't make my tool, feeble and round like an egg, new again"].[54] Cerquiglini has demonstrated that in Machaut's work old age, impotence and the cleric's poetic identity are intimately connected.[55] In Dunbar's case, too, such hints are apparent, both in "Sanct saluatour" (B61) and elsewhere in the begging-poems. The "magryme" (B35, 3) leaves the sufferer's "curage sleipeing" (12), and we may recall Langour's "instrument full lamentable and deid" (B75, 22). Whether we take Dunbar's painful purse to suggest venereal disease or a figurative castration less easily localized, the poems make it clear that the lassitude induced by poverty is unmanning. In contrast to "men that hes pursis in tone," Dunbar is, in the evocative words of the second wife in his own *Tretis,* "a right lusty schadow" (B3, 191).

All the features we have noted in connexion with the petitioner's body are signs both of humility and of humiliation; the poet as suppliant reveals his lack of status, his "dependence on a highly-placed person."[56] That dependence takes especially interesting form in what is perhaps Dunbar's richest figuration of the petitioner's body, "Schir, lat it neuer in toune be tald" (B 66). Bawcutt has finely discussed the "comical-pathetical" and "witty" qualities of the poem;[57] while these are certainly present, there may be a case for modifying unduly cheerful readings. Here I find myself anachronistically recalling D. A. Miller's point that Dickens's characters derive their "charm" from "the debt of gratitude we pay to their fixity for giving us, in contrast, our freedom. We condescend to praise these characters as 'inimitable' because they make manifest how safe we are from the possibility of actually imitating them."[58] It is in such a comfortable distance between imagined audience and speaker that the poem's "playfulness" resides. Dunbar here is comically bestial, a "talking animal" whose fear is of exclusion: "Gryt court hors puttis me fra the staw / To fang [*get*] the fog [*withered grass*] be firthe [*wood*] and fald [*field*]" (11–12).[59] He is also aged, with "maine ... quhyt" (21), at the wrong end of a "lyff ... miserabell" (28) and sacrificed opportunities (51–54). In this wintry poem,[60] time brings decay and exclusion; the body cut off from the court, the community in which it has its being, is abject, marginal and less than human. The reader beholds this figure from the safe distance of inclusion within the frame of the court.

Solidified in this poem is a relation not only between poet and reader, but also between poet and monarch. The *place* of its consolidation is the relation between stanza form and refrain. The stanzas work through a number of conceits in which the poet compares himself to a rejected "ald ȝaid auer [*worn-out pack-horse*]" (3), hoping to divert the sovereign with a variety of equine parallels to his own neediness. Yet the speaker's deepest anxiety appears to be that rumor and reputation, putting these conceits in the mouths of others, may give them a more pejorative cast, and that his own imaginative description of his situation will be transformed into the dismissive contempt of others. The stanzas of ambiguous authorship that conclude the poem in the Maitland Folio thus concretize Dunbar's conceits in a double-edged way:[61]

> Efter our wrettingis, thesaurer,
> Tak in this gray hors, auld Dumbar,
> Quhilk in my aucht with seruice trew   *possession*
> In lyart changeit is his hew.   *grey*
> (69–72)

At the last, the extended tropes of Dunbar's poem are replaced by the executive and administrative "wrettingis" of the king. These give Dunbar the reward he desires, but at the same time confirm finally the identity the poem simultaneously enacts and dreads, even going so far as to banish the fruitful gap between the suppliant and his fictions in a decisive act of closure ("this gray hors, auld Dumbar"). If the petition apparently succeeds, it does so by confirming the distribution of power between subject and sovereign. The subject is finally spoken for, and by the same token is decisively reduced to an animal voicelessness, ceasing of a sudden to be the talking creature of beast fable.

"THE KINGIS GRACE" V. "JOHNE THOMSOUNIS MAN"

Rivalry, emasculation and physical impotence deprive Dunbar of a clearly limned identity, reducing him to the zero term in the court's imaginative economy. In the poems on "feasts of benefices," the court obeys an insane arithmetic whereby "Quha monyast hes makis maist [*most*] requeist"(B43, 2). "[V]plandis Michell," with his two or three "curis," "playis with totum and I with nychell [*nothing*]" (B68, 71, 74). "Sir Iohne Kirkpakar," who has seven "kirkis" (88), boasts that "ȝitt I think thai grow sall till ellevin, / Or he be seruit in ane, ȝone ballet maker" (B75, 89–90). The player with no cards is a "syphir [*cipher*]" among the rapacious benefice seekers who metaphorically feast on their gains (B43, 20). Variations on the same theme appear in other poets: Deschamps, too, claims that at the banquets of the great he is "tousjours serviz d'oublie," punningly merging the host with the court servitor's perennial neglect.[62] In Dunbar's poems, this neglect will only be abolished with the very different economy of the Last Judgement: "Quha maist hes than sall maist repent, / With largest compt to pairt amang thame" (29–30).[63]

Liberation from this specular struggle, however, is held out by the promise of royal "grace," which here means something more than the mere fulfillment of endless requests for benefice or payment. The subject may be endowed with difference from his rivals, and thus with his very being, by the sovereign's look. From the thirteenth century we may compare Rutebeuf:

> Granz rois, c'il avient qu'a vos faille,
> A touz ai ge failli sans faille.
> Vivres me faut et est failliz;
> Nuns ne me tent, nuns ne me baille.
> Je touz de froit . . .[64]

[Great king, if I should lack you I lack everything. I lack livelihood; no one offers or gives me anything. I'm coughing from the cold . . .]

The variant forms of "faillir" press the point home. If the poet – who shares the Archpoet's cough – loses the king, he loses more than concrete benefits. He can only turn back to his ruler with "Et je n'ai plus que vos veeiz," a line which means something close to "All I have is the clothes on my back," but which in context carries a further implication ("All that I have – that I am – is conferred on me by your look").[65] The "simple" Dunbar also refers himself to the king's face that gives grace: "Methink his graciows countenance / In ryches is my sufficiance" (B5, 25–26).

This royal "grace" is, of course, quasidivine, given "of mercye and not of rycht" (B68, 52).[66] The king becomes intercessor; as *roi thaumaturge* he ministers to the supplicant's suffering body,[67] and with his "medecyne" (54) "Can best remeid" for the "malice" that afflicts the "panefull purs" (B61, 34). The conclusion of "Schir, ȝe have mony seruitouris," however, violently revises this common topos. Having conceded that reward would cure his melancholy, Dunbar begins to demand it with menaces that involve, once again, writing:

> with my pen I man me wreik.
> And sen the tane most nedis be –   *one*
> In to malancolie to de
> Or lat the vennim ische all out –
> Be war anone, for it will spout
> Gif that the tryackill cum nocht tyt   *medicine; soon*
> To swage the swalme of my dispyt.   *assuage; swelling; anger*
> (B67, 82–88)

This ferocious reworking of a common motif transfers power from the royal patron-physician's body to that of the petitioner-sufferer; the "I" bursts out with a new and disruptive violence.

It may seem that the rhetoric which appropriates the petitioner as metaphorically "sick," a diminished counterexample to the monarch's splendor, is being turned against itself. As Bawcutt notes, however,[68] these lines are paralleled in *The Tretis of the Tua Mariit Wemen and the Wedo*, in which one of the wives, a sexually voracious incarnation of medieval misogyny, prepares to vent her confessional spleen:

> Now sall the byle all out brist, that beild has so lang.
> For it to beir on my breist wes berdin our hevy.   *burden over heavy*
> I sall the venome devoid with a vent large
> And me assuage of the swalme that suellit wes gret.   *swelling*
> (B3, 164–67)

T. S. Dorsch has argued that the petitionary poems present an unattractive figure who sabotages his own case by going on for far too long. Dunbar, he says, was mistaken to depart from his own warning that "In asking sowld discretioun be" (B44, 5 etc.): that advice "is sensible and manly, and he ought to have followed it."[69] Dorsch here unveils the matrix of Dunbar's representational performance. For the poet of these petitionary poems is, quite precisely, "unmanly," the *mulier garrula et vaga* of clerical antifeminism.[70]

Such a subject position might seem discursively unpromising, but it opens on to some unexpected rapprochements. In "Schir, for ʒour grace, bayth nicht and day" (B63), Dunbar piously prays that some miracle turn the king into "Iohne Thomsounis man" – a hen-pecked husband. Even though his sovereign presumably remains obdurate, Dunbar's tone still has the effect of wittily feminizing both king and poet, uniting them as a couple of talkative gossips like the "cummaris [*gossips*] tua" of B57. As the poem proceeds, the king is figured in a variety of ways, split among various identifications. The poet's mock-profound longing "That ʒe had vowit to the swan, / Ane ʒeir to be Iohne Thomsounis man" (19–20) associates the monarch with those knights of romance and chivalric cult who replace action with "effeminate" devotion. Reference to the king's lack of "reuth" (9) works with the "danger" (B9, 74) he elsewhere displays to suggest a pitiless lady whose caprice must be humored. The desire that moves the petitioner amalgamates amatory motifs with pleas for preferment in a style that can certainly be situated on the continuum defined by Eve Kosofsky Sedgwick as "homosocial."[71]

As figured in these poems, James IV's queen is similarly multiple. She is the "sweit meik rose" (B63, 21) from *The Thrissill* (cf. B15, 6, 25–30; B52, 142, 148–82), identified with that "aduocat, bayth fair and sweit" (B63, 25), the Virgin.[72] She is the lady of romance, setting her lover exorbitant standards (B63, 17–20). B63, however, also sketches a narrative plot of another kind;

in the clashing tonalities of Dunbar's poem, the intercessory queen is a virago – John Thomson's legendary wife – who should rule her husband better. Elsewhere, the "sweit meik rose" presides over the court's punitive rituals; the second of the Doig poems withdraws the lampoons contained in the first with the words

> Thocht I in ballet did with him bourde   *jest*
> In malice spack I newir an woord
> Bot all, my dame, to do ȝou gam ...   *entertain you*
>   (B73, 5–7)

The petitionary poems yield a variety of gendered identifications. Within the frame of Dunbar's poem, petitioner and king are in intimate converse, like a pair of female gossips.[73] Elsewhere, the king is the object of the poet's desire, the disdainful lady whose "graciows countenaunce" is wealth enough for the loyal subject. For the petitioner, however, feminization is bound up with mortification, for the petitioner's aging body, diseased, fickle and mutable, is the very source of its "hysterical" outbursts. The queen, too, shifts between virgin mother – the intercessor for royal favor – and folkloric shrew.

The poet-as-woman thus uses his deviously won rhetorical status to cement a male relationship between poet and patron. The queen as John Thomson's wife, the woman on top, unites them in a bond not so far removed from the all-male "dirty joke" whose structure, as Freud recognized, turns on the scandalous exposure of the woman.[74] Both king and queen emerge in these poems in the context of violently opposed images; and the speaker of the poems moves abruptly from one to the other, with little mediation. These poems play out a scene of unstable sexual difference and metaphoric dissolution, nowhere more apparent than in the fantasized masochism with which the king is begged to hand Dunbar's malign plagiarist double, complete with "babile [*bauble*]," over to "Cuddy Rug, the Drumfres fuill," for a Yuletide celebration in which "ladis may bait him lyk a buill" (B64, 23–34, 27).[75]

One last poem evokes more orthodox generic coordinates. In appealing to the king's grace, the poems clearly reflect the literature of advice to princes. If Dunbar receives his benefice or his pension, then the Scottish court will indeed be the ideal court of the *speculum principis*, ruled by justice tempered with mercy. This intimate relationship between petitioner and court, invariably presented in hyperbolic terms, receives its most audacious formulation in the underrated "This hinder nycht, halff sliping as I lay" (B75). At the beginning, the best efforts of several personifications of a more cheerful cast cannot rouse a gloomy dreamer. Then Discretioun identifies his illness – melancholy – and announces that Nobilnes can cure him:

> Or euir this wicht at heart be haill and feir   *healthy, vigorous*
> Both thow and I most in the court appeir,
> For he hes lang maid service thair in vane.
> With sum reward we mane him quyt againe,   *must*
> Now in the honour of this guid New 3eir.
> (51–55)

The racked body of the petitioner mirrors the body politic of court and realm; if Discretion and Nobleness at last put in an appearance at court, all will be well. The point is further underlined when Affection – partiality, and so presumably favoritism – is overruled by Reason:

> I grant thow hes beine lord a sessioun
> In distributioun, bot now the tyme is gone.
> Now I may all distribute myne alone.
> Thy wrangous deidis did euir mane enschesoun.   *unjust deeds; every; injure*
> (62–65)

The court, as Reason's legal terminology betokens, will now oversee the just distribution of benefices that Dunbar's poems constantly request, and the man who has complained "humblie into ballat wyse" be rewarded. But the decorum of the poem has been abruptly broken. If Reason's intervention ("Now I may all distribute myne alone") is a metaphor for the reassertion of justice at court, then her words imply the very partiality that as Reason she should transcend.

This ethical and didactic allegory, in other words, is undoing itself, and it continues to unravel as the authoritative figure of Discretion delivers a most uncharacteristic rejoinder to Reason's words:

> "Weill spokin, Ressoun, my brother," quoth Discretioun;
> "To sett on dies with lordis at the Cessioun   *dais; session*
> Into this realme thow war worth mony ane pound."
> (73–75)

Discretion speaks the language of material advantage, and Reason's worth is measurable in pounds. And it is at this moment that the more disreputable Inoportunitie and the nightmare clerical pluralist Sir Johne Kirkpakar enter the picture.

Reason reasserts her more usual *persona*, and her final verdict is a familiar and a dejected one: "With gredines I sie this world ourgane [*overrun*], / And sufficience dwellis nocht bot in heavin" (99–100). However, the next stanza demolishes the notion that the petitioner is motivated solely by just offence at long service unrewarded:

> "I have not wyt thairof," quod Temperance,   *blame*
> "For thocht I hald him evinlie the ballance,
> And but ane cuir full micht till him wey,

> 3ett will he tak ane vther and gar it suey. *cause; sway*
> Quha best can rewll wald maist haue gouernance."
>
> (101–05)

Bawcutt sees these lines as a reference back to the greedy Kirkpakar, and punctuates accordingly. They cannot, however, be entirely divorced from the half-awake benefice seeker Dunbar, and they admit of a more unsettling reading. If he received a benefice, Dunbar would immediately want another; once again, he is no different from the rival-double. Dunbar's famous benefice is thus finally subsumed in a more general human appetitiveness that can never be fully satisfied. Having begun an allegorical analysis of the close relationship between the states of court and petitioner, the poem abruptly switches tactics, and the suppliant becomes less the victim of "gredines" than its embodiment. While Bawcutt glosses "Quha best can rewll wald maist have governance" as "Whoever can best rule should have most authority," the poem's one witness, the Reidpeth MS, reads "wald," not "suld." On such a construction Temperance's maxim proves not to resolve matters so much as to muddle them further, in a bafflingly opaque generality reminiscent of Molinet's self-dismantling fusillades of proverbial wisdom. It applies to benefice seeker and king at once; the vision of the perfect court has been replaced by the collapse of royal *voluntas* and the petitioner's greed alike into a lust for power ungrounded in any conception of good government or "common profit." Dunbar's miniature *speculum principis* flaunts once again the inauthenticity of the speaker of the petitionary poems, and the poem's abrupt and explosive ending (another demented cannon shot, as in *The Goldyn Targe*) leaves a distinct disquiet.

SOVEREIGN SHADOWS

Sir David Lyndsay praised James IV of Scotland as the "Lode sterne and lampe of libiralytie" and celebrated the renown of his household:

> And, of his courte, throuch Europe sprang the fame
> Of lustie lordis and lufesum ladyis ying,
> Tryumphand tornayis, justyng and knychtly game,
> With all pastyme accordyng for one kyng.
> He wes the glore of princelie gouernyng ...

Lindsay's aim is in part to construct James as an *exemplum* of vainglory, as his stellar court soon gives place to downfall at Flodden through "wylfull mysgovernance."[76] Yet his panegyric, however conventional, is borne out both by the records and by modern historical accounts. In what seems to have been a conscious attempt to displace the very different "art of rule" of the father he had supplanted, James's "behavior suggests a concern to make himself visible."[77] This is demonstrated in the architecture of his reign – the construction of Holyrood Palace,[78] the "kingis hous" at Stirling, additions to the Stirling chapel royal and Linlithgow Palace[79] – and even the building of his ship the "Great Saint Michael" seems to have had propagandist no less than military impact in view.[80] Such concerns are also reflected by the surviving accounts of his court ceremonial: they mark, as we have seen, his marriage to Margaret Tudor, and Macdougall points out that "no Scottish king before James IV appears to have been so committed to the staging of tournaments and to taking part in them himself."[81] His "libiralytie" involved a gift-giving that extended the reach of the royal body through contiguity.[82] He seems, too, to have taken care to maximize the royal presence by dispersing it, imposing on himself a fiercely demanding itinerary as he traveled around Scotland to dispense justice.[83] From this concern for sheer physical mobility – a desire to stand metonymically for his kingdom, by being everywhere at once – stems perhaps the tale, alluded to by Robert Lindsay of Pitscottie, that he would ride in disguise through the realm of Scotland to sound his subjects' minds and test their loyalties: a visual game with disguise and revelation that meshes with the romance motif of the *roi inconnu*.[84]

Spectacular monarchic presence would have been enhanced by the physical structure of the Scottish court, which contrasts with the developments leading to the English Privy Chamber. As Neil Cuddy points out, the court of Scotland did not undergo changes like those noted by Starkey; it remained organized along French lines, its distribution of rooms minimizing the degree of seclusion available to the monarch and retaining him in the public eye at all times.[85] This, I think, does more than myths of a democratic Scottish protonationalism to account for Dunbar's tone of familiarity with his sovereign, and his work's pervasive representation of a three-dimensional court, with its own "chalmers" and recognized personalities (James Doig, Sir Thomas Norny, "Mistress Musgrave").

James IV's strategic brilliance sheds light on Dunbar's tactical self-representation, for Dunbar's self-scattering is a mirror of the monarch's permeation of the polity with his presence. In his well-known gloss on Kantorowicz, Foucault has stated that "In the darkest region of the political field the condemned man represents the symmetrical, inverted figure of the king."[86] Dunbar's begging-poems may be said to stage a kind of informal self-criminalization. His vacillations of moral and social stance, and his rivalrous self-projection, now proclaim the speaker's bad faith, now dissolve any notion of sincerity and even identity. This slipperiness has its ground in a body enclosed by pain and poverty, and subject to time and decay.[87] His subjectivity is based in lack; Dunbar's benefice, like his purse, is a constant in a consistently inconsistent persona, a running joke. The subject insistently foregrounds his own powerlessness as physical debility, and even as alignment with the woman of clerical antifeminism.

These features make the petitioner into a dialectical stereotype, for they have counterparts in the *speculum principis* tradition. This is confirmed by Hay's abbreviated "Regiment off Princis" (III, 9463a) in *The Buik of King Alexander the Conquerour*. Against Dunbar's loquacity, we may set the ideal ruler's silence and self-restraint; he must

> seild spek, with wourdis all of witt,
> As all his wordis sould be put in wrette,
> And all of visdome speik in audience,
> And efter syne to clois, and kepe silence.   (10030–33)

Dunbar's fierce invective, too, is unkingly ("off na man mak scornyning, / For þat efferis nocht till ane nobill king," 10048–49). Above all, his self-professed insincerity and bad faith counter the good faith demanded of the monarch:

> quhat he spak, it suld be rate and stabill,
> And all his [w]ordis suld be veritabill.
> Ane kingis word suld ay be haldin dere –
> The wourd is euer þe hartis messingere . . .   (9917–20)

> fals of faith is defamit oure all;
> For fra gud faith anys defamit be,
> Cummys nevir agane til honoure of lawte.   (10077–79)

Hay's king has a transparency that the opacity of Dunbar's subject position studiously avoids. If the supplicant's body is constricted and tormented by pain, time and circumstance, the king's body is at once symbolically expansive – it governs the kingdom as the soul does the body (9813–14) – and required to "kepe abstinence, / Be m[e]s[u]rabill, and . . . liff sobirly" (10065–66). And if the petitioner must make entertainment out of his prodigality, the king must maintain the balance between getting and spending (9479–92) that is true magnificence.

We saw earlier that in Hay's text a king's people are his mirror, reflecting back to him his own defects. Such a perspective might imply that Dunbar's petitionary poems are an authentic critique of a king who harbors moral derelicts at court while neglecting old servants. However, the supplicant's self-construction works to vitiate, and thus neutralize, such criticism in advance. Once again, the *Fürstenspiegel* tradition is clear that commentary such as Dunbar's – or for that matter Hoccleve's or Deschamps's – is of its nature superfluous, and to be disregarded:

> Quha spekis oure oft, and ay is traitland new,
> He may never laik of lyere and vntrew .... (10336–37)

I pointed out in my introduction to this chapter that the process of modeling grants the model ontological priority; if the monarch *is* all, *is* substance, Dunbar must be – and must be seen to be – nothing: unstable, dispersed, fragmented. The figure that stands at the center of Dunbar's petitionary poems – so transparently and repetitiously "not superhumanly righteous, but fallible, unhappy, and self-interested"[88] – is on display so that the reader or auditor of the poem, occupying the position of the sovereign, can experience his distance from this flawed petitionary self. The petitionary poems are above all a flaunting, even a celebration, of the absence of power: a self-abjection through which the subject is figured at an aggressively visual court.

There are thus grounds for modifying Burrow's view that the petition witnesses a poetic "discovery of the individual." His argument stops short of addressing its own most suggestive implication – that an autonomous subjectivity enters English poetry on the basis of its apparent antitheses, limit and dependence.[89] His hypothesis that petitionary autobiography is intended as amusing play also asks to be examined further, since as Baudrillard observes, "the sphere of play is always the aesthetic sublimation of labour's constraints."[90] What is to be made of a literature in which the effects of the passing of time on the body – the processes of age and physical degeneration – are represented in so "playful" a fashion? Most importantly of all, what is the subject's own investment in the process, and what satisfactions are received?

The answer lies in the way in which such representations affirm the monarch's status as object of fantasy, and thus source of the subject's pleasures. The supplicant's self-humiliation renders him, as we have seen, the polar opposite of the king, and the single, suffering body to which he is consigned throws into relief the king's title to another body. The petitioner serves the royal "plaisir," which, as the words of Deschamps quoted at the beginning of this chapter reveal, can write itself on the body as pain. However, it is also the means by which the subject-poet acquires a "plaisir" of his own, the pleasure of an identification aroused in order to be thwarted. In bringing to the fore his own profoundly embodied miseries, and offering them to the sovereign as a source of amusement, the petitioner heightens by contrast the monarch's splendor, and thus identifies with the structure that makes of that splendor a necessity, and keeps ruler and subject apart. Even as Dunbar recedes spectacularly from view, he confirms all the more persuasively his dependence on the royal look that makes him, a look whose glory is the subject's own image of the ideal. In so doing, he opens the avenues of identification between subject and monarch that both uphold royal power and represent it as the sovereign's "love" for his subjects. In the petitionary poem, subject and sovereign affirm a mutual love. Guillaume Crétin's words to his own ruler are true in more ways than one: "Vous m'aymez mieulx, ce croy, paovre que riche."[91]

CHAPTER 4

Translative senses: Alexander Barclay's Eclogues *and Gavin Douglas's* Palice of Honour

To move from Dunbar to Gavin Douglas is to take a considerable leap in status and visibility within the Scottish court. Douglas presented his translation of the *Aeneid* to his kinsman Henry, Lord Sinclair, after completing it on July 22, 1513, nearly two months before the symbolically fraught battle of Flodden. In the dedication, he refers to another poem, *The Palice of Honour*, written twelve years before:

> To ȝou, my Lord, quhat is *th*ar mair to say?
> Ressaue ȝour wark desyrit mony a day;
> Quharin also now am I fully quyt,
> As twichand Venus, of myn ald promyt
> Quhilk I hir maid weil twelf ȝher*is* tofor,
> As wytnessith my Palyce of Hono*ur*,
> In *the* quhilk wark, ȝhe reid, on hand I tuke
> Forto translait at hir instance a buke:
> So haue I doyn abufe, as ȝe may se,
> Virgillis volu*m* of hir son Enee,
> Reducit, as I cowth, intill our tong.
> Be glad, Ene, thy bell is hiely rong ... .[1]

As we shall see, *The Palice* features, near its close, a scene in which Venus presents a "book" to Douglas, with a command to translate it. It has become customary to present Douglas's *Eneados* as the epitome of aristocratic and proto-imperialist epic,[2] and the actualities of Douglas's career would appear to substantiate this. A younger son of the fifth earl of Angus and thus connected to one of the most powerful of Scottish noble families, he was installed as provost of the collegiate church of St. Giles in Edinburgh in March 1503, and it is commonly implied that his elevation to this office, which was in the king's gift, may have been prompted by his authorship of *The Palice* and its dedication to James IV. After James's death at Flodden, Douglas, from 1516 Bishop of Dunkeld, was entangled in the politics of a royal minority and neighboring kingdoms, dying in exile in 1522.[3]

It is beyond the scope of this chapter to offer a detailed engagement with the *Eneados* itself, though it should be pointed out that I do not find the "imperialist" reading of the *Eneados*, for all Douglas's words about his aspiration to "the kny*ch*tlyke stile" (Prol. ix: 31), fully sustainable. The *Eneados*, with its elaborate apparatus of prologues refashioning the clerical *accessus ad auctores*,[4] is, to be sure, firmly assertive about its ambitions to extend Virgilian epic reach into "*the* langage of Scottis natioun" (Prol. 1: 103). It is, however, inescapably caught up in the instabilities of translation and temporality; if the *auctor*, as has been claimed, doubles Aeneas's wanderings, this is the inevitable fate of an epic subject haunted throughout the *translatio imperii* by "the narcissism that *is* exile."[5] My intent here is to examine *The Palice*'s own temporal relation to *translatio*. In its relation to the *Eneados*, it is at once proleptic and retrospective, a bid to accommodate, and yet disavow, the foreshadowings of epic desire in the erotic desire of allegorical dream vision and its language. *The Palice* thus becomes something of an anacrusis to the national and imperial ambitions of Scots in the *Eneados*.

This chapter, however, also imitates the early modern *cursus honorum* of Virgilian genres by turning first to a set of eclogues, those by Alexander Barclay. Barclay's ecclesiastical connexions offer a more jagged trajectory than Douglas's. Written, as far as can be determined, between 1509 and 1514, Barclay's *Eclogues* are the work of a monk whose monastic affiliations are, Lydgate-like, involved in other parts of the public sphere: the designs for the Field of Cloth of Gold in 1521, the print shop of Richard Pynson. Barclay discovers elements of what will come to be known as "nation" within the folds of a translated, "eclogic" clerical imaginary, whereas for Douglas the national abuts on to a projected epic space, a horizon that in *The Palice* is at once all-encompassing and – for the time being – absent.

STARK PASTORAL

Perhaps even more than Skelton, it is Alexander Barclay whose career asks with a special insistence where culture is located in the first two decades of the sixteenth century, throwing the plurality of markets and jurisdictions into clear relief. Ordained and appointed to a title (guaranty of support) by the collegiate church of Ottery St. Mary in Devon, he became a Benedictine monk of Ely Cathedral priory in 1513, evidently leaving it to enter the Franciscan order at some point between 1521 and 1528. His monastic identity, however, was in dialogue with multiple patrons and institutions.[6] Most of his works were produced in close collaboration with Richard

Pynson's printing shop; in April 1520 he was called on to embellish the English court's building for the Field of Cloth of Gold with historical and other themes. His career after 1520 betrays further oscillations: possible connexions with reforming circles, but also militant antireform activity before his death in 1552.[7] His shifts in vocational stance have been variously assessed; most relevant to my purpose is that his career, as well as his work, constitutes a series of translations. While there is a certain consistency in his adoption of the persona of the black monk – as he appears in the frontispiece to Pynson's print of his version of Sallust's *Jugurthine Wars* – there is also a certain elusiveness in the identity of an author who speaks entirely through the translated. I will be addressing this facet of Barclay's works, and suggesting that translation, the potential source of his cultural authority, also renders that authority a shifting and variable quantity. I will be especially concerned with the ways in which this manifests itself in the *Eclogues*, his most popular work later in the sixteenth century.

Barclay's work embraces every potential division offered him by the task of translation and the institutions of patronage. Outside the *Eclogues*, he produced several books in unusually close collaboration with Pynson: *The Ship of Fools* (1509), a verse *Life of St. George* printed about 1515 and translated from Mantuan, *The Mirror of Good Manners* from the *De quattuor virtutibus* of Domenico Mancini (around 1518) and a prose translation of Sallust's *Jugurthine Wars* (c. 1520). As David Carlson notes, these share a distinctive bicolumnar layout, with their originals printed beside Barclay's English translations except in the case of the *Ship of Fools*, where each chapter of the English is preceded by its equivalent in his source, John Locher's Latin translation of Sebastian Brant's original. What is noteworthy here is that several also share double dedications, which are, as William Nelson has pointed out, double in more ways than one. On the title page of *The Mirror of Good Manners*, Barclay alleges that he was "commanded" to translate Mancini's *De quattuor virtutibus* by Sir Giles Alington. His address to Alington, however, indicates that he adopted this task of his own accord, since Alington had in fact required him to "amende" an unknown work, "A Lovers confession." According to his own overt declaration, Barclay chose to go a different way, for fear that some might find it

> to my age and order muche inconvenient
> To write of thing wanton, not sad but insolent.

As Nelson indicates, however, Barclay is in part ghosting here the Augustinian Mancini's own prefatory statement that rather than write of love, to which he is ill-suited, he will produce a didactic treatise.[8] The *Life of*

St. George's title page claims that it was undertaken "at commaundement" of Thomas Howard, duke of Norfolk; Barclay's English dedicatory poem, however, states rather that Norfolk's "desire" *and* "renomyd fame" spurred him to translate it, and it also contains a Latin dedication to Nicholas West, bishop of Ely, putting him among several who urged Barclay to carry it out.[9] The same linguistic bifurcation appears most acutely in the Sallust translation, where a prose dedication in English, again to Norfolk, runs alongside a Latin one to John Veysey, bishop of Exeter.[10]

Barclay's double dedications serve various purposes, some of which resonate well beyond the literal. Alongside standard excuses – that nobles need to learn Latin, that great deeds should never die – Barclay's dedication to the Sallust translation draws attention once again to his own evident unsuitability to the task at hand: a monk compelled to explain why he should write of martial matters, he is heartened by Job's contention that "mans life upon yerth is but a warfare."[11] We glimpse here, repeatedly, a double movement of consolidation and extension. The continuities between Latin text, Latin dedication, and clerical addressee bestow on Latin a very specific location and sphere of cultural authority. Yet Barclay is still the self-promoting translator, in a move borne out by the metaphoric shifts in his own language, and by the way in which his authorial identity is interpolated chiefly to draw attention to his own efforts. In the preface to *The Ship of Fools* he confirms this: "I haue but only drawen into our moder tunge, in rude langage the sentences of the verses as near as the pareyte of my wyt wyl suffer me, some tyme addynge, somtyme detractinge and takinge away suche things a [*sic*] semeth me necessary and superflue."[12] "[T]he original," Nelson comments, "appears in order that the reader may know what changes Barclay has wrought."[13]

Barclay's enterprise, then, already bestrides two spheres. If one revolves around Latin and the monastic standing on which Lydgate had drawn – and, for that matter, the fraternal identities of Mantuan and Mancini – the other, vernacularizing, is more disseminatory, more prone to a studied kind of error. With this in mind I would like to look especially closely at the *Eclogues*, where the dialogic structure of the genre makes the location of the author unusually difficult to determine. It should be noted that these poems have a more uncertain textual history than others by Barclay. Though their editor, Beatrice White, assumes them to have been written between 1509 and 1514, all earlier editions are lost, and we do not know in what form they circulated, or whether they were gathered together at an early stage. Editions begin to appear in 1518, the first known being of the fifth *Eclogue*, and the earliest surviving edition of all five together is in John Cawood's 1570 collected edition of Barclay. They bring together several sources: Eneo Silvio Piccolomini's *De miseriis curialium epistola*; two of the increasingly popular *Eclogues* of Baptista Spagnuoli, or Mantuan; and, at one point, more remotely, Jean Lemaire de Belges's *Le Temple de Vertu et d'Honneur*.[14] Almost from the outset, Barclay ringfences his monastic identity with a series of defensive repudiations. He begins with an assertion that he does not seek the name of "Poete laureate" (104) and the fourth *Eclogue*, on the miseries of poets faced with grudging patrons, returns to this particular combat with singular violence. At the end of *The Ship of Fools*, the moralist-monk has already inveighed against Skelton's "wantones": "It longeth nat to my scyence nor cunnynge / For Phylyp the Sparowe the (Dirige) to synge" (841, lines 19–21). Less prominent is a possible thrust at *The Bowge of Courte*'s Skelton's and Hawes's reworking of exegetical terms in the second *Eclogue*, on courtly flatterers who "cloke the truth their princes to content" (295).[15] In the fourth *Eclogue*, however, Barclay embroiders on his original in Mantuan to launch an assault on "rascolde poetes" (680), one of whom is "decked as Poete laureate, / When stinking Thais made him her graduate" (685–86). Skelton's academic laureation, conferred in Barclay's formula by the Muse-as-courtesan, leaves the poet-laureate abjectly bound to a vilified female body.

Clerical misogyny, however, is not contained, but linked to a series of connected figures that extend a more general heterogeneity, though still one hostile to monastic maleness. This is already apparent in *The Ship of Fools*, where Barclay pictures the London printing of his text as a lively encounter between its encyclopedic categories and an urban promiscuity that risks breaking bounds:

> From London Rockes almyghty god vs saue
> For if we there anker, outher bote or barge
> There be so many that they vs wyll ouercharge.   (151, 12–14)[16]

The fifth *Eclogue* takes up this vision: "Baudes be suffered so where them lust to bide, / That the strete fadeth vpon the water side" (797–98). Here the courtly courtesan reemerges triumphant:

> Uile Thais was wont in angles for to be,
> Nowe hath she power in all the whole citie.   (801–02)

A sexuality both unbridled and commodified blurs jurisdictional bounds. Faustus, the city-loathing shepherd of this eclogue, implodes with inevitable allusions to the paradigmatic city of Sodom (1005), and the work ends as his interlocutor Amintas attempts to mollify him. The pacification of comic excess issues in a promise to take up the subject again the next day.

In creating a pastoral space defined against court and city, Barclay is building on earlier formulations of his clerical identity. In *The Ship of Fools*, he connects the metropolis with local margins through the insertion of anecdotes about his life and place in Devonshire, such as his caustic addition of the secondaries of his collegiate church to the fools "that nought can and nought wyll lerne" (332) and the inclusion, under the rubric, "The description of a wyse man," of reference to "his frende bysshop by name" (780, 13–14). Such interpolations thicken the geographical texture, giving Barclay a place (*topos*) of a very precise kind. That place spreads into the semifictive Ely that is his equivalent to his source's "creation" of the semiallegorical landscape around Mantua, with its city of Coitus (Coito) and its tower of sulphur (Solferino).[17] Barclay's identity is rooted in a rather more reassuring scenery, a clerical imaginary whose repertory of figures supplies his discursive position with affective support, and so with authority. Barclay's rural Ely is very much a textual world, one that seems to ask for exegesis, generated from the contingencies of translation, amplification of sources, interstitial allusions and the domestication of characters and places. Out of this, Barclay builds on the nostalgic and elegiac element in pastoral, producing a terrain shaped by a heavily masculine, quite literally patriarchal narrative of heroic discipline, desire, loss and sheep.

Barclay's transhistorical community brings dead *auctores* together with modern prelates. This is nowhere more apparent than in the memorable lament for John Alcock, bishop of Ely and founder of Jesus College, Cambridge, who had died in 1500. Indeed, Alcock is here one of a trio of dead clerics, set between Archbishop Morton of Canterbury, already described as "the patron of thinges pastorall" (1: 511) and Roger Westminster, Ely's prior until 1500. The lines on Alcock, "father of things pastorall" (1: 531), collect several components:

> My harte sore mourneth when I must specify
> Of the gentle Cocke whiche sange so mirily,
> He and his flocke were like an vnion,
> Conioyned in one without discention,
> All the fayre Cockes which in his dayes crewe
> When death him touched did his departing rewe,
> The pretie palace by him made in the fen,
> The maides, widowes, the wiues and the men,
> With deadly dolour were pearsed to the heart
> When death constrayned this shepheard to depart.
> Corne, grasse and fieldes mourned for wo and payne,
> For oft his prayer for them obtayned rayne,
> The pleasaunt floures for wo faded eche one

> When they perceyued this shepheard dead and gone,
> The okes, elmes and euery sorte of dere
> Shronke vnder shadowes, abating all their chere,
> The mighty walles of Ely monastery,
> The stones, rockes, and towres semblably
> The marble pillers and images echeone,
> Swet all for sorowe when this good cocke was gone ... (3: 469–88)

The death of Alcock produces a landscape quick with the sorrows of remembrance; he is a benevolent local deity whose loss has plunged the world into grief. But Barclay's landscape is also a very textual confection indeed. Its sweating stones, as White noted, may be borrowed from Book One of Virgil's *Georgics*, and the temple images which sweat at Caesar's death (250, note to 125). The play on Alcock's name, too, is subject to multiple influences. Mantuan refers to the papal treasurer Falcone di Sinibaldi, another "good shepherd," as "pastor ... quadam ducens ex alite nomen," a shepherd bearing the name of a bird – a line which, as Wilfred Mustard observed years ago, is behind Barclay's allusion.[18] However, there is also a more immediate reference, as Julie A. Smith notes, to Alcock's own rebus, the image of a cock on a globe, resonant with multiple connotations: the prelate's mandate to preach, Peter's remorse, Christ as Man of Sorrows.[19]

Stephen Guy-Bray notes that Virgilian pastoral inherits from Theocritus a "largely unbroken spectrum" of homosocial relations; in Virgil's *Eclogues* these are fragmented by power and status, so that "the men of the eclogue meet to mourn when they meet at all."[20] Barclay brushes against the intimate and idyllic; at the end of the third *Eclogue*, Corydon takes leave with "Adewe swete Cornix, departing is a payne, / But mirth reneweth when louers mete agayne" (3: 824–25), while Faustus hastens to return to his friend as they bed down together under the straw: "After great colde it is full swete God wot / To tumble in the strawe or in the litter hot" (5: 225–26). The real erotic weight of the *Eclogues*, however, belongs in the not so displaced homosocial content of the laments, as two men join in mourning for a lost father, powerful bonds between male generations and between shepherd and flock shrunken like the Ely oaks to a bleak fable of failed patrilineage, dead elders and wayward sons: "the yong be much vnlike the olde," says Corydon (1: 516). This is a genealogy made not by acts of begetting, but by disciplined celibacy: as Cornix puts it, "When he [Alcock] went faded the floure of all the fen, / I boldly dare sweare this cocke trode neuer hen" (1: 529–30). In case we miss the point, it is emphasized with the final member of this paternal group, Roger Westminster or "the Shephearde Roger":

> When he departed his flocke for wo was faynt,
> The fouldes sounded with dolour and complaynt,
> So that their clamour and crye bespred the yle,
> His death was mourned from Ely forty mile.
> These worthy heardes and many other mo
> Were with their wethers in loue conioyned so,
> That more they cured by witte and pacience,
> Than dreadfull drome[21] can do with violence. (3: 505–12)

This picture of a man in love with his wethers does not have the punning density of the lines on Alcock or Morton – earlier turned by metonymy into "the riche shepheard which woned in Mortlake" (1: 499) – but its allegorical quality echoes them. At moments like this, Barclay's England is itself a rebus, rather in the sense that Freud uses the term to describe the images produced by the dream-work. Ely here relates metonymically to Barclay's monastic *habitus*, and is the spatial configuration of the poet's ego, an amplification of a bodily surface.

As such, however, it cannot but bring with it its own *corps morcelé*, a mirage of a body in pieces. I refer to the vivid description of court's effect on the subject that enters the first three *Eclogues*. Even before the detail enters, it is anticipated in Barclay's relationship to his source texts, which in this instance do not appear alongside his own. In the first three *Eclogues*, which are in any case furnished with Mantuan allusions *not* belonging to those Mantuan eclogues Barclay translates in the fourth and fifth *Eclogues*, Barclay, as Mustard observed long ago, occupies a constantly shifting distance to his source.[22] Piccolomini's *De miseriis curialium*, an epistolary instance of curial satire, is broken down into dialogue. Sometimes the source is focused in a style that highlights its place in a chain of mediations. Where the original bleakly notes that princes reward courtiers as we fatten pigs for slaughter, the image – well suited to its pastoral Barclayan reception – is followed with "sic de Seneca Longinoque legimus, quos propter diuitias interemptos Iuuenalis affirmat his versibus," and adding the Juvenalian quotation.[23] Barclay highlights Piccolomini's role as transmitter, and adds a further voice:

> Like as Longinus and Seneca doubtlesse,
> Which as sayth Codrus were slayne for their riches,
> So writeth Pius (whom some Eneas call)
> A clause alleaging of famous Iuuenal. (1: 1253–56)

At others, the voice of the source is identified as "syr Sampson" (2: 1191), mapping the future pope on to a type-figure parish priest, or a citation in the source of Aristotle is ascribed to an anonymous Cambridge "scoller" ("[One of the same which go in copes gay]," 1: 865–66). By a series of shifts, source and mediation become indistinguishable.

The effects of this are most noteworthy in the second *Eclogue*. Barclay has underlined in the first the traditional curial complaint that the prince implicitly demands the absolute dedication of all the courtier's faculties. All senses and desires must be focused on the ruler:

> thou must all thing fulfill
> As is his pleasure, and nothing at thy will.
> None of thy wittes are at thy libertie,
> Unto thy master they needes must agree. (1: 1183–86)

"Will" and "pleasure" nuance significantly the Latin's terse "Nulla tibi aut in uerbis aut in operibus libertas supererit" (Mustard, 35).

This narrative of libidinal coding is played again in the second *Eclogue*, but here it has changed. The part of the source deployed has to do with the effect of the court on the five senses, and the result – outlined by Piccolomini, much expanded by Barclay – is phobic carnival, predicated on an absolute and catastrophic mismatch between the courtier's body and the time of the prince. When you wait for meals at table, they come too soon or too late to satisfy hunger (2: 597–628); the wine is too cold or too hot (629–31), while you are perpetually tormented, like Tantalus, by smells from the table of the great (901–04). You eat the worst food (737–812); the cups are only washed once a year, and then "of that vessell thou drinkest oft iwis / In which some states or dames late did pis" (2: 641–42: "in quibus saepe minxisse domini consueuerunt"; "dames," revealingly, is Barclay's addition). Just as the prince mediates desires for food, so he limits access to "fayre ladies" ("At thy princes pleasour thou shalt them onely see," 2: 171). The prince, in this transplanted account, controls the circulation of objects to which desire affixes itself, and, most crucially, the Other enjoys. Women at court are fickle ("none shalt thou loue of this sorte pardee, / But that she loueth another better then thee," 2: 413–14). As Piccolomini notes and Barclay repeats, it is a structural condition of court life, not an accident, that

> Though it to [lords] turne to no profite at all,
> If they haue pleasour the seruaunt shall haue small. (2: 793–94)

The court offers the script of unity; what it confers, however, is a horrific performance of missed encounter. The courtier's relation to his master, too, suggests nothing so much as R. Howard Bloch's familiar description of medieval misogyny. Whether he fornicates too much or too little, "vse[s] familiaritie" with a few men or is "common to all indifferent" (3: 431, 433), the prince is the cause of the servitor's inner turbulence, and is "a perpetually overdetermined signifier with respect to which man is always at risk." No more than the woman of medieval antifeminism can the lord get it right.[24] There is an excess of unregulated physical proximity; when the court travels, one is liable to share a bed with people who fart or scratch themselves all night, or even with a leper (3: 83–110). And Barclay goes further than his source in describing the likelihood that at dinner you may get mutilated by the knives of your fellow courtiers: "Ofte in such dishes in court is it seene. / Some leaue their fingers, eche knife is so kene" (2: 981–82). At the base of court existence lie fragmentation and an excruciating carnality. We are a long way from the court as the cradle of civility, and the world where the real is increasingly elaborated by the courtesy book's symbolic.[25]

Now we witness a curious doubling of this effect in Barclay's relationship to his source. At the beginning of the *Eclogues*, Barclay partially translates Mantuan (who called his eclogues his *Adulescentia*) to signal with full post-classical decorum that his pastoral poems are literary prentice-work (Prol.1–102; cf. 69–76 with Mantuan's prefatory letter to Paride Ceresara). His translation stages an associated reversion. In the *De Miseriis*, Piccolomini laments that there are few clerics nowadays who do not follow Epicureanism, and affirms this with a quotation from Cicero's *Pro Caelio*;[26] while Cicero and a few others will think the gods favor a man who can avoid the temptations of the senses, all of which Cicero lists, the majority are more likely to believe that such a man has incurred divine anger ("huic homini ego fortasse et pauci deos propitios, plaerique autem iratos putabunt" ["such a man I and some few others may account heaven's favorite, but most will think him the object of its wrath"]).[27] Barclay, here resolutely preserving the clergy even from rhetorical taint, reworks the latter point, particularly the "plaerique" ("*no* men count them of maners dull and rude", Prol. 2: 84, italics mine). Piccolomini launches at this point an exordium that announces he will now address the requirements and risks to which the five senses are exposed in the world of the court:

in oratione pro Marco Caelio Ciceronem dicentem inuenimus; quibus in uerbis omnes quinque sensus tetigit quibus voluptates hauriuntur. (Mustard, 37)

[we find Cicero saying this in his speech on behalf of Marcus Caelius; in these words he has touched on all the five senses to which our pleasures cling.]

While Barclay follows the general organization suggested by this *dispositio* – he traces in sequence Piccolomini's treatment of the five senses – he entirely omits the prefatory statement that announces it. Piccolomini's source text becomes rhetorically and sensorily ordered body, and Barclay's vernacular version is located in the movement "from insufficiency to anticipation," with the temporal twist that the symbolized and hierarchized body of the prior texts here precedes a violent and disordered insufficiency.[28]

The latter is most apparent in Barclay's savagely carnivalesque reversions to his source. He offers an amplification of *Philippians* 3, 18–19 hardly less devastating than that of Chaucer's Pardoner ("They been enemys of Cristes croys, / Of whiche the ende is deeth; wombe is hir god!," *CantT* VI, 532–33). Barclay's devotees of the belly-god are accorded a full-scale cultic peroration, which pictures a temple where the vessels are "Platters and dishes, morter and potcrokes, / Pottes and pestels, broches and fleshe hokes" (Prol. 2: 565–66). The curial satirist's vision is of being dismembered and eaten (even the servers "At euery morsell hath eye vnto thy hande" [2: 938]). This, of course, is part of the diabolical machinery of a court that is "in earth an ymage infernall" (1: 1260). At the start of the third *Eclogue* – in a passage that is pure Barclay – it transpires that this has haunted Corydon's dreams:

> Me thought in the court I taken was in trap,
> And there sore handled, God geue it an ill hap.
> Me thought the scullians like fendes of their lookes
> Came some with whittels, some other with fleshhokes.
> Me thought that they stoode eche one about me thicke
> With kniues ready for to flay me quicke.
> So had I (sleeping) as much of feare and dreade,
> As I should (waking) haue lost my skin in deede.   (3: 15–22)

If loss is elsewhere nobly distanced, we can hardly say the same of this ferocious, comic-traumatic excoriation.

Against the seething somatic nightmare of the court, an anthill of men behaving badly, are set the figures of the revered departed. Dead men walk the pages of the *Eclogues*: Morton, Alcock, Westminster, Sir Edward Howard, killed in an attack on the French off Brest in 1513 and mourned in "The Towre of Vertue and Honoure," the elegy perhaps set into the fourth *Eclogue* as a probable bid for Howard patronage.[29] And their number includes the poet himself. At the very outset, Barclay dourly opposes himself to the "laureate poets" of the court:

> But of their writing though I ensue the rate,
> No name I chalenge of Poete laureate.
> That name vnto them is mete and doth agree
> Which writeth matters with curiositee.
> Mine habite blacke accordeth not with grene,
> Blacke betokeneth death as it is dayly sene,
> The grene is pleasour, freshe lust and iolite,
> These two in nature hath great diuersitie.

> Then who would ascribe, except he were a foole,
> The pleasaunt laurer vnto the mourning cowle.   (Prol. 4: 103–12)

The black habit is set against the living green of the laurel wreath, in a thrust directed perhaps against Skelton, perhaps more generally against the rhetoricians who had found court favor under Henry VII and retained it under his successor. This is not the death of the author so much as the author as death, a figure whose boundary-haunting here takes on an uncanny quality.[30]

Barclay's *Eclogues* are among much else a curiously neglected resource in the current critical fascination with nation and region. From the depths of pastoral convention, Barclay produces an "authentic" England, dialectically related to yet distinct from a larger national frame, inhabited by benign clerical deities. His monastic identity is here suffused with a fantasy of England as local being, and in this creation of a stable point of discursive origin, he gives a new dimension to late-medieval writing on the court. However, the combination of clerical discourse and courtly address marks a synthesis that Barclay, and history, were not to sustain, as the little known about his subsequent career suggests. A letter sent to Wolsey by the informer Hermann Rinck from Cologne, dated October 4, 1528, links Barclay with Tyndale and the evangelical pamphleteers Jerome Barlowe and William Roy ("formerly Observants of the order of St. Francis, but now Apostates").[31] The next year another informer, John West, speaks of "brother Alysander Barkley, who has called Wolsey a tyrant and other opprobrious and blasphemous words."[32] The next surviving information puts Barclay once again at the political and geographical margins: in 1538 he was moving around Devon and Cornwall, fomenting dissent and speaking against the royal supremacy. He was ultimately to become one of Mary Tudor's chaplains before her accession, and thus "involved in conflict with the government almost until his death in June 1552."[33] The *Eclogues*, with their stylized depiction – and partial production – of the tensions between an English political center and monastic margins, clearly held in check forces that could not long survive history's entropic pull.

EMPIRE THROUGH THE LOOKING-GLASS

Douglas's *Palice of Honour* certainly shares Barclay's uneasy view of the imagined court, not least in its preoccupation with corporeal integrity. While Barclay's courtiers relive the press of courtly bodies in infernal dreams, the fears in Douglas's poem take on imaginative life in a dream vision, through a series of courts – some static, some peripatetic – that he passes through, or that pass him by. These fears, too, are of metamorphosis, and are bound up with the dream's deep involvement in the tropology of *fin amour*. The *Palice*'s Ovidianism has been well documented, usually in regard to a quite palpable strand of excess.[34] In the wild swerves of its narrative, the poem's dreamer-narrator has various traumatic experiences in a standard lover's *locus amoenus* and then at the (very literal) hands of Venus's court, before being rescued by Calliope and the Muses and conducted to the Palace of Honour. Since the poem stages a movement from Ovid to the promise of Virgil, from Scots vernacular to Scots as epic medium, its conclusion brings a covenant of liberation into an epic future. This, however, cannot come to pass without unresolved dissonances.

Readers have gravitated towards one disquieting episode in particular as the poem's culmination. Once in the palace, the dreamer, like the marginalized clerics of earlier French court poetry in his preoccupation with "seeing," peeps "In at a boir [*chink*]" (1903)[35] and glimpses "the gladdest represent / That euir in erth a wrachit catywe kend" (1904–05) – an opulently bejewelled palace, where "Rial Princis in plate and armouris quent [*intricately made*]" (1919) walk to and fro, while

> Intronyt sat a god armypotent,
> On quhais gloryus vissage as I blent   *looked*
> In extasy, be his brychtnes, atonys   *at once*
> He smate me doun and byrsyt all my bonys.
>
> (1921–24)

Much has turned here on the variant readings of line 1921; Copland's edition of *c*. 1553 styles the god "armypotent," whereas the 1579 print of Henry Charteris reads "omnipotent." Spearing offers the uncharacteristically bald assertion that this "represent" is "God," while for Fradenburg "The heroization of the 'represent'" recovers image for masculine action.[36] The episode suggests Barclay's sad tales of the body's *mésalliance* with ruler and court. If, however, the "represent" is, as some have argued, a transfiguration of an earthly king, this king brings a specific language. The epithet "Armypotent," passing through Statius, Boccaccio, Chaucer and Lydgate from Virgil's "armipotens," blends a vernacular literary tradition with an epic past of *translatio*.[37] Virgilian diction is no less endowed than Ovidian motif with the power to break bones. Here that power is exercised in a masculine agon through which Douglas, not for the first time in the poem, dramatizes by way of his dreamer's predicament a constant and disturbing – though also wildly funny – misalignment between body and the languages of the literary past.

Far more rhetorically ample and enigmatic, however, is the scene that precedes this crushing encounter. When the dreamer reaches the Palace of Honour, he encounters Venus enthroned. On "thre curius goldyn treis"

(1474) before her face stands a "fair myrrour" (1476), which shows "All thinges gone lyk as they wer present" (1497). We will return to this scene in due course; for the present I will simply outline the direction of Douglas's poem, which represents a series of translations of figure and space, an elaborate threshold at which Scots is made ready for Virgil. *The Palice*'s excesses arise because this highly bookish poem becomes, *avant la lettre*, a meditation on something close to Derrida's archive; a cultural memory that embodies authority as it issues commands, and comprehends an "anarchivic" death drive that annihilates the archive even as it seeks to construct it.[38] Only the pressure of this movement underlies the poem's achievement of a precarious equilibrium of "authority" – an authority which gestures both towards monarch and court, and towards an archive at once classical and vernacular. And the balance reached is, as we shall see, precarious indeed.

Like Dunbar's allegories, *The Palice* initially paints a vernacular landscape fused with Latinate artifice, the mother tongue with the language of the fathers. At its opening, Douglas's dreamer rises in May "to do my obseruance" (6) and traces his way through a thickly Chaucerian (or perhaps, once again depending on chronology, Dunbarian) landscape. It is heraldically "powderit" (11); Aeolus's intrusions are suspended, as they are in *The Thrissill and the Rois* (49–50); there is even an evocation of *The Legend of Good Women*'s daisy, according to Peter Travis Chaucer's "heliotropic" emblem of figuration (37).[39] The aureate landscape, however, is violently shaken by the intrusion of a voice "preclare [*clear*] as phebus schone" (63) – Derrida's archive in "jussive" mode.[40] It praises May as a figure allied with creating Nature; she is the "Maternall moneth" (65) and "verray ground tyl werking of nature" (69) which "small herbis constrenis tyl encres" (68), refresher of buds and birds alike. She also provokes the warrior impulses of "martis vassalage" (83) and "amorus lufe and armony" (84). This violent excess of presence – of voice and light – rephrases the generic and stylistic garden *topos* with its amorous overtones, but does so as a demand:

> Quha that constrenit ar in luffis rage
> Addressand þaim with obseruans ayrly
> Weil auchtyst the tyl glore and magnify.   *ought*
> (86–88)

The components of aureate diction – Latinate law, the mother tongue – are abstracted from the landscape and relayed as an order. The "maternall moneth" insists, as later will Venus, on the praise of a responsive voice supplying more of the same. This vocal intervention from an invisible source, with its maternal associations, disconcertingly anticipates a body of psychoanalytic and film theory in which a maternal "voice-object" conjoins fantasies of fusion with paranoiac terror.[41] The effect is not unlike that of the interrupted ekphrasis of *The Goldyn Targe*, but here it is a strident declamation that disrupts the relation between the eroticized garden and the dreamer-narrator who had been so "at home" there. The voice intrudes from without as alien object; the dreamer errs ("foruay[s]," 92) and is suddenly engulfed in a strange corporeal delirium, "With sprete arrasyt, and euery wit away. / Quakyng for fere, baith puncys [*pulse*], vane and neruis" (98–99). This dreamer's body can "not sustene so amyabyll a soun" (102); he is, literally, floored by an overwhelming excess of voice and genre.

Nor does this relationship between the speaker and the language of which he is a figure reach any kind of equipoise. The dreamer is transported from the garden of love to a "wyldernes abhomynable and wast" (155). Here the scenery shows us the future translator of the *Eneados*, and the author whose classical inclinations have frequently provoked critical debate about the nature and extent of his "humanist" impulses. Yet his "deserte terrybill" (136) is a syncretist's nightmare: a "stinking" stream "Lyke tyll Cochyte, the ryuer infernall" (138) contains yelling fish leaping from commentaries on *Revelations*.[42] Here the landscape's monstrosity is the very measure of its intertextual heterogeneity. It is no wonder that the dreamer bursts into a lament on transience and Fortune's unpredictabilities, glossing the metaphoric transformation of "veyr translat in wyntyr furyus" (190).

The metalinguistic nature of this lurch into dystopia is suggested in a number of ways. The artifice with which nature is shot through at the poem's opening gives place to a denatured wasteland where the vegetation is dead, yet still forces its way to light in a kind of negative life:

Not throu the soyl, bot muskan treis sproutyt	*rotten*
Combust, barrant, vnblomyt and vnleuyt.	*without flowers; without leaves*
Ald rottyn runtis quhairin no sap was leuyt	*stumps*
Moch, all wast, widdrit with granis moutyt …	*Decayed; withered; fallen*
	(149–52)

This terrain, where to be present at all is to be out of place, seems to generate its own contradiction in the catalogues that attend the courts of Minerva, Diana and Venus, pagan and Old Testament characters ordered and clustered as if in defense against the ground's decomposition and formlessness. Even then, however, the poem dwells on the waste matter rejected by these fragments of the archive. When Minerva's court passes – the wise on their way to the Palace of Honour, which draws all the poem's characters – attention is given not to the figures who accompany her, but to the "catiuis twane" (231) who bring up the rear, Sinon and Achitophel, the one with "a wedy [*noose*] about his mone [*neck*]" (232) and the other on "an hyddows hors" (233). These are the court's "abject" (240) who used their wisdom "lewdly" (275). And the abject of the archive come to include the dreamer himself, the "elrych grume [*elvish fellow*]" (299) who hides throughout in a hollow tree, as if in scapegoating citation of the "elvyssh" Chaucer who tells *Sir Thopas* (*CantT* VII, 703). When Venus's court surfaces, the very charm of its music drives him into melancholy, and the curse he utters on Venus and her court (607–36) brings their ire down on him.

This moment has figured for the poem's readers as its most Ovidian, since it is here that the dreamer, savagely mobbed by a cluster of very vernacular fairies, fears most for his form:

> For gret effere me thocht na pane to be.
> But sore I dred me for sum othyr Iape
> That Venus suld throw hir subtillyte
> In till sum bysnyng best transfigurit me.   *monster*
> As in a bere, a bair, ane oule, ane ape.   *bear; boar*
> I traistit so for till haue been myssape
> That oft I wald my hand behald to se
> Gyf it alteryt, and oft my vissage grape.   *groped*
> (737–44)

Despite his fear, the dreamer is already a "bysnyng" or monster (from ON *bysn*, "marvel" or "portent") throughout the poem's first part, whether in his own eyes (625) or in Venus's.[43]

The poem also touches on other kinds of vulnerability, as monstrosity is caught up in a constant and (in the poem's world) highly contingent mismatch between speaker and generic demand. Sometimes he falls comically short; David Parkinson has demonstrated how feebly he measures up to the aspirations of visionary literature, with its guides and revelations.[44] At others, his utterances come joltingly to the fore, disarranging the subordinations of narrative syntax. At all times, and in all senses, he is a spectacle. The contingency goes further, since in true Ovidian fashion his voice and figure are always at risk of "laps[ing] back, at the edges, into the natural world"[45] – or, more precisely, into a disfiguring mimesis of something which is not quite nature. (We might think of Douglas's contradictory and grisly desert in the light of Lacan's assertion that "there is no absence in the Real.")[46] The menace of a reversion to bestiality is an ever-present threat. In the fearful wilderness even Minerva's sober court approach "As heyrd of bestis stampyng with loud cry" (196), though on closer view they reveal themselves to be "ladyis fair and gudly men arrayit, / In constant weid" (202–03).

With this in mind, we can better appreciate the dreamer's habit of describing the abrupt transitions he undergoes in the terms of a medieval scientific materialism, usually signaled by citations from Bartholomaeus Anglicus. *The Palice* amplifies, repeatedly, the digression on sound supplied by the windy eagle in *The Hous of Fame*. At the very outset, another sensorium-in-verse of an aureate Middle Scots landscape, Douglas's "reparcust ayr" (25), pointing forward (or backward) to Dunbar's Latinate diction, sets this material register in place. The dreamer's brief trauma in love's garden is in turn interrupted by "ane impressioun" (105) ("a fiery impression or exhalation," according to Bawcutt's note) that overwhelms him. He takes the chance to tell us that this is not surprising, "for ouer excelland lycht. / Corruppis the wit and garrys [*causes*] the blud auaile [*descend*] / On tyl the hart that it no danger ale" (113–15). The extended gloss, offered half-apologetically, follows on the dreamer's collapse in the garden and itself brings on an equally explosive outburst of modesty. He apostrophizes his own "barrant wyt" (127), calling on it to show its "dull exhaust inanytee" (133) and its "beggit termis, mare than thryis" (131). This closes a metaphorical circle, barren wit prefiguring the wasteland's "barrant" growth (150), which appears both as a horrible infliction from without and as the sorry product of the poet's own "wyt." *The House of Fame* intrudes especially clearly when the music of love's court is carried to the dreamer's ears by water, and the acoustic phenomena take Douglas in bizarre directions: loud noise disturbs the water, but the fish do not hear it, "For as we se rycht few of thaym has Eris" (377). Raw sound and unadorned diction, like the violent swoons and collapses of Douglas's dreamer, mark a body bereft of any productive relationship to the signifier, driving a wedge between "wyt" and language.

These effects of language impel a dreamer who is debilitated in a number of regards. Not only is he set adrift by metaphor; his experiences also dislocate the metaphors of sexual difference. The Maytime dreamer, crushed by the disembodied voice, is shaken even more by the subsequent "impressioun": "Amyd the virgultis all in tyl a fary / As femynine so feblyt fell I doun" (107–8). Similarly, his narrow escape from the bodily metamorphosis threatened by Venus's retinue cannot quite conceal the very real metamorphosis he does undergo, and indeed has undergone. His desperate plea of clerical privilege before the love-goddess, noted for its pointer to the historical and well-connected churchman Gavin Douglas ("And, mare attour I am na seculare," 696), is perhaps more interesting for Venus's very precise demolition:

> Not of a clerk we se the represent
> Saue onely falsshed and dissaitfull talys,

> Fyrst quhen thow come with hart and hail entent
> Thow the submyttit till my commaundement.
> Now now thairof me thynk to sone thow falys
> I weyn nathyng bot foly that the alys.
> ȝe clerkis bene in subtyle wordis quent.
> And in the deid als scharpe as ony snalys. (710–17)

Douglas's clerical identity exists here only as a legal fiction to be used against him. At the beginning of the poem, this dreamer who entered the love-garden to do his "observaunce" as a lover was decisively dissociated from Gavin Douglas's historical and clerical being. This original appearance in the poem is now thrown back at him with contractual force ("Thow the submyttit till my commaundement"; we recall May's remonstrance about Dunbar's prior promise in *The Thrissill*). A generic lover has reneged on a purely literary promise. The dreamer has already spoken of the "frenesyis" which "nakyt" – stripped – him of his "sempyll cunnyng" (134–35), a trope literalized in the horror-comedy of his mobbing ("Pluk at the craw [*crow*] thay cryit, deplome the ruke" 651).[47] Now Venus subjects him to the ultimate dismantling. He is "clerkly" only in his production of fictions; he has fallen away from the lover role mandated by his original appearance in the garden; finally, his "quent" verbal skills do not disguise his absence of "manhood" when it comes to "the deid." The integrity of the dreamer's body may have been spared, but his tropical body is now hopelessly undone. After his final annihilating confrontation with the "god armypotent," his guiding Nymph reverts to the earlier terms: "My hede in wed [*I'll wager my head*] thow hes a wyfis hart. / That for a plesand sycht is so mysmaid" (1937–38). The dreamer is angered by further evidence of his "mismaking," but the Nymph, with wonderful condescension, proverbially calms him down: "kyrkmen wer ay Ientill to ther wyuys" (1944). "After this," Parkinson comments, "the dreamer could never be mistaken for a great spirit, a high mind, or even much of a man."[48]

The poem's final and most striking revision of love-poetry opens it out in new but unforeseeable directions. Critics have noted *The Palice*'s highly parodic view of the medieval encyclopaedic tradition. When Calliope and the Muses rescue the dreamer from Venus and fly him to the Palace of Honour itself, the organization of the world below them answers to bibliography rather than geography; the rivers they cross are not ordered according to any possible real-world journey, even in the terms of medieval cartography. The encyclopaedia, however, emerges at the poem's culminating point, in an episode that most readers have passed over in embarrassment or mystification, and it is here that we return to Venus's mirror.

The dreamer sees the entire contents of the Old Testament and the Apocrypha (1498–1567), the stories of Thebes, Hercules and Jason, the Matter of Troy (1607–29) and its extension in the *Aeneid* (1630–56), the subsequent Matter of Rome (1657–92), and even "al the cumming of the Antecrist" (1701). Closer to home, there are vernacular protagonists – "Raf Coilȝear" (1711), John the Reeve (1712), Robin Hood (1718), even "Peirs plewman" (1714)[49] – and tales of "Nigramansy" (1720), which Bawcutt nicely observes "read like a grotesque parody of Ovid" ("of a Nutmog, thay mayid a monk in hy, / A parys kirk of a small penny py," 1725–26).[50] After this demurely compendious account of all the styles, genres and "materes" known to medieval literary production, secular and sacred, it comes as something of a surprise when the dreamer's attendant nymph glosses the contents of the mirror's reflection:

> ȝone myrrour clere,
> The quhilk thow saw afore dame Venus stand
> Signifyes nothing ellis till vnderstand
> Bot the gret bewty of thir ladyis facis
> Quhairin louers thinkis thay behald all gracis. (1760–64)

Among the poem's editors, Bawcutt finds this explanation "lame and unconvincing" (xlv); Parkinson observes that the marginal note in Copland's edition, where these lines are glossed "the Auctors conclution of Venus merour," contradicts the poem, "in which the 'conclusion' (which does not offer an adequate description of the catalogue just finished) is the Nymph's."[51]

I am not sure that this passage can be so easily dismissed. The entire poem has unfolded from an opening within which the dreamer was designated as lover-protagonist. Now, like Guillaume de Lorris's Amant and Narcissus, he looks in a mirror – here, the mirror of Venus. What he "behalds," however, is a compilation that catches up an entire medieval library within the loose and permeable bounds of universal history, and which is then named, retroactively, as the face of the beloved. Caught within the reflection of the lover's look is another archive. The dreamer was liberated by Venus on condition that he fulfill "the nixt resonabil command" (997) she might put, and he accepts:

> Weil weil (said scho) thy wyll is suffycyent.
> Of thy bousoum answere I stand content,
> Than suddandly in hand a buke scho hynt
> The quhilk to me betaucht scho or I went
> Commandand me to be obedient.
> And put in ryme that proces than quyt tynt. (1747–52)

As we have seen, the "buke" is the *Aeneid*, destined to be translated into Scots as Douglas's *Eneados*, completed some twelve years later. The formerly hostile Venus reappears as a figure in a patrilineal chain of transmission – Aeneas's mother, and *mediatrix* passing an important foundational text between Latin and a mother tongue that Douglas will define as "Scottis." The alien voice lauding the "maternall Moneth" returns in the mirror of a love-poetry that contains an archive, and presages the exaltation to epic vehicle of a Scots vernacular that earlier episodes had brutally unmade.

The Palice of Honour accordingly affirms what Derrida calls the "patri-archive":[52] the final encounter with the "god armypotent" is framed by recuperative gestures – an allegorization of the household (1779–827), the limiting assertion that "Prosperite in erd is bot a dreme" (1983). Yet the dream sputters out amid a reversion to the punitive rituals of its earlier episodes. Told by the Nymph that he has just lost the opportunity to see how "trespassouris" against honor are rewarded (2056), the dreamer is seized by an aggravating desire to look back, for less than Orphic reasons:

> Madame (quod I) for goddis saik turn agane.
> My spreit desyris to se thair torment fane. (2058–59)

Returned to the garden, he is left praising honor, and the poem's final dedication to James IV follows. Yet *The Palice* is sent into the world not with an *envoi de quare*, but with an unusually explosive dismissal:

> Thy barrant termis, and thy vyle endyte
> Sall not be min, I wyll not haue the wyte.
> For as for me I quytcleme that I kend tha,
> Thow art bot stouth, thyft louys lycht but lyte.
> Not worth a myte, pray ilk man till amend tha.
> Fare on with syte, and on this wyse I end tha. (2164–69)

The poet suddenly turns into a "flyter" against his own text, rehearsing, with a barrage of internal rhyme, charges with which we are by now familiar. His poem is purloined, sterile, worthless – waste matter, in effect. The relation assumed here between poet and text mirrors the one we have already seen at work in Calliope's court of the Muses. Douglas here departs from his precedent in *The House of Fame*, where poets are pillars supporting the deeds of heroes. Of Skelton's *Garland of Laurel*, Seth Lerer has written that when Chaucer, Gower and Lydgate make their appearance, they are "voiced presences,"[53] embodied figures. Douglas, however, makes the poets embody their works. Ovid, clerk of the court, shows ("schew," 1216) the multiple contents of the *Metamorphoses*. Virgil in some way enacts the

Eclogues, or "playd the sportis of Daphnis and Coridon" (1226); Terence "play[s]" (1227) his comedies. The substitution of book for author is even more explicit in the case of satirists, epigrammatists and flyters:

Iuuynale lik a mower hym allone	*Juvenal; jester*
Stud skornand euery man as thay ȝeid by	*went*
Marcyall was cuyk, till rost, seith, fars or fry.	*Martial; seethe; stuff*
And Pogyus stude with mony gyrn and grone	*Poggio; sneer*
On Laurence Valla spyttand and cryand fy.	
	(1229–33)

Poggio Bracciolini's performed invectives look ahead to Douglas's final attack on his own text. That text has now come to stand for Douglas, replacing him, and the poet is caught in imaginary rivalry with his own poem. Douglas, the originary term now cleared (rhetorically) of a prefatory text, can look ahead to the monument that will be the *Eneados*.

Yet even this forward-looking conclusion encapsulates the same fears as the rest of the poem. *The Palice of Honour* began with a sequence of false starts and an unnamed imperative to write. Now Douglas has written himself into a goddess's patronage, in a fiction of *auctoritas*. He has, however, repudiated his embodiment in one text simply to accomplish it in another, one – as any number of European foundation myths can attest – that was constantly available for geographic translation, and that carried its own drive to annihilation, to Trojan and Roman ruin as well as to empire. Indeed, his patron, the source of his authority, is also the being whose servants have, on her orders, subjected his physical body and clergial being to harm. The newfound position of authority from which he can complete his translation of the *Aeneid* thus seems strangely precarious, and this instability of poetic authority catches up an odd historical irony in Douglas's departure to England, political maneuverings and final exile. His text is underwritten by the pathos of distance – an imperial assertion in suspension, its author banished from the nation it was to authorize, and that was to authorize it.

CHAPTER 5

Mémoires d'outre-tombe: *love, rhetoric and the poems of Stephen Hawes*

In his study of the *grands rhétoriqueurs* of France and the Low Countries, Paul Zumthor recurs regularly to the metaphor of clothing. The *rhétoriqueur* works in a "costume of language ... made out of the fabric of a protocol woven from ancient, exhausted feudal traditions": he also wears the poetic robes which are the prince's gift. However, both garments conceal the pains of economic vulnerability and constraint; the poet as court servitor is literally a sign of monarchic magnificence, no one regarding the miserable body beneath.[1] The point is not new to Zumthor; the *Curial* similarly remarks that "Oftymes the peple make grete wondrynges of the Ryche robe of the courtyour / but they knowe not by what labour ne by what dyffyculte he hath goten it."[2] However, it provides an apt point of entry into the life of Stephen Hawes, who belongs among those poets about whom little is known outside the sources that document such matters as royal donations of garments. In 1503 he received an allowance of four yards of black cloth for mourning on the occasion of the funeral of Henry VII's queen.[3] His name does not, however, appear among the list of those officers who received mourning for Henry VII's funeral, a fact to which I will return. One other record, in the accounts of John Heron, treasurer of the chamber, shows for January 10, 1506 a payment to Hawes of ten shillings "for a balett that he gave to the kings grace in rewarde."[4]

Other details about Hawes may be gleaned from the prints of his poems, all of which came from Wynkyn de Worde's press. The introduction to his religious allegory *The Example of Virtue* states that it was written in the nineteenth year of the reign of Henry VII, placing it between August 1503 and August 1504; by the same token, a similar note in *The Pastime of Pleasure*, his best-known poem, puts its composition between August 1505 and August 1506. All the Hawes poems published in the reign of Henry VII designate him "groom to the chamber," but there is no evidence to corroborate John Bale's later assertion that he was among those attendants closest to the king in the "secretum cubiculum" or Privy Chamber.[5] And in the sole surviving copy of what is probably his final poem, *The Comfort of Lovers*, the formula has changed – he is "somtyme grome" of the late king's chamber, presumably a sign that he had no similar post under Henry VIII. The print can be dated to 1515 on typographic grounds, though the poem was, according to the title page, written between 1510 and 1511, raising the possibility of earlier prints or manuscript circulation. All that is known further is that he was dead by 1529, when the earlier of two surviving prints of a poem by his admirer Thomas Feylde, *A Controversy between a Lover and a Jaye*, refers to "Yong Steuen Hawse whose soule god pardon."[6] If we take this to suggest that Hawes was at least in his twenties by the time he wrote his earlier poems, it seems reasonable to suppose that he may not long have outlived the composition of *The Comfort of Lovers*.

Hawes's double commitment to the Tudor line and an English poetic tradition are apparent in the words with which he dedicates his longest poem, *The Pastime of Pleasure*, to Henry VII:

> Your noble grace and excellent hyenes,
> For to accepte, I beseche ryght humbly,
> This lytell boke, opprest with rudenes,
> Without rethorycke or colour crafty.
> Nothynge I am experte in poetry
> As the monke of Bury, floure of eloquence,
> Whiche was in tyme of grete excellence
>
> Of your predecessour the .v. kynge henry,
> Vnto whose grace he dyde present
> Ryght famous bokes of parfyte memory,
> Of his faynynge with termes eloquent,
> Whose fatall fyccyons are yet permanent,
> Grounded on reason; with clowdy fygures
> He cloked the trouthe of all his scryptures.   (22–35)[7]

Through this modesty *topos* Hawes, with some adroitness, performs an act of twofold legitimation. By connecting his king with an illustrious Lancastrian precursor,[8] he validates the first Tudor's claim, built on divine "grace" (3) and his own "gouernaunce" (6). But the lines, a dedication miniature in words, also allude to a previous act of dedication by poet to king – that of the *Troy Book*[9] – with the effect that Hawes constructs a genealogy of poets conterminous with that of the ruler. Hawes sets himself in the line of Lydgate, the poet whom, of the triumvirate of Chaucer, Gower and Lydgate cited by later medieval English authors, he seems chiefly to have admired.[10] Lydgate further becomes the authority for a poetic practice that we have seen interrogated in Skelton's *Bowge*, in which "fatall fyccyons" cloak truths with "clowdy fygures."[11] Such terminology is resonant for the court poet: just as the "truth" of the exegetes is cloaked by the "cloudy fygures" of the poets, and may be cloudily foretold in books of prophecy, so political "truths" (accessions to thrones, royal marriages) can be foretold through the standard ploys of pageant-makers.[12] Hawes received cloth from a king, and gave "clokes."

Previous readers of Hawes's poems have found much to occupy them, both in Hawes's obvious identification of poetic with political and royal authority, and in his display of a rhetorician's passion for rhetoric. My own reading will follow these paths, but with a difference. It enters *The Pastime* through Hawes's handling of narrative voice and *prosopopeia*, to find authority behind a series of veils, unpredictably and chillingly located. It then leaves the poem by way of its more overt pronouncements on rhetoric, and its place amid some contemporary affiliations between rhetoric and politics on which we have already touched. The poetry of love is once again a presence, but in *The Pastime* it is the immediately apprehensible face of a deadly anamorphosis.

The Comfort of Lovers too turns on secrecy, but secrecy here resides in a bleak fragmentation of *The Pastime*'s already unstable synthesis of genres. *The Comfort* combines political prophecy and love complaint in what at this historical remove appears to have been a bid for reinstatement at a court from which the poet had been expelled. This results in a bizarre and fascinating hybrid, since it entails the marriage of two genres that might at first seem compatible in their representation of the speaking subject, but which in literary practice cancel one another out. The result is a text that avails itself of a cultural detritus of available literary languages and models, striving to name a loss that ultimately is not quite available to its consciousness.

LOVE IN THE TIME OF RHETORIC

The Pastime centers on a personified lover, Graunde Amoure, who is commanded by Fame to undergo an education in the Towers of Doctrine and Chivalry and thereby win the maiden La Bell Pucell. When the poem begins, however, this narrator has no name; he is the anonymous speaker of love-lyric or *chanson d'aventure*, appearing in "a medowe ... gaye and gloryus" (64), surrounded by all the trappings of the *dit* and its Chaucerian offspring. The speaker remains a lover (almost) throughout; the desire for which he stands moves the narrative, associating it with the modes of allegorized love-quest, and constantly propelling it onward with phrases such as "So forth I rode" and "So forth I went."

His subsequent encounter with Dame Fame, iconographically surrounded by "tongues of fyre" (157), conjoins love with the language of *gloire* so prominent in English court culture and its Burgundian antecedents. It is in reply to Fame's questioning that he announces his name for the first time ("What was my name, she axed me treuly. / To whome I sayde it was la graunde Amour," 185–86). Amoure, in short, only reveals his identity in response to Fame's promptings, and thereby underscores the intimate relationship between love and the pursuit of honor so common in *rhétoriqueur* writing.[13] When Fame with her "swete reporte" praises La Bell Pucell, Pucell immediately becomes the object of desire, as Amoure's heart is "set on fyre / With brennynge loue moost hote and feruent" (288–89). Now the amorous quest will be one with the quest for renown, Amoure's desire with desire for glory in the service of the "comyn welthe" (252). These initial encounters inaugurate a process that continues through Amoure's meetings with the didactic personifications of the Towers of Doctrine and Chivalry. He figures an erotic desire that his encounters with these representatives of powerful literary discourses model and refine.[14]

As such a mobile desire, Amoure echoes a number of literary predecessors. Again like the "I" most immediately implicated in the dream action of Guillaume de Lorris's *Roman de la Rose*,[15] he moves through the allegorical landscape "at a uenture" (2967) – a *tabula rasa*, an ingenuous narrator with no powers of prediction, continually open to new narrative event and meaning. Hawes's most pervasive narratorial debt, however, is to a poem itself influenced by the *Roman*, Deguileville's *Pèlerinage de la vie humaine*, and its continental successors.[16] In Deguileville's poem, the limited awareness of Guillaume de Lorris's narrator has theological significance, and he becomes the "naive narrative persona ... who has everything to learn, the universal human situation."[17] *The Pastime* links its Tower of Doctrine episodes with instructional and encyclopaedic works of the kind printed by Wynkyn de Worde,[18] so that Amoure's visit to Dame Grammar requires him to behave like a student straight from the interrogatory pages of Donatus:

> "Madame," quod I, "for as moche as there be
> Viii. partes of speche, I wolde knowe ryght fayne
> What a nowne substantyue is in his degre,
> And wherfore it is so called certayne." (582–85)

Yet such passages too are shaped by Amoure's identity as romance-lover, as pedagogic discipline replaces the romance-hero's statutory tribulations.

If Amoure has literary affinities with Deguileville's Pilgrim, however, the two are also some distance apart. For if the iconography and events of *The Pastime* often suggest the pilgrimage, other parallels remain veiled. Amoure initially follows a "fayre pathe" (71), a common enough feature of the landscape of love-allegory, but it leads not to its usual destination in a "pleasaunt herber,"[19] but to a divide in the road of ostentatious significance. His confrontation with the choice of two paths, one "the streyght waye / Of contemplacyon" (85), the other the road to "worldly dygnyte / Of the actyfe lyfe" (93–94), also orients the alert reader. Amoure takes the "actyfe waye" (112), and the alternative generic possibility remains latent for a long while. The split voice of this poem points to a knowing lover and an unknowing pilgrim.

There are, however, numerous points at which the fiction of a lover-narrator is simply dropped, and the "I" is the neutral mediator of a rhetorical *topos*. The Tower of Doctrine episodes, with their gestures toward popular encyclopaedic works, create abrupt alternations between the Amoure-narrator and the statutory expositor of a didactic text. Thus, a brief encounter with Dame Arithmetic terminates in a referral of the reader to more learned textbooks ("To reherse in englysshe more of this scyence / It were foly, and eke grete neclygence," 1448–49), and then moves directly back to Amoure as lover ("I thought full longe tyll I hadde a syght / Of la bell pucell ... ," 1450–51). The effect is to superimpose on Amoure's journey the author's and reader's own progress through the book, so that the temporalities of the act of reading and the represented narrative action intersect. We can instance the end of the Tower of Rhetoric episode, where after Dame Rhetoric has concluded a long oration with a tribute to Lydgate, the "I" returns:

> Now wyll I cease of lusty rethoryke.
> I may not tary, for my tyme is shorte,
> For I must procede and shewe of arysmetryke
> With dyuers nombres, whiche I must reporte.
> Hope inwardly doth me well conforte
> To brynge my boke vnto a fynysshment
> Of all my mater and my true entent.   (1289–95)

Amoure must continue his narration, as he moves on to the next chamber in the Tower of Doctrine; his inner "hope" recalls his role as lover, his desire for "a fynysshment" his longing for consummation. But the voice is also, once again, that of the expositor who must proceed to the next topic. All these effects merge in the topos of the rhetorician who must continue with his poem; the lover's desire and the process of writing become one.

Such sudden and unprepared movements from speaking lover to speaking book and back tend to be explained away either as authorial ineptitude (Hawes is a careless user of late-medieval narratorial devices) or as an innocently "medieval" cultural redundancy (Hawes the medieval author simply fails to make the distinctions a modern reader would find natural). They slowly acquire an importance of their own, however, for apparent discontinuity at the level of narratorial voice becomes a more inclusive continuity at the level of the printed book. The sense of the book itself as a larger unit, affiliated to other kinds of book, is as prominent as the narratorial fiction of Graunde Amoure. A fictional character from the realm of love-literature progresses through and past blocks of nonnarrative didactic matter, an illusion the woodcuts that articulate the early editions of the poem help to sustain.[20] In the poem's diffusely overlapping discourses and voices, distinctions between narratorial roles, genres and even writer and reader fold back into a general identification of the lover's desire with the writer's – and the reader's – physical progress through the book. And this in turn generates a complementary process by which the lover's desire is glossed in various ways, as the poem's citation of a multiplicity of genres – the pilgrimage, the literature of Fame, the popular encyclopaedia, didactic and love-allegory, romance – doubles back on it.

This is nowhere more apparent than in the explicit parallels drawn between Amoure's first encounter with Pucell and rhetorical *inventio*. Dame Rhetoric has lectured Amoure on the respective contributions to *inventio* of the ".v. inwarde wyttes" (703). "Comyn wytte" (706) selects the basic matter, and "ymagynacyon" is responsible for its amplification (708–09), "Clokynge a trouthe with colour tenebrous" (712). "Fantasy" (722), "good estymacyon" (736) and "the retentyfe memory" (750) also play their parts. When Amoure meets Pucell at the Tower of Music, these functions are recalled:

> The comyn wyt dyde full lytell regarde
> Of dame musyke; the dulcet armony
> The eres herde not, for the mynde inwarde
> Venus had rapte, and taken feruently.
> Ymagynacyon wrought full pryuely.
> The fantasy gaue perfyte Iugement
> Alway to to [*sic*] her for to be obedyent.
>
> By estymacyon, moche doubtfully I cast
> Wheder I shoulde by longe tyme and space
> Atteyne her loue, or else to loue in wast. (1485–94)

> Whan she was gone, inwardly than wrought
> Vpon her beaute my mynde retentyfe.
> Her goodly fygure I graued in my thought. (1506–08)

Pucell herself has become the "mater" (709) on which Amoure's five faculties work. It is impossible here to draw a useful distinction between *inventio* and falling in love, as rhetorical treatise and love-literature become different ways of reading what is at root the same desire. The passage reminds us that Dame Rhetoric has already spoken of the "fantasy" of the rhetoricians of old in terms that suggest Amoure's allegorical quest; they are driven "Newe thynges to fynde" (728), and to bring their invention to fulfillment, by "brennynge loue" (727) and "hole desyre" (735). And when the quest's end is reached, the link between rhetoric and love is once more underlined, as Pucell greets Amoure with "depured and … lusty rethoryke" (5267).

Such glossing, of course, is integral to the hermeneutic modes on whose lexis Hawes draws so readily. The views of rhetoric found in Hawes's prologues and in Dame Rhetoric's speeches are mutually sustaining; in both the poet, by touching a truth and "cloking" it subtly, wields an authority with both doctrinal and political foundation. In Hawes's earlier *The Example of Virtue*, the exegete's *id est* is explicitly built into the narrative, always pointing "vertically" to another sense:

> The water eclyped was vayneglory,
> Ever with yeopardy and tempestyous,
> And the shyp called was ryght truly
> The vessell of the passage daungerous. (134–37)

In *The Pastime*, however, the vocabulary of revelation and concealment also applies to the structural use of vernacular modes. Declaring a provisional allegiance to the literature of courtly love, it also makes use of that literature's wittily self-advertising approach to rhetorical trope, in particular *prosopopeia*. For an instance of this heritage we may turn to Machaut's *Remède de Fortune*. Esperance has just departed after her colloquy with the lover-narrator, and he is returning to the small wicket gate by which he originally reached his isolated "destour" in the Park of Hesdin:

> Mais je m'aperçu bien que nuls
> N'estoit alez par ceste voie,
> Depuis que venus y estoie;
> Qu'en riens n'i estoit depassée
> L'erbe poingnant, et la rousée
> Clere et luisant seur l'erbe drue
> N'estoit pas encor abatue …

[I saw clearly that no one has come that way since I'd entered, for the sharp-bladed grass had not been disturbed and the bright, sparkling dew was still on the thick grass]²¹

The untrodden grass reminds us that Esperance was only a fiction.

Hawes's poem too distances personification, showing it in changing perspectives. Godfrey Gobylyve, the grotesque dwarf who provides an antifeminist and antiromance counter to Amoure's courtly idealism, enters the picture with a peculiar low-style density and specificity, marked by Kentish dialect, doggerel rhymed couplets and a comic genealogy (3514–47). It is thus all the more surprising when Correction, galloping up with her "knotted whyppe" (4118), tells us who he "really" is, and introduces herself:

> "My name," quod she, "is called correccyon,
> And the toure of chastyse is my mancyon.
> This strong thefe, called false reporte,
> With vylayne courage and an other sorte
> And vyle perlers false coniecture,
> All these I had in pryson full sure.
> But this false reporte hath broken pryson
> With his subtyll crafte and euyll treason,
> And this Iourney pryuyly to spede,
> He hath cladde hym in this foles wede."   (4126–35)

Before he is subjected to any other punishments, the errant Godfrey is punished by personification, rewritten – or rather exposed beneath a textual "foles wede" – as False Report. The whole episode is richly reflexive. False Report has escaped the prison where he was held with False Conjecture. His crime, says his warden Correction, is speaking ill of women, but the level of literary self-consciousness suggests that False Report and False Conjecture stand for the uncontained menace of gossip, subversive and potentially anarchic if it invades love-allegory's circumscribed purlieus. Correction's chastisement of Gobylyve thus dramatizes through *prosopopeia* another rhetorical figure, that of *correctio*.²²

This "correction" of a potential misreading introduces other kinds of discipline. Dame Rhetoric has claimed that her science

> was founde by reason
> Man for to *gouerne* well and prudently,
> His wordes to ordre, his speche to puryfy.   (691–93; emphasis mine)

The rhetorician promotes good government and self-government, and his experiments with diction refine the language, both points on which Hawes aligns himself with Lydgate. The common term in these activities is reason;

Hawes's words express a traditional affinity between *ratio* and *oratio*, well-ordered words denoting order in humanity and state.[23] Here Godfrey's undisciplined and treasonous body, his crude vernacular dialect – the "barbary tongue" (920) that the rhetorician's *elocutio* refines[24] – and the "jangler"'s vulgar antifeminism are set against Amoure's courtliness and rhetoric's civilizing effects upon body and language, *fin amour* embracing the very virtues privileged by the rhetorician's endeavors. Rhetoric is here a force for coercion.

A similarly pointed foregrounding of *prosopopeia* appears as Amoure prays for guidance in the Temple of Mars, but here it seems rather to stress the limitations of poetic trope. Mars offers aid to Amoure, but behind him stands Fortune, who claims that her mutability constrains his power. Mars's twofold response is unexpected. Not merely is Fortune without substance ("The man is fortune in the propre dede / And not thou that causeth hym to spede," 3212–13), an essentially Boethian position, she derives her power solely from the labors of poets who have "made a fygure" (3208) of her, "of the truth to make relacyon" (3211). Mars's interpretative procedure opens up some alarming possibilities. So ruthless a collapsing of figures into their inceptions would, if pressed farther, issue in a world totally dominated by the planets, which would itself contradict Mars's concluding Boethian claim that "The man is fortune in the propre dede." Further, the general tenor of Mars's argument, divorced from its specific instance, suggests that figures bear no necessary relation to truth, and indeed can, as here, distort it. The poetic "fygure" is identified, however fleetingly, with Fortune herself; double-faced and potentially deceptive, masquerading as a cause where it may be no more than a gloss. The vocabulary with which Hawes regularly celebrates the poet's function is here, but the context strips it of its customary weight. The speech opens up serious questions about the ontological and epistemological status of the poetic trope; it is "nought," a cipher, its capacity to point beyond itself called into doubt.

Less portentously and more playfully, the poem consistently uses *prosopopeia* to display the fictive quality of its love-allegory. When Amoure and Pucell separate after their first extended scene together, Amoure comments that

> Neuer before, as I trowe and wene,
> Was suche departynge true louers betwene.   (2379–80)

As Spearing points out, these lines have an ironic dimension, since the allegory's point "is to generalize." However, if Amoure here seems to believe his experience "unique and unprecedented,"[25] his fellow personifications are under no such illusion, but regularly call attention to their "generalizing" function. Counsel leaves Amoure with the words

> fare you well, for I must frome you go
> To other louers whiche are in dyspayre,
> As I dyde you to confort them also. (2486–88)

and Dame Fame departs with a magnificently garbled "For I must hens to specyfy the dedes / Of theyr wortynesse, accordynge to theyr medes" (314–15).

The cumulative effect of such passages in this poem of love is paradoxical. Amoure himself is a personification on a quest moved by the desire for which he stands, and yet *The Pastime* recurrently queries the possibility of treating such a figure narratively at all. In the poem's closed allegorical world, Amoure's reputation has always gone before him; his name always assures him of a welcome (384–85, 2976–89, 3790–99, 4471–72) and each new group of allegorical ladies he meets has heard of him and his quest (491–97, 4473–79, 4885–90). The inner logic of this is revealed by the ladies who greet Amoure after his slaying of the seven-headed giant:

> They prayed me to shewe them my name;
> "La graunde amoure it is," I sayde, "in dede";
> And than sayde they, "No wonder though ye spede." (4883–85)

If Amoure is love embodied, his quest is already complete; personification here seems to circumvent narrative and leave it redundant.

While personification and narrative are somewhat uneasy companions in Amoure's text, its intercalated love-lyrics – which take the form of complaints, petitions and dialogues – generate different tensions. They explore at length Amoure's uncertainty as to the narrative's outcome, and their expansive musings pull against the succession of events, their static, ritual gestures seeming impervious to narrative context. This lyric self-containment is illustrated by a later manuscript, Bodleian MS Rawlinson C. 813, which includes six love-complaints that draw – one briefly, the other five extensively – on both *The Pastime* and *The Comfort of Lovers*.[26] Passages from several scenes are woven together in an elaborate *cento*, and are not materially altered by the loss of their narrative frame. Other episodes employed – Amoure's "supplycacyon" to Venus (3804–908), and the letter she sends to Pucell (3951–4086) – are highly self-contained in the first place and need still less alteration, and parts of the dialogue between Amoure and Pucell are transformed into a single-voiced complaint by the simple expedient of dropping Pucell's lines.[27] In particular, nos. 13, 14, 15 and 16 of the lyrics in the Rawlinson manuscript, on fos.14v–27v, can be read as one continuous complaint, the near seamless product of a skillful exercise in compilation; the last lines by Hawes that we hear in this group are Amoure's final words to Pucell in the open-ended *Comfort of Lovers* (923–24), to be addressed shortly.

The compiler of Rawlinson C. 813, or of the exemplar behind this section of the MS, was clearly able to envisage some of the lyric passages in *The Pastime* as a single monologue, cut off from narrative sequel or response.

Amoure's lyrics, then, posit an unsatisfied desire that suspends narrative, while the device of *prosopopeia* implies a narrative already complete. This is hardly surprising; in Nicolette Zeeman's words, the verse of courtly love, in its "hyperboles and tropes of endless possibility," "espouses a playful yet resolute commitment to youth, narrative atemporality and poetic stasis, and deals evasively with all material which might contradict this."[28] However, this once again raises generic tension; while the lover may be committed to narrative atemporality, the pilgrim's very identity, defined by the span of man's earthly existence, is acutely "plotted." The poem's conclusion, however, gradually brings *persona* and personification into disambiguating conjunction, in the process giving a new meaning to Hawes's poetics of "fayned fables" and "cloudy fygures."

THE DEATH OF THE COURTLY LOVER

The lyrics of *The Pastime* correspond to Amoure's eager anticipation of his final union with Pucell ("For nature thought euery houre a daye / Tyll to my lady I sholde my dette well paye," 5297–98). Their wedding, the ostensible climax of the poem, is reached, after 5,324 lines – and passed, barely noticed, in a breathless *occupatio* (5327–31). Amoure mentions the "Ioye" in which he lived with his lady "ryght many a yere" (5333), and then breaks into what seems to be another apostrophizing lyric:

> O lusty youth and yonge tender herte,
> The trewe companyon of my lady bryght,
> God let vs neuer frome other asterte
> But all in Ioye to lyue bothe daye and nyght.   (5334–37)

The recursion to a lyric optative ("God let vs neuer") suggests that the speaker wishes to transform his life up to this point into lyric, to maintain desire in a perpetual present. The narrative, however, is acquiring an almost unseemly dispatch; after the many lines expended on Amoure's quest, his descent into senescence occupies a mere thirty-five. As Death bids Amoure leave his earthly treasure (5388–89), Amoure's longing for the payment of his marital debt yields to the discharge of a grimmer one:

> "Alas," quod I, "nothynge can me ayde;
> This worldly treasure I must leue behynde.
> For erth of erthe wyll haue his dette now payde.

> What it [sic] this worlde but a blast of wynde?
> I must nedes dye; it is my natyf kynde."
> And as I was at this conclusyon,
> To me dyde come dame confessyon.   (5390–96)

"This conclusyon," indeed; the rhetoric of self-understanding here (the conclusion to which Amoure comes about himself) rests on the proximity of physical extinction. As J. A. W. Bennett reminds us, the Delphic injunction to "Know thyself" was in many late-medieval sermons a call to the recognition of inward sinfulness.[29] The various fictional modes of *The Pastime* are gradually giving place to a nonfictional mode of penitence. This shift carries the reader through confession, contrition and satisfaction (5396–403) and culminates in this startling stanza:

> Of holy chyrche, with all humylyte,
> My ryghtes I toke, and than incontynent
> Nature auayled in so lowe degre
> That dethe was come, and all my lyfe was spent.
> Out of my body my soule than it went
> To purgatory for to be puryfyed
> That after that it myght be gloryfyed.   (5404–10)

Amoure's narration of his own death near the end of this extended poem has long seemed to most readers the nadir of Hawes's ineptitude; Derek Pearsall's claim that the moment is "an extraordinary gaffe"[30] is typical. A more attentive response comes from *The Pastime*'s most careful reader, C. S. Lewis:

> even from the outset – perhaps because [Hawes's] imagination is so earnest and his conscious skill so weak – the good passages have had this peculiar quality, that they seem to come from nowhere, to be a disembodied voice, not always a perfectly articulate voice, coming to us out of a darkness; so that when, at last, it comes to us admittedly from the grave, it at once compels belief.[31]

Amoure's speech is the most dramatic of *The Pastime*'s configurations of the relation between lyric and narrative, as lyric stasis becomes deadly. The fluidity and openness of this speaking subject are radically recoded; a poem that has expanded the reader's horizon of expectations through unexpected combinations of existing genres suddenly becomes a devotional lyric, reminiscent of several nominally spoken from beyond the grave ("Speke softe, ye folk, for I am leyd aslepe!").[32] Through this lyric interpolation the poem is retrospectively organized as a hierarchy of literary discourses, with the penitential evidently at the apex. As the earlier suggestions of the *pèlerinage* genre come to dominate the poem, the subject of the *énoncé* and the subject of the *énonciation* finally merge,[33] and the poem's eschatological implications emerge into thematic consciousness. This is in every sense a "fatal fiction"; a pleasant pastime becomes a *memento mori*.

"Out of my body my soule than it went": in such a statement, who am "I"? If Amoure is the "I" of penitential lyric, he also recalls the revenants who in some popular late-medieval narratives describe purgatory. Like Amoure, the protagonist of *The Spreit of Gy* is caught in a pronominal whirl, shifting uneasily between "we" and "I" as his soul awaits the resurrection of a body to which it is still tied:

> Gyes body has now na skathe,
> And I am pyned to saue vs bathe.
> And efter, when we com to blys,
> What joy sa I haue, sall be his
> ...
> if I answer for Gy,
> I do him no velany.
> Mi spekyng es all for his spede,
> That I may neven to yhow his nede ...[34]

Such passages are illuminated by Roland Barthes's point that the words "I am dead" constitute "a true hapax of narrative grammar, a staging of words impossible as such."

"In the ideal sum of all the possible utterances of language," Barthes writes, "the link of the first person (I) and the attribute 'dead' is precisely the one which is radically impossible." His understanding of this utterance as an "empty point," or a "blind spot of language,"[35] has other suggestive resonances in Hawes's case. *The Pastime* emerges as an instance of anamorphosis – a distorted or deformed perspective, first associated with early-modern painting, that requires the use of special equipment (such as a lens) or a particular vantage point to reform the image. Lacan's own favored example of the technique is Holbein's *The Ambassadors*, painted around thirty years after Hawes's poem. The skull which in Holbein's painting hovers in the foreground before his subjects amid their multiple artifacts, a "strange, suspended, oblique object," suggests for Lacan "simply the subject as annihilated."[36] In Sarah Kay's words, the viewer is enabled to see "that what he or she takes for 'reality' is one particular take on a 'real' that exceeds it."[37] Here, the disturbing "return of the 'real'" – the skull hidden in plain sight looks back – becomes the site of the poem's authority. In late-medieval terms, Barthes's "impossible utterance," with its penitential and purgatorial burden, does not query language's referential capacities so much as redouble them; in Lewis's words, the voice "at once compels belief." The doubling attests a move away from poetic fiction to a vantage point from which the discrete episodes that have preceded it, with their discontinuous treatment of narratorial voice, can form an intelligible ensemble.

The narrator's gestures of gradual withdrawal also illuminate the poem's earlier treatment of *prosopopeia*. The playfulness with which personifications read and interpret one another – Mars "reads" Fortune, Correction "retracts" Gobylyue – are now seen to have foreshadowed an unexpected ending in which Amoure himself is reread. Since the narrative has hurried over the wedding of Amoure and Pucell, Amoure's romance desire seems to find satisfaction and full closure only in the death that terminates his role in the poem. He is left in Purgatory, awaiting the Last Judgement; but his narration of his own death has already forced a last judgement on the reader, who is compelled to read the poem's love-fiction anew and reconsider the ambiguities that formerly surrounded the poem's genre. The reader is left buried alive with Hawes's repentant sinner, awaiting resurrection, and the act of reading the poem itself takes on the aspect of an intercessory prayer.

The poem does not end here, however; and the concluding triumphs further Hawes's displacement of poetic fiction. Fame, the first to appear, proclaims that the "famous actes" (5588) of Graunde Amoure will be immortal, and calls on Remembraunce,

> Commaundynge her ryght truely for to wryte
> Bothe of myn actes and my gouernaunce,
> Whiche than ryght sone began to endyte
> Of my feates of armes ...   (5594–97)

If we assume, as I think we can, that the record she begins is *The Pastime* itself, the result is a striking *mise en abîme*. Throughout, we have been reminded of the physical book that is *The Pastime*; now, a figure within the poem begins to write the poem. We simultaneously observe, however, that the "book" is not finished yet. Fame's words represent the poem as chivalric romance, and we may recall that early in the poem Amoure's quest is proleptically pictured in just this way on a "clothe of aras" (413) in the Tower of Doctrine: as "a full noble story" (414) in which his "passage daungerous" (473) ends with his marriage to Pucell. But as Time appears to counter Fame's declaration of "Infenyte I am, nothynge can me mate" (5604), the poem's generic strand of chivalric romance is in turn put aside by the homiletic elements that have now come to the fore.

Time reminds us that he is the precondition of all earthly existence, and of everything pertaining to it, including the sacral history of man's fall and redemption. He also continues the literary reflections begun by Fame:

> Withouten tyme is no erthely thynge:
> Nature, fortune, or yet dame sapyence,
> Hardynes, clergy, or yet lernynge,
> Past, future, or yet in presence. (5677–80)

"Dame sapyence": Time personifies. Just as Hawes's personifications are fictions, so the qualities and attributes they represent are themselves, being time-bound, only shadows. Having thrown aside its love-fiction, *The Pastime* in its concluding stanzas presses forward from a conception of literary allegory as cloak for truth toward a vision of time and the cosmos as an allegory of "cloudy fygures." Once the triumph of Time has presented the temporal as itself a fiction – a fiction which bound in time the composition of the poem, Graunde Amoure's quest and indeed the king's guidance of the state (2–4, 883–84) – Eternity, with the line "Tyme renneth alwaye his ende to enbrace" (5758), finally dismisses both time and narrative, using in the process what could be read as literary terminology:

> Now I my selfe shall haue none endynge,
> And my maker had no begynnynge. (5759–60)

Fame's apotheosis of Graunde Amoure, whose name will endure in writing, thus prompts an extended meditation that moves from the word's impermanence in time to Time's own insignificance before Eternity. Commenting implicitly on the word as sign, the passage ends in the absolute presence of divine being, in which word and thing, "fygure" and "trouthe," can no longer be told apart.

While *The Pastime* has often been described as an assemblage of archaic conventions, it has also been noted that the conventions are hardly combined in commonplace fashion. As Edwards points out,[38] Middle English literature offers no formal analogues for Hawes's poem. Gordon Kipling, finding affinities between *The Pastime* and the Burgundian chivalric and heraldic romances of Hawes's day, notes parallels with *Le Chevalier délibéré* by Olivier de la Marche, but dismisses Hawes's poem as a clumsy and banal imitation of Burgundian trends.[39] The connexion, however, is a suggestive one, for *Le Chevalier*, like *The Pastime*, turns on an unforeseen structural disclosure. This first-person allegorical romance is also shaped around a combination of narratorial identities, but de la Marche's narrator is explicitly both pilgrim and knight from the outset, when he is told by Pensée that he must go to joust with "Accident" and "Debile" in the "merveilleux pas de la mort" ["monstrous Tourney of Death"].[40]

A new narrative focus, however, is foreshadowed when the narrator arrives at a hermitage, "La Demeurance de Raison" (34.8). Up to this point he has been both knight and Christian subject, clad in the Pauline armor of *Ephesians* 6, 13–18.[41] But when the hermit speaks of the knight's homeland, the knight acquires a more specific identity:

> Du paÿs es et de la marche
> Ou Fortune, Douleur et Rage
> Ont entreprins de faire rage.   (36.6–8)

[You are from the country and of the marches where Chance, Misery and Rage have set about to wreak havoc.]

Through wordplay, de la Marche becomes a synecdoche of a suffering land; like Hawes's poet-rhetorician, this *rhétoriqueur* is a figure of the state he serves. This is reinforced when the author devolves from the place of protagonist to become a mere spectator at a tournament in which Accident and Debile overcome "Phelippe, que l'on ama tant" (225.7) – de la Marche's lord Philip the Good, along with Charles the Bold and Mary of Burgundy. The poem proves to be a ceremonial elegy, its centerpiece not the narrator's private encounter with death – the destiny of the individual Christian faced with frailty and old age, represented in Hawes's poem – but an act of public mourning.

The tournament episode culminates in an apostrophe to the reader:

> O vous qui ce livre lisés,
> Assavourez ceste adventure.
> En ce beau miroir vous mirez:
> Par ce trespas vous passerez …   (265.1–4)

[O you who read this book, take well into account this adventure. Look at yourself in this fine mirror: through this transition you shall go …]

De la Marche also utters his bitter sorrow ("desplaisance dure") at the death of the patrons who sustained him ("soubz eulx j'ay pris nouriture," 266.6). Susie Speakman Sutch and Anne Lake Prescott find in this intervention by de la Marche *in propria persona*, as avowed servant of the Burgundian ducal house, a reintegration of the tournament episode into the narrative frame. As a homiletic reminder of mortality, the address to the reader corresponds morally with the pilgrimage mode of the surrounding text; as nostalgic praise of de la Marche's deceased patrons, it promotes Burgundian chivalric ideology through the noble deaths it privileges. The passage "gives moral legitimacy to an episode that by all internal signs appears to be self-sufficient and autonomous, residing outside the narrative boundaries of the pilgrimage of life allegory (or, we could say more precisely, deeply embedded within the frame as a self-contained specular *récit*, a mise-en-abîme)."[42] If Hawes does indeed borrow the generic framework of *Le Chevalier* and its crucial device of structural disclosure – and the absence of English analogues, along with Kipling's demonstration of Burgundian cultural connections, makes this a real possibility[43] – then he displays a literary sensibility that is not backward-looking but distinctly *au courant*. However, Hawes's comparable moment of *mise en abîme* reverses de la Marche's generic ratio. The poetry of fame and chivalry promoted in de la Marche's words is, in Hawes's poem, finally discarded for piety, in what may be seen as a calculated "outdoing" of the Burgundian precursor text. Remembrance begins to write *The Pastime* as the romance of the knight Graunde Amoure, only for the text to privilege a poetry that both includes romance – and all the other genres it cites – and at the last reaches beyond them.

There is a notable negativity in the affirmations that conclude *The Pastime*, and it presents us with some puzzling paradoxes. "As narration," writes Jonathan Goldberg, "allegory embodies death, a realm that the mind represents to itself as a space in which the human dilemmas of time and otherness are overcome because they are finally beside the point."[44] Goldberg's words seem a curiously accurate description of Hawes's allegorical art, which validates itself at the point of its own extinction.[45] As we have seen, the evocation of Eternity exposes the fictionality of all things, and Hawes's art of cloudy figures turns out to embrace nothing less than the sensory world itself. This disclosure, however, is also, and inevitably, the poem's closure; where, after all, can it go after this? Hawes's art asserts its own authority at the moment, and indeed through the very act, of submission to the highest of all authorities in the semantic structures that produce allegory, and so is a form of poetic self-annihilation.

EVERYTHING THAT DIES SOMEDAY COMES BACK

The analogy just drawn might suggest that Hawes displaces de la Marche's accent on worldly honor and service to the state in favor of a more parochially devotional closure. Hawes's narrative and rhetorical strategy in *The Pastime*, however, is hardly so innocent. Let us recall Lewis's observation that Graunde Amoure's narration of his death, however immediately unexpected, nevertheless seems to emerge quite naturally from the rest of the poem, given that the narration throughout has suggested "a disembodied voice ... coming to us out of a darkness." I have tried here to define the elements of Lewis's "darkness." In some respects, *The Pastime* cultivates a generic indeterminacy whose resolution in the form of Amoure's death is hidden from the reader; in others – allusion to the pilgrimage genre, lyric stasis, the use of personification – the poem consistently prefigures that resolution. A multiplicity of successive generic speakers render the source of a specific utterance difficult to locate. The poem shifts unpredictably between the narrative teleology of chivalric romance, the consumption of time in extended passages of love-lyric, and those passages, noted above, in which the foregrounding of the acts of writing and reading introduces a near isochrony between events within the narrative and the narration itself. It may be added that a ruthlessly literal-minded reading of the narrative tense Amoure employs throughout the poem – a simple past, punctuated by present-tense rhetorical statements – might imply that the entire narration has been delivered by Amoure from a purgatorial present uneasily suspended between time and eternity. In short, the "death" spelt out in the final pages has been immanent in the text throughout, but in secret, veiled form.

Hawes's overt portrayal of the rhetorician's art foregrounds a *dispositio* that encompasses not only the arrangement of topics, but also the origin of states: "By dysposycyon, the rethorycan / To make lawes ordynatly began" (860–61). In *The Pastime*, however, the rhetorician has another and concealed face, and it is here that Hawes's "fatal" hermeneutics of "trouthe" and "fygure" reveals a darker purpose. The poem is studded with impassioned defenses of figuration and diatribes against "dull and rude" readers who cannot perceive concealed meanings (806–12). The specific examples that Hawes gives of such a reading throw out an immediate and vernacular line of connexion to print culture, for they are euhemeristic exempla drawn for the most part from Caxton's *Recuyell of the Historyes of Troye*.[46] Atlas bears the heavens upon his shoulders to signify his "connynge" in astronomy (988–94); hell, ruled by Pluto, was in reality a Greek city inhabited by wicked and rapacious giants (1002–12; *Recuyell*, 323, 327),[47] and Cerberus's three heads are moralized to figure the "thre vyces" of "pryde / auaryce / and also rapyne" (1023, 1026; *Recuyell*, 330–31). The culminating instance in Hawes's catalogue is the tale of Hercules's slaying of the Lernaean hydra, which Hawes claims is drawn from "the cronycles of Spayne."[48] Following Lefèvre, who himself here follows Boccaccio's *Genealogie deorum gentilium libri*, he makes the Hydra into a half-human creature, who, Sphinx-like, poses insoluble "sophisms" to passers-by, and kills them if they fail to supply the correct answers:

ffor as moche as I am the moste wyse creature that euer nature maad. and that I am acustomed to make a questyon to suche men as I fynde / and them destroye yf they can not answer therto . and for as moche as I ne fynde in my royame / but peple as bestes & with oute entendement / I haue therfore destroyed their blood and so shall I do thyn yf thou canste not assoylle or sophyme that I shal make to the (392)

The initial battle between Hercules and the Hydra is one of words and wits rather than might:

the monstre maad vnto hercules seuen sosymes oon after an other so fallacious and so subtyll / that whan hercules had gyuen solucion to oon / the monstre replyed by seuen argumentes / All way hercules that was full of philosophie and expert in all scyence . Answerd so solempnly to all his fallacious argumentes that he surmounted hym / And for this cause the poetes fayne that this ydre had seuen heedes as hyt appereth in the first tragedye of seneca / and sayen that whan hercules had smiten of oon of his heedes . that seuen other heedes cam agayn in the sameplace (392)

Hawes follows this description closely, but with an addition:

>   Seuen sophyms, full harde and fallacyous,
>   This Ydre vsed in perposycyon
>   Vnto the people, and was full rygoryous
>   To deuoure them where lacked responcyon.
>   And whan one reason had conclusyon,
>   An other reason than incontynent
>   Began agayne with subtyll argument.
>
>   For whiche cause the poetes, couertly,
>   With .vii. hedes doth this Ydre depaynt,
>   For these .vii. sophyms, full ryght closely.
>   But of rude people the wyttes are so faynt
>   That with theyr connynge they can not acquaynt;
>   But who that lyst theyr scyence to lerne,
>   Theyr obscure fygures he shall well decerne.   (1037–50)

The movement from Lefèvre's moralization to a typical Hawesian denunciation of foolish and unwary readers gives the analogy a new dimension. Lefèvre's source in Boccaccio, and its own source, Jerome's continuation of Eusebius's *Chronicle*, imply a critique of sophistical rhetoric.[49] Hawes's transition, however, has the effect – not, I think, accidental – of aligning the *auctor*'s didactic but obscurely oracular voice with the hydra proposing the sophisms, and the reader with his unwary victims. Caxton's Hydra depicts the unsubtle people he kills in terms which prefigure Hawes's "rude," faint-witted audience; they die because they are short on hermeneutic skills, "as bestes & with oute entendement."

The workings of Hawes's own poem replicate this metaphor. While *The Pastime* finally reveals a doctrinal sense, it does not point the reader to this openly. Instead, its deployment of popular vernacular genres associated with the theme of love – the very "balades of feruent amyte" (1391) the poem deplores – serves in part to mislead, distracting the reader from a meaning that is finally sprung like a trap. Hawes's poem works by indirection, sifting out those who can read rightly and consigning the others to the outer darkness of "ygnoraunce" and "slouth" (1142). It also supplies this imagined relation between book and reader with a clear political analogue. After his Caxton-derived *exempla*, Hawes embarks on a description of the "redolent well of fomous poetry" (1051) from which spring four rivers. One of them is the river of "vnderstondynge" (1056), a faculty that is, in Hawes's account, deployed on a public and political rather than an intellectual stage; its proper exercise entails the recognition that resignation and withdrawal are to be preferred to impulsive and warlike action (1075–99). The falls of Troy and Rome both exemplify the dangers of disrupting peace, and bringing ruin, for "a lytell cause / grounded on vanyte" (1081) or a "contrauersy" (1098). This commonplace has a precise fifteenth-century heritage, for as Hawes's reference to Troy reminds us, it was familiar from the various speeches of the counsellors to caution and reason in the *Roman de Troie* and its derivatives.[50]

Mervyn James has associated such political quietism with a late-medieval "moralization of politics," arguing that the "loss of nerve" discernible in the magnates of the later fifteenth century, and their increasing unwillingness to take significant political risks, are at once mediated and shaped by the period's literary taste for providentialist history.[51] It is not going too far to suggest that Hawes, by providing political analogues to long-established modes of reading, represents his art as allegorical interpellation. Obedience and conformity are bound up with the reading of allegory, a genre which arouses in the reader an illusory sense of interpretative autonomy. Moralization of the "lytterall censes trewe" (677) is an active process, in which the reader, making connexions, drawing parallels, perhaps mastering a particular iconography, must invest much labor. Yet this occurs within clearly defined boundaries; the reader is offered a subject position that seems to bestow a large share in determining the allegory's meaning, and the result is misrecognition. Poetry thus becomes, for Hawes, a mode of policing "the errynge people / that are retractyf" (1123): "euyll treason" characterizes both subjects who rebel against their king and Godfrey Gobylyve with his treacherous tongue, subjected to Correction (888, 4133).

The Pastime of Pleasure frames a relation between rhetorician and audience which replicates that between monarchy and political subject. The secrecy on which its narrative turns is doubled by the secrecy and coercion that underwrite the poem's discussions of rhetoric, where rhetoric as Ciceronian force for law and civil order is linked to a secret text that presents the rhetorician as Hydra-headed *auctor* and wellhead of meaning. Grande Amoure's narration of his own death mirrors Hawes's pursuit of a literary practice that establishes his authority through a secret withdrawal from his text. In the wake of Roland Barthes's famous essay, we are perhaps overaccustomed to viewing the death of the author as the birth of the reader, as though antiauthorial iconoclasm were only ever a liberatory gesture, releasing the reader into the production of meaning.[52] Hawes's poem, however, raises the real possibility that the "death of the author" can have the reverse effect; the poem's narrator vanishes from the text in order that discursive authority may finally be more powerfully established. Death here allows a new form of revenance – concealed and diffuse, as rhetorical effect and affect. The author "dies" to this text in one way in order to effect an uncanny return in others – covertly, in multiple fashion, by side and back doors.[53]

The authority that Hawes proclaims is a vernacular authority, supported by allusion to Chaucer, Gower and of course Lydgate. As we have seen, however, the domain in which he asserted it contained other alignments of rhetoric, language and authority, in particular those embodied by Bernard André, his colleagues and other humanist scholars. There is, David Carlson writes, no evidence that Henry VII "adopted a grand strategy for patronizing humanists, on the basis of an intuitive grasp of the deep, long-ranging political implications of a movement still only emergent in England."[54] However, the poetry promoted by this "'closed shop' of continental *literati*"[55] did, as we have seen, gain prestige; Green detects at this point "a tendency for English to lose ground to Latin as the vehicle for courtly propaganda."[56] When Hawes speaks of the relation between the status of the courtly humanists and "the makyng of Lydgate," that relation is, as we have noted, seen as explicitly oppositional. Yet his work makes its own contribution to *étatiste* ideology, albeit one less overt than the poems of Bernard André or Pietro Carmeliano, and in the process endows his own English poetic lineage with a new political importance. If in *The Pastime* Hawes rehearses the familiar praise of Chaucer, Gower and Lydgate, he does so in support of a poetry that both advocates and adopts a rhetoric of secrecy, existing ambiguously within the margins of public discourse. Hawes is thus able to establish a new and powerful space for a vernacular voice. In *The Pastime of Pleasure* his narrative effects, at the heart of the public sphere of rhetorical persuasion, a replication of the instrumentality of secrecy.

FAR FROM HEAVEN: *THE COMFORT OF LOVERS*

As we have seen, the compiler of Rawlinson C. 813 or its exemplars implicitly abolishes the narrative determinism of the pilgrimage of life, replacing it with a continuous lyric complaint, a luxuriant consumption of tropes yearning for a consummation that never arrives. In the face of the unknown reverses that evidently jeopardized Hawes's place at court around the accession of Henry VIII in 1509, a similar reading of *The Pastime* is performed in Hawes's own *Comfort of Lovers*. Like its precursor, *The Comfort* opens with a prologue in which Hawes professes his desire to imitate "the makyng of Lydgate" (12) and the authors of obscure "poetycall scryptures" (3). A chronographia sets the poem in May or June "Whanne fayre was phebus with his bemes bryght / Amyddes of gemyny" (29–30). We encounter a lover alone and "musynge in a medowe grene" (36), sorrowing over the inauspicious course of his fortunes and the plotting of mysterious adversaries. He falls asleep and dreams he is in a garden. Here he meets a "lady of goodly age" (76) who asks him to confess his griefs to her. He tells his story; he once fell in love with a "lady fayre of syght" (90) above his station, and wrote "dyuers bokes" (93) to communicate the passion he dared not voice. The lady, holding out hope of a future "Ioyfull daye" (196) when his sufferings will be past, directs him to a tower (219) where he finds a "goodly temple" (233). He enters this elaborately decorated building and bewails his situation once more.

At this point he is confronted by three magic mirrors. From one hangs a sword; from the second a flower in which is set an emerald; from the third "an ymage ... of the holy goost" (452–53). Both the second and the third mirrors are accompanied by "scrypture" (359) which the lover reads; after so doing he sees beside him a sword and shield, and takes them up. He begins to lament his lady's distance once again, but almost immediately she arrives on the scene. A dialogue follows in which the lover-dreamer, previously nameless, is designated as "Amour," while the lady similarly becomes "Pucell." This obvious gesture back towards *The Pastime* concludes with Pucell's affirmation that Venus and Fortune must settle the fate of their love between them. "Amour" agrees and then wakes up, to write the poem describing his dream.

This summary gives very little idea of how odd the poem is. The lover's opening lament, "Remembrynge well / [his] lady excellent" (33), is almost immediately turned in a different direction:

> To god I sayde, "Thou mayst my mater spede
> And me rewarde accordynge to my mede.

> Thou knowest the trouthe; I am to the true;
> Whan that thou lyst thou mayst them all subdue." (39–42)

In an unexplained shift, God has been set up in the lady's place as recipient of the lover's complaint, and allusion made to a mysterious "them," presumably the lover's opponents, though as yet we are not certain. Mention of God's power and protection leads to meditation on their former beneficiaries:

> Who dyde preserue the yonge edyppus
> whiche sholde haue be slayne by calculacyon?
> To deuoyde grete thynges the story sheweth us,
> That were to come by true revelacyon,
> Takynge after theyr hole operacyon
> In this edyppus, accordynge to affecte,
> Theyr cursed calkynge holly to abiecte. (43–49)

The motif of prophecy arises through memory, in the field of the lover's desire; here as throughout the poem, remembering entails looking to the future to establish temporal continuity. A distinction is apparently drawn between those prepared to wait on the divinely moved outcome of events, and those who misguidedly attempt to predict that outcome and so act to forestall it. But the Oedipus story hardly provides the most obvious proof of mistaken prophecy. As the editors of the *Minor Poems* put it, in understandable bafflement: "Hawes seems to be saying that Oedipus was preserved in order to demonstrate the folly of foretelling events. Yet the example is equally well suited to supporting the validity of divination."[57] In this moment of aporia, an *exemplum* cited to prove one thing barely suppresses a countertext proving its complete opposite.[58]

This, however, is as nothing to the difficulties of the lover's colloquy with the "lady of goodly age." Her first request is reminiscent of psychoanalyst speaking to analysand:

> Tell me your mynde now shortly euerydele;
> To layne the trouthe I charge you to beware.
> I shall for you a remedy prepare. (80–82)

The lover's response here has the quality of free association, structured by a rigorous but inaccessible symbolic net of meanings. It is held together, ironically, by a series of plays on the word "trouthe." He affirms that his "trouthe and loue" (88) are the cause of his trouble, as he has "watched many nyghtes" (95) for his lady, "To her and hers my trouthe well to take" (96). He then moves into an apparent digression on how nature constantly tests the "trouthe" of origins, culminating with the romance *topos* that noble blood will reveal itself in the most unlikely places. Another rapid switch leads into the claim that in this world there are only love and hate "the trouth for to tell" (121), which becomes a roundabout way of expressing continued fidelity. There follows a magnificently bizarre stanza:

> Thretened with sorowe of ma[n]y paynes grete,
> Thre yeres ago my ryght hand I dyde bynde;
> Fro my browes for fere the dropes doune dyde sweet.
> God knoweth all, it was nothynge my mynde;
> Vnto no persone I durst my herte untwynde,
> yet the trouthe knowynge, the good gretest P
> Maye me releace of all my /p/p/p/ thre.   (134–40)

This is extraordinary, but perhaps no more so than his next words:

> Now ryght fayre lady, so sadde and demure,
> My mynde ye knowe in euery maner thynge;
> I trust for trouthe ye wyll not me dyscure
> Sythen[s] I haue shewed you without lesynge,
> At your request, the cause of my mournynge.   (141–45)

What, one feels entitled to ask, has this mourning lover disclosed "without lesynge," and how could the lady conceivably "dyscure" him when nothing has been revealed? The historical circumstances behind the poem have so far remained a mystery. There is allusion to some form of compelled verbal betrayal on its narrator's part:

> "Alas madame," vnto her then sayd I,
> "Aboue .xx. woulues dyde me touse and rent
> Not longe agone, delynge moost shamefully
> That by theyr tuggynge, my lyfe was nere spent.
> I dyde perceyue somwhat of theyr entente;
> As the trouthe is knowen vnto god aboue,
> My ladyes fader they dyde lytell loue.
>
> Seynge theyr falshode and theyr subtylte,
> For fere of death where I loued best,
> I dyde dysprayse to knowe theyr cruelte
> Somwhat to wysdome, accordynge to behest.
> Though that my body had but lytell rest,
> My herte was trewe vnto my ladyes blood.
> For all theyr dedes I thought no thynge but good."   (162–75)

In view of the reference to "my ladyes fader," and two allusions to the lover's continued allegiance to "the reed and the whyte" (189, 193), most speculation has positioned itself in relation, whether close or more distant, to the editors' contention that the lady is Henry VII's daughter Mary Tudor.[59] In this case the passage would imply that under attack from enemies of the ruling line – or perhaps under vigorous cross-questioning from such people to ascertain where his own true loyalties stood ("by theyr tuggynge, my lyfe was nere spent") – Hawes professed disloyalty ("I dyde disprayse") in order to find out how the land lay. We perhaps need, however, to abstract more positivist perspectives from a broader sense of the cultural symbolism surrounding the figure of the royal patroness. There is evidence for a form of courtly cult centered on Mary Tudor in the last years of Henry VII's reign. In 1506 a Greenwich tournament challenge took the form of a letter sent to the Princess Mary by the Lady May, claiming "free licence" from "my Ladye and Soveraigne Dame Sommer ... during the tyme of my short Raigne ... and a fortnight in the moneth of my sister June" to spend her time as it shall be to her "comfort and most solace."[60] More material survives for the "Justes of the Moneth of May" of 1507, in the form of an invitation to this tournament at Kennington – also a letter sent by the Queen of May, "yeven vnder our signet at our castell of Comphorte in our citie of Solas."[61] Here we find, in Kipling's words, "an allegorical cast of characters and a romantic *mise en scène* for the essentially dramatic show."[62] Several of the realm's most noted knights, Charles Brandon, Thomas Knyvet, Giles Capell and William Hussey, entered the lists dressed in green, wearing their queen's badges about their necks; the role of May Queen during these jousts was played by Mary Tudor, wearing a green and florally adorned dress. She presided over the month-long tournament from a stage built beside a hawthorn tree "tymberde with our armes off flowres of all sortes," which bore upon its branches "a shyld of whyt and grene, whyche collours be moste comfortable and plesande for all seasons."[63] Henry VII's symbolic hawthorn bush with its shield of Tudor green and white transformed the Queen of May into a Tudor figure of dynastic renewal and continuity. Here Mary's body figures the body politic, as she oversees a chivalric "flowering" of "thys noble realme of Englonde";[64] a verse account of the jousts printed by de Worde at the time refers to "This confortable blossome named Mary,"[65] and amplifies the imagery of May and the red and white Tudor rose.

This, if the 1506 reference to a "ballett" given to the king tells us anything, is the kind of activity in which Hawes may well have been involved. If Hawes indeed lost his post after 1509 and was seeking some form of restoration to court, Mary Tudor, with her probable relation to cultic amatory verse, may have appeared a self-recommending potential intercessor. However, we do not know – and at this remove probably never will – whether the poet may have become entangled in all too real political difficulties, or whether he was called to account for transgression in a courtly "game of love" of the kind so memorably described by John Stevens.[66] Hawes in any case touches on the defective "vnderstandynge" (186) of those who had "wened for to haue made an ende / Of my bokes before [t]he[y] hadde begynnynge" (183–84). This suggests a *Legend-of-Good-Women*-like misconstruction of the poet's earlier writing, and we may either imagine that in court circles groups involved in amorous "play" and political and factional affiliations may have overlapped, or learn from recent criticism of both Chaucer and (almost a century and a half later) Wyatt to be more warily alert to the political subtexts of such "play."[67] Either way, the uncertain historical referent of *The Comfort*'s ambiguities – whether it be love-play, the formal rituals of early Tudor patronage in the lists or in the chamber, or darker plottings – is surely of less interest than the strange, jagged poetic surfaces those ambiguities produce.

If one reads the text as a covert petition, addressed to a patron such as Mary Tudor, then the "three Ps" lines do yield up some sense. We could construe thus: Hawes never really "hated" his lady; at some point he stopped writing for fear of powerful enemies ("my ryght hande I dyde bynde"). "The good gretest P" (139) may be Pucell from *The Pastime of Pleasure*,[68] reentering the scene as a fictional surrogate for the female patron addressed. Hawes perhaps suggests that if she knew the truth behind his apparent *peccata* (the three Ps as sins, like those engraved on Dante's forehead as he journeys up the mount of Purgatory),[69] she would "releace" him of his sins – in other words, forgive and absolve him.

This is all possible; it is not, however, the poem Hawes actually wrote. The whole episode remains disconnected, and it is a paradox that most of its inner fractures seem to stem from its play on "truth," a word whose signifieds one might have expected to be mutually affirming. At various points "truth" seems to connote political loyalty, nobility of blood and sincerity in love, the lover's "troth." The truth about the lover's situation is known to God above (167) and should be made known to his lady. In another important stanza (183–89), the word also suggests the "truth" of the lover's earlier books, which some had tried to prevent from being written although

> Who lyst the trouthe of them for to ensu[e]
> For the reed and the whyte they wryte full true.   (188–89)

We will return later to the claim that Hawes's earlier texts – including *The Pastime of Pleasure* – conceal some form of unitary meaning, although as in Dunbar's *The Thrissill and the Rois*, "the reed and the whyte" conveniently blend the Tudor rose with the lady's countenance. These versions of truth might appear to converge in an emphatic if coded profession of devoted service misunderstood, but such a view is curiously foreign to the experience of reading the poem, in which their referent at any given moment is slippery. In the face of the lady's approving "I knowe your thought, / your worde and dede and herte to be one" (148–49), the lover's word seems to be the last place where any such unitary meaning is to be found. This lover's speech does not attest the truth and integrity of his inmost self, his single-hearted "entente"; on the contrary, it would seem that the "truth" of this subject is always differing from itself, is never quite where he says he is.

His complaints, however, also contain far more overt linguistic disruptions. The mysterious "Aboue xx. woulues" of the passage quoted earlier (162–68) are followed by his declaration that "Thoughe in meane season of grene grasse I fede, / It wolde not greue me yf she knewe my heuynesse" (204–05). There are unexplained references earlier to a house to be swept and a broom set on fire (176–77). The words "Let the mou[n]t with all braunches swete / Entyerly growe; god gyue vs grace to mete" (181–82) drift past spectrally, tracing for an instant the "rich mount" of Tudor iconography, an erotic fantasy mingling dynastic fertility (the patroness's body) and royal bounty, and a restoration to a court which is the fount of being. The sources of this referential scattering are wide-ranging; if the poet is indeed hinting at a misspent past in which he feigned disloyalty, it may be noted that "wylde wolves" appear in the moral allegory *The Court of Sapience*, which Hawes certainly knew, haunting the narrator's passage through this world before he reaches Dame Sapience's haven.[70]

This rich supply of letters, numbers, heraldic emblems and enigmatic colloquialisms, however, has its main source in the abundant storehouse of political prophecy.[71] Students of this weird and invigorating genre have identified several strands, notably the tradition of "prophecies of Merlin" with its "heraldic or totemistic" symbolism of animals and plants (e.g. Hawes's "xx. woulues"); riddles, proverbs and *impossibilia*; and the "pseudo-Methodian" tendency (named after St. Methodius the third-century bishop of Lycia) to steer away from figures towards literal evocation of the spectacle of apocalypse.[72] As contemporaries noted, the internal logic of the more figurative prophecies carries contradictions. The prophetic figure's meaning will not emerge until the prophecy has been fulfilled in history, and the gap between word and thing vanishes with that "apocalyptic closure" when all things will be revealed and all meanings decisively disambiguated[73] (Alan of Lille speaks of the period prior to revelation as a *dilatio* or deferral).[74] This produces its own paradox for that relatively humble form of prediction, the political prophecy. On the one hand, prophecies, because they do not mean once for all, can come to mean almost anything. This is especially apparent in the fifteenth and early sixteenth centuries, when what might initially have been "allusive, topical meanings"[75] come to take on new references. If the forms of apocalyptic thought remained fairly constant, their content was fluid and indeterminate; changing circumstances changed possible signification. The narrator of "Twelve Letters Save England," who stumbles across a woman in Cheapside setting "xii. letteris in order on a rowe" on a garment, promptly proceeds to give a detailed point-to-point exposition;[76] the tale of "wolves" and other emblematic beasts in "When cuckow time cometh oft so soon," in BL Lansdowne MS 762, remains scrupulously impenetrable.[77]

On the other hand, the very openness of prophetic fictions severely limits their practical utility. This is a point on which Robert Mannyng of Brunne waxes distinctly sardonic. Of Merlin's prophecies, he writes that

> Some men haue them mykel in hande,
> That con nought them wel vnderstande.
> Y sey for me, y naue no wyt
> To open the knottes that Merlyn knyt.
> Men may sey more than he hath seyd,
> That nothyng ther-to may be leyd.
> Merlyn spak on swylk a manere,
> That til hit be gon, non may hit lere.[78]

A prophecy only yields its historical truth when it is too late.

How does this bear on Hawes's combination of genres in *The Comfort*? There is a basic structural homology between love-complaint and political prophecy, since both entail the deferral of a closure that can only be imposed from without by an other, whether the mistress or the divinity who brings about the event foretold. The desired sexual consummation with the lady thus stands in the same relation to the love-fiction as the Apocalypse does to human history, an intervention from outside time, an epiphany in which signs are no longer covert. In Hawes's text, the love-complaint finds itself increasingly engorged by a grand narrative of prophecy and fulfillment, in which anything legible seems to figure the sorrowing lover's own state.

Books themselves are well to the fore in this. Given Hawes's avowed love of Lydgate, it it hardly far-fetched to perceive here a revision of the opening of *The Temple of Glas*, that exquisite intertextual echo chamber where lovers from Virgil, Ovid and Chaucer convene. The lover laments his plight:

> Two thyngs me conforte euer in pryncypall:
> The fyrst be bokes made in antyquyte
> By Gower and Chaucers, poetes rethorycall,
> And Lydgate eke, by good auctoryte
> Makynge mencyon of the felycyte

> Of my lady and me, by dame fortunes chaunce,
> To mete togyders by wonder[f]ull ordynaunce.
>
> The seconde is, where fortune dooth me brynge
> In many placys, I se by prophecy,
> As in the storyes of the olde buyldynge,
> Letters for my lady, depeynted wonderly,
> And letters for me, besyde her meruayllously
> Agreynge well vnto my bookes all
> In dyuers placys I se it in generall. (281–94)

No less than in *The Bowge of Courte*, the dreamer is inside a living modesty topos. The convention we witness at the end of a fifteenth-century poem like *The Isle of Ladies* – where the display of "letters" on a wall becomes a means of occult communication between true lovers[79] – is here writ very large indeed, as this amatory bush telegraph appears "in many places." All the world, it would seem, loves a lover. In this all-engulfing erotic textuality, the poetry of England's poetic fathers augurs and authenticates a lover-author's "felycyte" as if shadowing forth a historical truth, in a preposterous genealogy.

Prophecy looms largest as the lover confronts the three mirrors. Whereas the earlier part of the poem presented a profoundly impaired relation between past and present, the mirrors show their connexion as an imaginary continuity. They are a transposition into narrative of the advisory commonplaces from the end of *The Pastime*; as Ashby puts it,

> Thinges past, remembre & wele deuide;
> Thinges present, considre & wele governe;
> For things commyng, prudently prouide ... (*Active Policy*, 912–14)

and they have advice texts attached to them. The first shows the lover's misspent youth ("As vnto wyldnesse alway affirmatyf," 325) and is itself full of *Distich*-like precepts. The second returns to "cursed calkynge"; the lover's opponents are envisaged as astrologers and false prophets, and the accents become increasingly obsessive and paranoid ("I sawe there trappes, I sawe theyr gynnes all," 407) as he foresees the perils that lie ahead. Hawes here echoes earlier representations of the *losengier* of love-poetry as diabolical, "practicing the art of divination." *The Comfort* set up a series of equivalences – between lover and prophet, the lover's sincerity and the prophet's truth – in such a way that the "calkers" of the prophetic narrative have the same function as the "faitours" of love-poetry: their ability to mimic the voice of sincerity or "truth" deprives that voice of any claim to authenticity.[80]

In the third mirror the language of prophecy once again comes to the fore. The mirror contains "an ymage of the holy goost with flaumbes ardaunt[ly]" (453), with a "meruaylous scripture" (455) describing the three manifestations of the Holy Spirit in visible form – at Christ's baptism, his Transfiguration, and in the tongues of fire at Pentecost. In a profane ecstasy of hyperbole, the Pentecostal diffusion of the divine Word into many languages through the gift of tongues contracts in this mirror-writing into the lover's elaborations of self:

> where I lyst by power dyuyne
> I do enspyre oft causynge grete prophecy,
> Whiche is mysconstrued whan some do enclyne
> Thynkynge by theyr wytte to perceyue it lyghtly,
> Or elles calke with deuylles the trouthe to sertyfy,
> Whiche contrary be to all true saynge,
> For deuylles be subtyll and alwaye lyenge.   (484–90)

A little later, the lover sees in the mirror a star with two beams, one of which goes straight to the sun while the other doubles back on its source. The lover meditates, then supplies a gloss:

> This sterre it sygnyfyeth the resynge of a knyght;
> The bowynge beame agayne so tournynge
> Betokened rattones of them which by myght
> wolde hym resyst by theyr wronge resystynge.
> The beame towarde Phebus clerely shynynge
> Betokened many meruaylous fyres grete
> On them to lyght that wolde his purpose lete.
>
> In the fyre clerest of euery element,
> God hath appered vnto many a one,
> Inspyrynge them with grete wytte refulgent
> (who lyst to rede) many dayes agone.
> Many one wryteth trouthe, yet conforte hath he none.
> Wherfore I fere me, lyke a swarme of bees
> wylde fyre wyll lyght amonge a thousande pees.   (547–60)

The language here echoes that of prophecy of a more literal kind:

> Wanne the hilles smoken,
> Thanne Babilon schal haue an ende;
> But whan they brenne as the fyyr,
> Thanne erthe schal henus wende ...[81]
>
> The sone shall shyn The ster that stydly stode
> That called is fixe Shall mevabull be annonne

> The sun and the mone on the sterre shall gone
> That after shall it neuer shyn ne couer[82]

As the editors point out, it seems that the failure to comfort this prophet in the wilderness will ignite a holocaust (the writing concludes with references to the Psalms). The lover has already spoken of his books as forms of prediction; now he is also prophet, whose "/p/p/p/ thre" may also be the "paynes" of which the "good gretest P" (Pater, as God the Father: cf. Gluck and Morgan, note to 139) will release him. Pater or Pucell: the miseries of the persecuted prophet compassed about by foes are superimposed on the frustrations of the complaining lover, and the lover's desire is bound up with a fantasy of apocalyptic vengeance.

"The resynge of a knyght" follows as the "ymage" has foretold. The sword nearby has been set there in a steel hand by "a grete lady a hondred yeres ago," and, we learn,

> No maner persone maye[st hol]de this swerde
> But one persone, chosen by god in dede
> Of this ladyes kynred ... (504–06)

> But yf that he be not of the lygnage,
> The hand wyll sle hym, after olde vsage. (510–11)

We are again close to the allegorical tournament; the shield, which the lover in good heraldic fashion "blase[s]," contains the Tudor colors of green and white, and an olive tree. At the same time, it recalls earlier reflections on the thematics of *nobilitas*. A romance motif marking a knight's election to a quest[83] coincides with the idea of "lygnage," the prophetic pattern with the symbolics of blood. In this recursion, echoing the direction towards the "sun" or source which is doubled by return, the lover takes the sword by "auctoryte" (710).

The lover's encounter with the temple and the mirrors has offered to close the sense of loss in his desire through a narrative of origin and prophetic destiny, to construct a smooth and linear temporal continuity. The lady, however, now arrives, and her first words are brusque and dismissive.

> "Ihesu," sayd she than, "who hadde wende? To fynde
> Your selfe walkynge in this place all alone
> Full lytell thought I; ye were not in my mynde." (701–03)

Though he has obtained the sword and shield, she repudiates him with "it was no thynge to you ordynate" (717). The incipient romance has been cut short before it has even begun.

And like the previous meeting with the "lady of goodly age," the encounter with Pucell herself is characterized by verbal obliquity and inexplicable redundancies, signs of excess. The lady asks if Amour's love is in the vicinity, and seems to acknowledge (773–75) that she knows herself to be the lady in question. But Amour mysteriously claims that at this time he can only contemplate his love's beauty "inwardly" (781), since his eyes are dimmed by weeping. A little later, Pucell's "Tell me who it is ye loue so sure" (800) continues as though this exchange had not taken place, and Amoure must actually inform her that "It is your grace that hath the intresse / In my true herte" (808–09). His love is acknowledged twice, and Pucell asks further questions to discover what she already knows. The situation points back to the similar treatment of the Black Knight's acknowledgement of loss in *The Book of the Duchess.* Hawes, assiduous builder of lines of communication with an English literary past, seems to recollect one of that past's most influential texts at what is – however we choose to gloss Chaucer's strategy – its own most desolate moment of failed communication and narrative disjunction. The words with which Amour initially prompts the exchange – "I speke vnknowen" (770) – prove to be all too accurate.

Recognition emerges through the mention of a text. The passages are separated by the following dialogue:

> PUCELL
> Of late I sawe aboke of your makynge
> Called the pastime of pleasure, which is wond[rous],
> For I thyn[k]e and you had not ben in louynge,
> Ye coude neuer haue made it so sentencyous.
> I redde there all your passage daungerous;
> Wherfore I wene for the fayre ladyes sake
> That ye dyd loue, ye dyde that boke so make.
>
> AMOUR
> Forsothe, madame, I dyde compyle that boke,
> As the holy goost I call vnto wytnes,
> But ygnoraüntly, who so lyst to loke;
> Many meruelous thynges in it I do expresse,
> My lyue and loue to enserche well doub[t]lesse.
> Many a one doth wryte I know not what in dede,
> Yet the effecte dooth folowe the trouthe for to spede.   (785–98)

Not until this point is Amour fully identified with the historical being of Stephen Hawes. Pucell, like Gower's Venus, furnishes the lover with a signature, which writes the prior poem into *The Comfort*'s own logic of prophecy and fulfillment. As such, it is the poem's fullest act of authentication:

"Stephen Hawes" has become his own authority *après coup*, a figure generated by the conjunction of two distinct but connected poems. As such, he guarantees the truth of both amatory and prophetic discourses; love inspires the poet to write unintentional spiritual truths. *The Comfort* too becomes a "fatal fiction," allowing the possibility that a text may be unconsciously prophetic[84] – as Hawes perhaps hopes his own petition will be answered.

But an answer does not and cannot come. The lady, promised by her kin to "a myghty lorde," rejects Amoure's suit. In so doing, she rejects the fictions that the lover urges, claiming kin with the ladies of Chartier's *La Belle dame sans merci* and the fifteenth-century *The Craft of Lovers*:[85]

> Me for to loue I dyde not you constrayne.
> Ye knowe what I am; I knowe not you certayne. (816–17)

Furthermore, Hawes's riddling low style returns, leading to some of the most enigmatic lines in the entire poem:

> Surely I thynke I suffred well the phyppe,
> The nette also dydde teche me on the waye.
> But me to bere I trowe they lost a lyppe,
> For the lyfte hande extendyd my Iournaye,
> And not to call me for my sporte and playe.
> Wherfore by foly yf that they do synne,
> The holy goost maye well the batayle wynne. (890–96)

The possible readings that have been suggested here – rivalry with Skelton the poet of *Phyllyp Sparowe*, the continuation of Hawes's writing by covert means, further rivalry with persons unknown[86] – only underline how far Hawes has fallen back into something close to silence. Above all, the mysterious enmity of the "calkers" is now articulated *with* the lady's "danger," both serving only to hinder the lover. In Chartier's *La Belle dame*, we may recall, the lover whose claim that he is dying of love is so sensibly rejected by the lady goes home and reads his own metaphors literally by actually dying for love. In the poem's final masculinist turn, the lady who has offered entirely rational objections to the lover's fictions is shown up as a callous and insensitive reader.[87] But this does not occur here; in an ending reminiscent again of *The Temple of Glas*, the lover is persuaded to abide by the judgement of Venus and Fortune. The poem ends in deferral, its prophecies still far from fulfillment.

Hawes's poem traces a path among several sources of authority, at once related and distinct, with which it seeks to identify. There are the authors of the past, Gower, Chaucer and above all Lydgate, whose works inspire to imitation. There is the lady, perhaps the text's substitute for a real patroness, who inspires the lover with love and its "troth." And there is the Holy

Ghost, the spirit moving the poet-prophet to write his "fatall fictions." The three are linked by the absent monarch whose dynasty is affiliated with the lineage of the poets, who may be "my lady's father," and who is himself authorized by "grace." Exclusion from the court seems to have given rise in Hawes's poem to a drastic attempt to merge all three authorities in one, by inscribing his amorous texts and the works of his predecessors into the sphere of prophecy, and seeking to make all three authenticate each other and consequently his own vernacular writing. Alienated from that source of power which the court embodies, Hawes makes his own bid for power, by producing a poetic closed system in which the poet's word alone counts.

The petitionary logic of its structure is not in itself difficult to grasp. If the lover's first interlocutor points to the desired outcome of Hawes's suit – she is able to read his perplexing hints, and draw from them a single purposeful utterance – the encounter with Pucell herself returns us to Hawes's present position, and to the unsatisfied anticipation to which he is unwillingly constrained. The combination of poetic, amatory and prophetic discourses aims to affirm the absolute moral integrity of the speaker. The prophetic elements also signal a desired future when all will be well, and this divided speaker, with his differing generic commitments, will be "re-membered," healed by the (female) patron's word, which will make thought, word, deed and heart one.

The conflicts that emerge from those commitments, however, far exceed any pragmatic aim. Hawes's multiple identifications, his attempts to empower his voice, do not lead to an especially settled text, to that "conforte" which moves uneasily between spiritual *consolatio* and the "comfort and solace" of love-allegory and tournament. The "trouth" that reaches utterance becomes divided and unstable. And while Hawes's premise that love and prophecy share patterns of deferral is structurally justified, there is a vast difference between the love complaint, with its sophisticated refinements for exploring the lover's desire, and the prophecy, in which the speaker is merely the mouthpiece of a being altogether exterior to him. The political prophecy of the early sixteenth century enshrined fantasy; the riven human subjects of history could find imaginary satisfactions in teleological narratives. Endeavoring to be restored to the center of power, Hawes struggles to create a seamless fantasy in which origins are harmonized with consequences, beginnings with ends, integrating disparate material through prophetic and genealogical structures. His text is a veritable art of memory, striving through commemoration to heal loss.

The true nature of that loss has not been clearly articulated, even at the end. In this text of "mournynge" (250, 720), the lady's diagnosis of the lover's condition is immediate: "I thynke some thynge be from you past and gone" (705). His response – "I am not hole / your mercy maye me ease" (824–25) – seems clear enough. But if his loss really has so simple a narrative referent, we may still wonder what to make of the extraordinarily haunting and disquieting close of Amour's final speech, with its characteristic insistence on memory:

> Of my herte I wolde ye knewe the preuyte.
> Forgete not me; remembre loue dere bought.
> Than as I thynke ye wolde remembre me. (922–24)

Amour has by now fully revealed his passion to Pucell – the "preuyte" of his heart – so what can remain of which she is unaware? The lines, positioned as they are, clearly have a petitionary aim, but there is also a hint that Amoure's loss lies deeper than the poem has revealed, or can reveal.

There is, indeed, a parallel here to Freud's conception of that "object-loss which is withdrawn from consciousness" and which results in melancholia, a phenomenon associated by Freud with the strange workings of narcissism.[88] Hawes's text is a ceaseless, often broken reshaping of genres straining towards the construction of narratives which, whether they employ romance, advice or prophetic conventions, repeatedly attempt to identify with patterns that link origins and ends, and to combine genres in a manner that reinforces his lover's word. It directs its energies to the concealment of a loss it is unable to acknowledge. This process cannot be conceived of outside those forms of authority and societal power outlined above, intimately bound up with the narrative patterns I describe, with which as ego-ideals the poem seeks a kind of narcissistic identification. The third mirror, with its sword placed there by a "grete lady in antyquyte," promises to authenticate Hawes's ambitions through association with lineage and divine influence. We might speculate that the poem seeks to close the gap generated by expulsion from court, the poet's enforced removal from the sphere of a royal power that could empower his own voice; its strenuous attempts at this may mark a mourning substituting for the one which in history – as the records tell us by their silence – Hawes was not offered a chance to attend. But this collapsing of past, present and future is undercut by a petitionary structure that must mark temporal *difference* – Hawes is now outside the court, complaining perhaps to a former patron – and must consequently end in postponement and indecision. The embryonic romance narrative and the predictions inspired by the Holy Ghost of "the resynge of a knight" come to nothing, since to fulfil its function as petition the text cannot show a satisfied petitioner.

This final deferral is itself underwritten by an act of identification with literary "auctoryte," since *The Comfort*'s echoes of Lydgate's *Temple of Glas* culminate in an open-endedness similar to that of the earlier poem. In another interesting conjunction of literary and royal authority, Pucell, the court's voice, ends by suggesting the solution to love's troubles offered in Lydgate's poem. Amour is left abiding the judgement of Venus and Fortune, but Venus's judgement in *The Temple* is itself an injunction to wait ("Abide awhile, and þan of þi desire / The time neigheth þat shal þe most delite").[89] If Lydgate is named among those authors who in *The Comfort* foretell Amoure's plight, the tangled prophetic relationship between Lydgate's past text and Hawes's present text becomes one of potentially endless deferral, dissolving chronology altogether. Authority, once again, undoes itself. In the one surviving print, the stanza that closes the dream is, symptomatically, half-effaced, but seems to imply that the lover's conversation is interrupted "that tyme" (927), a hint that it remains to be taken up again – and again.

Hawes's final poem is thus left in exhausted and isolated pathos. It encrypts a loss it cannot securely translate into metaphor. Imaginary lady and imaginary rivals alike supply objects and obstacles on which the poem desperately fastens, while in the distance the fires of annihilation beckon, at once desired and feared (560). But if *The Comfort of Lovers* tries out multiple modes with a view to constructing various narratives, it is on another level not a narrative at all, merely a series of dialogues and complaints surrounded by obscure intimations of greater things. *The Pastime of Pleasure*'s relationship between lyric and narrative is here recast as one between a lyric present in which the lover and his lady perhaps endlessly rehearse the standard figures of complaint and dialogue, and a completely different – prophetic – temporality grounded in radical discontinuity, in which the lover's past texts, written before the action begins, point across a void towards an apocalyptic horizon. In its simultaneous confirmation and denial of the validity of prophecy, the opening allusion to Oedipus thus foreshadows a deep division. As petitioner, Hawes tries to make his love-poetry reenter the historical world of the court; as prophet, he makes the most all-encompassing claims for the poet's authority in his work. In this curiously moving poem, though, the attenuated authority on show has no support from any position in the world of politics, king and court, not even that of a groom to the chamber. Indeed, its claims to absolute power are a function of its very powerlessness. Hawes's struggle to make all other texts conform to his own fictions only ends by reminding us all the more poignantly that the self-reflexive solipsism of his poem, intended to influence history, is ultimately, and in spite of itself, an escape from history.[90] Hawes's "preuyte," it is implied, may not be revealed until the end of time and its human and historical tribulations, when all is revealed. It is perhaps in this sense alone that Hawes's "fatal fictions" in *The Comfort of Lovers* hold out a remote hope of "comfort."

CHAPTER 6

Mapping Skelton: "Esebon, Marybon, Wheston next Barnet"

To move from a Hawes stranded by the accession of Henry VIII to the Skelton of the early 1520s is to cross a narrower gap than might be imagined. Both poets engage with a similar crisis of symbolic investiture, revealed in discursive flights from erotic to apocalyptic and to metapoetic. My aim in this chapter is to suggest that in Skelton's case, this anxiety of location is addressed through a poetics that seeks to multiply and disperse the grounds of authority, while finding new figures for the relations among them. In contrast to André's classically "foreign" England and Barclay's Englishing of the alien, Douglas's thresholding of the epic, Dunbar's performances of disappearance and the retreats of Hawes and the earlier Skelton himself, Skelton at this stage of his career embraces a poetics that deranges spheres of authority altogether, providing intersections and divergences between them with a bewildering rapidity.

While the known facts are few, readers of Skelton's career at this period have noted a certain insecurity. The royal tutor rusticated to Diss in 1503 looks to have returned to the center of royal power in the early 1510s, but in what capacity is not known. The title of *orator regius*, which he assumed in or just after 1512, reveals little. Works that cannot be securely dated oscillate between laureate pretension (*Calliope*), royal counsel (the interlude *Magnyfycence*) and the flytings and invectives of less exalted court entertainment. Greg Walker, whose account I follow here, has suggested that the multiple attacks on Wolsey were moved neither by personal grudge nor noble support (the Howard sponsorship of earlier accounts), but rather by political misreading; *Speke Parott* shows a Skelton operating on the assumption that Wolsey is falling out of royal favor, only to discover belatedly that he is not; *Collyn Cloute* and *Why Come Ye Nat to Courte?*, also directed against Wolsey, are accordingly a hunt for new patrons among urban mercantile élites.[1] In fact Skelton, is, as Carlson notes, ἄτοπος – "unclassifiable" or "unplaced,"[2] whether as client-poet or as conflicted cleric, fiercely opposed to prelacy and eager to shame bishops back into the pulpit, yet

145

wary of surrendering clerical prerogative or crossing lines between anticlerical commonplace and Lollardy or Lutheranism.[3] And the poet who reads clerical authority and jurisdictional boundaries so alertly from within the sanctuary of Westminster, in the teeth of the disputes over sanctuary between Wolsey and Abbot John Islip, is also a past master in the pleasures of transgression, whether they involve hawks defecating on the church altar of Diss (*Ware the Hauke*) or Philip Sparrow's "nomadic" perambulations over the body of Jane Scrope.[4]

In *Speke Parott*, Skelton *atopos* authors a complex enfolding of prophecy, love-complaint, academic satire, travel writing and multiple other textual kinds. These either evade hierarchy and order, or allow it into the poem in the inevitably violent form of Cardinal Wolsey. Parrot's paradisal origins in the realm of the marvelous and his linguistic facility generate a desire which pulls in other genres, but which also throws into relief their limits, so that the poem unfolds in multiple, superimposed temporalities. In so doing it also complicates the imagining of "the court," since one of its deepest currents is urban and mercantile. In *The Garlande of Laurell*, first printed in 1523, similar tactics delve into a different archive – autobiographical, autobibliographical – under the sign of another marvelous bird. In the top of the "goodly laurell tre" (665) at the poem's center roosts the "byrde of Araby / Men call a phenix" (667–68). This avian figure of self-generating poetic prowess is, like Parott, ensconced in a specifically female space: as "men" have sent Parott from "Ynde" to "greate ladyes of estate" (6), so in *The Garlande* Skelton is led to "a goodly chaumber of astate" where a countess sits enthroned (768). From the nests of these bowers, Skelton's poems range across history, mythology, language and genre, powered by a desire that overcomes place but is compelled in the end to concede limit.

CARDINAL OPPOSITIONS

The risks of using Skelton to conceptualize a categorically defined "court" poetry, as against a variety of interlocking urban subcultures, are already visible in the textual witnesses of *Speke Parott*.[5] The version printed by current Skelton editors is a composite; while lines 58–224 are drawn from later printed editions, the one witness from Skelton's lifetime – which contains lines 1–57 and 238–513 – is BL MS Harley 2252, the commonplace book of the London mercer John Colyns. Ulrich Frost, on palaeographic grounds, raises the tantalizing possibility that "Colyns's exemplar may have been a holograph manuscript of Skelton's circulating in London."[6] Not the least striking feature of *Speke Parott* is that it flaunts the heterogeneity that characterizes the commonplace book more generally. It would be entirely possible to schematize the poem's relations to the other genres around it in its physical context: Arthurian and other romances (the stanzaic *Morte d'Arthur*, *Ipomydon*) and variously fragmentary courtly lyrics ("O Mystres, Why," at fol. 84v, the two-line "Yet am I bonde" on the recto side of fol. 133*v, where *Speke Parott* begins), other satires directed against Wolsey ("Of the Cardinall Wolse," "Thomas, Thomas, All Hayle" at fol. 158r, Skelton's own *Collyn Cloute*), fragments of prophecy (fol. 1v) and excerpts from laws regulating trade. In the nature of the commonplace book, *Speke Parott* draws in all these genres, but turns them inside out, setting an apocalyptic horizon to the city itself and its various mobilities.

These flows, which seem both to seek and elude containment, are immediately apparent in the Latin distich that opens the work:

> Lectoribus auctor recipit opusculy huius auxesim
> Crescet in immensem me vivo pagina presens;
> Hinc mea dicetur Skeltonidis aurea fama.

[By his readers an author receives an amplification of his little poem. This book will grow in boundless extent while I am alive; Thence may my golden fame of Skelton be proclaimed.][7]

We may wonder whether the lines promote the reader, requested to "amplify" the work, or the power of the *auctor*. The distich, I think, strikes in multiple directions. The "author" may "make" or "increase" his book,[8] but he also "receives" [*recipit*] increase by his readers. *Auxesis*, a term that points to rhetorical amplification and to economic growth,[9] implies that the book is capital which through its readers will bring symbolic return, *aurea fama*. The *pagina presens*, however, will grow *in immensum* in the author's lifetime – not, it should be stressed, solely to "greatness," but, as Kinsman's version (which I quote here) and the etymology of *immensum* have it, to "boundlessness," the immeasurable. Not only does the book's potential reach have no end once readerly subjectivities come into play, it may even exceed its own nature as a book. The author here is ancillary, his living body (*me vivo*) to one side of the book's own organic growth (*crescit*), his fame's increase a mere consequence (*hinc*). Rather than simply privileging either author or reader, Skelton's syntax queries the very notion of their mutual alterity, and refuses to settle the matter. Here the book itself, as well as its author, is alive, poised to go beyond its identity and slough off material form.

The poem, then, is an Eco-esque open work, a "litelle quayre, named the Popagay" (278), which at its outset immediately conjures up another form of boundary. Parott is "a byrde of Paradyse" (1), endowed by Dame

Philology with "a gyfte in my neste when I lay, / To lerne all langage and hyt to speke aptlye" (44–45). "Langage," as Parott learns it in Paradise, is singular. The *Glossa ordinaria* points out that the "division of tongues" that came with the Tower of Babel did not entail creation *ex nihilo*: "God made nothing new, but divided the modes of speaking and forms of language among different peoples. Whence we find the same syllables and letters of the same meaning joined in different ways in different tongues, and often the same nouns or verbs other in significance."[10] Parrot may have learned language, but must speak languages and experience the madness of division: "Now *pandes mory*, wax frantycke som men say" (46).[11]

Created in the earthly paradise, Parott is an exile from a domain of nameless "pleasure perdurable" (186), driven now to feed "*in valle* Ebron" (188), the place of refuge.[12] For Kathy Lavezzo, Parott's paradisal origins bring a "sublime geographic identity"[13] into his place as English subject ("Cryste save Kyng Herry the viiith, owur royall kyng," 34); for Jane Griffiths, they assert "his long perspective on the abuses which he chronicles" and his "title to be believed."[14] The praise that Parott addresses to the English king and queen, however, is only one of a series of similar expressions that Parott, with his notorious facility in hailing those in power with due reverence, reels off ("Parot can say '*Cesar, ave*,' also," 110). Framed by a catalogue of the languages Parott can use aptly – Latin, Hebrew, "Caldee" (25), "Greke tong" (25–26), Castilian, even the *lingua franca* that points into the Ottoman Empire ("in Turke and in Trace," 39) – the English plaudit becomes oddly arbitrary, especially coupled with one of the ambiguous glosses accompanying the poem in Harley 2252, which recalls that "Katherine" breaks down etymologically into "universal ruin."[15] Even Parott's national-political identification, then, is when viewed in another light – as the poem often encourages us to do – merely one in a series of substitutions, carried along by postlapsarian linguistic caprice.

Parott's purchase on Paradise – on an infinitude which doubles the poem's open principle of potentially infinite extension – is illuminated by Michael Uebel's recent discussion of the "utopian desire" which shapes medieval Europe's apprehension of its eastern others. Uebel contends that figurations of the earthly paradise respond to the Fall as disruption of "the fluid relation of the sacred and profane." One way in which the narrative of Edenic loss is managed is through "utopic representation of an allegorical type," in which "the radical differences of wonders are always repressed so that their universal and timeless value can emerge."[16] Parott, who embodies the wonders of "Ynde," thematizes precisely the point of intersection between such utopian desire and the "timelessly" frozen, repressive scenarios that grasp it. Skelton's patronal dislocation, his aggression (however motivated) against Wolsey, his allusions to European politics find expression in a utopian desire that is not easily distinguished from the boundless conditions of reception, the uncertain line of demarcation between author and reader, sketched in Skelton's distich.

It has been suggested that Parott is the figure of the court poet, compromising the high and noble destiny of a vocation by entertaining ladies. Parott's courtly role, however, becomes indissociable from his status as allegorical author and reader. Skelton criticism is familiar with the lover Parott, and my aim here is to bring out the style in which his role as erotic object – "a fayre byrd for a lady" (211) – is bound to "the dynamic, often rhythmical oscillation between the poles of conservation and loss, achievement and interdiction" that Uebel finds in the paradisal-utopian subject,[17] and that here refuses to allow a clear distinction between Parott as Amant Vert and Parott as tongue-in-beak "bybyll clarke" (119). Parott's first appearance stresses the glittering, playfully autoerotic bird "given to knowing, phallic innuendo":[18]

> Wythe my beke bente, and my lytell wanton iye,
> My fethyrs fresshe as ys the emerawde grene,
> Abowte my necke a cerculett lyke the ryche rubye,
> My lytell legges, my fete bothe fete and clene,
> I am a mynyon to wayte apon a quene ...   (15–19)

This is the amatory bird of Ovid and of Jean Lemaire de Belges's *Les Épîtres de l'amant vert*, so far from jealousy that when his mistress Margaret of Austria is with her two successive royal spouses he shows "grand joye ... En devisant et faisant noise et bruit / Pour n'empescher de ton plaisir le fruit."[19] As Henrician minion embodying the love-speech of an entire tradition, he complements the ladies in an idealized circularity, becoming a pedagogic and prosthetic aid to love ("With ladyes I lerne and goe with them to scole," 21).[20] A veritable stock of parrot-lore (green feathers, "rubye" circlet), he is thoroughly self-contained – "With my beke I can pyke my lyttel praty too" (107) – and certainly legible at first as ambitious courtier, there to procure ambiguous pleasure for ladies and through ladies for male readers. His identification with the languages bestowed on him often has a wildly polymorphous perversity; at times, as Richard Halpern notes, he "dislocates the speaking subject" parrot-style, "referring to himself by name and in the third person, as if he were elsewhere, not in this voice that emerges from his body."[21] Parott's "wantonness," however, soon begins to run through the poem in an ebb and flow that is of a piece with his hermeneutic activities.

As court pet, Parott is enclosed in "A cage curyowsly carven" (8), which serves him as a "coverture" (9) – a tent, but also a defense. An exotic fetish object found in the parrot's legendary habitat of "Ynde" (4), near the earthly paradise, he has been sent to "greate ladyes of estate" (6), who bedeck his "bowur" (12) with (perhaps rhetorical) flowers. Its centerpiece is "A myrrour of glasse, that I may tote [*peek*] therin" (10). This might appear to be just another amatory adornment, but it comes to acquire some remarkably far-reaching properties:

> The myrrour that I tote in, *quasi diaphonum*,
> Vel quasi speculum, in enigmate,
> Elencticum, or ells *enthimematicum*,
> For logicions to loke on ... (190–93)

The clear allusion to the Pauline *speculum* points to the kinds of parallelism that Parott is able to "speak" across sacred history in order to address the inconvenient historical fact of Wolsey; the cage's "coverture" becomes "*metaphora, alegorica* withall ... his protectyon, his pavys and his wall" (202–03).

This direction is visible at Parott's first allusion to Wolsey. Parrott is equipped with an impressively mobile and accommodating tongue ("With Dowche, with Spaynyshe, my tonge can agree," 32). His preening multi-lingualism easily falls into the courtly verbal "play" that is conspicuous consumption, the entertainment of ladies. To be sure, Parrott's own verbal expense is often remarkably regulated. If he seems ready to expend language in the right circumstances, he also hints warily at retention in a storehouse of memory, or more accurately at a kind of recycling in which he gathers the "shredis of sentence, strowed in the shop" (92) of old philosophers and passes them through the "crop" of his "wanton conseyt" (94–95), an erotically restless cluster of parrot-faculties. Nevertheless, the apt speech derived from Dame Philology may sometimes be flung away in a dismissal that overthrows "aptness" in homage to a world and time out of joint. Linguistic expansionism points to postlapsarian signs that have lost their originary points of reference. The surplus of carnival ("In *Salva festa dies, toto* ys the beste" ["On holiday, to have everything is best"], 49) gives place to the reestablishment of law: "*Moderata juvant,* but *toto* dothe exede" ["Moderation gratifies, but everything is too much"] (50). It is in this more sober frame that Wolsey makes his first appearance:

> But reason and wytte wantythe theyr provynciall,
> When wylfulnes ys vicar generall. (53–54)

In the face of such aptness, there is applause ("*Hec res acu tangitur*, Parrott, *par ma foye*" ["You have hit the nail on the head, Parrott, truly"]) followed by nervous admonition ("*Tycez-vous*, Parrott, *tenes-vous coye*" ["Be quiet, Parrot, keep still," 55–56]). The ladies' whispers suggest courtly learning and division, overlapping with sexuality (Parott has aroused a response) and secrecy.

The pattern continues, and subterranean temporalities begin to rise in a disquieting groundswell of Old Testament narratives. The butcher's son from Norwich is suddenly the Golden Calf ("*Vitulus* in Oreb," 59) the obscene bull-god nourished by an overmercifull priest-king and *roi fainéant* ("Melchisedeck mercyfull made Moloc mercyles," 60).[22]

> Jereboseth is Ebrue, who lyst the cause dyscus.
> "Peace, Parrot, ye prate as ye were *ebrius*!
> Howst the, *lyuer god van hemrik, ic seg*;
> In Popering grew peres, whan Parrot was an eg.   (67–70)

Interpretation here is a delirium that runs along curious roads. Jeroboseth (Gideon), the hero awaited by a neglected and downtrodden kingdom, is "Ebrue" (67), only to prepare a swerve into another kind of "truth" – the drunkenness ("*ebrius*") to which parrots were notoriously prone, Parrott's swift dance to a national stereotype (the drunken Fleming), and the double pun on "Popering." Wolsey's libidinousness and supposed papal ambitions shape Parott's own verbal extravagance, his provocation of fictional courtly ladies and historical London mercers. Asked where this is tending, Parrot cuts back with "Over in a whynnymeg!" (71), which Kinsman suggests is a reference to a song "of sexual encounter and dispatch." At the same time, it shrinks into "places" where the sacral and the soteriological contract into, but also pull against, the local and dialectal:

> Hop Lobyn of Lowdeon wald have e byt of bred;
> The Jebet of Baldock was made for Jack Leg ...   (72–73)

Threats of Scottish invasion meet *Esther* and folk legend, the hanging of a wicked counsellor in Baldock that of a giant outlaw in Hertfordshire.

The poem's alliteration enhances the carnivalesque qualities of such popular reference. Repeated consonants and vowels insist on the material body of sound, which also becomes here the material body of the all-pervading usurper of the body politic. Yet that body is ironically the "native" resonance of Skelton's own poetic. Meanwhile, political allusions suggest, through a landscape reminiscent of Hieronymus Bosch, a lover's impotence and a weak king: "A narrow unfethered and without an hed, / A bagpype without blowynge standeth in no sted" (74–75). A theater of corporeal fragments generates analogues both to Skelton's psittacine language, which wanders without an organizing center and generates terror, and a disordered, headless and split body politic. Out of all this there somehow surfaces a temporarily triumphant culmination, in which Parott's identity as "green lover" can hardly be overlooked:

> *Collustrum* now for Parot, whyte bred and swete creme!
> Our Thomasen she doth trip, our Jenet she doth shayle;
> Parrot hath a blacke beard and a fayre grene tayle. (82–84)

As he reads Wolsey's depredations in the frame of typology, Parott is clearly in thrall to a hermeneutic power not which he possesses but by which he is possessed, assembling references "*Confuse distributyve*" (198). Parott's "marvelous" being, in brief, invigorates, but is also not altogether identical with, the more circumscribed patterns of erotic courtly exchange and the desire of the exegete, three planes conjoined like the sides of a Möbius strip, in all of which distinctions between subject and object seem to vanish.

Parott's moments of figurative breakthrough are oral ones; once, it seems, he was "Deyntely dyetyd with dyvers delycate spyce" (3), and in the poem this marks his relation to speech. A hungry Parott who "hathe not dyned of all this long day" (23) has all too clearly forsaken the paradisal "gyfte" economy of his nest – dainty diet and language – for an exchange in which he receives tidbits for the *frisson* induced by pointed comments about cardinals (an "almon" [7, 48], "nutmeg ... *cum gariopholo*" [183], "synamum stickis and *pleris cum musco*" [185]). Even the levels of exegesis are held together by small pieces of food: the "bit of bread" sought by Hob Lobbin of Lothian catalyzes the shift to the southern tale of Jack o' Legs, hanged by Baldock bakers. If as Marx claims a commodity's value is only recognized in its mirroring by another commodity, these items, like Parott himself dear because far-fetched, are such mirrors,[23] though some are also therapeutic, "For Parrot to pyke upon, his brayne for to stable" (184). Parott's predicament cannot but recall Abraham and Torok's depiction of the "communion of empty mouths" in which speech is substituted for the missing breast.[24] Parott's speech must complete the desires of the ladies (hence the poem's title) while their continual solicitations also strive to draw from him the historical signifiers that will tie him to the present. After this movement of demand and desire, it is Parott's final bid for a "date" that brings the economy of John Colyns's London down on him:

> Now, Galathea, lett Parrot, I pray yow, have hys date –
> Yett dates now are deynte, and wax very scante,
> For grocers were grugyd at and groynyd at but late;
> Grete reysons with resons be now reprobitante,
> For reysons ar no resons but resons currant –

> Ryn God, ryn Devyll! Yet the date of Owur Lord
> And the date of the Devyll dothe shurewlye accord. (439–45)

If Parrott is bringing God's timelessness into juncture with Wolsey's diabolical time-serving,[25] then the poem has finally contracted into its own historical moment.

Various motives have been ascribed to Skelton's hostility to Wolsey: revulsion at an accumulation of privilege and power, jealousy that the King's cardinal was usurping the true counsellor or poet's place close to the monarch, the misrecognition that could make Wolsey alone responsible for absolutist arrogation of power and deflect attention from the king. Along with this has gone a tendency to observe the various ways in which Wolsey mirrors Parott, or his creator.[26] My narrower point here is that as the poem's initial pattern of paradisal loss and intermittent recuperation supplies its energies to the more bounded circles of drive and desire that associate Parott the courtly lover with Parott the allegorist, so Wolsey's roles become equally diverse. He is the matter to be glossed, and saturates the poem's symbolic field, so that he is there at every turn. In this doubling, Parott's appetites are oral, while wolves (like Wolsey, the "wolf of the sea" or "wolvys hede" [434]) love parrots with a special love.[27] Both antagonists make allegorization an exercise in consumption, but if Parott nibbles in return for producing the occasional scrap of meaning, Wolsey devours, historically and allegorically.[28]

Here, Skelton's approach to constructing his poem brings us to the duality of "strategy" and "tactic" outlined by Michel de Certeau. De Certeau's "strategy" comes into being when "a subject of will and power ... can be isolated from an 'environment.'" A strategy "assumes a place that can be circumscribed as *proper (propre)* and thus serve as the basis for generating relations with an exterior distinct from it." A "tactic," on the other hand, cannot count on such a "proper," or "a borderline distinguishing the other as a visible totality"; it operates in time rather than space, dependent on the opportune and the provisional. De Certeau's main analogy for this distinction is *reading*. In opposition to the relentless and ruthless spectacularization of contemporary culture, reading is silent production in which the reader "insinuates into another person's text the ruses of pleasure and appropriation: he poaches on it, is transported into it, pluralizes himself in it ... Ruse, metaphor, arrangement, this production is also an 'invention' of the memory." De Certeau offers what for our purposes is a striking genealogy for this dimension of modernity's spectacle. Reading in his view resembles "that art whose theory was developed by medieval poets and romancers: an innovation infiltrated into the text and even into the terms of a tradition." The active readers envisaged by de Certeau are able "to insinuate their countless differences into the dominant text. In the Middle Ages, this text was framed by the four, or seven, interpretations of which it was held to be susceptible. And it was a book." [29]

De Certeau's medieval analogizing bears on *Speke Parott* in several regards, not least suggestively at the points of difference. Parott is in a way a dispossessed consumer, but is also the creation of an author working from a complex intersection of privations, restraints and privileges. Evidently excluded from court and at odds with the cardinal, who himself conjoins church and *polis* in unprecedented ways, he is still heir to the privileged traditions of clerical hermeneutics. He is not so much de Certeau's *remanieur* as the self-appointed terminus in an authorial chain; if Wolsey has misread God's book, apparently unaware that he is himself no more than a figure in eschatological history, Skelton's task is to correct such a blindly self-enacted misreading. Yet Skelton, in terms that are not quite detachable from Wolsey's own – and do indeed sometimes mirror them – does counter Wolsey's encroachments on power by infiltrating himself into them and recombining their elements.

As de Certeau's "subject of will and power," Wolsey's consumption is relentless. *Speke Parott* is an attack on Wolsey which in reading him as Antichrist, manifested through history under multiple guises, prefigures apocalypse as carnival. Wolsey, framed in the text of Skelton's poem, ensures the *convertibility* of registers into one another, in a poem that is, if we are to follow Walker and consider that Skelton is here seeking patronage, a speculative enterprise. There is a deep identity between Parott's various amorous and interpretive assays, as Skelton seeks readers, and the figurative Wolsey's implacable advance across time and place. A privileged locus of this conflict is the city. One of Parott's transports of prophetic, avian and erotic excitement ("Lyke a wanton, whan I wyll, I rele to and froo," 109) gives place to a lament suffused with loss:

> *Ulula*, Esebon, for Jeromy doth wepe!
> Sion is in sadness, Rachell ruly doth loke;
> Madionita Jetro, our Moyses kepyth his shepe;
> Gedeon is gon, that Zalmane undertoke ...   (113–16)

The accents shift; from urban prophecy (Jeremiah) to the laments of Rachel, to the disappearance of Gideon. Nelson offers the glosses that endowed the biblical city of Heshbon with a double significance: the city under the rule of the heathen "Seon" (121), and the "new city rise[n] on the ashes of the old" after Gideon's victory. If the reference to sanctuary ("assilum," 124) points to Heshbon as the Church, a common reading, the next lines render the city literal and a site of substitutions:

> Esebon, Marybon, Wheston next Barnet;
> A trym-tram for an horse myll it were a nyse thyng,
> Deyntes for dammoysels, chaffer far-fet ... (126–28)

Characteristically, the hinge of an internal rhyme translates the biblical prototype into London, then pushes it northwards.[30] Wolsey's expansionism is transmuting the city as sacred space; sanctuaries and nunneries are traded for "trym-trams," "chaffer far-fet." Once again, Wolsey, the agent of conversion and commutation, is converting ritual space to his own ends. Yet this commutation happens in Parott-speech; the means by which Wolsey transforms Esebon to Marybon is aural. It is Parott's mode of using language that enacts Wolsey's alteration, and through this the likeness between the two is emphasized. Wolsey is making visible a logic which, as Lavezzo has superbly argued, underscores similarities between two alien creatures, the paradisal Parott and Wolsey the embodiment of "Rome in England." It also, however, brings to sight another kind of *auxesis* by which the economics of Wolsey's dissolution of several houses is grasped through both the Antichrist's seizure of sacred ground and Parott's own magical properties.

Like Parott himself, then, Wolsey, the great encroacher, is at once interpreter and vehicle of sacral history. His touch strikes everything with a deadly literalism. "*Aurea lyngua Greca*," like the poet's *aurea fama*, should be "magnyfyed" (142), but distinctions have been lost in the so-called Grammarians' War, the collision between pedagogies of precept and imitation sponsored, in Skelton's reading, by Wolsey's endowment of the first chair in Greek at Oxford.[31] The result is a carnival in which Latin mingles promiscuously with the vernacular ("*silogisari* was drowned at Sturbrydge Fayre," 165). For Skelton, the intrusion of imitation leads to a brutal carnival of scapegoating, in which Donatus is "dryven out of scole" (170), Alexander ("a gander of Menanders pole," 173) cast out of the gate. In such a context, "breaking Priscian's head," a phrase Skelton may have coined in English ("Prisians hed broken now, handy-dandy," 171), is far from being the dead metaphor it was to become. The passage is profoundly reminiscent of the "scholastic battle play" of medieval *disputationes* described by Jody Enders, the bellicose theatricalizing of academic display with its personified *imagines agentes*.[32]

The poem's penultimate section, covering Skelton's distant perceptions of Wolsey's conduct at the Calais conference and his supposed papal aspirations, carries forward the mapping of Wolsey's curious peregrinations:

> Go, litelle quayre, namyd the Popagay,
> Home to resorte Jerobesethe perswade;
> For the cliffes of Scaloppe they rore wellawey,
> And the sandes of Cefas begyn to waste and fade,
> For replicacion restles that he of late ther made;
> Now Neptune and Eolus ar agreed of lyclyhod,
> For Tytus at Dover abydeth in the rode;
>
> Lucina she wadythe among the watry floddes,
> And the cokkes begyn to crowe agayne the day;
> *Le tonsan de Jason* is lodgid among the shrowdes;
> Of Argus revengyd, recover when he may,
> Lyacon of Libyk and Lydy hathe cawghte hys pray … (278–89)

Skelton sends his book to follow Wolsey's travels, yet retracing his steps requires imitation, and Parrott is again caught up in rivalrous emulation of Wolsey. Consensus is fairly clear; Jerobeseth (Wolsey) is called home while Calais looks on in horror at his diplomatic hyperactivity; Henry VIII (Neptune) and the Emperor Charles V (Aeolus) have agreed to keep the Channel open so that Charles (this time Titus), who is to land at Dover, will have access to Spain; Wolsey has returned with his goal (the emperor's support in his bid for the papacy) achieved after negotiating with Charles at Bruges (hence the allusion to the Burgundian Order of the Golden Fleece as well as the myth of Jason) and the hundred-eyed Argus is the peacock-like François I. Wolsey finally appears as Lycaon, the king turned into a wolf for serving Zeus with a dish of human flesh. The landscape Skelton creates here is overlaid by Ovidian mythography; European potentates vanish and reappear under multiple divine guises, while sands and cliffs are animated. Wolsey's name once again furnishes puns, but here his lupine identity, which near the end of the poem offers a splendidly chilling visual vignette ("Hys wolvys hede, wanne, bloo as lede, gapythe over the crowne," 434) turns him into one of the framing figures of Ovid's *Metamorphoses*. Lycaon is the quintessential human monster turned predator, and in Ovid predators, sexual and other, often force metamorphosis. Here, as Wolsey passes through the landscape, cliffs lament and historical monarchs become gods.

When Parott comes close to narrating his own nature, it is elusive:

> Parot is my owne dere harte, and my dere derling.
> Melpomene, that fayre mayde, she burneshed his beke:
> I pray you, let Parrot have lyberte to speke.
>
> Parrot is a fayre byrd for a lady;
> God of his goodnes him framed and wrought;
> When Parrot is ded, he dothe not putrefy;

> Ye, all thyng mortall shall torne unto nought
> Except mannes soule, that Chryst so dere bought;
> That never may dye, nor never dye shall:
> Make moche of Parrot, the popegay ryall. (208–17)

The apparent *gravitas* of these haunting lines leads one to expect a major programmatic statement, and in a sense, that is what we get. For all that, however, what Parrott stands for here has never been satisfactorily explained. He is "the poetic faculty," the soul, an uncorrupted saintly body:[33] all are possibilities, but none have exclusive purchase. If Parrot is a figure for poetry, then he can only be adjudged an uncanny one, confounding categories: split between spiritual and carnal, a dead yet not putrefying body whose proximity to the soul (the two seem teasingly close, yet not quite identical) surrounds it with an aura not easily described. (We might compare another of his Greek and Latin interpolations, in which "*Vita et Anima / Zoe ke psiche*" ["Life and Soul"] [267–68] are followed by more dubious copulations of both terms and tongues: "*Concumbunt Grece. Non est hic sermo pudicus*" ["They lie together in the Greek manner. This is not a modest way of speaking"] [269].) Parrott, not surprisingly, evades designation, and the question of interpreting him turns the mirror on the reader: the "pereles prynce that Parrot dyd create, / He made you of nothynge by his magistye" (218–19). In the provisional moment of reading, the reader, like Parrott, is created *ex nihilo*, summoned to "Poynt well this probleme that Parrot doth prate" (220) and remember mortality.

Galathea, a reader herself made up of many prototypes,[34] enters to hear the lament of Pamphilus, marginally glossed as "the all-loving," when he "lost his mate." Parott's response is a version of the lyric "Come over the burne, Besse, to me." The poem exists in a moralized version in which "Bess" is "mankynde" summoned by Christ. It can thus be read as entirely continuous with what has gone before – where "wylfulnes ys vicar generall," Christ calls an erring church back to him. In the other version, however, Bess is a young woman "Goten with child" by "A wanton chyld."[35] Parrot reasserts the identity of the green lover:

> I wyl be ferme and stabyll,
> And to yow servyceabyll,
> And also prophytabyll … (246–48)

As Griffiths notes, this sudden phallic reinvestment may draw Galathea into a temporal continuum that will be "prophytabyll" and so "profit" her. Griffiths suggests that this may be a "double *double entendre*,"[36] finding closure in a triple pun. However, behind this petition there suddenly appears a specter whose meanings are disquietingly unsettled:

> Alas, I am dysdayned,
> And as a man halfe-maymed,
> My harte is so sore payned ... (252–54)

The Christological identification of the lyric offers us something close to a monologue of the "Woefully arrayed" Christ speaking directly to the sinner, as pained and rejected body of the Passion. If we also follow earlier readings in suggesting that Parrott echoes Psittacus – the son of Deucalion and Pyrrha, transformed by the gods into a parrot after his death – there may be another reason for the mutation and metamorphosis of this figure; like the incarnate Christ, he is "as a man halfe-maymed." As Christ, Psittacus and "halfe-maymed" lover, Parott, at least at this point, has only the authority of a logos itself maimed, a figure of verbal lack. Even Wolsey, scrambled into a farrago of scriptural and other types, a batch of joltingly polysyllabic verbs (432) and a wolf's head, has more substance; indeed, he challenges Parott for the position of the poem's ontological center.

The last part of the poem has often drawn accusations that it lacks the imaginative texture of its previous sections in its drift into the standard mode of "abuses" satire. Admonished by Galathea to "sette asyde all sophisms, and speke now trewe and playne" (448), Parrott finally moves into a series of ponderous antitheses. Yet these lines, for all their sententiousness, are no less oblique than much that has gone before, and they draw on similar forms of prophetic symbolism. "So myche newe makyng, and so madd tyme spente" (450) might suggest a conservative fear of Wolsey's administrative innovations, but the "newe makyng" most evident here – seemingly perceived as such by uncomprehending contemporaries – is Skelton's own, and the "madd tyme spente" doubles back on the poem's carnivalesque propensities. Similarly, the reference to "So myche translacion into Englyshe confused" (451) works as a highly accurate gloss on the entire poem, in which translation, the dominant figure of metaphor as movement and transformation, shapes both Parrott's practice of allegory as a shuttling between orders and levels of meaning (the ghosts of the exegetical four levels are very present here) and Wolsey's processions and diplomatic perambulations. Even the antitheses of political clamor recall another kind of complaint; the reversions to "So many," "So myche" and "so lytell" take up the earlier erotics of privation and excess manifested in Parrot's dealings with the "ladyes" of the court.

Skelton may – though perhaps we shall never know how far this is the case – have intended the poem as a petition to return to favor. In practice, however, it sums up multiple allegiances: to king; to a court we cannot clearly envisage; to the overweening cardinal it ostensibly detests but structurally requires, and his radical reformings and deformings of church and state; to textual bodies as privileged as Scripture and as popular as outlaw legend; finally, and most crucially, to the multiplying "properties" of figuration. Skelton's career might seem to locate him in some instances as the early Tudor Virgil, aspiring to the status of laureate poet. He may also be seen, however, as his period's Ovid, producer of texts and metaphors and unpredictable discourses of sexuality, whose work defies ready ascription to a prior authority and what it represents, and whose metamorphoses outrun their subjects.

ROMANCING THE LAUREL

Chaucer's *Hous of Fame* ends enigmatically with the approach of a "man of gret auctoritee" (2158) whose identity remains undisclosed. Readers of the *Garlande of Laurell*, however, know that the "man" is John Skelton. And they know this on grounds that meet the only standard of proof admitted by positivist scholarship – Skelton tells us so himself. *The Garlande of Laurell*, long read as a response to Chaucer's precursor text,[37] narrates Skelton's progress to the final honor of a laurel crown conferred before the Queen of Fame and an assembly of great poets of the past. Yet its beginnings are troubled enough: the melancholy poet drifts into a dream in "the frythy forest of Galtres" (22) near Sheriff Hutton castle in Yorkshire, and hears his right to a place in Fame's court questioned in a long and heated debate between Fame herself and Dame Pallas. His fortunes, however, then take a turn for the better, as the wild press of poets struggling for Fame's favor clears to allow the arrival of Chaucer, Gower and Lydgate – a Chaucer, we might suppose, miraculously liberated from the House of Rumor in which his own poem leaves him stranded, and in one of those giddying spatial transformations it so often delivers, brought face to face with Skelton, having picked up Gower and Lydgate somewhere along the intervening years. The three are garbed as befits their status as the revered elders of an English poetic heritage; indeed, says Skelton, "Thei wantid nothynge but the laurell" (397) – which he, of course, covets.

If we leave aside the clichés about Skelton's gigantic ego, there is much to note about this encounter. Chaucer, Gower and Lydgate, previously only names in what is by Skelton's day a topical roll call of the three major fathers of English poetry, are here real men with real bodies who greet the newcomer to Fame's "collage" (403) with their vernacular eloquence. They are there to establish Skelton's own name, his title to a signifier that will represent the subject for other signifiers, be heard and read universally. Voice and body guarantee – quite literally, substantiate – a transmission of poetic authority both patrilineal and national.

But the fathers, of course, are there not to beget, but to stand by and applaud an act of self-creation, whose own gendering takes unpredictable paths. Critics have drawn attention to the identity the poem asserts between Skelton's crown of laurel and the work that bears its name.[38] Appropriately, the poem's central emblem of poetic craft is a phoenix sitting in the heights of a laurel[39] – determinedly a "She" (669), as if in polemical reclamation from the legend, figured in Claudian and Ovid, according to which this immortal bird is its own son and its own father.[40] In a similar style, Skelton's self-authoring is witnessed and approved by the fathers, but goes one step beyond biological reproduction, transfiguring and sublimating the body of paternity in a spectacular gesture of imaginary self-enfolding, gendered female, which becomes the poem's own extraordinary reflexiveness. All is not so simple, however, for the legitimation the English poets offer is evidently not theirs to give; having greeted him, they quickly ditch him for reasons unexplained ("From you most we, but not long to tary," 520) and hand him over to the care of Occupation, the Queen of Fame's "regestary" (522), who leads him to the presence chamber of Elizabeth Tylney Howard, countess of Surrey, and her attendant ladies. Here he receives his crown of laurel, a very public emblem that is woven and bestowed on him in a curiously private ceremony. Only after this can he be honored by the court of Fame, where Occupation reads a long and bizarre catalogue of his works. The labor so neatly summed up in the richly allusive figure of the phoenix, in other words, proves somewhat harder to perform by narrative means, and to establish the supramaterial nature of poetic inspiration Skelton's poem has to map a course through, and past, a scene of very material origins.[41] This scene centers on a female patron, and it condenses a number of terms – matter, material labor, the maternal tongue – which suggest that the endurance of Skelton's name may be a more contingent matter. I want to address here the multiple intertexts – for the most part Ovidian and, as we have seen, Chaucerian – which both further and complicate Skelton's endeavor, and their connexion with the aesthetic and economic institutions that shape the poem's strange textual history.

That history is both revealed and concealed in the poem: revealed as a long list of writings – an autobibliography; concealed in a scholarly problem of dating. The only existing text of the poem that can be dated with assurance is Richard Faques's print of October 1523, but since the 1960s it has been demonstrated that the poem probably originated much earlier, perhaps in a celebration of Skelton's academic laureation by the Countess of Surrey and her ladies. Skelton was laureated by the universities of Oxford, Louvain and Cambridge in 1488, 1492 and 1493 respectively, while Melvin J. Tucker has shown that the only period during which the countess and other members of the Howard *familia* were in residence at Sheriff Hutton castle was 1489–99, and that the women addressed in the *Garland*'s lyrics "were to be identified with a generation of Howard women and their compeers who flourished in the 1480s and 1490s."[42] Overall, it would seem that the lyrics to the countess and her ladies were written in the 1490s, followed quite shortly by the Sheriff Hutton narrative frame in which they are set; other parts of the poem came later, and Skelton evidently added to and revised the poem throughout his career, the bibliography appearing last.

In accordance with this palimpsestic temporal accretion, Skelton's bid to specify his relationship to the signifier is marked by a fierce imaginary rivalry. If half the poem tries to sustain a fantasy of its phoenix-like self-sufficiency, the other half seeks as energetically to explode that fantasy. The poem has been variously read as proud statement of the Renaissance poet's prophetic inspiration,[43] as a humanist orator's self-promotion, and as an attempt to construct an "implied reader" who "belongs to a conspicuously national [i.e. English] community."[44] All these views have a point, but are not quite the poem we read. *The Garland* proclaims the integrity of Skelton's name and corpus, and yet its very existence is rhetorically dependent on other voices that crowd its pages, or, to judge by its sputtering aggression, seem to threaten it from without. By the same token, talk of the rhetorical construction of a unified audience sorts oddly with a poem whose identifiable addressees include – on a conservative estimate – the Countess of Surrey, assorted ladies, Henry VIII, Cardinal Wolsey, the mysterious Roger Statham who is so cryptically attacked at 742–51, and – probably – Alexander Barclay (1257–1375). Nor is it quite clear how the profile of "the oratorical performing self"[45] is enhanced by a catalogue that includes such gems as "The Balade … of the Mustarde Tarte" (1245), "The Gruntyng and the Groynninge of the Gronnyng Swyne" (1376) and "the Murnyng of the Mapely Rote" (1377). The poem unpredictably mixes genres (dream vision, debate, lyric, catalogue, invective), rhetorical identities (Juvenalian satirist, courtly maker in the mode of Machaut and Chaucer), meters, stanza forms and indeed languages. The laurel, with its post-Petrarchan academic and political sanctions, thus becomes the paradoxical sign of an extremely heterogeneous text, a strange litter of cultural grammars in which several different literary and historical models are overlaid.

These models return us to an early sixteenth-century patronage market in which multiple economies, both real and symbolic, and multiple models for identification circulate and compete. The difficulties of Skelton's vocational place at this point have already been noted. Also relevant here is the question of medium: the Faques text is a rare instance of Skelton's selective resort to print, while the lyrics suggest private coterie circulation in manuscript.[46] Kate Harris points out that in a patronage culture the book is "an object to be created, to a degree now difficult to envisage, in the patron's image and *The Garland*'s relation to both script and print complicates that relation still further."[47] Skelton's is thus the pursuit of an ambivalent sign indeed: the laurel crown that asserts the poetic and political authority once assigned to Petrarch might also assert, at this historical conjuncture, the very dissolution of that same authority into multiple readings and contexts, be a laurel without an aura.

My concern here is not with the vexed question of Skelton's relations to Howard patronage, but rather with autobiography of a more deflected kind. If we accept the dating just outlined, then we have a text which contains a journey from origins in intimate manuscript circulation and a scene of regional aristocratic patronage to the wider and more mixed reading public of print, for whom the catalogue of Skelton's works will be the sign that puts the author-function "Skelton" in circulation. Yet in narrative terms, the text seems to move in the direction of the lyrics that mark the earliest phase of its composition, revisiting its beginnings in female patronage in a movement defined by the trope of *hysteron proteron*.[48] The Countess of Surrey episode itself has undergone a bizarre structural translation; chronologically the poem's origin, it has now become an instance of the narrative dilation or deferral described by Patricia Parker as a troping of the female body, a digression on Skelton's path to the phallus, full of lyric address and courtly leisureliness. This quest, however, frames a rather more troubled relationship to the signifier, and it is here that Skelton's Ovidian allusions come into play.

Skelton's *Garlande* introduces his self-projection as laureate through citation of its hidden side – the dimension which, as Lynn Enterline has forcefully reminded us, speaks to language as the scene of privation.[49] The laurel crown's Ovidian aetiology is recapitulated when the great company of Skelton's poets enters, led by Orpheus and Apollo. If Orpheus, the son, exuberantly animates objects – the very stump against which Skelton is leaning begins to dance – Apollo, his father, is trapped in lamentation for Daphne ("I have lost now that I entended, / And may not atteyne it by no medyacyon," 318–19). Mediation, of course, is the purpose of the laurel garland, signifier of loss:

> in remembraunce of Daphnes transformacyon,
> All famous poetis ensuynge after me
> Shall were a garlande of the laurell tre.   (320–22)

With hindsight, even the poem's opening, in which "hartis belluyng, embosyd with distres" (24) are pursued by foresters and hounds, evokes an Ovidian prototype. Skelton is cast as Actaeon home on the English range, about to slip into a dream where he will hear, rather than see, the secrets of goddesses.

As it turns out, however, the castration and mutilation to which Skelton may be exposed affects name rather than body. Fame complains that while "auncient poetis" (65) were industrious, and wear the laurel crown "In figure" of their toil (68), "Skelton is wonder slake, / And, as we dare, we fynde in hym grete lake" (69–70).[50] Pallas justifies this distinctly emasculated figure on the grounds that the nature of writing *per se* puts any writer in a no-win situation; it is constantly struggling to recover an impossible relation. The outspoken panegyrist may be accused of flattery, while satire and the riddling tropes of political prophecy may offend the powerful. "Another manes mynde diffuse is to expounde," she says, "Yet harde is to make but sum fawt be founde" (111–12). But the material sign, abstracted from the body of its producer and subjected to multiple readings and meanings, is also the source of literal thraldom. "Beware, for wrytyng remayneth of recorde!" (89) says Pallas proverbially, and the point recurs throughout the poem; whether or not you stick to your word, your word will surely stick to you.[51] And once again the bondage is erotic, for the whole debate stems from Fame's complaint that Skelton "wyll not endevour hymselfe to purchase / The favour of ladys with wordis electe" (75–76). Here, the common opposition between poetry (the works of the classical *auctores*) and making (writing as ephemeral courtly entertainment)[52] disappears; poetry proves to be grounded in making, and at the heart of Skelton's attempt to enter the transcendent canon of what Chaucer called "alle poesye" we find a courtly scenario more appropriate to *The Legend of Good Women* and its French predecessors. The poet bound to the uncertain shifts of the signifier that are the inevitable concomitant of spreading one's name, the errancy of Fama underlying the renown of Fame, is simultaneously bound to the will and desire of female readers.

The drive to arrest this mobility is figured in the topography of Skelton's poem, which is illuminated by Carolyn Dinshaw's association of Chaucer's "queyntelych"-wrought house of Rumour with female sexuality and the female body.[53] At first the risks seem great. The three English poetic fathers conduct Skelton to the palace of Fame through gates of "elephantis tethe" (468), portal of false dreams and uncanny prolepsis of the *vagina dentata*. Once they have ceded their tutelage to Occupation, she leads Skelton up "a windyng stayre" (767) into the secret recesses of Sheriff Hutton and to "a goodly chaumber of astate" (768) – a metonym for the body of the patroness, which is also, in a real sense given the probable chronology of its composition, the matrix of the poem.

In the ladies' chamber of Sheriff Hutton, we observe, in flat contradiction to that strand in the poem that figures poetry as self-making, a poetic reputation woven under the fingers of ladies, in an economy of exchange. Skelton, the Countess says, deserves his reputation because

> "of all ladyes he hath the library,
> Ther names recountyng in the court of Fame;
> Of all gentylwomen he hath the scruteny,
> In Fames court reportyng the same;
> For yet of women he never sayd shame,
> But if they were counterfettes that women them call,
> That list of there lewdnesse with hym for to brall."   (780–86)

In this trade-off, we are once again back to the archaic scene of patronage of *The Legend of Good Women*; poetic fame for women's good names is the order of the day. As phallic mother, who has something that Skelton wants, the countess is clear that Skelton must also return thanks to the ladies "With proper captacyons of benevolence" (815); if they work for his "pleasure" (810), he must also pleasure them with "some goodly conseyt" (814).

Critics have referred to the ensuing scene as "delightful," "enchanting," and "charming," suggesting a distinct readiness to fall in with the text's narcissistic reconstruction of its originary scene of patronage.[54] For the women show how far they deserve the good names that Skelton will give them. They settle to an intimate scene of spinning and weaving – a male fantasy of female interiority and domesticity, a gathering of women in labor. "With fingers smale, and handis whyte as mylk" (797) supple enough to assuage the lack of any slack poet, they exchange cheerful gossip ("Reche me that skane of tewly sylk," 798; "Wynde me that botowme of such an hew," 799). Skelton, however, gives his exchange with the ladies a distinctly asymmetric twist; while the ladies weave the text of his laurel crown and thus his reputation, he "sharpe[s his] pen" (823) and with his "dredfull tremlyng fist" (828) covertly undoes theirs.

Skelton's lyrics have puzzled most commentators on the poem, and attempts to explain away the manifest indecorousness of their Ovidian subtexts have usually succeeded only in drawing attention to their own strenuousness. Lady Anne Dacre is linked with Deianira, to whose jealousy the downfall of Hercules was ascribed (901);[55] Margaret Tilney with the fables of the incestuous Canace (934)[56] and Phaedra (940);[57] Gertrude Statham is "Lyke to Dame Pasiphe" (1048), whose intercourse with a bull bred the Minotaur.[58] Meanwhile, allusions to the *Heroides* name Laodamia (972), faithful to her husband beyond death itself,[59] and Hypsipyle ("fayre Isaphill," 1025), loyal to a father whose life she saves, betrayed by her husband Jason.[60] And in the extended and faintly voyeuristic retelling of the story of Cydippe in the lyric addressed to Lady Muriel Howard, Skelton allegorizes his own procedure in these short poems. Cydippe arouses the passion of Acontius, who is visiting Delos to celebrate the feast of Diana. He throws her an apple carved with the words "I swear by the sanctuary of Diana to marry Acontius"; she reads them aloud, and the goddess takes them as a binding vow.[61] If at the outset Skelton is in Cydippe's position – bound by a letter which is a feminized source of authority – here a male inscription takes hold of female desire, finds gratification by devious means.

Skelton thus translates the figure of the female patron into a doublet of related types: women outrageously transgressive, women whose fidelity traps them in death and desertion. Women are simultaneously vested with immense danger and shown to be not so dangerous. The most complete undoing of the sign of the patroness falls to Isabel Pennell, compared to a nightingale, lyric tropes reduced to familiar Philomelan sounds:

> Dug, dug,
> Jug, jug,
> Good yere and good luk,
> With chuk, chuk, chuk, chuk. (1000–03)

Skeltonics celebrate this lady through what Jonathan Goldberg calls "the Ovidian etiology of song in rape and violation."[62] Under the veil of courtly compliment, Skelton appropriates the women's powers to make his name, while subjecting their names to semiotic mutilation. It is after this unmaking of the patroness that Skelton's three forefathers appear once more, to conduct him before the poets' conclave. The chamber scene issues in an empowered Skelton and bonds solidified across time among male poets.

This, however, is not quite the end of the matter. To be sure, Skelton's autobibliography boasts an insane and virtuosic inclusivity, covering a range from his most politically worthy enterprises – such as his *Speculum principis* and translation of Diodorus Siculus – to his most salacious lyrics. Sandwiched between a description of the morality play *Magnyfycence* and the Latin verses which, according to John Norton-Smith, encode another reference to Skelton's birth from his own verses,[63] we find a mention of "Manerly Margery Mylke and Ale," Skelton's low-style dialogue between a clerk and a protesting serving-maid. The *Garland* allusion deserves to be quoted in full:

> Of Manerly Margery Maystres Mylke and Ale;
> To her he wrote many maters of myrthe;
> Yet, thoughe I say it, therby lyith a tale,
> For Margery wynshed, and breke her hinder girth;
> Lorde, how she made moche of her gentyll birth!
> With, "Gingirly, go gingerly!" Her tayle was made of hay;
> Go she never so gingirly, her honesty is gone away.
>
> Harde to make ought of that is nakid nought;
> This fustiane maistres and this giggisse gase
> Wonder is to wryte what wrenchis she wrowght,
> To face out her foly with a midsomer mase;
> With pitche she patchid her pitcher shuld not crase;
> It may wele ryme, but shroudly it doth accorde,
> To pyke out honesty of suche a potshorde.   (1198–211)

A knowing classical allusion that exposes the woman is Dunbarically replayed in the language of what Freud calls smut ("die Zote"). Amid more exalted genres we find "manerly Margery" whose unmannerly body, textually dilated – she has a longer entry than previous, much more edifying works – is bursting with the most profligate polysemy (her poorly patched pitcher, her "tayle / tale" that "lyith" and is "made of hay," Skelton's usual equine metaphors). At the same time, she is contained within the masculine word of social satire, for her deferrals have no carnivalesque dynamism; rather, her resistance is caricatured as the exaggerated delicacy of a girl with ideas above her station ("go gingirly"). The text, having appropriated the generative powers of the female body, can expose women's genitals as "nakid nought," of which, even for Skelton, it is "harde" to make anything.

In Skelton's poem, the woman's body tropes several forms of material contingency – the "occasionality" of the poem's origin, its dependence on a patron's demand, the sliding signs of the mother tongue. There are, however, three reasons why *The Garlande* may in the end be more than the sum of such antifeminist discursive strategies. One is that recent historicizations of Skelton's antifeminism in other contexts have found in it an oppositional and critical force: Elizabeth Fowler's reading of the grotesque body of Elynour Rummynge as parodic critique of a money economy,[64] Halpern's of the body of Jane Scrope in *Phyllyp Sparowe* as the site of a "regime of pleasure" running counter to the bodily codings of emergent Tudor absolutism.[65] A second is that if the song of the nightingale and the linguistic grossnesses of Manerly Margery suggest a repudiation of the material body of the English language, the Skeltonic by which the poet is remembered is itself, as Roland Greene points out, "a poetry turned inside out, in which theme and imagery are ... determined by the material patterns of sound."⁶⁶ The excesses of Skelton's poem may perhaps be seen as a scandalous exposure, rather than an endorsement, of the rhetorical bases of humanist oratory, a revelation of its foundations in linguistic violence.

The third and final reason why I am reluctant to claim the last word here is that Skelton does not allow it to himself. Occupation's catalogue, we recall, comes to rest on the mysterious "Item Apollo that whirllid up his chare" (1471). Skelton is "halfe sodenly afrayd" (1477) and asks her to erase the line, but no – it is subject to the conditions of fame, she says, and what is once written "must nedes after rin all the worlde aboute" (1483). Editors have assumed yet another reference to a satirical work now lost, but the line also, of course, quotes the point at which Chaucer's *Squire's Tale* is interrupted by the Franklin. The poem that supplies such decisive closure to one Chaucerian text concludes with allusion to another whose digressions and lacunae suggest, as Elizabeth Scala has persuasively argued, compulsive and repeated return to an origin "which is barred from signification," and which, therefore, "demands construction over and over again."⁶⁷ (The Squire's last line before the one Skelton cites, of course, is "And ther I lefte I wol ayeyn bigynne.") The gesture reflects Skelton's final bibliography, where works of instruction and propaganda alternate with low-style verse, obscure hints, and pieces whose very existence is in question, so that Skelton's "name" is founded on an absent text, a catalogue of ghosts. And this disturbance is mirrored in the end of the dream. When Occupation "ma[kes] rehersall" of "the laurel" (1503), and the *Garlande of Laurell* becomes one with the poem we read, the poets cry "*Triumpha, triumpha!*" (1506), but Fame – whether in approval, irritation or boredom we never know – orders the book to be "shett fast" (1510), waking the dreamer up. In this laureation *interruptus*, *The Garlande of Laurell*'s endeavors to erase origin issue in a final recognition of limit.

Conclusion

This study breaks off – with, as we shall see shortly, one exception – in 1528. Much critical attention, of a high order, has homed in on the 1530s, and Puttenham's "new company of courtly makers," who, chiefly in the persons of Wyatt and Surrey, "polished our rude and homely maner of vulgar Poesie."[1] The immediate causes of this distinctiveness have not been far to seek. Greg Walker sees in the 1530s generation in England a voice "created out of the intense political pressure of Henrician tyranny," a tyranny that even in the 1520s had seemed scarcely imaginable. The result is a poetry that suggests "a wider instability in the very categories of knowledge prompted by the unfixing of the realm" and "a fluidity of sexual relationships" that bespeaks a "moral and political amnesia" at its heart.[2] Robert Meyer-Lee finds in Wyatt's poetry an intersection between Lydgate's "laureate poetics" and the verse of *fin amor* which "had served the elite as a demonstration of their facility with language and their deep capacity for refined sentiment."[3] Yet the poetic traditions of England and Scotland – traditions that cannot be considered apart from the shaping significance of the European versions of *dit* and love-allegory – had long been inflected with *amour courtois* by the time Wyatt reached them, and the love-lyric, as Boffey shows, had moved some way from its elite pretensions. Moments of poetic signature – "Geffrey"'s woeful distance from love-tidings in the *Hous of Fame*, Gower's final recognition by Venus – are profoundly inflected by the figure of the cleric-poet and his complex relationship to desire and writing. It has been part of my project to argue that the work of Skelton and his contemporaries is in part motivated by a bid to counterpoint the neo-Latin writing dominant at the English court at the sixteenth century's beginning with an erotic language of secrecy that imports significant revisions in its imagining of the authority to which it subscribes.

As significantly, however, I have tried to show that the generic fragmentation that presents itself as part of these poets' enterprises is not well served by an historicism that has often domesticated them. In 1990, reviewing

Alistair Fox's *Politics and Literature*, Colin Burrow breezily imputed an essential misguidedness to Fox's privileging of Skelton and his immediate contemporaries.[4] Meyer-Lee, too, declares that despite Skelton's far greater formal and thematic range, and Wyatt's narrowness, "to declare Wyatt's work regressive in comparison with Skelton seems odd" – a view, moreover, that is imbued with the self-evidence of an "intuition."[5] Some, however, have seen Skelton, Hawes and Barclay as protomodern, with *Speke Parott* understood as a 1520s *Waste Land*. Such readings risk being accused of misrecognition (such poets are perfectly transparent when placed within a properly formulated historical understanding) or relocated in conservative generalities (a poem in chaos embodies a perception of the world in chaos, "all coherence gone").

It is certainly true that this period sees in English and Scottish court poetry the explosion of a fragmenting and abrasive eclecticism, in which signification goes violently awry, and the forms of love-allegory and dream vision, along with imported forms of satire and pastoral, threaten to collapse into incoherence under the pressure of something unspoken. Yet it will not do, I think, simply to reduce what is going on here to the impact of political terror on a presumed norm of "plain speaking." The effect of a rather exhausting bricolage might rather be traced to the workings of allegory itself, as preferred mode of self-presentation. Gordon Teskey, working from Walter Benjamin's reading of allegory as the realm of the corpse – the space where the body dies into signification – sees in personification the concealment of a violence. He writes, however, that "the violence inside personification is exposed when that figure is ... turned inside out." What becomes visible is "the truth over which allegory is always drawing its veil: the fundamental disorder out of which the illusion of order is raised." Writing emerges as a material trace that marks a "violent" distance from an allegorical center.[6] Working, as I have tried to do throughout, from such a sense of what allegory might mean, with its interchange of partial objects and absent centers, I would like to close with two figural bodies, one English, one Scottish, which seem to summarize some important cultural differences.

Skelton's last poem, *A Replycacion Agaynst Certayne Yonge Scolers Abjured of Late*, printed in 1528, has been noted for its programmatic statement of the disembodied nature of poetic inspiration:

> ... there is a spyrituall,
> And a mysteriall,
> And a mysticall
> Effecte energiall,
> As Grekes do it call,

> Of suche an industry
> And suche a pregnacy,
> Of hevenly inspyracion
> In laureate creacyon,
> Of poetes commendacion,
> That of divyne myseracion
> God maketh his habytacion
> In poetes whiche excelles,
> And sojourns with them and dwelles. (365–78)[7]

Disembodiment here, however, is purchased at a price. These lines are appended to an attack on Thomas Arthur and Thomas Bilney, both denounced as heretics and commanded to carry symbolic faggots at Paul's Cross in public penance. Skelton's poem is particularly forceful in its denunciation of their attack on "that glorious mayde and mother" Mary (257). The poem, however, also sinks into onomatopoeic alternations that nominally denote the heretics' "Wytlesse wandring to and fro!" / With "te he, ta ha, bo ho, bo ho!" (74–75), approximating once again to sound at its most material in the "wandering" region of unlikeness. Similarly, Skelton catches one of the heretics laughing

> whan he dyd pas
> With his fagot in processyon.
> He counted it for no correction,
> But with scornefull affection
> Toke it for a sporte,
> His heresy to supporte. (187–92)

This brief moment of unregulated bodily sound cannot but double Skelton's own torrent of monosyllabic invective. The doubleness of Skelton's enterprise is at its most apparent when Skelton bids to recall the heretics from their error:

> Wherfore make ye no mo restrayntes,
> But mende your myndes that are mased;
> Or els doutlesse ye shalbe blased,
> And be brent at a stake,
> If further busynesse that ye make. (293–96)

Disembodied "inspiration" and the smoke of the fires from the Lollard's Pit outside Bishopsgate, where Bilney was later burned as a relapsed heretic, mingle in the murderous, punning blazonings of Skelton's pen.

From this preface to a literary history of the Reformation in England we turn finally to a different act of poetic disembodiment, one far closer to the corporeal exchanges we have seen in Dunbar. As Skelton constructed a

Conclusion

private calendar dating from his entry into the royal service, so Sir David Lyndsay entered the service of James IV's third and only surviving son, later James V, on "The day of thy natyvitie" (*The Complaynt of Schir David Lindesay*, 16). As Master Usher, he presents himself as a constant presence in the young prince's life, noting that he "lay nychtlie be thy cheik" (80), and in *Ane Dreme* Lyndsay amuses the young James by pulling faces, while at the same time he stresses the instability of his own form faced with the sovereign's imaginary unity:

> sumtyme lyke ane feind tranfegurate
> And sumtyme lyke the greislie gaist of Gye,
> In divers formis, oft tymes disfigurate,
> And sumtyme dissagyist full plesandlye.   (15–18)

Lyndsay picks up the fears of bodily transformation that have plagued Dunbar and Douglas, but incorporates them for the pleasure of his monarch.

In *The Complaynt*, Lyndsay describes his care for the young prince's body.

> as ane chapman beris his pak,
> I bure thy grace upon my bak
> And sumtymes strydlingis on my nek,   *astride*
> Dansand with mony bend and bek.   *leap*; *bow*
> The first sillabis that thow did mute
> Was, 'Pa, Da Lyn'.   *play (?) David Lyndsay*
>   (87–92)

The king also figures as prelinguistic; it is, as R. James Goldstein points out, Lyndsay who figures as the Name of the Father. Goldstein observes that "the body mystic of the sovereign offers an ego-ideal for the identity formation of a subject (in both the political and psychoanalytic senses of the word) while the adult offers an ego-ideal to the body natural of the child-king."[8] For a time the sole locus of royal authority was in Lyndsay's charge, entertained in more than one aspect by the poet's performances of identity.

In Lyndsay's *Answer to the Kingis Flyting*, written around 1535, the king has found new bedfellows. The king, through his flyting, has – in a reversal of the poet–patron relationship that we have seen pertain previously – attempted to inaugurate a relationship of equality between himself and Lyndsay by allowing, or rather mandating, competition. Irrespective of whatever real affection may have existed between king and poet, this is a scripted *communitas*. Lyndsay's strategy of response resists it by admitting the king's superiority, but depicting it as an imperative. In what will turn into a reflection on the king's amatory habits, Lyndsay removes himself from rivalry in order to occupy the position of adviser – and his concern with the king's body, ironically, requires a profession of his own inadequacy. The scene the poem stages is a response to scurrilous verses the king has written, attacking Lyndsay's reputation as a lover. As a result, it transpires, ladies refuse to have anything to do with him:

> Thay banis me, sayand I am nocht able
> Thame to compleis, or preis to thare presence. *please; advance*
> (12–13)

Lyndsay, however, ostensibly refuses to engage the king, pleading a lack of poetic competence and art:

> Wer I ane poeit, I suld preis with my pen
> To wreik me on your vennemous wryting,
> Bot I man do as dog dois in his den, *must*
> Fald baith my feit, or fle fast frome your flyting
> (15–18)

The modesty topos returns; the poet will not venture further because of his inability. But here there is a difference; the poet's impotence allows him to speak from a position of authority. Lyndsay's response to the king's taunts is to figure himself as a venerable greybeard:

> Quhat can ye say forther, bot I am failyeit
> In Venus werkis? I grant, schir, that is trew.
> The tyme hes bene, I wes better artailyeit *provided with artillery*
> Nor I am now.
> (29–32)

Lyndsay also cedes to the king superiority in poetry, calling him "of flowand rethorik the flour" (70), as Dunbar did Chaucer, and proclaiming him "prince of poetry" (21), a title, as Janet Hadley Williams notes, more often given to Virgil. By positioning himself beyond a rivalrous relationship with the young king, Lyndsay is able to reverse traditional symbolism and place himself in a paternal – and patronal – role. In a reorientation of Dunbarian tropes, the unregulated and fragmented body is that of the sexually promiscuous king, "strang lyke an elephand / And in till Venus werkis maist vailyeand" (25–26). Lyndsay thus builds to a ferocious culmination

> like ane boisteous bull, ye rin and ryde *boisterous*
> Royatouslie, like ane rude rubatour, *Riotously; scoundrel*
> Ay fukkand lyke ane furious fornicatour. *raging*
> (47–49)

Yet a rivalry still exists for him; he specifically blames the king's unbounded sexual activity on "your counsale … That wald nocht of ane princes [*princess*] yow provide" (43–44).

Such imaginary rivalry, in 1535, looks forward to a distant future. The court poets who briefly clustered around the young James VI worked with their own combination of erotics and politics. And as Roderick J. Lyall has recently argued, such practice raises multiple possibilities for a model of late sixteenth-century culture that embraces two centers and two nations. The possible grounds for comparison are numerous. English Protestant nationalism, and its internal counternarratives, needs to be weighed against Reformation Scotland and the subsequent degree of tolerance during the Lennox ascendancy, and the cult of Elizabeth against the intimacy surrounding the youthful James VI, after another long royal minority.[9] The period between 1485 and 1528 fabricates a multiplicity of literary cultures, in a more capacious manner than Puttenham's retrospective account of the Tottel generation was inclined to grasp. It also lays the ground, as Lyall has argued, for a triangular understanding of English, Scottish and European writing. It is to be hoped that this book has played some part in opening up such prospects.

Notes

INTRODUCTION

1. For the circumstantial evidence for the 1495 edition, see Kenneth Varty, *Reynard, Renart, Reinaert and Other Foxes in Medieval England* (Amsterdam, 1999), 98–99.
2. William Caxton, trans., *The History of Reynard the Fox*, ed. N. F. Blake, EETS 263 (Oxford, 1970), 13.
3. The fate of the royal summons varies through the Renart tradition. Caxton, following Gherard Leeu's prose *Reinaert*, does not mention a document: see W. Gs. Hellinga, *Van den Vos Reynaerde: 1 Teksten* (Zwolle, 1952), 33. In the French texts, Noble's first two messengers, both ill-fated, clearly do not carry it. It is Grimbert the badger, sent next, who insists that the royal seal is needed, and who eventually reads the king's brief and performative letter: "s'il veoit vostre seel ... Lors sai je bien que il vendroit, / Ja nule essoigne nel tendroit" (IX, 927, 929–30; "once he sees your seal, I know he'll come without a single excuse"). The document promises Renart "honte et martire, / et grant anui et grant contraire" ["shame and torture, great suffering and harsh reprisals"] should he fail to show (IX, 988–89). I cite the edition of Gabriel Bianciotto, ed., *Le Roman de Renart* (Paris, 2005), based on a gamma family manuscript.
4. I am indebted here to Luke Sunderland, "*Le Cycle de Renart*: From the *Enfances* to the *Jugement* in a Cyclical *Roman de Renart* Manuscript," *French Studies* 62 (2008), 1–12 (11).
5. For the last book-length comparative treatment, see Gregory Kratzmann, *Anglo-Scottish Literary Relations 1430–1550* (Cambridge, 1980).
6. On *auctoritas*, see A. J. Minnis, *Medieval Theory of Authorship: Scholastic Literary Attitudes in the Later Middle Ages*, 2nd edn (Philadelphia, 1988), 10–12. On authority and the more general use of "legitimate language" see Pierre Bourdieu, *Language and Symbolic Power*, ed. and intro. John B. Thompson, trans. Gino Raymond and Matthew Adamson (Cambridge, MA, 1991), 57–61.
7. These versions present themselves as masculine; for a different focus, see Jennifer Summit, *Lost Property: The Woman Writer and English Literary History, 1380–1589* (Chicago, 2000). On the unsettling effects of the tropes of love-poetry, see Nicolette Zeeman, "The Verse of Courtly Love in the Framing Narrative of the Confessio Amantis," *Medium Aevum* 60 (1991), 222–40.

8. Walter Map, *De nugis curialium: Courtiers' Trifles*, ed. and trans. M. R. James, rev. edn. C. N. L. Brooke and R. A. B. Mynors (Oxford, 1983), 2–3. Map here cites Augustine, *Confessions*, xi.25; see the edition by James J. O'Donnell, 3 vols. (Oxford, 1992), 1, 160.
9. Greg Walker, "John Skelton and the Royal Court," *Vernacular Literature and Current Affairs in the Early Sixteenth Century: France, England and Scotland*, ed. Jennifer and Richard Britnell (Aldershot, 2000), 1–15 (2). Walker's sensitive adjudication of the matter suggests multiple subcultures and a "courtly-metropolitan ecosystem" (4).
10. G. R. Elton claims the "true Court" to be an essentially Tudor phenomenon, not seen until the reign of Henry VII. See "Tudor Government: The Points of Contact III. The Court," *Transactions of the Royal Historical Society* 5th series 26 (1976), 211–28 (212).
11. D. A. L. Morgan defines the beginnings of courtly self-consciousness in England as a Yorkist legacy: "The House of Policy: the Political Role of the Late Plantagenet Household, 1422–1485," *The English Court: From the Wars of the Roses to the Civil War*, ed. David Starkey et al. (London and New York, 1987), 25–70 (67–68). C. Stephen Jaeger, *The Origins of Courtliness: Civilizing Trends and the Formation of Courtly Ideals 939–1210* (Philadelphia, 1985), describes the Carolingian and clerical formation of a "courtly" *mentalité*.
12. The idea that medieval England possesses a distinctive "court culture" is questioned in *English Court Culture in the Later Middle Ages*, ed. V. J. Scattergood and J. W. Sherborne (London, 1983). In particular, see Scattergood's own "Literary Culture at the Court of Richard II," 29–43; Denton Fox, "Middle Scots Poets and Patrons," 109–27; A. I. Doyle, "English Books in and out of Court from Edward III to Henry VII," 163–81. At the latter end of the fifteenth century – the period covered by this study – distinguishing between reading audiences on a social basis is in any case notoriously problematic. Derek Pearsall notes that "'court poetry' by provenance becomes 'courtly poetry' by dissemination, in turn providing models for provincial composition": *Old English and Middle English Poetry* (London, 1977), 213. In *Manuscripts of Courtly Love Lyrics in the Later Middle Ages* (Cambridge, 1985), Julia Boffey stresses that of the hundred or so English manuscripts containing love lyrics she discusses, "genuinely 'courtly' associations – with members of the royal family or the higher nobility – are very few" (116). On the complex social affiliations of so-called "courtly" poetry in the fifteenth century, see further Boffey, *Manuscripts*, 113–41; Richard Firth Green, *Poets and Princepleasers: Literature and the English Court in the Later Middle Ages* (Toronto, 1980), esp. 8–10; Peter J. Lucas, "The Growth and Development of English Literary Patronage in the Late Middle Ages and Early Renaissance," *The Library*, 6th series 4 (1982), 219–48 (242–44); Carol M. Meale, "Patrons, Buyers and Owners: Book Production and Social Status," *Book Production and Publishing in Britain 1375–1475*, ed. Jeremy J. Griffiths and Derek Pearsall (Cambridge, 1989), 201–38. For a reading of the Henrician court, see Seth Lerer, *Courtly Letters in the Age of Henry VIII: Literary Culture and the Arts of Deceit* (Cambridge, 1997).

13. For Scotland, see Sally Mapstone, "Was there a Court Literature in Fifteenth-Century Scotland?," *Studies in Scottish Literature* 26 (1991), 410–22, and "Older Scots Literature and the Court," *The Edinburgh History of Scottish Literature*, 3 vols. (Edinburgh, 2007), I, 273–85. On fifteenth-century English courts, see *inter alia* John Watts, "Was There a Lancastrian Court?," *The Lancastrian Court: Proceedings of the 2001 Harlaxton Symposium*, ed. Jenny Stratford (Donington, 2003), 253–71; David Starkey, "Henry VI's Old Blue Gown: The English Court Under the Lancastrians and Yorkists," *Court Historian* 4 (1999), 1–28; Steven Gunn, "The Court of Henry VII," *The Court as a Stage: England and the Low Countries in the Later Middle Ages*, ed. Steven Gunn and Antheun Janse (Woodbridge, 2006), 132–44. Paul Strohm contends that the title of "court poet" acquires maximal descriptive force if "the court is understood less as an entity or even a font of material reward than as an imaginative stimulus and emotional aspiration." "Hoccleve, Lydgate and the Lancastrian Court," *The Cambridge History of Medieval English Literature,* ed. David Wallace (Cambridge, 1999), 640–61 (641).
14. James Simpson similarly links Foucault's notion of "discourse" to the more literary one of "genre": "while denoting the formal characteristics of a way of writing or speaking in the way 'genre' does, the word 'discourse' also denotes ... the claims to power made by a given genre." *"Piers Plowman": An Introduction to the B-Text* (London, 1990), 15. Simpson draws here on Michel Foucault, *The Archaeology of Knowledge*, trans. A. M. Sheridan-Smith (London, 1972), 33–34, 50–52.
15. On the permeability of boundaries between the court and the wider reading public of printed books in Scotland, see Denton Fox, "Middle Scots Poets," 125. On Wynkyn de Worde's printing of poems by both Skelton and Hawes and its implications for the relationship between court circles and print culture, see A. S. G. Edwards, "From Manuscript to Print: Wynkyn de Worde and the Printing of Contemporary Poetry," *Gutenberg Jahrbuch* (1991), 143–48.
16. Stephen J. Greenblatt, *Renaissance Self-Fashioning from More to Shakespeare* (Chicago, 1980), 11–156.
17. P. N. Medvedev and M. M. Bakhtin, *The Formal Method in Literary Scholarship: A Critical Introduction to Sociological Poetics*, trans. Albert J. Wehrle (Baltimore, 1978), 133; and see the further discussion of "Genre and Reality" on 133–35. The true authorship of this work remains an open question. For its canonical introduction into medieval studies, see Strohm, *Social Chaucer* (Cambridge, MA, 1989), 49–50.
18. Medvedev and Bakhtin, *Formal Method in Literary Scholarship*, 134.
19. Sigmund Freud, *The Standard Edition of the Complete Psychological Works*, ed. and trans. James Strachey et al., 24 vols. (London, 1953–73), IV, 177.
20. Ibid., IV, 48: "the scene of action of dreams is different from that of waking ideational life." Freud here draws on G. T. Fechner, *Elemente der Psychophysik*, 2 vols., 2nd edn. (Leipzig, 1889), II, 520–21.
21. George Puttenham, *The Arte of English Poesie*, ed. Gladys Doidge Willcock and Alice Walker (Cambridge, 1936), 186.
22. Ibid., 186–87.

23. Cf. Paul de Man's distinction between symbol, which "postulates the possibility of an identity or identification," and allegory, which "designates primarily a distance in relation to its own origin": "The Rhetoric of Temporality," *Blindness and Insight: Essays in the Rhetoric of Contemporary Criticism*, 2nd edn., Theory and History of Literature 7 (Minneapolis, 1983), 187–228 (207).
24. Such "fables of patronage" have already proved a significant resource: see Seth Lerer, *Chaucer and his Readers: Imagining the Author in Late Medieval England* (Princeton, 1993), 61.
25. Michel Foucault, *The History of Sexuality: An Introduction*, trans. Robert Hurley (New York, 1978), 148.
26. Timothy J. Reiss makes the comparable suggestion that Montaigne reads the private subject of absolutism as by definition "inconstant and constantly mutable," a "motion" or "passage," and implies that the political subject only "receives its being from its relationship to a sovereignty incarnate in the person of the prince": "Montaigne and the Subject of Polity," in *Literary Theory/Renaissance Texts*, ed. Patricia Parker and David Quint (Baltimore, 1986), 115–49 (140, 137, 139–40). The essay appears, significantly revised, in Reiss's *Mirages of the Self: Patterns of Personhood in Ancient and Early Modern Europe* (Stanford, 2003), 440–68.
27. On the "mobile, elastic and volatile" qualities of identifications, see Diana Fuss's indispensable *Identification Papers* (New York, 1995), 8.
28. A. C. Spearing, *Medieval to Renaissance in English Poetry* (Cambridge, 1985), 59–120 (esp. 105–10).
29. David Lawton, "Dullness and the Fifteenth Century," *ELH* 54 (1987), 761–99.
30. On Hoccleve, see Ethan Knapp, *The Bureaucratic Muse: Thomas Hoccleve and the Literature of Late Medieval England* (University Park, PA, 2001). On Lydgate, see most recently the essays in *John Lydgate: Poetry, Culture and Lancastrian England*, ed. James Simpson and Larry Scanlon (Notre Dame, 2006) and Nigel Mortimer, *John Lydgate's Fall of Princes: Narrative Tragedy in its Literary and Political Contexts* (Oxford, 2005).
31. This has been contended by Lee Patterson: see "Making Identities in Fifteenth-Century England: Henry V and John Lydgate," *New Historical Literary Study: Essays on Reproducing Texts, Representing History*, ed. Jeffrey N. Cox and Larry J. Reynolds (Princeton, 1993), 69–107, and "'What is Me?': Self and Society in the Poetry of Thomas Hoccleve," *Studies in the Age of Chaucer* 23 (2001), 437–70. Patterson finds similar tendencies at work in the Ricardian court, where they are seen as constitutive of the "literary" itself: "Court Politics and the Invention of Literature: The Case of Sir John Clanvowe," *Culture and History, 1350–1600: Essays on English Communities, Identities and Writing*, ed. David Aers (Detroit, 1992), 7–42. See too Scott-Morgan Straker, "Rivalry and Reciprocity in Lydgate's *Troy Book*," *New Medieval Literatures* 3 (1999), 119–47; Sarah Tolmie, "The *Prive Scilence* of Thomas Hoccleve," *SAC* 22 (2000), 281–309; Nicholas Perkins, *Hoccleve's "Regiment of Princes": Counsel and Constraint* (Cambridge, 2001).
32. For alternative views, see Derek Pearsall, "Hoccleve's *Regiment of Princes*: The Poetics of Royal Self-Representation," *Speculum* 69 (1994), 386–410; Larry Scanlon,

Narrative, Authority, and Power: The Medieval Exemplum and the Chaucerian Tradition (Cambridge, 1994), 298–350. Maura Nolan describes a Lydgate who emerges "less as a subject, and more as an aesthetic function": *John Lydgate and the Making of Public Culture* (Cambridge, 2005), 10–14, and "'Now wo, now gladnesse': Ovidianism in *The Fall of Princes*," *ELH* 71 (2004), 531–58 (536).

33. Paul Strohm, *England's Empty Throne: Usurpation and the Language of Legitimation 1399–1422* (New Haven, 1998), 194–95.
34. Robert Meyer-Lee, *Poets and Power from Chaucer to Wyatt* (Cambridge, 2007).
35. R. F. Yeager, *John Gower's Poetic: The Search for a New Arion* (Cambridge, 1990), 234. See too J. A. Burrow, "The Portrayal of Amans in *Confessio Amantis*," *Gower's Confessio Amantis: Responses and Reassessments*, ed. A. J. Minnis (Cambridge, 1983), 5–24; Zeeman, "Verse of Courtly Love."
36. *The English Works of John Gower*, ed. G. C. Macaulay, 2 vols., EETS ES 81, 82 (London, 1900–01). All further references to the *Confessio Amantis* are to this edition, and are by book and line number.
37. For recent treatments, see Sian Êchard, "Pre-Texts: Tables of Contents and the Reading of John Gower's *Confessio Amantis*," *Medium Ævum* 66 (1997), 270–87; Frank Grady, "Gower's Boat, Richard's Barge, and the True Story of the *Confessio Amantis*: Text and Gloss," *Texas Studies in Literature and Language* 44 (2002), 1–15.
38. For Chaucer's importance as vernacular authority in Hoccleve's poem, see Larry Scanlon, "The King's Two Voices: Narrative and Power in Hoccleve's *The Regement of Princes*," *Literary Practice and Social Change in Britain, 1380–1530*, ed. Lee Patterson (Berkeley, 1990), 210–47 (226, 233–42). On the Lancastrian promotion of the English language, see John H. Fisher, *The Emergence of Standard English* (Lexington, 1996), 16–35, and Malcolm Richardson, "Henry V, the English Chancery, and Chancery English," *Speculum* 55 (1980), 726–50. On the "Lancastrian poetics" of literature and nation, see Green, *Poets and Princepleasers*, 187–90; Paul Strohm, "Saving the Appearances: Chaucer's 'Purse' and the Fabrication of the Lancastrian Claim," *Hochon's Arrow: The Social Imagination of Fourteenth-Century Texts* (Princeton, 1992), 75–94, and *England's Empty Throne*.
39. John Lydgate, *The Fall of Princes*, ed. Henry Bergen, 4 vols., EETS ES 121–24 (London, 1924–27). All references are to this edition, and are by book and line number.
40. The most noteworthy instance appears in BL MS Additional 29729, fol. 177v:

> his nobles bene spent / I leue ychon
> and eke his shylinges nyghe by
> his thred bare coule / woll not ly
> ellas ye lordis / why nill ye se
> and reward his pouerte   (40–44)

This is cited in Eleanor Prescott Hammond, ed., *English Verse Between Chaucer and Surrey* (Durham, 1927). On Shirley, see Margaret Connolly, *John Shirley: Book Production and the Noble Household in Fifteenth-Century England* (Aldershot, 1998).

41. *Boethius: De consolatione philosophiae: Translated by John Walton*, ed. Mark Science, EETS OS 170 (London, 1927). All references are given by stanza number, following the editor's practice.
42. Ian R. Johnson notes that Walton finds a "violence" in his subordination to a female patron and her "unnatural" demand for philosophy: *The Idea of the Vernacular: An Anthology of Middle English Literary Theory, 1280–1520*, ed. Jocelyn Wogan-Browne, Nicholas Watson, Andrew Taylor and Ruth Evans (University Park, 1999), 37 n. 4. On Walton and Chaucer, see Johnson, "Walton's Sapient Orpheus," *The Medieval Boethius: Studies in the Vernacular Translations of "De consolatione philosophiae"*, ed. A. J. Minnis (Cambridge, 1987), 139–68.
43. John Lydgate and Benet Burgh, *Secrees of Olde Philisoffres*, ed. R. Steele, EETS ES 66 (London, 1894). All references are to this edition. Pearsall comments that "Here, we are led to believe, the pen slipped limply from [Lydgate's] fingers, and the aged monk slumped to the floor": *John Lydgate* (London, 1970), 297.
44. Burgh, with a wit not usually allowed him, conflates the attendant dwarf of romance with Bernard of Chartres's well-known remark that medieval authors were dwarves standing on the shoulders of giants, the classical ancients: cited in John of Salisbury, *Metalogicon*, ed. J. B. Hall, Corpus Christianorum Continuatio Mediaevalis XCVIII, III.4 (Turnhout, 1991). On this trope, see Jacqueline T. Miller, *Poetic License: Authority and Authorship in Medieval and Renaissance Contexts* (Oxford, 1986), 9–15.
45. J. Laplanche and J.-B. Pontalis, *The Language of Psycho-Analysis*, trans. D. Nicholson-Smith (London, 1988), 205.
46. See Green, *Poets and Princepleasers*, 203–05. On Renaissance *imitatio* and some of its major precursors, see Thomas M. Greene, *The Light in Troy: Imitation and Discovery in Renaissance Poetry* (New Haven, 1982).
47. Thus in the *Troy Book*, Lydgate claims to "obeie with-oute variaunce" the command of Henry Prince of Wales, "Whiche hath desire, sothly for to seyn, / Of verray knyʒthod to remembre ageyn / The worthynes." This obedient vessel of his lord's desire and memory is literally self-effacing, both before his Lancastrian lord ("I wante connyng his hiʒe renoun tendite") and Chaucer, whose authority enables Lydgate's text. See Lydgate's *Troy Book*, ed. Henry Bergen, 4 vols., EETS ES 97, 103, 106, 126 (London, 1906–35), I, 75–77, 92, 3527–30.
48. All quotations from Chaucer's work are from *The Riverside Chaucer*, ed. Larry D. Benson et al., 3rd edn. (Boston, 1987). Quotations from the *Canterbury Tales (CantT)* are by group and line number.
49. John Cooper Mendenhall, *Aureate Terms: A Study in the Literary Diction of the Fifteenth Century* (Lancaster, 1919), 61–67.
50. "Even when they ... are oriented towards non-material stakes that are not easily quantified, as in 'pre-capitalist' societies or in the cultural sphere of capitalist societies, practices never cease to comply with an economic logic": Pierre Bourdieu, *The Logic of Practice*, trans. Richard Nice (Cambridge, MA, 1990), 122.

51. David Starkey's comments reveal the element of "symbolic capital" in Lydgate's amplification, noting its analogues: "as adjectives and figures of speech come cheap in comparison with gold plate (or even with well-carved stone), considerations of prudence put far less of a brake on the tendency to extravagance in literature than they did in most other areas of artistic activity." "The Age of the Household: Politics, Society and the Arts *c.* 1350–*c.* 1550," *The Later Middle Ages*, ed. Stephen Medcalf (New York, 1981), 225–90 (260).
52. Antony J. Hasler, "Hoccleve's Unregimented Body," *Paragraph* 13 (1990), 164–83 (177).
53. R. James Goldstein, *The Matter of Scotland: Historical Narrative in Medieval Scotland* (Lincoln, 1993), 239.
54. All references are to Hary, *Wallace*, ed. Matthew P. McDiarmid, 2 vols., STS 4th series 4, 5 (1968).
55. Norman Macdougall, *James III: A Political Study* (Edinburgh, 1982), 117–18.
56. Mapstone, "Was there a Court Literature?," 410–22.
57. On Chaucer's audience, see Strohm, *Social Chaucer*, 47–83.
58. George Ashby, *Works*, ed. Mary Bateson, EETS ES 76 (London, 1899), *Dicta & Opiniones Diversorum Philosophorum*, 911–17. All references to Ashby's works are to this edition, and take the form of the name of the relevant work followed by line numbers. To clarify Ashby's handling of the maxim, some contextual information may be helpful. Ashby's "Dicta" gathers and translates a small number of the many maxims in the *Liber Philosophorum Moralium Antiquorum*. This collection of *sententiae*, first compiled in Arabic, was subsequently translated into Spanish, and from Spanish into Latin: Ezio Franceschini, "Il '*Liber Philosophorum Moralium Antiquorum*,'" *Atti della Reale Accademia Nazionale dei Lincei*, anno CCCXXVII, 6th series, Memorie della Classe di Scienze Morali, Storiche e Filologiche 3 (1930), 354–99. A French translation of the Latin *Liber* was made by Guillaume de Tignonville towards the end of the fourteenth century, and a number of English prose translations of the *Liber* are based on de Tignonville's: see Curt F. Bühler, ed., *The Dicts and Sayings of the Philosophers: The Translations made by Stephen Scrope, William Worcester and an Anonymous Translator*, EETS OS 211 (London, 1941), ix–xiii. For each maxim that he translates, Ashby gives the Latin first, following it with his own version. In the *sententia* cited in the text, he omits the Latin's interesting implication of a mutual play of looks between servant and master. The servant must not inadvertently permit the master to perceive him as aspiring to an outward as well as inward "equality": "cum servies alicui domino, noli fieri equalis sibi nisi in fide, sensu et patiencia; in aliis vero nequaquam, *cavens ne te aspiciat equalem* in statu aut vestitu vel in suis deliciis" ["when you serve any master, do not become his equal except in faith, wit and patience: in no other way do so, *taking care lest he see you as his equal* in standing, dress or in his pleasures"] (emphases mine). (I cite the *Liber* in the edition by Franceschini, "Il 'Liber philosophorum moralium antiquorum': Testo critico," *Atti del Reale Istituto Veneto di Scienze, Lettere ed Arti* 91.1, pt. 2 [1931–32], 393–597 [472–73]; the Latin original that heads Ashby's English

translation, Cambridge University Library MS Mm.4.42, fols. 19r–84r, differs from this in several minor details, but the sense is not altered.) De Tignonville's version places still more emphasis on the servant's self-fashioning under the master's eye: instead of "noli fieri equalis sibi," it has "quant tu serviras aucun seigneur *garde que tu ne te monstres son pareil* [take care that you do not show yourself his equal] fors en .iii. choses cestassavoir en foy en sens & en pacience. Et garde sur toutes choses quil ne te appercoyve vouloir estre pareil en estat aluy en vestemens & en delices" (emphases mine). For de Tignonville's version, I have consulted BL MS Royal 19. A. viii, fol. 32r and BL MS Royal 19. B. iv, fol. 34r; here I cite the former.

59. John Scattergood, "Fashion and Morality in the Late Middle Ages," *England in the Fifteenth Century: Proceedings of the 1986 Harlaxton Symposium*, ed. Daniel Williams (Woodbridge, 1987), 255–72 (259–64).

60. Freud, *Standard Edition*, XIX, 1–66 (34); on the super-ego in this essay, indistinguishable from the ego-ideal, "formed through identification with the parents as a corollary of the decline of the Oedipus complex," and "combin[ing] the functions of prohibition and ideal," see Laplanche and Pontalis, *Language of Psycho-Analysis*, 144–45.

61. Louise Olga Fradenburg, *City, Marriage, Tournament: Arts of Rule in Late Medieval Scotland* (Madison, WI, 1991), 68; see canonically Ernst H. Kantorowicz, *The King's Two Bodies: A Study in Medieval Political Theology* (Princeton, 1957).

62. See Fradenburg's discussion of the use of "communitarian experience" for this purpose in *City, Marriage, Tournament*, 73–74. Fradenburg here draws on Victor Turner, *The Ritual Process: Structure and Anti-Structure* (1969; Ithaca, 1977), 106–07.

63. The proverb is added by Ashby to the adage from the *Liber* translated at this point, in the form "Qualis rex, talis populus": Curt F. Bühler, "The *Liber de dictis philosophorum antiquorum* and Common Proverbs in George Ashby's Poems," *PMLA* 65 (1950), 282–89 (285–86). It was widespread in the Middle Ages in the form "Qualis rex, talis grex": Hans Walther, *Proverbia Sententiaeque Latinitatis Medii Aevi*, 9 vols. (Göttingen, 1963), IV, no. 23250, and IX, 39840 a17a.

64. Daniel Poirion, *Le Poète et le prince: l'évolution du lyrisme courtois de Guillaume de Machaut à Charles d'Orleans* (Paris, 1965), 11.

65. Sir Gilbert Hay, *The Buik of King Alexander the Conquerour*, ed. John Cartwright, 3 vols., STS 4th series 16 (1986), vol. II, textual introduction, text, lines 1–9264; 18 (1990), vol. III, text, lines 9265–19369; vol. I (forthcoming), general introduction, commentary and glossary. I cite here vol. III.

66. On this tradition see Mario Grignaschi, "L' Origine et les métamorphoses du 'Sirr-al-'asrâr'" and "La Diffusion du *Secretum secretorum ('Sirr-al-asrâr')* dans l'Europe occidentale," *Archives d'Histoire Doctrinale et Littéraire du Moyen Âge* 43 (1976), 7–112 and 47 (1980), 7–70; Wilhelm Kleineke, *Englische Fürstenspiegel vom Policraticus Johanns von Salisbury bis zum Basilikon Doron König Jakobs I* (Halle, 1937); Mahmoud Manzalaoui, "The *Secreta secretorum*:

The Medieval European Version of 'Kitab Sirr-ul-Asrar,'" *Bulletin of the Faculty of Arts, University of Alexandria* 15 (1961), 83–107 (95). Recent perspectives are provided by Perkins, *Hoccleve's "Regiment of Princes"*, 93–99, and Judith Ferster, *Fictions of Advice: The Literature and Politics of Counsel in Late Medieval England* (Philadelphia, 1996).

67. In "The Advice to Princes Tradition in Scottish Literature, 1450–1500" (1986), Sally Mapstone notes the presence of a "moral and social fusion of thought," "the idea of kings as men and as kings" (116), in several advice texts of the period, and suggests that it connects, by way of the ideology of "common profit," with the tone and content of legislation produced at this time by the Scottish parliament (115).

68. Shakespeare, *Hamlet*, III, i, 61–62. On the special powers of the king's body politic, see Sir John Fortescue, *The Governance of England*, ed. Charles Plummer (Oxford, 1885), c.vi, 121: "the kyngis pover... is no poiar to mowe synne, and to do ylle, or to mowe to be seke, wex olde, or that a man may hurte hym self. Ffor all thes poiars comen of impotencie ... Wherfore the holy sprites and angels, that mey not synne, wex old, be seke, or hurte ham selff, haue more poiar than we, that mey harme owre selff with all thes defautes. So is the kynges power more ... "

69. Thomas Hoccleve, *The Regiment of Princes*, ed. Charles R. Blyth (Kalamazoo, 1999), 2027–28.

70. See David Aers, "A Whisper in the Ear of Early Modernists, or, Reflections on Literary Critics Writing the 'History of the Subject,'" *Culture and History 1350–1600: Essays on English Communities, Identities and Writing*, ed. David Aers (Detroit, 1992), 177–202; Lee Patterson, "On the Margin: Postmodernism, Ironic History, and Medieval Studies," *Speculum* 65 (1990), 87–108.

71. I do not here overlook the extent to which this self-scrutiny is already figured in other discourses, in particular those – in many ways cognate – of the confessional and penitential writing, and of the literature of *fin amour*. On the devotional self, see now Jennifer Bryan, *Looking Inward: Devotional Reading and the Private Self in Late Medieval England* (Philadelphia, 2008). Lee Patterson points out that "medieval anthropology defined the subject as desire ... as *amor*, an inward sense of insufficiency that drives the Christian self forward on its journey through the historical world": *Chaucer and the Subject of History* (London, 1991), 8.

72. Mikkel Borch-Jacobsen, *The Freudian Subject*, trans. Catherine Porter (Stanford, 1988), 21.

73. *A Familiar Dialogue of the Friend and the Fellow: A Translation of Alain Chartier's "Dialogus familiaris amici et sodalis,"* ed. Margaret S. Blayney, EETS OS 295 (Oxford, 1989), 21. For the original, see Pascale Bourgain-Hemeryck, ed., *Les Oeuvres latines d'Alain Chartier* (Paris, 1977), 245–325 (282).

74. Green, *Poets and Princepleasers*, 12, 203.

75. Poirion, *Poète et le prince*, 175–77.

76. Zumthor writes that "The poet's role on the court stage is to be the delegate of the prince himself: this act of delegation can be revoked at any time but,

temporarily at least, it clothes the poet in habits of such pomp that no one inquires about the person beneath them. A costume of language is made out of the fabric of a protocol woven from ancient, exhausted feudal traditions ... Although prisoners of courts where they were, for better or worse, dependents, these men had one place in which they could hide from this alienation – the inside of the poetic universe, i.e., the act of constituting the text." See "The Great Game of Rhetoric," trans. Annette and Edward Tomarken, *New Literary History* 12 (1981), 493–508 (495, 507). For the original, see *Le Masque et la lumière: la poétique des grands rhétoriqueurs* (Paris, 1978), 48–49, 54.

77. See "The Manciple's Servant Tongue: Politics and Poetry in the *Canterbury Tales*," *ELH* 82 (1985), 85–118 (91). As Fradenburg points out, the ambiguity is nicely caught in Lydgate's admonition that "prayer of princes is a commaundement. See "Isopes Fabules," *The Minor Poems of John Lydgate*, ed. Henry Noble MacCracken, 2 vols., EETS ES 107, OS 192 (London, 1911, 1934), 2 (813).

78. Louise O. Fradenburg, "Spectacular Fictions: The Body Politic in Chaucer and Dunbar," *Poetics Today* 5 (1984), 493–517 (516). The phrase "the exigencies of the political" is cited from Zumthor, "Great Game of Rhetoric" (496). The original has "le politique": *Le Masque et la lumière*, 52. Zumthor's book along with Poirion's (see notes 64 and 75, above) remain important resources; see also Alexandre Leupin, "The Powerlessness of Writing: Guillaume de Machaut, the Gorgon and *Ordenance*," *Yale French Studies* 70 (1986), 127–49.

79. Lacan, "Aggressiveness in Psychoanalysis," *Ecrits*, 82–101 (92–93).

80. *Fifteenth-Century English Translations of Alain Chartier's "Le Traité de l'espérance" and "Le Quadrilogue invectif*," ed. Margaret S. Blayney, 2 vols., EETS OS 270, 281 (Oxford, 1974, 1980), 1, 38. For the original, see Alain Chartier, *Le Livre de l'espérance*, ed. François Rouy (Paris, 1989), 45.

81. Ranald Nicholson, *Scotland: The Later Middle Ages* (Edinburgh, 1974), 575.

82. Leslie J. Macfarlane, *William Elphinstone and the Kingdom of Scotland: The Struggle for Order* (Aberdeen, 1985), 235, whose discussion the remainder of this paragraph follows.

83. Ibid.

84. Elton, "Tudor Government"; David Starkey, "Intimacy and Innovation: The Rise of the Privy Chamber, 1485–1547," *The English Court: From the Wars of the Roses to the Civil War*, ed. David Starkey et al. (London, 1987), 71–118. Recent work has pointed to the absolutist proclivities even of the earlier Tudors: T. F. Mayer, "Tournai and Tyranny: Imperial Kingship and Critical Humanism," *Historical Journal* 34 (1991), 257–77. Mayer argues that Henry VIII's maneuverings over the occupation of Tournai between 1513 and 1519 were in fact proto-absolutist, and refers this in part to "Henry's taste for French models" of sovereignty. Mayer suggests that he was "following the example of his own father, who probably drew heavily on his Breton experience in shaping his 'new monarchy'" (269). On Henry VII's time in Brittany, see Anthony Goodman, "Henry VII and Christian Renewal," *Studies in Church History* 17 (1981), 115–25, who speaks of Henry VII's "admiration for the French 'royal religion'" (121). For opposing viewpoints in the debate as to whether Henry VII's

accession inaugurated a new style of rule, see *The Reign of Henry VII: Proceedings of the 1993 Harlaxton Symposium*, ed. Benjamin Thompson (Stamford, 1995), especially Christine Carpenter, "Henry VII and the English Polity" (11–30) and John Watts, "'A New Ffundacion of is Crowne': Monarchy in the Age of Henry VII," 31–53. For alignment of Henry VII's reign with other European patterns of nascent absolutism, see Perry Anderson, *Lineages of the Absolutist State* (London, 1974), 22, 118–28.

85. Discussion in the last decades was stimulated by Elton's privileging of Thomas Cromwell's bureaucratizing work of the 1530s, the so-called "Tudor Revolution in Government": see Elton's book of that name (Cambridge, 1953). For a useful overview of responses to Elton, see *Political Thought and the Tudor Commonwealth: Deep Structure, Discourse and Disguise*, ed. Paul A. Fideler and T. F. Mayer (London, 1992), 1–18.
86. William Kuskin, *Symbolic Caxton: Literary Culture and Print Capitalism* (Notre Dame, 2008), and the essays edited by Kuskin in *Caxton's Trace: Studies in the History of English Printing* (Notre Dame, 2006).
87. Harry Berger, Jnr., "Bodies and Texts," *Representations* 17 (1987), 144–66 (164) repr. in *Situated Utterances: Texts, Bodies, and Cultural Representations* (New York, 2005), 99–128.
88. Ibid., 149.

1 BEGINNINGS: ANDRÉ'S *VITA HENRICI SEPTIMI* AND DUNBAR'S AUREATE ALLEGORIES

1. On humanism as "gesture" or "activity" rather than identity, see David R. Carlson, *English Humanist Books: Writers and Patrons, Manuscript and Print, 1475–1525* (Toronto, 1993), 5; Daniel Wakelin, *Humanism, Reading and English Literature 1430–1530* (Oxford, 2007), 3–9.
2. See David R. Carlson, "Politicizing Tudor Court Literature: Gaguin's Embassy and Henry VII's Humanists' Response," *Studies in Philology* 85 (1988), 279–304, which includes Gaguin's invective and the responses; John M. Currin, "Persuasions to Peace: the Luxembourg-Marigny-Gaguin Embassy and the State of Anglo-French Relations," *English Historical Review* 113 (1998), 882–904 (899–903).
3. Roberto Weiss, *Humanism in England During the Fifteenth Century*, 3rd edn. (1941; Oxford, 1967).
4. *Memorials of King Henry the Seventh*, ed. James Gairdner, Rerum Britannicarum Medii Aevi Scriptores (Rolls Series) 10 (London, 1858), 56. All translations of André, Gigli and Carmeliano are my own, though in the current passage I have benefited from Carlson's at "Politicizing," 287. On Carmeliano, Gigli and Vitelli, see most recently the *DNB* entries by J. B. Trapp.
5. Stephen Hawes, *The Comfort of Louers*, in *The Minor Poems*, ed. Florence W. Gluck and Alice B. Morgan, EETS OS 271 (Oxford, 1974), 19–21. All further references to Hawes's poems other than *The Pastime of Pleasure* are to this edition.
6. Green, *Poets and Princepleasers*, 209. Meyer-Lee reads André's laureate presence as decisive for the practice of other poets: *Poets and Power*, 174–76.

7. André is so described in Bibliothèque Nationale MS Arsenal 418, fol. v: cited in William Nelson, *John Skelton, Laureate* (New York, 1939), 25 note 46. On the post's possible Burgundian origins, see Gordon Kipling, "Henry VII and the Origins of Tudor Patronage," *Patronage in the Renaissance*, ed. Guy Fitch Lytle and Stephen Orgel (Princeton, 1981), 117–64 (131).
8. On "the derogatory attitude toward the vernacular characteristic of this period," see Richard Foster Jones, *The Triumph of the English Language* (Stanford, 1953), 3–31 (10). For an admirably full account of the complexities surrounding the vernacular and various Latinities, see the essays and material in Wogan–Browne et al., *Idea of the Vernacular*.
9. See A. F. Pollard, *The Reign of Henry VII from Contemporary Sources*, 3 vols. (1913–14; rpt. New York, 1967), II, 233–34; Henry R. Plomer, "Bibliographical Notes from the Privy Purse Expenses of King Henry the Seventh," *The Library* 3rd series 4 (1913), 291–305.
10. David R. Carlson, "The Writings of Bernard André (*c*. 1450–*c*. 1522)," *Renaissance Studies* 12 (1998), 229–50.
11. For Bourdieu, the symbolic forms – including language – which receive the greatest value and profit are those most unequally distributed, in two senses: the conditions of acquiring them and the capacity to reproduce them are restricted, and the expressions themselves are relatively rare on the "markets" where they appear: *Language and Symbolic Power*, 55–56.
12. David R. Carlson, "The 'Opicius' Poems (British Library, Cotton Vespasian B.iv) and the Humanist Anti-Literature in Early Tudor England," *Renaissance Quarterly* 55 (2002), 869–903 (880).
13. David R. Carlson, "King Arthur and Court Poems for the Birth of Arthur Tudor in 1486," *Humanistica Lovaniensia* 36 (1987), 147–83 (156, 158–59, 166). References to Gigli's *Genethliacon* and Carmeliano's *Suasoria Laeticiae* are to the edited texts of the poems appended by Carlson to this article.
14. Fradenburg, *City, Marriage, Tournament*, 74–83.
15. Temporary obstacles to the marriage included not only the parties' relationship in the fourth degree of kinship, and perhaps also affinity, but also – highly problematically – the fact that Richard III's parliament had declared Elizabeth illegitimate: S. B. Chrimes, *Henry VII*, 2nd edn., introduced by G.W. Bernard (1972; New Haven, 1999), 65–66.
16. A point I make cautiously, and in full cognizance of Naomi Schor's powerful depiction of the "catastrophic diminution" that is evaded by the metaphorization of blindness and the figure of the "blind person as *seer*": "Blindness as Metaphor," *differences* 11 (1999), 76–105 (88, 103).
17. On fantasy's tendency to "create what it purports to conceal," see Slavoj Žižek, *The Plague of Fantasies* (London, 1997), 7.
18. BL Cotton MS Domitian A.xviii, fols. 126r–228r; described in Gairdner, pp. xiii–vi. Gairdner thinks it likely, and I agree, that André "dictated his compositions to an amanuensis" (xiii). On the immediate political imperatives behind the *Vita*, see Daniel Hobbins, "The Poet Laureate as Stabilizer: Bernard André

and the *Vita Regis Henrici Septimi*," *Proceedings of the Medieval Association of the Midwest* 4 (1997), 61–79.
19. Carlson, *English Humanist Books*, 64.
20. On André's Sallustian techniques, see C. W. T. Blackwell, "Humanism and Politics in English Royal Biography: The Use of Cicero, Plutarch and Sallust in the *Vita Henrici Quinti* (1438) by Titus Livius de Frulovisi and the *Vita Henrici Septimi* (1500–03) by Bernard André," *Acta Conventus Neo-Latini Sanctandreani*, ed. I. D. McFarlane, Medieval and Renaissance Texts and Studies 38 (Binghamton, 1986), 431–40 (438).
21. Ned Lukacher, *Primal Scenes: Literature, Philosophy, Psychoanalysis* (Ithaca, 1986), 24. See Fradenburg, *City, Marriage, Tournament*, 9; Paul Strohm, *Theory and the Premodern Text* (Minneapolis, 2000), 110.
22. Patricia Parker, "Virile Style," *Premodern Sexualities*, ed. Louise Fradenburg and Carla Freccero (New York, 1996), 201–22 (201).
23. Jacques Derrida, reading Freud, claims that the substitutive logic of dissemination "entrains" castration in "the affirmation of ... nonorigin, the remarkable empty locus of a hundred blanks no meaning can be ascribed to": *Dissemination*, trans. Barbara Johnson (Chicago, 1981), 268 note 67. We might note here that the gaps in the MS of the *Vita* connote other breaks in lineal transmission. André was tutor to Prince Arthur, Henry's heir, whose death in 1502 may have dealt a political and personal blow to the poet's hopes: Daniel Hobbins, "Arsenal MS 360 as a Witness to the Career and Writings of Bernard André," *Humanistica Lovaniensa* 50 (2001), 161–98 (175).
24. At fol. 163r. Gairdner, xv, suggests that André's scribes "had little of the author's scholarship."
25. Fradenburg, *City, Marriage, Tournament*: "sovereignty promises a fantastic, a perfect but imaginary closure to the very yearning it brings into being: this is 'sovereign love'" (71). The narratives of sovereign love also inform Sarah M. Dunnigan, *Eros and Poetry at the Courts of Mary Queen of Scots and James VI* (Basingstoke, 2002).
26. Gabrielle Spiegel, *Romancing the Past: The Rise of Vernacular Prose Historiography in Thirteenth-Century France* (Berkeley, 1993). The "oppositional" Lucan's influence is reviewed by Edward Paleit, "Lucan in the Renaissance, Pre-1625: An Introduction," *Literature Compass* 1 (2005).
27. Carlson, "'Opicius' Poems," 879–80.
28. Walter Benjamin, "Theses on the Philosophy of History," *Illuminations*, ed. and intro. Hannah Arendt, trans. Harry Zohn (New York, 1992), 245–55 (253).
29. *The Testament of the Papyngo*, in Sir David Lyndsay, *Selected Poems*, ed. Janet Hadley Williams (Glasgow, 2000), lines 476–78.
30. Norman Macdougall, *James IV* (Edinburgh, 1989), 250; that progress is most memorably narrated in the "Fyancells of Margaret, eldest Daughter of King Henry VIIth to James King of Scotland," written by John Younge, Somerset Herald, and printed in John Leland, *De rebus Britannicis collectanea*, 6 vols. (London, 1770), IV, 258–300. On earlier events, see Nicholson, *Scotland*, 549–55. For a brilliant analysis of the symbolism of the marriage and

Dunbar's poem, to which my own discussion is much indebted, see Fradenburg, *City, Marriage, Tournament*, 67–149.

31. The poem's unique text, in the Bannatyne MS, has no title; it owes the one by which it is generally known to Allan Ramsay, who printed it in *The Ever Green* in 1724.
32. Spearing, *Medieval to Renaissance*, 212; see, too, Deanna Delmar Evans, "Ambivalent Artifice in Dunbar's *The Thrissill and the Rois*," *Studies in Scottish Literature* 22 (1987), 95–105 (104).
33. All quotations from Dunbar are from William Dunbar, *The Poems of William Dunbar*, ed. Priscilla Bawcutt, 2 vols. (Glasgow, 1998), and are signalled by B and the poem's number in the edition.
34. James I of Scotland, *The Kingis Quair*, ed. John Norton-Smith (Oxford, 1971), lines 372–413.
35. David F. Hult, *Self-Fulfilling Prophecies: Readership and Authority in the First Roman de la Rose* (Cambridge, 1986), 252.
36. The term "aureate," introduced by Lydgate, has a wealth of connotation in fifteenth-century poetry, which has tended critically to translate into what Bawcutt calls "conceptual vagueness": *Dunbar the Makar* (Oxford, 1992), 353. John Norton-Smith, more careful than most, well describes its movement between the metaphoric fields of "rhetorical skill," "the spoken sound of eloquent language" and "rhetorical skill giving rise to eloquence": John Lydgate, *Poems*, ed. John Norton-Smith (Oxford, 1966), 192–95. Both Meyer-Lee (*Poets and Power*, 54–61) and Lois Ebin address the provenance of the term "aureate licour," marking the literal "influence" of poetic inspiration, in Lydgate's *Balade in Commendation of Our Lady* (line 13): Ebin, *Illuminator, Makar, Vates: Visions of Poetry in the Fifteenth Century* (Lincoln, 1988), 27. Norton-Smith, like Mendenhall's early study, limits the term's critical range to diction in some degree Latinate, an emphasis with which I concur. See, too, Arne Zettersten, "On the Aureate Diction of William Dunbar," *Essays Presented to Knud Schibsbye*, ed. Michael Chesnutt et al. (Copenhagen, 1979), 51–68. Dunbar retains the crucial association of poetic inspiration with *vocal* presence in his own, highly aureate and vocative Marian lyric "Hale, sterne superne" (B16), just as the metonymic "sugurit lippis and tongis aureate" of *The Goldyn Targe* (line 263) recall Lydgate (see Ebin, *Illuminator*, 28). In the latter case, however, Dunbar, as we shall see, treats such vocal immediacy as lost, available only to a kind of *post hoc* reconstruction.
37. R. J. Lyall, "The Stylistic Relationship between Dunbar and Douglas," *William Dunbar, the "Nobill Poyet": Essays in Honour of Priscilla Bawcutt*, ed. Sally Mapstone (East Linton, 2001), 69–84.
38. Pamela M. King, "Dunbar's *The Golden Targe*: A Chaucerian Masque," *Studies in Scottish Literature* 19 (1984), 115–31 (127). See, too, Frank Shuffleton, "An Imperial Flower: Dunbar's *The Goldyn Targe* and the Court Life of James IV of Scotland," *Studies in Philology* 72 (1975), 193–207.
39. Jacques Lacan, "The Instance of the Letter in the Unconscious," *Écrits: The First Complete Edition in English*, trans. Bruce Fink in collaboration with Héloïse Fink and Russell Grigg (New York, 2006), 412–41 (419).

40. "First inspect the mind of a word, and afterwards its face": Geoffrey of Vinsauf, *Poetria Nova*, in Ernest Gallo (ed. and trans.), *The "Poetria Nova" and its Sources in Early Rhetorical Doctrine* (The Hague, 1971), lines 744–45. All references to the *Poetria Nova* are to this edition. See, too, Richard Finkelstein, "Amplification in William Dunbar's Aureate Poetry," *Scottish Literary Journal* 13 (1986), 5–15; Isabel Hyde, "Primary Sources and Associations of Dunbar's Aureate Imagery," *MLR* 51 (1956), 481–92; Ebin, *Illuminator*, 75–79.
41. David Lawton, *Chaucer's Narrators* (Cambridge, 1985), 132.
42. Noted, too, by A.C. Spearing in *Medieval Poet as Voyeur: Looking and Listening in Medieval Love-Narratives* (Cambridge, 1993), who sees here a "humanization and sexualization" of the landscape (246). We might point out that Dunbar's *translationes* have become Matthew of Vendôme's "reversible" figures: "Ars Versificatoria," in *Les Arts poétiques du XIIe et du XIIIe siecle: recherches et documents sur la technique littéraire du moyen âge*, ed. Edmond Faral (Paris, 1924), 173.
43. Chrétien de Troyes, *Le Chevalier de la Charrette ou Le Roman de Lancelot*, ed. Charles Méla (Paris, 1992), lines 1457–99.
44. Priscilla Bawcutt, note to lines 145 ff., observes Presence's relative rarity among the persons of medieval love-allegory.
45. Christopher Pye, *The Regal Phantasm: Shakespeare and the Politics of Spectacle* (New York, 1990), 92.
46. *DOST* s.v. desolat, 1 (a).
47. The connections between the exile mapped by the Fall – "the *persona* banished from his proper place to an alien one" – and the transfer and displacement narrated by classical theories of metaphor are examined in Margaret W. Ferguson's excellent "Saint Augustine's Region of Unlikeness: The Crossing of Exile and Language," *Georgia Review* 29 (1975), 842–64 (842).
48. Nicolette Zeeman, "The Idol of the Text," *Images, Idolatry, and Iconoclasm in Late Medieval England: Textuality and the Visual Image*, ed. Jeremy Dimmick, James Simpson and Nicolette Zeeman (Oxford, 2002), 44.
49. Sarah Tolmie notes that "a usurper re-creates the originary moment of a monarchy," since "The regal abstractions that accompany dynastic rupture point to the real foundation of royal power in contingent, violent pre-eminence and to the massive cultural project of its mystification into the guarantee of law and order." "Kingmaking: The Historiography of Bruce and Lancaster in Royal Biography, Ceremonial and Document" (1998), 4.
50. On its history, see Priscilla Bawcutt, "Dunbar's use of the Symbolic Lion and Thistle," *Cosmos* 2 (1986), 83–97 (89–94).
51. Fradenburg, *City, Marriage, Tournament*, 142–43.
52. D. Vance Smith, *Arts of Possession: The Middle English Household Imaginary* (Minneapolis, 2003), 199, 202.
53. Joanna Martin reads *The Thrissill* in this light, associating it with "This hindir nycht in Dumfermeling" (B76) and "Madam, ȝour men said thai wald ryd" (B30), poems which evoke the sexual undercurrents of the Stewart court: *Kingship and Love in Scottish Poetry, 1424–1540* (Aldershot, 2008), 154–59.

54. Roland Barthes, *Mythologies*, trans. Annette Lavers (New York, 1972), 114–15.
55. We may compare Joan Copjec's account of the Lacanian gaze as the point "at which something appears to be *in*visible ... at the moment the gaze is discerned, the image, the entire visual field, takes on a terrifying alterity ... When you encounter the gaze of the Other, you meet not a seeing eye, but a blind one": *Read my Desire: Lacan against the Historicists* (Cambridge, MA, 1994), 34–36.
56. Jacques Lacan, *The Four Fundamental Concepts of Psycho-Analysis*, ed. Jacques-Alain Miller and trans. Alan Sheridan (London, 1977), 96.
57. Fradenburg, *City, Marriage, Tournament*, 146.
58. Smith, *Arts of Possession*, 201, citing the testimony of "John Suffolk le heraud" in the *Curia Militaris* trials (National Archives, PRO C 47/6/1 mem. 3). On heraldry at the Scottish court, see Fradenburg, *City, Marriage, Tournament*, 79–81; Carol Edington, *Court and Culture in Renaissance Scotland: Sir David Lindsay of the Mount* (Amherst, 1994), 26–32.

2 *THE BOWGE OF COURTE* AND THE BIRTH OF THE PARANOID SUBJECT

1. Nelson, *John Skelton*, 161–65.
2. See Lerer, *Chaucer*, 19–56, 147–208; Meyer-Lee, *Poems and Power*; and on the difficult relation between laureate and *vates*, Griffiths, *John Skelton*, 25–37. On the relevant iconography, see Julie A. Smith, "The Poet Laureate as University Master: John Skelton's Woodcut Portrait," *Renaissance Rereadings: Intertext and Context*, ed. Maryanne Cline Horowitz et al. (Urbana, 1988), 159–83 (163–66). In addition to the works already cited, see on laureation, J. B. Trapp, "The Owl's Ivy and the Poet's Bays," *Journal of the Warburg and Courtauld Institutes* 21 (1958), 227–55, and "The Poet Laureate: Rome, *Renovatio* and *Translatio Imperii*," in P. A. Ramsey (ed.), *Rome in the Renaissance: The City and the Myth* (Binghamton, 1982), 93–130; Priscilla Bawcutt, "Henryson's 'Poeit of the Auld Fassoun,'" *Review of English Studies* n.s. 32 (1981), 429–34 (431–34); Green, *Poets and Princepleasers*, 209–11.
3. *Caxton's Own Prose*, ed. N. F. Blake (London, 1973), 80.
4. Wakelin, *Humanism*, 148–49.
5. Except where otherwise stated, all references to Skelton are to John Skelton, *The Complete English Poems*, ed. John Scattergood (Harmondsworth: Penguin, 1983).
6. Kuskin, *Symbolic Caxton*, 257–83 (270, 279).
7. Edwards, "From Manuscript to Print."
8. Lynn Enterline, "Embodied Voices: Petrarch Reading (Himself Reading) Ovid," *Desire in the Renaissance: Psychoanalysis and Literature*, ed. Valeria Finucci and Regina Schwartz (Princeton, 1994), 120–45 (121).
9. Antony J. Hasler, "Cultural Intersections: Skelton, Barclay, Hawes, André," *John Skelton and Early Modern Culture: Papers Honoring Robert S. Kinsman* (Tempe, 2008), 63–84 (69–71).

10. Roland Greene, "Calling Colin Clout," *Spenser Studies* 10 (1992), 229–44 (234).
11. A. W. Barnes, "Constructing the Sexual Subject of John Skelton," *ELH* 71 (2004), 29–51.
12. *The Bowge of Courte* was printed in 1499: Helen Stearns Sale, "The Date of Skelton's *Bowge of Court*," *MLN* 52 (1937), 572–74. Greg Walker has persuasively argued that it was written in that year: *John Skelton and the Politics of the 1520s* (Cambridge, 1988), 13. Melvin J. Tucker, "Setting in Skelton's *Bowge of Courte*: A Speculation," *ELN* 7 (1970), 168–75, and F. W. Brownlow, "The Date of *The Bowge of Courte* and Skelton's Authorship of 'A Lamentable of Kyng Edward the IIII,'" *ELN* 22 (1984), 12–20, claim an earlier date, chiefly on the basis of astrological interpretation of the opening chronographia. I concur with Walker: astrological dating, as he points out, is vulnerable to the charge that the chronographia is a thematic device, not an external pointer to actual time and date (11). Furthermore, the astrological evidence, as Tucker concedes, fits 1499 as well as 1480.
13. A. R. Heiserman, *Skelton and Satire* (Chicago, 1961), 63. On conventions, see John Scattergood, "Insecurity in Skelton's *Bowge of Courte*," *Genres, Themes and Images in English Literature from the Fourteenth to the Fifteenth Century. The J. A. W. Bennett Memorial Lectures, Perugia, 1986*, ed. Piero Boitani and Anna Torti (Tübingen, 1988), 186–209.
14. See Stanley Fish, *John Skelton's Poetry* (New Haven, 1965), 15; Alistair Fox, *Politics and Literature in the Reigns of Henry VII and Henry VIII* (Oxford, 1989), 26; and cf. Nelson, *John Skelton*, 81. Fox, *Politics and Literature*, deduces Skelton's own discontent with a court that he seems, for whatever reason, to have left soon after the poem was printed (26).
15. Sydney Anglo, "Ill of the Dead: The Posthumous Reputation of Henry VII," *Renaissance Studies* 1 (1987), 27–47.
16. Sir Robert Clifford, a probable informer, was paid £500: Ian Arthurson, "Espionage and Intelligence from the Wars of the Roses to the Reformation," *Nottingham Medieval Studies* 35 (1991), 134–54 (143–44). For Henry VII's reign, Arthurson points out that "In the main payments to spies are found before 1499" (144). On the Stanley conspiracy, see W. E. J. Archbold, "Sir William Stanley and Perkin Warbeck," *EHR* 14 (1899), 529–34.
17. David Starkey, *The Reign of Henry VIII: Personalities and Politics* (London, 1991), 25–26; on the Privy Chamber under Henry VII, see, too, David Starkey, "Intimacy and Innovation: The Rise of the Privy Chamber, 1485–1547," *The English Court*, ed. David Starkey et al. 72–76. S. J. Gunn, "The Courtiers of Henry VII" points out that a privy chamber is already mentioned in 1493: *EHR* 108 (1993), 23–49 (38 note 4). See, however, David Grummitt, "Household, Politics and Political Morality in the Reign of Henry VII," *Historical Research* 82 (2009), 393–411 (400 note 26), which re-evaluates the connection with the Stanley conspiracy.
18. *The Statutes of the Realm: Printed from Original Records and Authentic Manuscripts*, ed. A. Luders, Sir T. E. Tomlins and J. France et al., 11 vols. in 12 (London, 1810–28; rpt. London, 1963), II, 521–22; J. R. Lander, *Government and Community: England, 1450–1509* (Cambridge, MA, 1980), 334.

19. J. R. Lander, "Bonds, Coercion and Fear: Henry VII and the Peerage," *Crown and Nobility, 1450–1509* (London, 1976), 267–300 (282).
20. B. P. Wolffe, *The Crown Lands, 1461 to 1536: An Aspect of Yorkist and Early Tudor Government* (London, 1970), 51–75.
21. A view that has survived several vicissitudes: see David Grummitt, "Henry VII, Chamber Finance and the 'New Monarchy': Some New Evidence," *Historical Research* 72 (1999), 229–43 (241).
22. M. M. Condon, "Ruling Elites in the Reign of Henry VII," *Patronage, Pedigree and Power*, ed. Charles Ross (Phoenix Mill, 1979), 109–42 (127). Arthurson notes the intelligencing value of the royal Issue Books ("Espionage and Intelligence," 143).
23. David Starkey, "The King's Privy Chamber" (1973), 357–65.
24. Grummitt, "Household, Politics and Political Morality" which appeared too late for me to take full advantage of it, outlines a reading of Henry VII's court style close to the one I offer here, drawing on Paul Strohm, *Politique: Languages of Statecraft between Chaucer and Shakespeare* (Notre Dame, 2005). Grummitt tellingly notes that "the physical space of the court acted as a place where the king could keep watch on his subjects" (401). See, too, Hasler, "*Allegories of Authority*", 39–45. My own reading of Skelton's poem has been much assisted by Marc Shell's comments on power, secrecy and money: see *The Economy of Literature* (Baltimore, 1978), 13–48.
25. A copy of *L'Abuzé* was owned by Thomas Kebell, "kynges seriaunt at Lawe," who died in 1500: see Eric W. Ives, *The Common Lawyers of Pre-Reformation England: Thomas Kebell, A Case Study* (Cambridge, 1983), 367.
26. Stephen Dickey, "Seven come Eleven: Gambling for the Laurel in *The Bowge of Courte*," *Yearbook of English Studies* 22 (1992), 238–54 (253).
27. Pearsall, *John Lydgate*, 58–59.
28. Alongside these lines, Ebin cites the Prologue to *Isopes Fabules* as the only place in his output at which Lydgate "explicitly articulates the theory of poetry as a veil" ("Lydgate's Views," 96 note 37). This is not strictly accurate; Lydgate's reference here is to poetic fictions as "blak erþe" (22) concealing jewels, and "muscle shellys blake" (27) within which pearls lie: *The Minor Poems*, II. Lydgate also refers to "a manere / lyknesse and ffigure, / Dirk Outward / mysty for to see ... As it were seyd / in Enigmate" in the *Secrees of Olde Filisoffres* (729–30, 732). It remains true that the trope is rare in his work when compared to the lexis of illumination and aureation; see, too, Meyer-Lee, *Poets and Power*, 183.
29. *The Curial made by Maystere Alain Charretier*, ed. F. J. Furnivall, EETS ES 54 (London, 1888). All references are to this edition.
30. For a similar suggestion, see Spearing, *Medieval to Renaissance*, 265.
31. Augustine, *De doctrina Christiana* CCSL XXXII, ed. I. Martin (Turnhout, 1962), III, vii, ix.
32. *L'Abuzé en court*, ed. Roger Dubuis (Paris, 1973), 103, lines 41–42.
33. Ambrosius Theodosius Macrobius, *Commentarii in Somnium Scipionis*, ed. Iacobus Willis (Leipzig, 1970), 1.2.19–20. The translation is taken from W. H. Stahl (ed., intro. and trans.), commentary on the *Dream of Scipio* (New York, 1952), 87.

34. Hult, *Self-Fulfilling Prophecies*, 124.
35. R. Howard Bloch, "Silence and Holes: The *Roman de Silence* and the Art of the Trouvère," *Yale French Studies* 70 (1986), 81–99 (95).
36. On the fetish as compensation that ameliorates fear of castration, see Freud, *Standard Edition*, XXI, 147–57 (152–53).
37. Paul D. Psilos, "'Dulle' Drede and the Limits of Prudential Knowledge in Skelton's *Bowge of Court*," *Journal of Medieval and Renaissance Studies* 6 (1976), 297–317 (312).
38. "Youre key is mete for every lok, / Youre key is commen and hangyth owte; / Youre key is redy, we nede not knok / Nor stand long wrestyng ther aboute" (22–25): see John Skelton, *Poems*, ed. Robert S. Kinsman (Oxford, 1969), 137, note to lines 22 ff. The dreamer's state as he falls asleep in a named location recalls the "thoghty" Hoccleve at the beginning of the *Regement of Princes*. Dickey notes that the inn's name "is perfectly apt for the poem's allegory on all its levels, mercantile, courtly and metapoetic" (240 note 9).
39. Cf. Spearing, *Medieval to Renaissance*, 265.
40. Leigh Winser, "*The Bowge of Courte*: Drama Doubling as Dream," *English Literary Renaissance* 6 (1976), 3–39, suggests that *The Bowge* "was conceived as a dramatic entertainment intended for performance" (3). Whilst this argument is open to question, Skelton certainly evokes the visual trappings of early Tudor courtly entertainment in his meditation on subjection, symbolism and power. Klaus Uhlig, *Hofkritik im England des Mittelalters und der Renaissance: Studien zu einem Gemeinplatz der europäischen Moralistik* (Berlin, 1973), refers directly to Dame Sans-Pere as "die Personifikation der königlichen Majestät" (287).
41. Sarah Kay, *Courtly Contradictions: The Emergence of the Literary Object in the Twelfth Century* (Stanford, 2001), 153.
42. *The Seminar of Jacques Lacan, Book VII: The Ethics of Psychoanalysis 1959–1960*, ed. Jacques-Alain Miller, trans. Dennis Porter (London, 1992), 69: "the distance between the subject and *das Ding* . . . is precisely the condition of speech." All references to *The Ethics of Psychoanalysis* are to this edition.
43. It is hardly surprising that some critics, avoiding the temptations of the poem's courtly *topoi*, have suggested that *The Bowge* might owe a debt to nominalism. See J. Stephen Russell, "Skelton's *Bowge of Court*: A Nominalist Allegory," *Renaissance Papers* 2 (1980), 1–14; Helen Cooney, "Skelton's *Bowge of Court* and the Crisis of Allegory in Late-Medieval England," *Nation, Court and Culture: New Essays on Fifteenth-Century English Poetry*, ed. Helen Cooney (Dublin, 2001), 153–67.
44. *MED*, s.v. bouche, n.1 (1); see also Skelton, *Poems*, ed. Kinsman, 138.
45. *L'Abuzé en court*, 115, line 7.
46. I owe this suggestive analogy to Ben Jones.
47. Geoffrey de Vinsauf, *Poetria Nova*, 28–29, lines 266–67, 270–71.
48. Itself a trope associated with the disciplining of rhetoric; in Lucian's *Lexiphanes*, Lycinus and a doctor called Sopolis administer a violent emetic to the eponymous hero to purge his vocabulary of *recherché* words and phrases,

pretentious Atticisms and Homeric tags. See Lucian, [*Works*], ed. A. M. Harmon, vol. v of 8, Loeb Classical Library (Cambridge, MA, 1913, 1967), 291–327 (316–20).
49. *MED*, s.v. bouche n.(2), 1(a), bouge, n.(1), 1(a); also bouget (a leather bag or wallet).
50. *MED*, s.v. mal (e), n.(2), 1(a), which can also mean "The belly, digestive tract," 2.
51. See Scattergood, "Fashion and Morality," 269, and "Skelton's 'Ryotte': 'A Rusty Gallande,'" *Notes and Queries* 219, n.s. 21 (1974), 83–85.
52. The curial satires here provide the historical grounding of Elias's observation that "The court is a kind of stock exchange" where the individual's value lies solely "in the favour he enjoys with the king, the influence he has with other mighty ones, his importance in the play of courtly cliques": *Power and Civility*, vol. II of *The Civilizing Process*, trans. Edmund Jephcott, 2 vols. (New York, 1982), 271. On the dispensability of court servitors, see John of Salisbury, *Policraticus*, ed. Clemens C. I. Webb, 2 vols. (Oxford, 1909), I, 214.
53. R. Howard Bloch describes money as "a form of property whose purpose is to catalyze substitution in a kind of metalanguage akin to logic itself": *Etymologies and Genealogies: A Literary Anthropology of the French Middle Ages* (Chicago, 1983), 170. Augustine, designating money as a measure which makes entities commensurable and so reduces them to equality, derives the word *cuneus* (coin) from *couneus*: *De ordine*, ed. W. M. Green, CCSL XXIX (Turnhout, 1970), 87–137 (133).
54. Francis Petrarch, *The Life of Solitude*, trans. Jacob Zeitlin (Urbana: University of Illinois Press, 1924), 172–73, 174.
55. Quintilian, *Institutio oratoria*, trans. H. E. Butler, 4 vols., Loeb Classical Library (Cambridge, MA, 1921; rpt. 1976), 8. Pr. 20–22; [Cicero], *Rhetorica ad Herennium*, trans. Harry Caplan, Loeb Classical Library (Cambridge, MA, 1954; rpt. 1968), 4.10.15–16; *Alberici Casinensis Flores Rhetorici*, ed. D. Mauro Inguanez and H. M. Willard (Monte Cassino, 1938), 31–59 (II, 5).
56. Rita Copeland, "The Pardoner's Body and the Disciplining of Rhetoric," *Framing Medieval Bodies*, ed. Sarah Kay and Miri Rubin (Manchester, 1994), 138–59 (146–47).
57. For discussion of this subject in the earlier Middle Ages, see Jaeger, *Origins*, 54–66; on the later period, Uhlig, *Hofkritik*.
58. *Curial*, 10–11. Chartier here anticipates with remarkable precision Elias's account of the process by which the violence of warring feudal barons is transformed, under centralized sovereignty, into mutual surveillance and self-surveillance under the ruler's watchful eye. "[C]areers and social success are contested with words" rather than swords, and courtiers ascribe psychological depth to themselves and their rivals in an increasing "psychologization" of aristocratic culture (271, 273–75).
59. Fish, *John Skelton's Poetry*, 67.
60. On the contending perils of speech and silence, see Frank Whigham, *Ambition and Privilege: The Social Tropes of Elizabethan Courtesy Theory* (Berkeley, 1984), 50–51.
61. J. M. Archer, *Sovereignty and Intelligence* (Stanford, 1993), 10.

62. Karma Lochrie, *Covert Operations: The Medieval Uses of Secrecy* (Philadelphia, 1999), 55.
63. Ad Putter, "Animating Medieval Court Satire," *The Court and Cultural Diversity*, ed. E. Mullally and J. Thompson (Cambridge, 1997), 67–76 (73).
64. C. Stephen Jaeger, "The Barons' Intrigue in Gottfried's *Tristan*: Notes Toward a Sociology of Fear in Court Society," *JEGP* 83 (1984), 46–66. "In the face of threat, insult, and intrigue, the cleric could not reach for his sword, but could only defend himself by the superiority of his mind and manners, by spinning counter-intrigues, and in the last resort by appealing to the ruler. But in general clerics were physically vulnerable in a way that knights were not" (60–61). Jaeger suggests that anticourt polemic originates in the protest of orthodox clergy against court clergy, who were not strictly part of the church hierarchy and were thus not subject to episcopal authority. The survival of this distinctively clerical image of court life is clear in *The Bowge*. Drede's "connynge," as has been frequently noted, is often cast back at him by his opponents, in terms alternately flattering and derisive (153–54; 261; 447–49; 454), while Disdayne offers a very physical threat to Drede ("By Goddis syde, my sworde thy berde shall shave!," 339). Drede's self-identification encodes the identity of the literate cleric, and thus of the "dull" author of the prologue, with his secretive clerical hermeneutics.
65. Winser suggests, on grounds different from those advanced here, that this figure may be Drede's "own double" (23). Dickey notes the reference back to the prologue's anxieties of influence, but assumes the "teder man" to be identical with Disceyte, a possibility that Skelton's poem neither confirms nor denies (248).
66. Richard Lanham, *The Motives of Eloquence: Literary Rhetoric in the Renaissance* (New Haven, 1976), 3–9.
67. On the uncanny as response to fear of castration, see Freud, *Standard Edition*, xvii, "The Uncanny," 217–56 (233).
68. Lacan, *Ethics*, 163.
69. James Simpson has, on different grounds, traced a process by which paranoia is in this poem ultimately elevated to the status of authority. See "The Death of the Author?: Skelton's *Bouge of Court*," *The Timeless and the Temporal: Writings in Honour of John Chalker by Friends and Colleagues*, ed. Elizabeth Maslen (London, 1993), 58–77 (75).
70. Uhlig, *Hofkritik*, 175; see also Jaeger, *Origins*, 54–66.
71. Uhlig, *Hofkritik*, notes that the commonplace nature of much curial satire limits its value as historical evidence (21).
72. Matthew of Vendôme characterizes Satire's look as self-consciously devious, "with oblique eyes attesting to a mind askew": "*Ars Versificatoria*," *The Art of the Versemaker*, trans. Roger P. Parr (Milwaukee, 1981), 63.
73. The phrase, which is Starkey's ("Intimacy and Innovation," 77), adapts Sir Francis Bacon's well-known remark on Henry VII's style of rule, "It was ... but keeping of distance, which indeed he did towards all": *History of the Reign of King Henry VII*, ed. J. Rawson Lumby (Cambridge, 1902), 214–15.
74. Fish, *John Skelton's Poetry*, 79.
75. Spearing, *Medieval Dream-Poetry*, 91.

76. On the press and the dissemination of obedience, see Patricia Clare Ingham, "Losing French: Vernacularity, Nation, and Caxton's English Statutes," in Kuskin (ed.), *Caxton's Trace*, 275–98.
77. Chaucer, *Parliament of Fowls*, 168; and see Spearing, *Medieval Dream-Poetry*, 91.

3 "MY PANEFULL PURS SO PRICLIS ME": THE RHETORIC OF THE SELF IN DUNBAR'S PETITIONARY POEMS

1. Eustache Deschamps, *Oeuvres complètes*, ed. A. Queux de Saint-Hilaire and Gaston Raynaud, 11 vols., SATF (Paris, 1878–1904) VI, MCLXVIII, 22–25. All references to Deschamps are to this edition, henceforth cited as Deschamps.
2. *Registrum Secreti Sigilli Regum Scotorum: The Register of the Privy Seal of Scotland*, ed. M. Livingstone, D. H. Fleming, J. Beveridge et al. (Edinburgh, 1908), I, 80, 563.
3. *Compota Thesauriorum Regum Scotorum: Accounts of the Lord High Treasurer of Scotland*, ed. Thomas Dickson, Sir John Balfour-Paul and C. T. Innes, 12 vols. (Edinburgh, 1877–1916), IV, 69. Henceforth all references cited as *LHTA*. See also J. W. Baxter, *William Dunbar: A Biographical Study* (Edinburgh, 1952), 142.
4. *Registrum Secreti Sigilli*, I, 323, 2119 (entry for 26 August).
5. Priscilla Bawcutt, "The Earliest Texts of Dunbar," *Regionalism in Medieval Manuscripts and Texts*, ed. Felicity Riddy (Woodbridge, 1991), 183–98 (191). On relations between the Maitland and the Reidpeth MSS, see Julia Boffey, "The Maitland Folio Manuscript as a Verse Anthology," *William Dunbar, "The Nobill Poyet": Essays in Honour of Priscilla Bawcutt*, ed. Sally Mapstone (East Linton, 2001), 40–50.
6. Priscilla Bawcutt, *Dunbar the Makar* (Oxford, 1992), 115.
7. Ibid., 108–09; Baxter, *William Dunbar*, 142.
8. Bawcutt, *Dunbar*, 104–05; see also Anne Betten, "Lateinische Bettellyrik: Literarische Topik oder Ausdruck existentieller Not? Eine vergleichende Skizze über Martial und den Archipoeta," *Mittellateinisches Jahrbuch* 11 (1976), 143–50 (150).
9. Christine Scollen-Jimack, "Marot and Deschamps: The Rhetoric of Misfortune," *French Studies* 42 (1988), 21–32 (29). For a brilliant reading of an earlier case, see Jill Mann, "Satiric Subject and Satiric Object in Goliardic Literature," *Mittellateinisches Jahrbuch* 15 (1980), 63–86.
10. The texts cited frequently in this chapter are as follows: *Die Gedichte des Archipoeta*, ed. Heinrich Watenphul and Heinrich Krefeld (Heidelberg, 1958), cited as *Gedichte*; *Oeuvres poétiques de Guillaume Crétin*, ed. Kathleen Chesney (Paris, 1932), cited as *Crétin*; Machaut, *Poésies lyriques*, ed. V. Chichmaref, 2 vols. (Paris, 1909), cited as *Machaut*; *Les Faictz et Dictz de Jean Molinet*, ed. Noël Dupire, 3 vols. SATF (Paris, 1936–39), cited as *FD*; *Oeuvres complètes de Rutebeuf*, ed. Michel Zink, 2 vols. (Paris, 1989–90), cited as *Rutebeuf*; *Moralisch-satirische Gedichte Walters von Châtillon*, ed. Karl Strecker (Heidelberg, 1929), cited as *M-S G*.

11. On the "polyvocal" element in Dunbar's work, see John Leyerle, "The Two Voices of William Dunbar," *University of Toronto Quarterly* 31 (1961/62), 316–38; my own "William Dunbar: The Elusive Subject," *Bryght Lanternis: Essays on the Language and Literature of Medieval and Renaissance Scotland,* ed. J. Derrick McClure and Michael R. G. Spiller (Aberdeen, 1989), 194–208; Joanne Norman, "William Dunbar: Grand Rhétoriqueur," in *Bryght Lanternis*, 179–93.

12. For cross-border analogues, see Wendy Scase, *Literature and Complaint in England 1272–1553* (Oxford, 2007), in particular 170–86 on the formal "dictaminal" complaint.

13. Bawcutt, *Dunbar*, 241.

14. On flyting, see Priscilla Bawcutt, "The Art of Flyting," *Scottish Literary Journal* 10 (1983), 5–24; Douglas Gray, "Rough Music: Some Early Invectives and Flytings," *English Satire and the Satiric Tradition*, ed. Claude Rawson and Jenny Mezciems (Oxford, 1984), 21–43.

15. *Regement*, 7–14, 80–112; cf. B29, 4; B26, 12. We may also note Rutebeuf's obsessively recurring "Ce je m'esmai, je n'en puis mais" ["It's my fear, I can do nothing about it"] in his complaints ("Complainte," 68; cf. "Mariage," 20, 80).

16. Cf. Edmund Reiss, *William Dunbar* (Boston, 1979), 39. We may compare Rutebeuf's "Griesche d'Yver," in Michel Zink's view a poem built on a reflexive pun: "The poet claims not to have sufficient intellectual resources to invent or recall a fine, splendid story, a 'rich story'; his intellectual poverty compels him to settle for describing his own life, a poor man's life, a 'poor story.'" *The Invention of Literary Subjectivity*, trans. David Sices (Baltimore, 1999), 96–97.

17. "Comme Colin Muset et Rutebeuf qui amusaient les autres en racontant leurs soucis d'argent ou de ménage, Deschamps joue pour la cour la comédie du Moi" ["Like Colin Muset and Rutebeuf who entertain others by telling of their financial or domestic woes, Deschamps performs for the court the comedy of the self"]. Poirion, *Poète et le prince*, 232.

18. René Girard, *To Double Business Bound: Essays on Literature, Mimesis and Anthropology* (Baltimore, 1988), 140.

19. So described in the title given to B4 by Bannatyne.

20. See Bryan S. Hay, "William Dunbar's Flying Abbot: Apocalypse Made to Order," *Studies in Scottish Literature* 11 (1973/74), 217–25. On the dangerous "modernity" of alchemy, perhaps not unconnected with Dunbar's *animus* towards Damian, see Sheila Delany, "Run Silent, Run Deep: Heresy and Alchemy as Medieval Versions of Utopia," *Medieval Literary Politics: Shapes of Ideology* (Manchester, 1990), 1–18, and Lee Patterson, "Perpetual Motion: Alchemy and the Technology of the Self," *Studies in the Age of Chaucer* 15 (1993), 25–57.

21. On this sequence, see David Parkinson, "Mobbing Scenes in Middle Scots Verse: Holland, Douglas, Dunbar," *JEGP* 85 (1986), 494–509.

22. Fradenburg, *City, Marriage, Tournament*, 149; Tom Scott, *Dunbar: A Critical Exposition of the Poems* (Edinburgh, 1966), 19; Gary Waller, *English Poetry of the Sixteenth Century* (London, 1986), 108.

23. On Dunbar's stance here, see A. E. Christa Canitz, "A Benefice for the Prophet: William Dunbar's Petitionary Poems," *SSL* 33–34 (2004), 42–61.

Greenblatt points out that the satirist's ostentatious rectitude "may be itself a kind of pose taken in response to the dictates of power": *Renaissance Self-Fashioning*, 135. For a later poet confronted with the demands of patronage, where plain style rather than plain speaking is at issue, see Stanley Fish, "Authors-Readers: Jonson's Community of the Same," *Representations* 7 (1984), 26–58. Fradenburg suggests that some instances of the "advice to princes" tradition, along with other texts in which the sovereign becomes the recipient of "plain speech," provide an instance of "the power of communitas to mystify status." See *City, Marriage, Tournament*, 289 note 22.

24. Jacqueline Cerquiglini, "'Le Clerc et le louche': Sociology of an Esthetic," *Poetics Today* 5 (1984), 479–91.
25. Martin le Franc, *Le Champion des Dames, Part I*, ed. Arthur Piaget (Lausanne, 1968), 276, 281–84, 289–90.
26. Jean de la Mote, *Li Regret Guillaume comte de Hainaut: poème inédit du xive siècle, par Jehan de la Mote*, ed. Auguste Scheler (Louvain, 1882). All references are to this edition.
27. Cerquiglini, " 'Le Clerc et le louche,'" 488.
28. Putter, "Animating Medieval Court Satire," 69.
29. In Froissart's "Dit dou florin," the poet alternately harangues and cajoles a talking coin, which puts its owner's losses down to the money he has spent on writing materials. This, the "florin" reassures him, has been money well spent, for "fait en avés mainte hystore / Dont il sera encor memore / De vous ens ou temps à venir, / Et ferés les gens souvenir / De vo sens et de vos doctrines" ["with it you have written many histories through which you'll still be remembered in times to come, and you will make people remember your wisdom and learning"]. *Oeuvres de Froissart: Poésies*, ed. Auguste Scheler, 3 vols. (Brussels, 1870–72), II, 199–207.
30. Spearing, *Medieval to Renaissance*, 205.
31. *Rutebeuf*, "La repentance Rutebeuf," 37.
32. J. A. Burrow, *Medieval Writers and their Work* (Oxford, 1982), 40, and "The Poet as Petitioner," *Studies in the Age of Chaucer* 3 (1981), 61–75 (64).
33. *Gedichte*, no. 1 ("Lingua balbus"), st. 36, 1–2.
34. *Deschamps*, 5, DCCCLXXIII, 11.
35. *Crétin*, XLV, 9–10, 23–28.
36. For a similar strategy, compare Michault Taillevent, who, overtaken by night in the midst of a wood, begins to meditate on the transitoriness of worldly possessions (65–72) and consider how he will appear as an example to others if he dies (73–80). See "La Destrousse Michault Taillevent," in Robert Deschaux, *Un Poète bourguignon du xve siècle, Michault Taillevent* (Geneva, 1975), 97–120.
37. The stance of "auld servand" unrewarded is, as Bawcutt notes, an inevitable commonplace; cf. Deschamps, threatened with the abolition of his rank of *huissier d'armes* (6, MCCVI).
38. Such poems directed at financial institutions of the court are common in Deschamps's work: see, for instance, 4, DCCLXXXV, with its refrain "Et quant vendra le Tresorier?," and the attacks on the "manieurs d'argent" of 5, MXIII, and 7, MCCCI, and cf. B22.

39. See also *Rutebeuf,* "De Brichemer," who invokes mythic distance, reproachfully telling a patron that he will have to wait as long for payment as the Britons for King Arthur's return from Avalon (15–16).
40. John Bossy, *Christianity in the West 1400–1700* (Oxford, 1985), 57. Cf. Rutebeuf: "Du duel son voisin ne li membre / Més le sien pleure" ["He forgets his neighbour's sorrow, but weeps for his own"]. The speaker is the impoverished, dice-obsessed "I" of "La griesche d'yver," 83–84.
41. Burrow, *Medieval Writers,* 43. Cf. another notable instance of the court servitor's symptomatology, the more loquacious Deschamps's toothache ("Mal de teste telle doleur ne fait," 5, IV, 9).
42. *Gedichte,* no. 3 ("Omnia tempus habent"), 18–20.
43. See *Machaut,* I, Complainte VII ("Sire, à vous fais ceste clamour"), 23–26; *FD,* II, XLIV (806–07), 2 (806).
44. *Crétin,* XLV, 39–43, 32–33. Perhaps the nearest analogue to the petitioner's diseased and tortured body can be detected in medieval religious lyrics on the body isolated before death, in which, as Douglas Gray observes, "a fundamental materialism seems to assert itself through layers of penitential comment" (183). On poems that describe the body in decay, and the *Proprietates Mortis* or "Signs of Death," see Douglas Gray, *Themes and Images in the Medieval English Religious Lyric* (London: 1972), 190–199; Rosemary Woolf, *The English Religious Lyric in the Middle Ages* (Oxford, 1968), 94–95, 317–18.
45. "Male Regle," 409.
46. *M-S G,* "Tanto viro locuturi" (st. 10, 5–6).
47. *Deschamps,* 4, DCCXCVII, 1–10.
48. "Lydgate's Letter to Gloucester," *Minor Poems of John Lydgate,* II, 6–8, 13–15, 18, 20. For an especially telling reading of the body's "subjection to the flows of monetary representation, and . . . its concomitant disappearance into semiotic flux," see D. Vance Smith, "Body Doubles: Producing the Masculine *Corpus,*" *Becoming Male in the Middle Ages,* ed. Jeffrey Jerome Cohen and Bonnie Wheeler (New York, 2000), 5–19 (9).
49. *Regement,* 684–85.
50. *Deschamps,* 5, DCCCLVII, 8. Cf. Deschamps, 4, DCCXCVII, 9; DCCXCIV, 13.
51. Similarly, Reiss, *Dunbar,* 42; Scott, *Dunbar,* 94.
52. Bawcutt, *Dunbar,* 111.
53. *FD,* 2, XXXV, 778, 13–18.
54. *FD,* 2, XXXV, 778, 8–10.
55. Jacqueline Cerquiglini, *"Un engin si soutil": Guillaume de Machaut et l'écriture au XIVe siècle* (Geneva, 1985), 143–47.
56. I follow here Cerquiglini, "'Le clerc et le louche,'" 482.
57. Bawcutt, "Dunbar's Christmas Carol," *Scottish Language and Literature, Medieval and Renaissance: Fourth International Conference 1984, Proceedings,* ed. Dietrich Strauss and Horst W. Drescher (Frankfurt, 1986), 381–92.
58. D. A. Miller, *The Novel and the Police* (Berkeley, CA, 1988), 208.
59. Cf. Deschamps's transmutation into a "vieil roncin" (old nag) through age: *Deschamps,* 5, XC, 10. Slightly later, Marot compares himself to a sheep

excluded from the fold, in a begging-poem addressed to François I asking to be put on the court payroll after the death of his father, also a court poet:

> L'Estat est faict, les Personnes rengées,
> Le Parc est clos, et les Brebis logées
> Toutes, fors moy, le moindre du Trouppeau,
> Qui n'a Toyson ne Laine sur la Peau.

["The estate is settled, all persons ranked, the park is closed and the ewes in their pens, all except me, the littlest of the flock, who has neither fleece nor wool on his skin."] Clément Marot, *Les Epîtres*, ed. C. A. Mayer (London, 1958), 136 (13–16). In another epistle, to the Chancelier Du Prat, he uses the same metaphor, punning this time on the Chancellor's name:

> Ce temps pendant à pasturer m'ordonne;
> Et pour trouver plus d'Herbe franche et bonne,
> M'a adressé au Pré mieulx florissant
> De son Royaulme ample, large et puissant.   (140, 15–18)

["This present time commands me to go out to pasture; and to find more good fresh grass, I turn to the most flourishing meadow in his wide, vast and powerful kingdom."]

60. Cf. *Deschamps*, 5, DCCCCIII: "Or est au bois, a la froidure, mis / Le suppliant qui trop doubte la glace" ["Now this suppliant, who has great fear of the frost, is put out in the woods and the cold"]. This proves to be no way to treat another aged and balding poet "Qui sur sa teste a grant froit a la fois / Pour ses cheveulx qui s'en sont departis" ["whose head is now very cold on account of the hair which has left it"].
61. On "concretization," the reader's activity of "removing or filling out the indeterminacies, gaps, or schematized aspects in the text," see Robert C. Holub, *Reception Theory: A Critical Introduction* (London, 1984), 25–29 (26).
62. *Deschamps*, 4, DCCCIX; see also 7, MCCCI, where he likens himself to a seller of "oublies," complete with appropriate street-cry.
63. Cf. Walter of Châtillon's "A la feste sui venuz," written to celebrate the carnivalesque "Feast of the Staff," in which the satiric poet adopts the voice of God at the Last Judgement: "et edos ab ovibus veni segregare" ["I come to separate the sheep from the goats"]. *M-S G*, no.13, st. 1, line 4.
64. *Rutebeuf*, "La pauvreté de Rutebeuf," 25–29.
65. Deschamps is troubled by an inverse relationship between the gaze of all and his sense of self (5, DCCCCXXI):

> Dont puet venir tele desordonnance
> Encontre moy et tele descongnoissance? ...
> Plus me voit on, tant sui je moins prisiez.   (26–27, 30)

["How is it that such disorder should come to me, and such disregard? The more they see me, the less they prize me."]
66. This widely used figure is perhaps most fully developed by Deschamps, 6, MCIX, an allegory in which "Medecin prince terrien / Figure" (21–22).

67. On royal healing by touch, see Keith Thomas, *Religion and the Decline of Magic* (London, 1971), 192–99; Marc Bloch, *The Royal Touch: Sacred Monarchy and Scrofula in England and France*, trans. J. E. Anderson (London, 1973). The Lord High Treasurer's Accounts for 30 April 1508 show a payment of three shillings "to ane pure barne that tuke the King be the hand": *LHTA*, IV, 114. The editor asks: "May we see in this the Royal power of touching for scrofula?" (lxxxii).
68. Bawcutt, *Dunbar*, 117.
69. T. S. Dorsch, "Of Discretioun in Asking: Dunbar's Petitionary Poems," *Chaucer und seine Zeit: Symposion für Walter F. Schirmer*, ed. Arno Esch (Tübingen, 1968), 285–92 (292).
70. On this figure, see G. R. Owst, *Literature and Pulpit in Medieval England*, rev. edn. (Oxford, 1961), 385–90; the phrase adapts Proverbs 7, 10–12.
71. Eve Kosofsky Sedgwick, *Between Men: English Literature and Male Homosocial Desire* (New York, 1985).
72. On lyric treatment of Mary as intercessor with Christ and "benevolent interventrix in the affairs of the world," see Woolf, *English Religious Lyric*, 118–20 (118).
73. On the ambivalence of gossip as "female vice of extraordinary power," see Lochrie, *Covert Operations*, 60.
74. Freud, *Standard Edition*, VIII, 99–100.
75. While Bawcutt's glossary (s.v. "lad") construes "ladis" as "boys" or "serving men," it is worth noting that *DOST* gives "ladis" as a possible plural of "lady," suggesting, in accordance with the reading advanced here, a more explicitly sexual element to this bull-baiting.
76. "The Testament of the Papyngo," in *Selected Poems*, 491–92, 500–04, 513. Fradenburg notes that this narrative of glory and fall has dominated the subsequent historiography of James IV's reign: *City, Marriage, Tournament*, 153–60.
77. Fradenburg, *City, Marriage, Tournament*, 161. My comments on James's strategic "visibility" are indebted to Fradenburg, to whose account of James's "arts of rule" it is central.
78. *LHTA*, II, lxxx–lxxxii, 87, 269ff.
79. For the Palace at Stirling, see *LHTA*, I, cclxv–cclxvi, 276–84 passim, 286, 291, 297, 303, 306–07 passim, 322–23 passim, 336, 355, 364, 367, 370, 372, 377, 384, 386–87 passim, 389–90 passim; II, lxxx, 81–85, 269–81. For its Chapel Royal's new decorations, lxxix–lxxx; for Linlithgow, I, cclxiii–cclxiv, 195, 204. See also R. L. Mackie, *King James IV of Scotland: A Brief Survey of his Life and Times* (Edinburgh, 1958); 113–16.
80. Norman Macdougall, "'The Greattest Scheip that ewer Saillit in Ingland or France': James IV's 'Great Michael,'" *Scotland and War, AD 79–1918*, ed. Norman Macdougall (Edinburgh, 1991), 36–60 (57).
81. *James IV*, 294. Macdougall cites the jousting in honor of Perkin Warbeck's marriage in 1496 (*LHTA*, I, cxxx–cxxxi, 257, 262, 263); the tournament to celebrate James's own wedding, in 1503, which continued for three days in Holyrood palace courtyard ("Fyancells," 298–300; *LHTA*, II, 390); and the spectacular jousts of June 1507 and May 1508, in the former of which the king may have played the role of the "wyld knycht," entering combat against all

challengers. In both, the object of the tourneying was the "black lady." On the jousts of 1507 and 1508, see *LHTA*, III, xlv–lii, 257–61; IV, lxxxiii–lxxxiv, 22, 119; and, for a full analysis, Fradenburg, *City, Marriage, Tournament*, 225–64.
82. Fradenburg, *City, Marriage, Tournament*, 74, 167.
83. Ibid., 156, 161, 167. Macdougall points out that there was "a world of difference between the remote, aloof James III amassing money from profits of justice without moving from Edinburgh in the process, and his energetic son, who ... might be expected to appear rapidly in any area in which unrest was likely to have damaging effects on Crown resources or prestige." *James IV*, 304.
84. Robert Lindesay of Pitscottie, *The Historie and Cronicles of Scotland, From the Slaughter of King James the First To the Ane thousande fyve hundreith thrie scoir fyftein ʒeir*, ed. A. J. G. Mackay, 3 vols. (Edinburgh, 1899–1911), I, 231; Fradenburg, *City, Marriage, Tournament*, 69–70.
85. Neil Cuddy, "The Revival of the Entourage: The Bedchamber of James I, 1603–1625," in Starkey et al., *The English Court*, 173–225 (178–81). Hugh Murray Baillie points out that the Privy Chamber was not distinguished from the Bedchamber and Closet in the Scottish court, as it was in the English: even when, in the reign of James V, French masons completed the palace at Stirling Castle and altered that of Linlithgow at about the same time, "both provide a Royal Apartment consisting only of a Garde Hall, Presence Chalmer and Bedchamber with a garde-robe and oratory behind it. As there is no room to enlarge or develop these closets, it is clear that the King and Queen of Scots were expected to live, as their ancestors had done, in their Bedchamber." "Etiquette and the Planning of the State Apartments in Baroque Palaces," *Archaeologia* 101 (1967), 169–99 (180).
86. Michel Foucault, *Discipline and Punish: The Birth of the Prison*, trans. Alan Sheridan (New York, 1977), 28–29.
87. Fredric Jameson draws a connection between the emergence of personalizing narrative detail in the context of "a life" with bourgeois capitalism: "realism is par excellence the moment of the discovery of changing time ... at one with ... a world of worn things ... and those discarded objects that are used-up human lives": "Beyond the Cave: Modernism and Modes of Production," *The Horizon of Literature*, ed. Paul Hernadi (Lincoln, 1982), 157–82 (176).
88. Bawcutt, *Dunbar*, 115.
89. On this aspect of the petitionary poem, see also my "Hoccleve's Unregimented Body."
90. Jean Baudrillard, *Selected Writings*, ed. Mark Poster (Cambridge, 1988), 109.
91. "You love me better poor than rich": *Crétin*, XLV, 50.

4 TRANSLATIVE SENSES: ALEXANDER BARCLAY'S *ECLOGUES* AND GAVIN DOUGLAS'S *PALICE OF HONOUR*

1. Gavin Douglas, *Virgil's Aeneid*, ed. D. F. C. Coldwell, STS 3rd series 25, 27, 29, 30 (Edinburgh, 1951–56), IV, 191, lines 117–28. All references are to this edition.

2. See e.g. Christopher Baswell, *Virgil in Medieval England* (Cambridge, 1995), pp. 276–79. For an account of the *Eneados* as uncompromisingly imperial *translatio*, see James Simpson, *Reform and Cultural Revolution* (Oxford, 2002), 78–86.
3. On Douglas's life, see Priscilla Bawcutt, *Gavin Douglas: A Critical Study* (Edinburgh, 1976), 1–22.
4. On this tradition, see Minnis, *Medieval Theory*, 9–72.
5. Elizabeth J. Bellamy, *Translations of Power: Narcissism and the Unconscious in Epic History* (Ithaca, 1992), 81.
6. See "Alexander Barclay," entry by Nicholas Orme, *DNB*. R. J. Lyall suggests that Barclay may have used *The Fall of Princes* as a source: see "Tradition and Innovation in Alexander Barclay's 'Towre of Vertue and Honoure,'" *Review of English Studies* n.s. 23 (1972), 1–18 (7). For a full examination of Barclay's Lydgateanism, see Meyer-Lee, *Poets and Power*, 190–204.
7. The biographical outline is given in Orme, *DNB*. On Barclay and Pynson, see David R. Carlson, "Alexander Barclay and Richard Pynson: A Tudor Printer and His Writer," *Anglia* 113 (1995), 283–302. On the later career: R. J. Lyall, "Alexander Barclay and the Edwardian Reformation 1548–52," *Review of English Studies* 20 (1969), 455–61.
8. See Alexander Barclay, *The Life of St. George*, ed. William Nelson, EETS OS 230 (London, 1955 [for 1948]), xv. For an alternative reading working from the assumption that Barclay was referring to Gower's *Confessio Amantis*, see Candace Barrington, "Misframed Fables: Barclay's Gower and the Wantonness of Performance," *Medievalia* 24 (2003), 195–225.
9. *Life of St. George*, 1, 7–9, Prol. 44–45.
10. *Here begynneth the famous cronycle of the warre / which the romayns had against Iugurth* (STC 21627), a.iv–A1.
11. STC 21627, a.vi.
12. David Rollin Anderson, "A Critical Edition of Alexander Barclay's *Ship of Fools* (1509)" (1974), 157, lines 1–5. All further references to *The Ship* are to this edition.
13. *Life of St. George*, xx, where Nelson engagingly labels Barclay "a very skittish pony." See too Meyer-Lee, *Poets and Power*, 194–95.
14. The dating of the *Eclogues* is discussed in *The Eclogues of Alexander Barclay*, ed. Beatrice White, EETS OS 175 (Oxford, 1928 [for 1927]; rpt. 1961), xxiv–xxv, lvi–lx. All references to the *Eclogues* are to this edition. See also Carlson, "Barclay and Pynson," 297–98. On Barclay and Eneo Silvio, see *Aeneae Silvii de curialium miseriis epistola*, ed. Wilfred P. Mustard (Baltimore, 1928), 15–16; for Barclay and Mantuan, I have consulted *The Eclogues of Baptista Mantuanus*, ed. Mustard (Baltimore, 1911), and Baptista (Spagnuoli) Mantuanus, *Adulescentia: The Eclogues of Mantuan*, ed. Lee Piepho (New York, 1989). On Lemaire de Belges, see Lyall, "Tradition and Innovation," 1–5.
15. It may be noted that White's edition of the *Eclogues* prints the immediate Latin source texts on the same page as Barclay's translations, using a 1578 Frankfurt edition of the *De Miseriis* and a first edition of Mantuan. In her preface, she

notes that "the punctuation of the English and Latin originals has been preserved, as contributing to the interest of the text." The early texts, however, sometimes render the Latin less intelligible, and when reproducing parts of it here I have silently emended in accordance with Mustard's editions for the convenience of the reader. Barclay's interpolation here deflects Piccolomini's original complaint that "Viros autem sapientes qui de moribus ac Naturis secretis disputent, quique historias referant, non nisi per adulationes apud principes accipies" ["But you will not find wise men who can discuss manners and the secrets of Nature, or tell histories, among princes except by flattery"]: cf. Barclay, *Second Eclogue*, 291–96. If I refer to any passage as Barclay's without further qualification, the reader may take it that the passage is Barclay's own addition to his source.

16. For a brief but perceptive discussion of Barclay's urban discourse, see Lawrence Manley, *Literature and Culture in Early Modern London* (Cambridge, 1995), 79–80.
17. See *Adulescentia*, ed. Piepho, xxxiii, 107, 108 notes to 28–30 and 60. The puns, as Piepho notes, foreshadow the fate of the lustful shepherd Amyntas.
18. See Mantuan, Eclogue IX, line 213, and on Falcone Piepho's detailed commentary at xxiv note 52. Mustard draws the connection with Barclay at *Eclogues*, 48–49, though White (228) is skeptical.
19. Julie A. Smith, "An Image of a Preaching Bishop in Late Medieval England: The 1498 Woodcut Portrait of Bishop John Alcock," *Viator* 21 (1990), 301–22.
20. Stephen Guy-Bray, *Homoerotic Space: The Poetics of Loss in Renaissance Literature* (Toronto, 2002), 38.
21. White's supposition that "'Dreadfull Drome' may be a reference to James Stanley, Bishop of Ely, 1506–1515, or to his deputy" (250, note 3 to 126) seems entirely plausible; see H. G. Newcombe's *DNB* entry on Stanley.
22. *Aeneae Silvii*, ed. Mustard, 15–16. Fox, *Politics and Literature*, notes that Barclay "deliberately obscures the careful structure of the original by introducing Coridon as an interlocutor" (46).
23. For these lines, see *Aeneae Silvii*, ed. Mustard, 35–36.
24. R. Howard Bloch, *Medieval Misogyny and the Invention of Western Romantic Love* (Chicago, 1991), 17–18.
25. Elias, *History of Manners*, I 53 ff. See, too, Fradenburg, "Manciple's Servant Tongue," 89–90.
26. Not, as the tradition reproduced in White has it, the *Pro Marcello*.
27. Cicero, "Pro Caelio," *The Speeches*, trans. R. Gardner, Loeb Classical Library (Cambridge, MA, 1958), XVII, 46–47.
28. Lacan, "The Mirror Stage as Formative of the *I* Function as Revealed in Psychoanalytic Experience," *Écints*, 75–81 (78).
29. Fox, *Politics and Literature*, 53–55.
30. Barclay perhaps builds his self-construction here on the Lydgate who enters Canterbury "In a cope of blak and not of grene, / On a palfrey slender, long and lene" – a pale horseman who according to the Host is "al devoyde of blood" (73–74, 89): John Lydgate, *The Siege of Thebes*, ed. Robert R. Edwards (Kalamazoo, 2001).

31. *Letters and Papers, Domestic and Foreign, of the Reign of Henry VIII*, ed. J. S. Brewer, 21 vols. (London, 1872), IV, 2083. The translation is White's (xlii). Lyall notes that Barclay "was probably associated with Tyndale because of their shared dislike of Wolsey and the English government rather than because of any agreement over religious matters": Lyall, "Alexander Barclay and the Edwardian Reformation," 455.
32. *Letters and Papers*, IV, 2405–06.
33. See White, xlvi–li, and Lyall, "Alexander Barclay," 457.
34. Bawcutt notes the poem's "element of bravura": *Gavin Douglas*, 67. For Spearing, the poem shows the sexual disquiets of Douglas the supposedly celibate cleric, who in the face of an angry love-goddess's judgment pleads benefit of clergy (*Medieval to Renaissance*, 239). Fradenburg analyzes Douglas's participation in the Scottish court's culture of honor and its drive to ground phenomenal exterior in an "inner" essence; the poem shows "the desire to recover protection and plenitude through a redemption of violence" and the risk of mutilation, polarities realized in *The Palice*'s alternately menacing and accommodating female figures (*City, Marriage, Tournament*, 187).
35. All references to *The Palice of Honour*, except where otherwise indicated, are to the London edition of c. 1553 printed in *The Shorter Poems of Gavin Douglas*, ed. Priscilla J. Bawcutt, STS 4th series 3 (Edinburgh: William Blackwood, 1967).
36. Spearing, *Medieval to Renaissance*, 232; Fradenburg, *City, Marriage, Tournament*, 190.
37. Virgil, *Aeneid*, IX.717; Statius, *Thebaid*, VII.78; Boccaccio, *Teseida*, VII.32; *CantT* I: A 1982.
38. Jacques Derrida, *Archive Fever: A Freudian Impression*, trans. Eric Prenowitz (Chicago, 1995), 10.
39. See Peter W. Travis, "Chaucer's Heliotropes and the Poetics of Metaphor," *Speculum* 72 (1997), 399–427 (402–16).
40. Derrida, *Archive Fever*, 1.
41. For a recent overview, see Mladen Dolar, *A Voice and Nothing More* (Cambridge, MA, 2006), p. 41.
42. Alicia K. Nitecki, "Gavin Douglas's Yelling Fish: *The Palice of Honour*, Lines 146–8," *Notes and Queries* 226 (1981), 118–19.
43. Bawcutt, *Gavin Douglas*, 59; Fradenburg, *City, Marriage, Tournament*, 189.
44. David Parkinson, "The Farce of Modesty in Gavin Douglas's *The Palis of Honour*," *Philological Quarterly* 70 (1990), 13–25 (14–15).
45. Lynn Enterline, *The Rhetoric of the Body from Ovid to Shakespeare* (Cambridge, 2000), 34.
46. Jacques Lacan, *The Seminar: Book II. The Ego in Freud's Theory and in the Technique of Psychoanalysis, 1954–55*, trans. Sylvana Tomaselli, notes by John Forrester (New York, 1988), 313.
47. Parkinson, "Mobbing Scenes in Middle Scots Verse."
48. Parkinson, "Farce of Modesty," 21.
49. This single stanza, missing from Copland's print, is supplied from the later Charteris print.

50. Bawcutt, *Gavin Douglas*, 59.
51. *The Palis of Honoure*, ed. David Parkinson (Kalamazoo, 1992), 121, note to line 1761. John Norton-Smith reads Venus as an "apt patroness of history," but contends that she "ought not to be associated with the creation of the Angels, or the fall of Satan": "Ekphrasis as a Stylistic Element in Douglas's *Palis of Honoure*," *Medium Aevum* 48 (1979), 240–53 (241).
52. Derrida, *Archive Fever*, 4 note 1.
53. Lerer, *Chaucer and his Readers*, 204.

5 *MÉMOIRES D'OUTRE-TOMBE*: LOVE, RHETORIC AND THE POEMS OF STEPHEN HAWES

1. Zumthor, "Great Game," 495; see *Le Masque et la lumière*, 48–49.
2. *Curial*, 10.
3. Stephen Hawes, *Minor Poems*, xiii. Unless otherwise indicated, all biographical and bibliographical information is taken from this edition.
4. National Archives PRO E 36/214, fol. 28r. This is the sole mention of Hawes in the surviving portions of Heron's accounts kept in the Public Record Office. For discussion of this material, see Sydney Anglo, "The Court Festivals of Henry VII: A Study Based upon the Account Books of John Heron, Treasurer of the Chamber," *Bulletin of the John Rylands Library* 43 (1960/61), 12–45.
5. John Bale, *Scriptorum illustrium maioris Brytannia . . . catalogus* (Basle, 1557–59; rpt. Farnborough, 1971), 632: see S. J. Gunn, "Literature and Politics in Early Tudor England," *Journal of British Studies* 30 (1991), 216–21 (218). David Starkey finds no mention of Hawes among the names of the Grooms of the Privy or Secret Chamber, though he concedes that the "missing members of the Secret Chamber can never . . . be identified with absolute certainty": "King's Privy Chamber," 26–58 (45). See, too, Lerer, *Courtly Letters*, 51. I am most grateful to Dr. Gunn for initial pointers towards *The Comfort of Lovers*'s possible connections with Mary Tudor's role at the center of the burgeoning chivalric cult of Henry VII's last years.
6. Thomas Feylde, *A Contrauersye bytwene a Louer and a Iaye*, 22 (STC 10838.7). The phrase "Yonge Hawes" also appears in the prologue to Robert Copland's 1530 edition of Chaucer's *Parliament* (here *The Assemble*) *of Fowles*, A1v (STC 5092); see A. S. G. Edwards, "An Allusion to Stephen Hawes, *c.* 1530," *Notes and Queries* 224 n.s. 26 (1979), 397.
7. Stephen Hawes, *The Pastime of Pleasure*, ed. W. E. Mead, EETS OS 173 (London, 1928). All references to *The Pastime* are to this edition.
8. On Henry VII's propagandist use of his Lancastrian lineage, see Sydney Anglo, *Spectacle, Pageantry, and Early Tudor Policy* (Oxford, 1969), 36–43.
9. Depictions of Lydgate presenting the work to Henry V are common to all illustrated manuscripts of the *Troy Book* apart from BL MS Royal 18.D.ii: see Lesley Lawton, "The Illustration of Late Medieval Secular Texts, with Special Reference to Lydgate's *Troy Book*," *Manuscripts and Readers in Fifteenth-Century*

England: *The Literary Implications of Manuscript Study*, ed. Derek Pearsall (Cambridge, 1983), 41–69 (55). On this gesture, see too Meyer-Lee, *Poets and Power*, 181–82.
10. For Hawes's praise of Lydgate, see *Pastime*, 48, 1163–76, 1338–86, 1394–407, 5810–16.
11. Some of the implications of Hawes's poetic vocabulary are discussed by Ebin, *Illuminator, Makar, Vates*, 146–47. See too *MED* s.v. "fatal," 1 (a) predestined; 2. predetermined, fated; 3 (a) fateful or (b) (of a wound) mortal.
12. Gordon Kipling suggests that Hawes may have written *The Receyt of the Lady Kateryne*, the account of the events surrounding Catherine of Aragon's arrival in England in October and November 1501: EETS OS 296 (Oxford, 1990), xlviii–l.
13. See Françoise Joukofsky, *La Gloire dans la poésie française et néolatine du XVIe siècle des Rhétoriqueurs à Agrippa d'Aubigné* (Geneva, 1969), 31, 48, 53, 132, 175–76 and *passim*; on the early Tudor cult of honor and its Burgundian antecedents, Gordon Kipling, *The Triumph of Honour: Burgundian Origins of the English Renaissance* (Leiden, 1977).
14. Cf. Peter Brooks: "One could no doubt analyze the opening paragraph of most novels and emerge in each case with the image of a desire taking on shape, beginning to seek its objects, beginning to develop a textual energetics": *Reading for the Plot: Design and Intention in Narrative* (1984; rpt. Cambridge, MA, 1992), 38. The very name of this romance hero is a figure for desire. For Deanne Williams, Hawes "expresses his sense of domination by French textual exemplarity as a form of control by French women": *The French Fetish from Chaucer to Shakespeare* (Cambridge, 2004), 133.
15. Evelyn Birge Vitz, "The *I* of the *Roman de la Rose*," *Genre* 6 (1973), 49–75 (54).
16. On this genre, see Siegfried Wenzel, "The Pilgrimage of Life as a Late Medieval Genre," *Mediaeval Studies* 35 (1973), 370–88.
17. Rosemond Tuve, *Allegorical Imagery: Some Medieval Books and their Posterity* (Princeton, 1966), 168. For a brilliant recent discussion of how the self is constituted in the *Vie humaine*, see Sarah Kay, *The Place of Thought: The Complexity of One in Late Medieval French Didactic Poetry* (Philadelphia, 2007), 70–94.
18. See H. S. Bennett, *English Books and Readers, 1475–1557*, 2nd edn. (Cambridge, 1969), 85–89; N. F. Blake, "Wynkyn de Worde: The Later Years," *Gutenberg Jahrbuch* (1972), 128–38 (135–36).
19. See "Le Dit dou Lyon," *Oeuvres de Guillaume de Machaut*, ed. Ernest Hoepffner, 3 vols., SATF (Paris, 1908–21), II, 185; "The Floure and the Leafe," *The Floure and the Leafe and The Assembly of Ladies*, ed. Derek Pearsall (London, 1962), lines 43, 47, 49 (49).
20. A. S. G. Edwards notes the high degree of collaboration between Hawes and de Worde in "Poet and Printer in Sixteenth-Century England: Stephen Hawes and Wynkyn de Worde," *Gutenberg Jahrbuch* (1980), 82–88. Edwards draws a distinction between those woodcuts that were evidently commissioned for *The Pastime* and those from stock that were "presumably intended to stress the didactic and expository aspect of . . . . the 'Pastime,'" and whose appropriateness is of a more general kind (84). The woodcuts alluded to are Hodnett, nos. 987,

1010 and 1258. I suggest that the woodcuts from stock create visual connections between the prints of Hawes's poem and other nonfictional, instructional texts.
21. Machaut, II, lines 797, 2974–80; the translation is from Machaut, *Le Jugement du roy de Behaigne and Remede de Fortune*, ed. James I. Wimsatt and William W. Kibler (Athens, 1988), 332, 334.
22. As a rhetorical figure, *correctio* "retracts what has been said and replaces it with what seems more suitable": *Ad Herennium*, IV, xxvi, 36. The gradation so achieved is intended to heighten persuasive effect.
23. On the bond ("vinculum") between *ratio* and *oratio* established as a first principle of human society, see Cicero, *De officiis*, trans. Walter Miller, Loeb Classical Library (Cambridge, MA, 1913; rpt. 1968), 52–54. On Lydgate's own association of rhetorical and political order, see Ebin, *Illuminator, Makar, Vates*, 40–48.
24. Seth Lerer, "The Rhetoric of Fame: Stephen Hawes's Aureate Diction," *Spenser Studies* 5 (1985), 169–84 (175). The episode is also discussed in Williams, *French Fetish*, 142–49.
25. Spearing, *Medieval to Renaissance*, 255.
26. See Edward Wilson, "Local Habitations and Names in MS Rawlinson C 813 in the Bodleian Library, Oxford," *Review of English Studies* n.s. 41 (1990), 12–44. For a full edition of the MS, see *The Welles Anthology: MS. Rawlinson C. 813. A Critical Edition*, ed. Sharon Jansen and Kathleen Jordan (Binghamton, 1991). For a provocative reading of its principles of compilation, see Lerer, *Courtly Letters*, 129–43.
27. The manuscript's Hawesian borrowings are discussed in *Welles Anthology*, 22–25, and tabulated on 300–03.
28. Zeeman, "Verse of Courtly Love," 223. See also Vitz's comment that in the *Roman de la Rose*, "the experience undergone by the hero is, in many respects, extra-temporal ... although at the outset rooted in time, the dream unfolds along an indefinite and unreal time axis": "*I* of the *Roman de la Rose*," 54.
29. J. A. W. Bennett, "*Nosce te ipsum*: Some Medieval and Modern Interpretations," *The Humane Medievalist, and Other Essays in English Literature and Learning, from Chaucer to Eliot*, ed. Piero Boitani (Rome, 1982), 135–72 (150). See also Gray, *Themes and Images*, 172–75.
30. Pearsall, *Old English and Middle English Poetry*, 267.
31. C. S. Lewis, *The Allegory of Love: A Study in Medieval Tradition* (Oxford, 1936), 284–85.
32. See Gray, *Themes and Images*, 199–206; Woolf, *English Religious Lyric*, 19, 88–89, 92, 312–26, 354–55, 401–04.
33. Tzvetan Todorov provides a succinct statement of this widely used distinction: "The individual who says *I* in a novel is not the *I* of the discourse, otherwise called the subject of the *énonciation*. He is only a character and the status of his utterances (the direct style) gives to them a maximum objectivity, instead of bringing them closer to the subject of the actual *énonciation*. But there exists another *I*, an *I* for the most part invisible, which refers to the narrator, the 'poetic personality,' which we apprehend through the discourse." See Tzvetan

Todorov, "Language and Literature," *The Languages of Criticism and the Sciences of Man: The Structuralist Controversy*, ed. Richard Macksey and Eugenio Donato (Baltimore, 1970), 125–33 (132).
34. *"The Gast of Gy," Three Purgatory Poems*, ed. Edward E. Foster (Kalamazoo, 2004); see lines 335–38, 353–56.
35. Roland Barthes, "Textual Analysis of Poe's 'Valdemar,'" trans. Geoff Bennington, *Untying the Text: A Post-Structuralist Reader*, ed. Robert Young (London, 1981), 133–61 (153).
36. Lacan, *Four Fundamental Concepts of Psycho-Analysis*, 88.
37. Kay, *Place of Thought*, 47.
38. A. S. G. Edwards, *Stephen Hawes* (Boston, 1985), 28.
39. See Kipling, *Triumph of Honour*, 22–23.
40. Olivier de la Marche, *Le Chevalier délibéré (The Resolute Knight)*, ed. and trans. Carleton W. Carroll and Lois Hawley Wilson (Tempe, 1999), 5.5. All references are to this edition and translation, and are by stanza and line number.
41. See Samuel C. Chew, *The Pilgrimage of Life* (1962; rpt. Port Washington, 1973), 140–43.
42. Susie Speakman Sutch and Anne Lake Prescott, "Translation as Transformation: Olivier de la Marche's *Le Chevalier délibéré* and its Hapsburg and Elizabethan Permutations," *Comparative Literature Studies* 25 (1988), 281–317 (284).
43. A possibility reinforced by other evidence: another route by which Hawes might have come to know *Le Chevalier délibéré* leads via Wynkyn de Worde to the printers of Gouda and Schiedam, where an edition of de la Marche's poem, splendidly illustrated with woodcuts, was produced in 1498. The use of woodcuts to articulate Hawes's narrative which Edwards discerns in *The Pastime of Pleasure* and *The Example of Virtue* might therefore have been suggested by de Worde himself. In *The Woodcutters of the Netherlands in the Fifteenth Century* (Cambridge, 1884), W. M. Conway notes de Worde's use, in an edition of the *Expositio hymnorum* printed at Westminster in 1499, of a woodcut originally made for an *Opusculum grammaticale* printed by Gotfridus de Os in 1486 (141–42); de Worde also obtained other material from Gouda, as is demonstrated in Lotte and Wytze Hellinga, *The Fifteenth-Century Printing Types of the Low Countries* (London, 1966), 82, plate 182. Lotte Hellinga points out that "In the context of inferred relations between printers (inferred on the basis of their typographic material) it is quite likely that Wynkyn could be aware of books produced in Gouda, or Schiedam ... in particular such spectacular books [as *Le Chevalier*]. Hawes's *Pastime* would be an extremely interesting example to demonstrate the point" (personal communication, 7 June 1990).
44. Jonathan Goldberg, *Voice Terminal Echo: Postmodernism and English Renaissance Texts* (London, 1986), 31.
45. In *The Example of Virtue*, Hawes offers a more sociohistorical signature in a similar style. Dame Sapience appoints him as groom to her chamber, while telling him that if he observes her precepts, "A moche better rome ye do deserve": *Minor Poems*, 16, line 406. The courtier's ambition is asserted in the very gesture by which it is transcended.

46. For the detailed parallels with Caxton's *Recuyell of the Historyes of Troye*, see Vernon Blair Rhodenizer, "Studies in Stephen Hawes's *Pastime of Pleasure*" (1918), 66–71.
47. All references are to William Caxton, *The Recuyell of the Historyes of Troye*, ed. H. Oskar Sommer, 2 vols. (London, 1894).
48. Edwards says that Hawes "mentions the 'cronycles of Spayne' (1030), a compilation that cannot be identified" (*Stephen Hawes*, 28). Hawes's mention of the "cronycles of Spayne" provides further evidence of his use of Caxton. In the *Recuyell*, Caxton faithfully duplicates four allusions in his source to the "Croniques d'Espaigne": see Raoul Lefèvre, *Le Recoeil des Histoires de Troyes*, ed. Marc Aeschbach (Berne, 1987), 341, 372, 375, 393; Caxton, *Recuyell*, II, 346, 390, 394, 421. Over two decades ago, Gerd Pinkernell identified the text referred to, and drawn on, by Lefèvre as the *Sumas de historia troyana* of Leomarte, a medieval Spanish version of the Trojan cycle; see Pinkernell's article on Lefèvre in *Dizionario critico della letteratura francese*, 2 vols. (Turin, 1972), 654–55. Leomarte's work is edited by Agapito Rey: *Sumas de historia troyana* (Madrid, 1932). G. R. Keightley points out that "there is no ground whatever for supposing that [Caxton] himself knew the texts to which Le Fèvre refers": "The *Cronyques of Spaygne* in Caxton's Version of the Trojan History of Raoul Le Fèvre," *Medium Aevum* 49 (1980), 73–89 (79). There is no reason to suppose that Hawes did either, but his dogged adherence to Caxton's phrasing is proof of the borrowing.
49. As Aeschbach once again points out, the association of the Hydra with sophisms comes from Boccaccio, *Genealogia*, XIII, 1: "Eusebius autem in libro Temporum de hac ydra aliter dicit sentire Platonem, quem ait asserere Ydram callidissimam fuisse sophystam. Nam Sophystarum mos est, nisi quis advertat, adeo propositiones suas tradere, ut uno soluto dubio multa consurgant" ["But according to Eusebius in his Chronicles Plato judged otherwise, claiming the Hydra was a most cunning sophist. For it is the way of Sophists to convey their propositions to the unwary in such a manner that when one doubt is resolved many more swarm in"]. See Giovanni Boccaccio, *Genealogie deorum gentilium libri* (Bari, 1951), 640; Aeschbach, 518, note to 60.3). Boccaccio's own source here is Jerome's continuation of Eusebius, where the claim is once again ascribed to Plato: "Hydram autem callidissimam fuisse sofistriam adserit Plato." See Eusebius, *Werke*, 7 vols., ed. Rudolf Helm (Berlin, 1956), VII, 57b; for analogues, 307.
50. See Benoît de Sainte-Maure, *Le Roman de Troie,* 6 vols., ed. Léopold Constans, SATF (Paris, 1904–12), I, 3646–650; Guido de Columnis, *Historia destructionis Troiae*, ed. Nathaniel Edward Griffin (Cambridge, MA, 1936), 43–44, 56–57, 59–60; Lydgate, *Troy Book*, II, 119–38, 1797–899, 2229–54, 5209–25.
51. Mervyn James, "English Politics and the Concept of Honour 1485–1642," *Society, Politics and Culture in Early Modern England* (Cambridge, 1986), 308–415 (357).
52. Roland Barthes, "The Death of the Author," *Image/Music/Text*, trans. Stephen Heath (Glasgow, 1977), 142–48.

53. I follow here Rita Copeland's fine discussion in "Lydgate, Hawes and the Science of Rhetoric in the Late Middle Ages," *Modern Language Quarterly* 53 (1992), 57–82, which works from *The Pastime*'s explicit statements on rhetoric rather than from its narrative structure. Copeland suggests that "A rhetoric understood on the model of the 'veils of fiction' justifies its own exclusiveness and secrecy as instrument of both discursive and political control," supporting an ideology of "royal absolutism" and "state sovereignty" (79, 80).
54. Carlson, *English Humanist Books*, 56–57. The surviving manuscripts of Henry's own library include mostly French texts, though his Privy Purse expenses show that he bought English books too: Anglo, "Court Festivals"; Plomer, "Bibliographical Notes from the Privy Purse Expenses."
55. Walker, *John Skelton,* p. 38.
56. Green, *Poets and Princepleasers*, p. 193.
57. *Minor Poems*, 153.
58. For Oedipus and Fortune, see Lydgate, *The Fall of Princes*, I, 3277–97, 3517–41. For a survey of medieval Oedipus traditions, Léopold Constans, *La Légende d'Oedipe étudiée dans l'antiquité, au moyen âge et dans les temps modernes* (Paris, 1881), and Lowell Edmunds, "Oedipus in the Middle Ages," *Antike und Abendland* 22 (1976), 140–55. On "Thebanness" as a principle of recursiveness, "disordered memory and fatal repetition" in medieval historiography: Patterson, *Chaucer and the Subject of History*, 75.
59. The most detailed suggestions have come from Alistair Fox, who argues that Hawes was unwillingly privy to a conspiracy to endanger the succession among those immediately around him in the household, and was forced to feign disloyalty to the Tudor line. See Fox, "Stephen Hawes" and *Politics and Literature*, 56–72.
60. BL MS Harley 69, fol. 2v.
61. College of Arms MS R36, fol. 124v. The document is transcribed by Richard Firth Green, "A Joust in Honour of the Queen of May, 1441," *Notes and Queries* 225 n.s. 27 (1980), 386–89 (387). Green's dating of this cartel is corrected by Gordon Kipling, "The Queen of May's Joust at Kennington and the *Justes of the Moneths of May and June*," *Notes and Queries* 229 n.s. 31 (1984), 158–62. I would like to thank the College of Arms's archivist, Mr. R. C. Yorke, for his assistance with my own work on these materials.
62. Kipling, *Triumph of Honour*, 133.
63. College of Arms MS R36, fol. 124r–124v.
64. College of Arms MS R36, fol. 124r.
65. "The Justes of the Moneths of May and June," *Remains of the Early Popular Poetry of England*, ed. W. C. Hazlitt, 4 vols. (London, 1864–66), II, 123, line 65.
66. John Stevens, *Music and Poetry in the Early Tudor Court* (London, 1961), 154–202.
67. As Lerer (*Courtly Letters*, 54) notes, Stephen Greenblatt's canonical analysis of Wyatt's poetry – "power over sexuality produces inwardness" – resonates for Hawes's *Comfort*: see Greenblatt, *Renaissance Self-Fashioning*, 124–25. On the parallel with Wyatt, see, too, Colin Burrow, "The Experience of Exclusion: Literature and Politics in the Reigns of Henry VII and Henry VIII," *Cambridge History*, ed. Wallace, 793–820 (797), and Meyer-Lee, *Poets and Power*, 190.

68. For this suggestion, see P. Parker, "Stephen Hawes," *Times Literary Supplement*, 21 June 1928, 468.
69. *Divina Commedia*, Purgatorio, IX, 112–14, where they are the wounds ('piaghe") of sin (114).
70. *The Court of Sapience*, ed. E. Ruth Harvey (Toronto, 1984), 134–35.
71. *Minor Poems*, 158.
72. I cite here Alistair Fox, "Prophecies and Politics in the Reign of Henry VIII," *Reassessing the Henrician Reformation*, ed. Alistair Fox and John Guy, 77–94 (79–80). See, too, Rupert Taylor, *The Political Prophecy in England* (New York, 1911), 35; Erwin Herrmann, "Spätmittelalterliche englische Pseudoprophetien," *Archiv für Kulturgeschichte* 57 (1975), 87–116; Sharon L. Jansen, *Political Protest and Prophecy under Henry VIII* (Woodbridge, 1991); Lesley A. Coote, *Prophecy and Public Affairs in Later Medieval England* (Woodbridge, 2000).
73. See Patricia A. Parker, *Inescapable Romance: Studies in the Poetics of a Mode* (Princeton, 1979), 57–59, and especially "Deferral, Dilation, Différance: Shakespeare, Cervantes, Jonson," *Literary Theory/Renaissance Texts*, ed Patricia Parker and David Quint (Baltimore, 1986), 183–209. The latter essay in particular has much assisted my own, both in its discussion of the Apocalypse as "history's own deferred Recognition scene" (189), and its suggestive mapping of a movement in several Renaissance texts among various forms of deferral and closure – erotic, apocalyptic, rhetorical.
74. Alan of Lille, *PL* 210.137.
75. Fox, "Prophecies and Politics," 80.
76. "Political Poems of the Reigns of Henry VI and Edward IV, communicated by Sir Frederic Madden, K. H., in a Letter to John Gage Rokewode, Esq., Director S. A.," *Archaeologia* 29 (1842), 318–47 (330–31); see also R. H. Robbins (ed.), *Historical Poems of the* XIV*th and* XV*th Centuries* (New York, 1959), 218.
77. R. H. Bowers, "'When cuckow time cometh ofte so soon': A Middle English Animal Prophecy (Lansdowne MS 762, fols. 59–61)," *Anglia* 73 (1955/56), 292–98 (lines 24, 28).
78. *The Story of England, by Robert Manning of Brunne, AD 1338*, ed. F. J. Furnivall, 2 vols., Rolls Series 87 (London, 1887), I, lines 8221–28.
79. *The Isle of Ladies or the Ile of Pleasaunce*, ed. Anthony Jenkins (New York, 1980), lines 2229–32.
80. Sarah Kay, "The Contradictions of Courtly Love and Origins of Courtly Poetry: The Evidence of the *Lauzengiers*," *JMEMS* 26 (1996), 209–53 (224). Standing for other courtiers and other poets, the *losengiers* "constitute an uncanny double of the desired audience as well as of the perfomer, ready with their envious tongues to criticize his performance and prevent his fulfilment" (228). On the infernal *losengier*, see also Emmanuèle Baumgartner, "Trouvères et 'Losengiers,'" *Cahiers de Civilisation Médiévale* 25 (1982), 172 note 12.
81. MS St. Pauls's Cath. 8, fol. 47r, printed in *Reliquiae Antiquae*, ed. T. Wright and J. O. Halliwell, 2 vols. (London, 1841–43); see also Siegfried Wenzel, "Unrecorded Middle English Verses," *Anglia* 92 (1974), 55–78 (76).

82. BL MS Cotton Cleopatra Civ. Fol. 123v; printed as "A Prophecy by the Stars" in Rossell Hope Robbins, "Poems Dealing with Contemporary Conditions," in *A Manual of the Writings in Middle English, 1050–1500*, ed. Albert E. Hartung, vol. v (New Haven, 1967–93), 1530. The poem exists in three other MSS.
83. Gerald Bordman, *Motif-Index of the English Metrical Romances* (Helsinki, 1963), H31.1. (46).
84. This view is taken by Spearing, *Medieval to Renaissance*, p. 259.
85. See Richard Firth Green, "The *Craft of Lovers* and the Rhetoric of Seduction," *Acta* 12 (1985), 105–25.
86. *Minor Poems*, 160–61; Fox, *Politics and Literature*, 66–67; Lerer, *Courtly Letters*, 80–82.
87. See William Calin, *The French Tradition and the Literature of Medieval England* (Toronto, 1994), 250–62 (258).
88. Freud, "Mourning and Melancholia," 244. In "'Processe of Tyme': History, Consolation and Apocalypse in the Book of the Duchess," *Exemplaria* 2 (1990), 659–83, Richard Rambuss links psychoanalysis and apocalypse in his reading of Chaucer's poem, on the grounds that they "work the same terrain: both depend upon the uncovering of secrets as the necessary key to effecting a solution or cure" (669).
89. John Lydgate, "The Temple of Glas," *Poems*, ed. John Norton-Smith (Oxford, 1966), lines 1203–04.
90. Alistair Fox observes that the poem "resembles the specially contrived entertainments put on before foreign ambassadors that emblematically and symbolically foreshadowed the desired outcome of the negotiations at hand" (*Politics and Literature*, 72). On such a showing, we might say, Hawes appropriates the publicly emblematic discourse of royal power for privately motivated symbolism.

6 MAPPING SKELTON: "ESEBON, MARYBON, WHESTON NEXT BARNET"

1. See Walker, *John Skelton and the Politics of the 1520s*, 35–52, 100–23.
2. *John Skelton and Early Modern Culture*, ix.
3. W. Scott Blanchard, "Skelton: The Voice of the Mob in Sanctuary," *Rethinking the Henrician Era: Essays on Early Tudor Texts and Contexts*, ed. Peter C. Herman (Urbana, 1994), 123–44.
4. Richard Halpern, *The Poetics of Primitive Accumulation: English Renaissance Culture and the Genealogy of Capital* (Ithaca, 1991), 113–20.
5. See further A. S. G. Edwards, "Dunbar, Skelton and the Nature of Court Culture in the Early Sixteenth Century," *Vernacular Literature and Current Affairs*, ed. Britnell and Britnell, 120–34.
6. Ulrich Frost, *Das "Commonplace Book" von John Colyns: Untersuchung und Teiledition der Handschrift Harley 2252 der British Library in London* (Frankfurt-on-Main, 1988), 276. See, further, Carol M. Meale, "The Compiler at Work: John Colyns and BL MS Harley 2252," *Manuscripts and Readers in Fifteenth-Century*

England, ed. Derek Pearsall (Cambridge, 1983), 82–103; David R. Parker, *The Commonplace Book in Tudor London. An Examination of BL MSS Egerton 1995, Harley 2252, Lansdowne 762, and Oxford Balliol College MS 354* (Lanham, 1998), 89–127. A. S. G. Edwards rigorously argues the implications of the poem's multiple witnesses in "Deconstructing Skelton: The Texts of the English Poems," *Leeds Studies in English* 36 (2005), 335–53.

7. For Skelton's Latin, I cite Kinsman, *Poems*, which also includes the marginal glosses appended to the parts of the poem in Harley 2252.
8. So Lerer, *Chaucer and his Readers*, 201–02.
9. Quintilian, *Institutio oratoria*, 8.4.3; Lisa Kallet-Marx, *Money, Expense and Naval Power in Thucydides' History 1–5.24* (Berkeley, 1993), 23.
10. *PL* 113.115; I cite John Fyler's translation in *Language and the Declining World in Chaucer, Dante and Jean de Meun* (Cambridge, 2007), 43. On Babel and fallen language more generally, see Fyler, *Language and the Declining World*, 35–59.
11. On Parott's "frantycke" speech: Nathaniel Owen Wallace, "The Responsibilities of Madness: John Skelton, 'Speak, Parrot,' and Homeopathic Satire," *Studies in Philology* 82 (1985), 60–80.
12. I follow here the reading of F. W. Brownlow in "*Speke Parrot*: Skelton's Allegorical Denunciation of Cardinal Wolsey," *Studies in Philology* 65 (1968), 124–39 (135).
13. Kathy Lavezzo, *Angels on the Edge of the World: Geography, Literature and English Community, 1000–1534* (Ithaca, 2006), 133.
14. Griffiths, *John Skelton*, 87.
15. For the fullest examination of these glosses, of uncertain provenance, see ibid., 107–08, 113–17.
16. Michael Uebel, *Ecstatic Transformation: On the Uses of Alterity in the Middle Ages* (New York, 2005), 117.
17. Ibid., 119.
18. Halpern, *Poetics of Primitive Accumulation*, 127.
19. Jean Lemaire de Belges, *Les Épîtres de l'amant vert*, ed. Jean Frappier (Lille, 1948), lines 126–28 ("great joy … in inventing and making noise and sound in order not to hinder the fruit of your pleasure"). On classical and medieval parrot lore, see Bernard Ribémont, "Histoires de perroquets: petit itinéraire zoologique et poétique," *Reinardus* 3 (1990), 155–71; more generally, Bruce Thomas Boehrer, *Parrot Culture: Our 2,500-Year-Long Fascination with the World's Most Talkative Bird* (Philadelphia, 2004), 1–82.
20. On the resonances of "mynyon" at the Henrician court, see Greg Walker, "The Expulsion of the Minions Reconsidered," *Historical Journal* 32 (1989), 1–16; also Jonathan Goldberg, *Sodometries: Renaissance Texts, Modern Sexualities* (Stanford, 1993), 48, and Lerer, *Courtly Letters*, 34–86.
21. Halpern, *Poetics of Primitive Accumulation*, 133.
22. I once again follow Brownlow, "'Speke, Parrot,'" here at 125–27.
23. Karl Marx, *Capital: A Critique of Political Economy*, trans. Samuel Moore and Edward Aveling, 4 vols. (London, 1954), I, 59.

24. See Nicolas Abraham and Maria Torok, "Mourning *or* Melancholia," *The Shell and the Kernel* (Chicago, 1994), I, 125–38, on the channeling of desire "through language into a communion of empty mouths" (127–28).
25. See Kinsman, *Poems*, note to lines 445 ff.
26. See, *inter alia*, Halpern, *Poetics of Primitive Accumulation*, 130–35, Lavezzo, *Angels*, 129–34, Meyer-Lee, *Poets and Power* 210–12.
27. [Pseudo-] Oppian, *Cynegetica*: *Oppian, Colluthus, Tryphodorus*, trans. A. W. Mair (London, 1928), II, lines 408–09. Wolsey is the "maris lupus" in the *Decastichon* of Skelton's *Why Come Ye Nat to Courte?*, 1.
28. This is the "allelophagy" which is allegory's special violence: Gordon Teskey, *Allegory and Violence* (Ithaca, 1996), 8.
29. Michel de Certeau, *The Practice of Everyday Life*, trans. Steven Rendall (Berkeley, 1984), xix, xxi–xxii.
30. *Contra* Nelson, *John Skelton, Laureate*, 181, who asserts the identity of Heshbon with the Church, Brownlow, "'Speke, Parrot,'" reads it as "'the earthly city' (hence London)" (129). Skelton effects the transition within the text.
31. David R. Carlson, "The 'Grammarians' War' 1519–21, Humanist Careerism in Early Tudor England, and Printing," *Medievalia et Humanistica* 18 (1992), 157–81. Carlson argues that the contention was driven on both sides by the quest for patronage and publicity.
32. See Jody Enders, *Rhetoric and the Origins of Medieval Drama* (Ithaca, 1992), 93; on *imagines agentes*, 49–50, and *The Medieval Theater of Cruelty: Rhetoric, Memory, Violence* (Ithaca, 1999), 68–69.
33. Spearing, *Medieval to Renaissance*, 271.
34. On Galathea, see Nancy Coiner, "Galathea and the Interplay of Voices in Skelton's *Speke, Parrot*," *Subjects on the World's Stage: Essays on British Literature of the Middle Ages and the Renaissance* ed. David G. Allen and Robert A. White (Newark, 1995), 88–99.
35. For both versions, see John Stevens, *Music and Poetry in the Early Tudor Court* (Cambridge, 1961), 346–48.
36. Griffiths, *John Skelton*, 98.
37. The connection has been assumed by most critics of *The Garland*. For specific commentary, see A. S. Cook, "Skelton's *Garlande of Laurell* and Chaucer's *House of Fame*," *MLR* 11 (1916), 9–14; John Scattergood, "Skelton's *Garlande of Laurell* and the Chaucerian Tradition," in *Chaucer Traditions: Studies in Honour of Derek Brewer*, ed. Ruth Morse and Barry Windeatt (Cambridge, 1990), 122–38.
38. See, e.g., Spearing, *Medieval Dream-Poetry*, 218.
39. H. L. R. Edwards, *Skelton: The Life and Times of an Early Tudor Poet* (London, 1949), 230; Spearing, *Medieval Dream-Poetry*, 215, and *Medieval to Renaissance*, 245; *The Book of The Laurel*, ed. F. W. Brownlow (Newark, 1990), 184, note to line 668.
40. On the phoenix, see Claudian, *Phoenix*, in Claudian, trans. Maurice Platnauer, 2 vols. (London, 1922), 23–26, 69–70; Ovid, *Metamorphoses*, trans. Frank Justus Miller, 2 vols. (Cambridge, MA, 1966), xv, 401–07. All references to the *Metamorphoses* are to this edition.

41. Cf. Skelton's *Replycacion Agaynst Certyne Yong Scolers*, where the "spyrituall," "mysteriall" and "mysticall / Effecte energiall" of "laureate creacyon" (365–73) is generated dialectically from menaces of a very material punishment, to be inscribed on the bodies of heretics ("doutlesse ye shalbe blased, / And be brent at a stake" [294–95]; the grim pun on "blased" merges the penalty for heresy with the murderously "blazoning" activities of Skelton's own pen).
42. I cite and follow here the overview of and contribution to the debate in David R. Carlson, ed., *The Latin Writings of John Skelton* (Chapel Hill, 1991), 102–09 (102). For Tucker's researches, see "Skelton and Sheriff Hutton," *English Language Notes* 4 (1967), 254–59, and "The Ladies in Skelton's 'Garlande of Laurell,'" *Renaissance Quarterly* 22 (1969), 333–45; see also Owen Gingerich and Melvin J. Tucker, "The Astronomical Dating of Skelton's Garlande of Laurell," *Huntington Library Quarterly* 32 (1969), 207–20. A somewhat strained case for a later date is argued in Fox, *Politics and Literature*, 147–55.
43. Spearing, *Medieval to Renaissance*, 245–46.
44. Andrew Hadfield, *Literature, Politics and National Identity: Reformation to Renaissance* (Cambridge, 1994), 36.
45. Lerer, *Chaucer and his Readers*, 203.
46. Julia Boffey, "'Withdraw your hande': The Lyrics of *The Garland of Laurel* from Manuscript to Print," *John Skelton and Early Modern Culture*, ed. David Carlson (Tempe, 2008), 135–46; Edwards, "From Manuscript to Print," 143–48, and *John Skelton: The Critical Heritage* (London, 1981), 3–5.
47. Kate Harris, "Patrons, Buyers and Owners: The Evidence for Ownership and the Role of Book Owners in Book Production and the Book Trade," in Griffiths and Pearsall, *Book Production and Publishing in Britain*, 163–99 (183).
48. On this trope and hierarchies of gender, see Patricia Parker, *Literary Fat Ladies: Rhetoric, Gender, Property* (London, 1987), 67–69 (69).
49. Lynn Enterline, *Rhetoric of the Body*, 31–32, 67–69 and *passim*. See, too, the fine examination of this episode in Philip Hardie, *Ovid's Poetics of Illusion* (Cambridge, 2002), 45–50.
50. For a similar reading, see, now, Maura Tarnoff, "Sewing Authorship in John Skelton's *Garlande or Chapelet of Laurell*," *ELH* 75 (2008), 415–38.
51. Scattergood, "Skelton's *Garlande of Laurell*," interprets this line as an allusion to the risky "stability of print" (131).
52. See Glending Olson, "Making and Poetry in the Age of Chaucer," *Comparative Literature* 31 (1979), 272–90; Anne Middleton, "Chaucer's 'New Men' and the Good of Literature in the *Canterbury Tales*," *Literature and Society. Papers from the English Institute, 1978*, ed. Edward Said (Baltimore, 1980), 15–56.
53. Carolyn Dinshaw, *Chaucer's Sexual Poetics* (Madison, 1989), 78–79.
54. H. L. R. Edwards, *Skelton*, 234; Spearing, *Medieval Dream-Poetry*, 216; Brownlow, *Book of the Laurel*, 76.
55. Ovid, *Heroides*, IX; *Metamorphoses*, IX, 1–272. All references to the *Heroides* are to the text in *Heroides and Amores*, trans. Grant Showerman, Loeb, 2nd edn. (Cambridge, MA, 1977).
56. *Heroides*, XI.

57. *Heroides*, IV; *Metamorphoses*, XV, 500–03.
58. *Heroides*, IV, 57–58; *Metamorphoses*, VIII, 131–37, IX, 735–40. For a suggestive commentary on the transgressive fictional potentialities of this figure in the Middle Ages, see Renate Blumenfeld-Kosinski, "The Scandal of Pasiphae: Narration and Interpretation in the *Ovide Moralisé*," *Modern Philology* 93 (1996), 307–26.
59. *Heroides*, XIII.
60. *Heroides*, VI, XVII, 193.
61. *Heroides*, XX, XXI.
62. Goldberg, *Voice Terminal Echo*, 70. See *Metamorphoses*, VI, 424–674.
63. John Norton-Smith, "The Origins of 'Skeltonics,'" *Essays in Criticism* 23 (1973), 57–62 (62).
64. Elizabeth Fowler, *Literary Character: The Human Figure in Early English Writing* (Ithaca, 2003), 245–73.
65. Halpern, *Poetics of Primitive Accumulation*, 126.
66. Greene, "Calling Colin Clout," 234.
67. Elizabeth Scala, *Absent Narratives: Manuscript Textuality and Literary Structure in Late Medieval England* (New York, 2002), 71–98.

CONCLUSION

1. Puttenham, *Arte of English Poesie*, 60.
2. Greg Walker, *Writing under Tyranny: English Literature and the Henrician Reformation* (Oxford, 2005), 426.
3. Meyer-Lee, *Poets and Power*, 226.
4. C. Burrow, "Tudor Sanctuaries," review of Fox, *Politics and Literature in the Reigns of Henry VII and Henry VIII*, *Essays in Criticism* 41 (1991), 51–61.
5. Meyer-Lee, *Poets and Power*, 226.
6. Teskey, *Allegory and Violence*, 19; and see Walter Benjamin, *The Origin of German Tragic Drama*, trans. John Osborne (London, 1998), 159–235.
7. For recent commentary, see Griffiths, *John Skelton*, 130–35, and Vincent Gillespie, "Justification by Faith: Skelton's *Replycacion*," *The Long Fifteenth Century: Essays for Douglas Gray*, ed. Helen Cooper and Sally Mapstone (Oxford, 1997), 273–312.
8. R. James Goldstein, "Normative Heterosexuality in History and Theory: The Case of Sir David Lindsay of the Mount," *Becoming Male in the Middle Ages*, ed. Jeffrey Jerome Cohen and Bonnie Wheeler (New York, 2000), 349–65 (355).
9. Roderick J. Lyall, *Alexander Montgomerie: Poetry, Politics and Cultural Change in Jacobean Scotland* (Tempe, 2005), 336–49; see, too, Dunnigan, *Eros and Poetry*.

Bibliography

PRIMARY SOURCES

L'Abuzé en court. Ed. Roger Dubuis. Paris: Droz, 1973.
Aeneas Silvius. *Aeneae Silvii de Curialium Miseriis Epistola*. Ed. Wilfred P. Mustard. Baltimore, MD: Johns Hopkins University Press, 1928.
Alan of Lille. "Summa de arte praedicatoria." *PL* 210: 110–98.
Alberic of Monte Cassino. *Alberici Casinensis Flores Rhetorici*. Miscellanea Cassinese 14. Ed. D. Mauro Inguanez and H. M. Willard. Monte Cassino: s.n., 1938.
André, Bernard. "De vita atque gestis Henrici Septimi . . . historia." *Memorials of King Henry the Seventh*. Ed. James Gairdner. Rerum Britannicarum Medii Aevi Scriptores (Rolls Series) 10. London: Longman, 1858. 1–75
[Archpoet.] *Die Gedichte des Archipoeta*. Ed. Heinrich Watenphul and Heinrich Krefeld. Heidelberg: Carl Winter Verlag, 1958.
Ashby, George. *Works*. Ed. Mary Bateson. EETS ES 76. London: Kegan Paul, Trench, Trübner, 1899.
Augustine. *Confessions, Introduction and Text*. Vol. 1 of 3. Ed. James J. O'Donnell. Oxford: Clarendon Press, 1992.
　De doctrina christiana. Ed. I. Martin. CCSL XXXII. Turnhout: Brepols, 1962. 1–167.
　De ordine. Ed. W. M. Green. CCSL XXIX. Turnhout: Brepols, 1970. 87–137.
Bacon, Francis. *History of the Reign of Henry VII*. Ed. J. R. Lumby. Cambridge University Press, 1902.
Bale, John. *Scriptorum illustrium maioris Bryttania . . . catalogus*. Basle, 1557–59. Farnborough, Hants.: Gregg International, 1971.
Barclay, Alexander. "A Critical Edition of Alexander Barclay's *Ship of Fools* (1509)." Ed. David Rollin Anderson. PhD dissertation, Case Western Reserve University, 1974.
　The Eclogues of Alexander Barclay. Ed. Beatrice White. EETS OS 175. Oxford University Press, 1928, 1960.
　Here begynneth the famous cronycle of the warre / which the romayns had against Iugurth. STC 21627. London: R. Pynson, n.d. [1520].
　The Life of St. George. Ed. William Nelson, EETS OS 230. Oxford University Press, 1955 [for 1948].

Benoît de Sainte-Maure. *Le Roman de Troie*. 6 vols. Ed. Léopold Constans. SATF. Paris: Firmin-Didot, 1904–12.

Boccaccio, Giovanni. *Genealogie deorum gentilium libri*. 2 vols. Ed. Vincenzo Romano. Bari: G. Laterza, 1951.

Bowers, R. H. "'When cuckow time cometh oft so soon': A Middle English Animal Prophecy (Lansdowne MS 762, fols. 59–61)." *Anglia* 73 (1955/56): 292–98.

Bühler, Curt F., ed. *The Dicts and Sayings of the Philosophers: The Translations Made by Stephen Scrope, William Worcester, and an Anonymous Translator*. EETS OS 211. Oxford University Press, 1941.

Caxton, William. *Caxton's Own Prose*. Ed. N. F. Blake. London: André Deutsch, 1973.

The History of Reynard the Fox. Ed. N. F. Blake. EETS 263. Oxford University Press, 1970.

The Recuyell of the Historyes of Troye. 2 vols. Ed. H. Oskar Sommer. London: D. Nutt, 1894.

Chartier, Alain. *The Curial made by Maystere Alain Charretier*. Trans. William Caxton. Ed. F. J Furnivall. EETS ES 54. London: N. Trübner & Co., 1888.

A Familiar Dialogue of the Friend and the Fellow: A Translation of Alain Chartier's "Dialogus familiaris amici et sodalis." Ed. Margaret S. Blayney. EETS OS 295. Oxford University Press, 1989.

Fifteenth-Century English Translation of Alain Chartier's "Le Traité de l'Espérance" and "Le Quadrilogue Invectif." Ed. Margaret S. Blayney. 2 vols. EETS OS 270, 281. Oxford University Press, 1974, 1980.

Le Livre de l'espérance. Ed. François Rouy. Paris: H. Champion, 1989.

Les Oeuvres latines d' Alain Chartier. Ed. Pascale Bourgain-Hemeryck. Paris: Editions du Centre National de la Recherche Scientifique, 1977.

[Chaucer, Geoffrey.] *The Riverside Chaucer*. Ed. Larry D. Benson et al. 3rd edn. Boston: Houghton Mifflin, 1987.

Chrétien de Troyes. *Le Chevalier de la Charrette ou Le Roman de Lancelot*. Ed. Charles Méla. Paris: Hachette, 1992.

Cicero. *Ad Herennium*. Trans. Harry Caplan. Loeb. Cambridge, MA: Harvard University Press, 1954, 1968.

De inventione, De optimo genere oratorum, Topica. Trans H. M. Hubbell. Loeb. Cambridge, MA: Harvard University Press, 1949, 1968. 349–73.

De officiis. Trans. Walter Miller. Loeb. Cambridge, MA: Harvard University Press, 1913, 1968.

"Pro Caelio." *The Orations*. 9 vols. Trans. R. Gardner. Loeb. Cambridge, MA: Harvard University Press, 1958. 398–522.

Claudian. *Phoenix*. 2 vols. Trans. Maurice Platnauer. Loeb. London: William Heinemann, 1922.

Compota thesaurariorum regum Scotorum. Accounts of the Lord High Treasurer of Scotland. 12 vols. Ed. Thomas Dickson, Sir James Balfour-Paul and C. T. Innes. Edinburgh: H.M. General Register House, 1877–1916.

The Court of Sapience. Ed. E. Ruth Harvey. University of Toronto Press, 1984.

[Crétin, Guillaume.] *Oeuvres poétiques de Guillaume Crétin.* Ed. Kathleen Chesney. Paris: Firmin-Didot, 1932.
Dante Alighieri. *La Divina commedia.* Ed. Natalino Sapegno. Florence: La Nuova Italia, 1955–57.
Deschamps, Eustache. *Oeuvres complètes.* 11 vols. Ed. A. Queux de Saint-Hilaire, and Gaston Raynaud. SATF. Paris: Firmin-Didot, 1878–1904.
Douglas, Gavin. *The Palis of Honoure.* Ed. David Parkinson. Kalamazoo, MI: Medieval Institute Publications, 1992.
  The Shorter Poems of Gavin Douglas. Ed. Priscilla J. Bawcutt, STS 4th series 3. Edinburgh: William Blackwood, 1967.
  Virgil's Aeneid. 4 vols. Ed. D. F. C. Coldwell. STS 3rd series. 25, 27, 29, 30. Edinburgh: William Blackwood, 1951–56.
Dunbar, William. *The Poems of William Dunbar.* Ed. Priscilla J. Bawcutt. 2 vols. Glasgow: Association for Scottish Literary Studies, 1998.
Eusebius. *Werke.* Ed. Rudolf Helm. 7 vols. Die griechischen christlichen Schriftsteller der ersten Jahrhundert 47. Berlin: Akademie-Verlag, 1956.
Faral, Edmond, ed. *Les Arts poétiques du XIIe et du XIIIe siècle: Recherches et documents sur la technique littéraire du moyen âge.* Paris: E. Champion, 1923.
Feylde, Thomas. *A Contrauersye bytwene a Louer and a Iaye.* STC 10838.7. London: Wynkyn de Worde, n.d. [1527].
The Floure and the Leafe and The Assembly of Ladies. Ed. Derek Pearsall. London: Nelson, 1962.
Fortescue, Sir John. *The Governance of England.* Ed. Charles Plummer. Oxford: Clarendon Press, 1885.
Franceschini, Ezio. "Il 'Liber philosophorum moralium antiquorum': testo critico." *Atti del Reale Istituto Veneto di Scienze, Lettere ed Arti* 91 pt. 2 (1931–32): 393–597.
[Froissart, Jean.] *Oeuvres de Froissart: poésies.* 3 vols. Ed. Auguste Scheler. Brussels: Victor Devaux, 1870–72.
[The Gast of Gy.] *Three Purgatory Poems: The Gast of Gy, Sir Owain, The Vision of Tundale.* Ed. Edward E. Foster. Kalamazoo, MI: Medieval Institute Publications, 2004.
Geoffrey of Vinsauf. *The "Poetria Nova" and its Sources in Early Rhetorical Doctrine.* Ed. and trans. Ernest Gallo. The Hague: Mouton, 1971.
[Gower, John.] *The English Works of John Gower.* Ed. G. C. Macaulay. 2 vols. EETS ES 81, 82. Oxford University Press, 1900–01.
Green, Richard Firth. "A Joust in Honour of the Queen of May, 1441." *Notes and Queries* 225 n.s. 27 (1980): 386–89.
Guido de Columnis. *Historia destructionis Troiae.* Ed. Nathaniel Edward Griffin. Cambridge, MA: Mediaeval Academy of America, 1936.
Hammond, Eleanor Prescott, ed. *English Verse between Chaucer and Surrey.* Durham, NC: Duke University Press, 1927.
Hary, *Wallace.* 2 vols. Ed. Matthew P. McDiarmid. STS 4th series. 4, 5. Edinburgh: William Blackwood, 1968–69.
Hawes, Stephen. *The Minor Poems.* Ed. Florence W. Gluck and Alice B. Morgan. EETS OS 271. Oxford University Press, 1974.

The Pastime of Pleasure. Ed. W. E. Mead. EETS OS 173. Oxford University Press, 1928.
Hay, Sir Gilbert. *The Buik of King Alexander the Conquerour.* 2 vols. Ed. John Cartwright. STS 4th series. 16, 18. Edinburgh: Scottish Text Society, 1986, 1990.
Hazlitt, W. C., ed. *Remains of the Early Popular Poetry of England.* 4 vols. London: J. R. Smith, 1864–66.
Hellinga, W. Gs. *Van den Vos Reynaerde: 1 Teksten.* Zwolle: Tjeenk Willink, 1952.
[Hoccleve, Thomas.] *Hoccleve's Works: The Minor Poems.* Ed. Frederick J. Furnivall, I. Gollancz, revised Jerome Mitchell and A. I. Doyle. EETS ES 61, 73. Oxford University Press, 1970.
  The Regiment of Princes. Ed. Charles R. Blyth. Kalamazoo, MI: Medieval Institute Publications, 1999.
The Isle of Ladies or the Ile of Pleasaunce. Ed. Anthony Jenkins. New York: Garland, 1980.
James I of Scotland. *The Kingis Quair.* Ed. John Norton-Smith. Oxford: Clarendon Press, 1971.
John of Salisbury. *Metalogicon.* Ed. J. B. Hall. Corpus Christianorum Continuatio Mediaevalis XCVIII. Turnhout: Typographi Brepols Editores Pontificii, 1991.
  Policraticus. Ed. Clemens C. I. Webb. 2 vols. Oxford: Clarendon Press, 1909.
La Marche, Olivier de. *Le Chevalier délibéré (The Resolute Knight).* Ed. and trans. Carleton W. Carroll and Lois Hawley Wilson. Medieval and Renaissance Texts and Studies 199. Tempe, AZ: Arizona Center for Medieval and Renaissance Studies, 1999.
Lefèvre, Raoul. *Le Recoeil des Histoires de Troyes.* Ed. Marc Aeschbach. Berne: Peter Lang, 1987.
Leland, John. *De rebus Brittanicis collectanea.* 6 vols. London: Gul. et Jo. Richardson, 1770.
Lemaire de Belges, Jean. *Les Épîtres de l'amant vert.* Ed. Jean Frappier. Lille: Giard, 1948.
Leomarte. *Sumas de historia troyana.* Ed. Agapito Rey. Madrid: S. Aguirre, 1932.
Letters and Papers, Foreign and Domestic, of the Reign of Henry VIII. 21 vols. Ed. J. S. Brewer et al. London: H.M. Stationery Office, 1872–1920.
Lindesay of Pitscottie, Robert. *The Historie and Cronicles of Scotland, from the Slauchter of King James the First to the Ane thousande fyve hundreith thrie scoir fyftein 3eir.* 3 vols. Ed. A. J. G. Mackay. Edinburgh and London: William Blackwood, 1899–1911.
Lucian. [*Works.*] Trans A. M. Harmon. Vol. v of 8. Loeb. Cambridge, MA: Harvard University Press, 1913, 1967.
Lydgate, John. *The Fall of Princes.* 4 vols. Ed. Henry Bergen. EETS ES 121–24. Oxford University Press, 1924–27.
  The Minor Poems of John Lydgate. Part II: The Secular Poems. Ed. Henry Noble MacCracken. EETS OS 192. Oxford University Press, 1934.
  Poems. Ed. John Norton-Smith. Oxford: Clarendon Press, 1966.

The Siege of Thebes. Ed. Robert R. Edwards. Kalamazoo, MI: Medieval Institute Publications, 2001.

Troy Book. Ed. Henry Bergen. 4 vols. EETS ES 97, 103, 106, 126. London: Kegan Paul, Trench, Trübner, 1906–35.

Lydgate, John and Benet Burgh. *Secrees of Olde Philisoffres*. Ed. R. Steele. EETS ES 66. London: Kegan Paul, Trench, Trübner, 1894.

Lyndsay, Sir David, *Selected Poems*, ed. Janet Hadley Williams. Glasgow: Association for Scottish Literary Studies, 2000.

Machaut, Guillaume. *Le Jugement du roy de Behaigne and Remede de Fortune*. Ed. James I. Wimsatt and William W. Kibler. Athens, GA: University of Georgia Press, 1988.

Oeuvres de Guillaume de Machaut. 3 vols. Ed. Ernest Hoepffner. SATF. Paris: Firmin-Didot, 1908–21.

Poésies lyriques. 2 vols. Ed. V. Chichmaref. Paris: H. Champion, 1909.

Macrobius, Ambrosius Theodosius. *Commentarii in Somnium Scipionis*. Ed. James Willis. Leipzig: B. G. Teubner, 1970. Trans., ed. and intro. William Harris Stahl, New York, 1952.

[Madden, Sir Frederic.] 'Political Poems of the Reigns of Henry VI and Edward IV, communicated by Sir Frederic Madden, K.H., in a Letter to John Gage Rokewode, Esq., Director S.A.' *Archaeologia* 29 (1842): 318–47.

[Manning of Brunne, Robert.] *The Story of England, by Robert Manning of Brunne, AD 1338*. 2 vols. Ed. F. J. Furnivall. Rolls Series 87. London: Longman, 1887.

Mantuan, Baptista. *Adulescentia: The Eclogues of Mantuan*. Ed. and trans. Lee Piepho. New York: Garland, 1989.

The Eclogues of Baptista Mantuanus. Ed. Wilfred P. Mustard. Baltimore, MD: Johns Hopkins University Press, 1911.

Map, Walter. *De nugis curialium: Courtiers' Trifles*. Ed. and trans. M. R. James, rev. edn. C. N. L. Brooke and R. A. B. Mynors. Oxford University Press, 1983.

Marot, Clément. *Les Epîtres*. Ed. C. A. Mayer. London: Athlone Press, 1958.

Martin le Franc. *Le Champion des Dames*. Ed. Arthur Piaget. Lausanne: Payot, 1968.

Matthew of Vendôme. "Ars versificatoria." *Les Arts poétiques du XIIe et du XIIIe siècle: recherches et documents sur la technique littéraire du moyen âge*. Ed. Edmond Faral. Paris: E. Champion, 1923.

Migne, J.-P., ed. *Patrologia cursus completus series Latina*. 221 vols. Paris: *s.n.*, 1844–64.

[Molinet, Jean.] *Les Faictz et Dictz de Jean Molinet*. 3 vols. Ed. Noël Dupire. SATF. Paris: Didot, 1936–39.

Ovid. *Heroides*. Trans. Grant Showerman. 2nd edn. Loeb. Cambridge, MA: Harvard University Press, 1977.

Metamorphoses. 2 vols. Trans. Frank Justus Miller. Loeb. Cambridge, MA: Harvard University Press, 1966.

Petrarch, Francis, *The Life of Solitude*. Trans. Jacob Zeitlin. Urbana: University of Illinois Press, 1924.

Plomer, H. R. "Bibliographical Notes from the Privy Purse Expenses of King Henry VII." *The Library* 3rd series 4 (1913): 209–305.

Pollard, A. F., ed. *The Reign of Henry VII from Contemporary Sources.* 3 vols. London: Longmans, Green, 1913–14.
"A Prophecy by the Stars." *A Manual of the Writings in Middle English, 1050–1500.* Ed. Albert E. Hartung. Vol. v. New Haven: Connecticut Academy of Arts and Sciences, 1967–93. 1530.
[Pseudo-] Oppian. *Cynegetica: Oppian, Colluthus, Tryphodorus.* Trans. A. W. Mair Loeb. London: William Heinemann, 1928.
Puttenham, George. *The Arte of English Poesie.* Ed. Gladys Doidge Willcock and Alice Walker. Cambridge University Press, 1936.
Quintilian. *Institutio oratoria.* 4 vols. Trans. H. E. Butler. Cambridge, MA: Harvard University Press, 1920–22, 1976.
The Receyt of the Lady Kateryne. Ed. Gordon Kipling. EETS OS 296. Oxford University Press, 1990.
Registrum Secreti Sigilli Regum Scotorum: The Register of the Privy Seal of Scotland. Ed. M. Livingstone, D. H. Fleming and J. Beveridge et al. Vol. 1 of 5. Edinburgh: H.M. General Register House, 1908.
Li regret Guillaume comte de Hainaut: poème inédit du XIVe siècle, par Jehan de la Mote. Ed. Auguste Scheler. Louvain: J. Lefever, 1882.
Robbins, R. H., ed. *Historical Poems of the XIVth and XVth Centuries.* New York: Columbia University Press, 1959.
Le Roman de Renart. Ed. Gabriel Bianciotto. Paris: Hachette, 2005.
Rutebeuf. *Oeuvres complètes de Rutebeuf.* Ed. Michel Zink. 2 vols. Paris: Bordas, 1989–90.
Shakespeare, William. *The Riverside Shakespeare.* Ed. G. Blakemore Evans et al. Boston: Houghton Mifflin, 1974.
Skelton, John. *The Book of The Laurel.* Ed. F. W. Brownlow. Newark, NJ: University of Delaware Press, 1990.
  The Complete English Poems. Ed. John Scattergood. Harmondsworth: Penguin, 1983.
  The Latin Writings of John Skelton. Ed. David R. Carlson. *Studies in Philology, Texts and Studies Series* 88.4. Chapel Hill, NC, 1991.
  Poems. Ed. Robert Kinsman. Oxford: Clarendon Press, 1969.
Statutes of the Realm: Printed from Original Records and Authentic Manuscripts. Ed. A. Luders, Sir T. E. Tomlins, J. France et al. Vol. 11 of 12. London, 1810–28; London: Record Commission, 1963.
Taillevent, Michault. *Michault Taillevent: un poète bourguignon du XVe siècle.* Ed. Robert Deschaux. Geneva: Droz, 1975.
[Walter of Châtillon.] *Moralische-satirische Gedichte Walters von Châtillon.* Ed. Karl Strecker. Heidelberg: Carl Winter Verlag, 1929.
Walther, Hans. *Proverbia Sententiaeque Latinitatis Medii Aevi.* 9 vols. Göttingen: Vandenhoeck & Ruprecht, 1963.
[Walton, John.] *Boethius: De consolatione philosophiae: Translated by John Walton.* Ed. Mark Science. EETS OS 170. Oxford University Press, 1927.
The Welles Anthology: MS. Rawlinson C. 813: A Critical Edition. Ed. Sharon L. Jansen and Kathleen H. Jordan. Binghamton, NY: Medieval and Renaissance Texts and Studies, 1991.

Wenzel, Siegfried. "Unrecorded Middle English Verses." *Anglia* 92 (1974): 55–78.
Wogan-Browne, Jocelyn, Nicholas Watson, Andrew Taylor and Ruth Evans, ed. *The Idea of the Vernacular: An Anthology of Middle English Literary Theory, 1280–1520*. University Park, PA: Pennsylvania State University Press, 1999.
Wright, T. and J. O. Halliwell, eds. *Reliquae Antiquiae*. 2 vols. London: William Pickering, 1841–43.

SECONDARY SOURCES

Abraham, Nicolas and Maria Torok. "Mourning or Melancholia." *The Shell and the Kernel*. Vol. 1. University of Chicago Press, 1994. 125–38.
Aers, David. "A Whisper in the Ear of Early Modernists, or, Reflections on Literary Critics Writing the 'History of the Subject.'" *Culture and History 1350–1600: Essays on English Communities, Identities and Writing*. Ed. David Aers. Detroit: Wayne State University Press, 1992. 177–202.
Aitken, Adam J., Matthew P. McDiarmid and Derick S. Thomson, ed. *Bards and Makars: Scottish Language and Literature, Medieval and Renaissance*. University of Glasgow Press, 1977.
Anderson, Perry. *Lineages of the Absolutist State*. London: New Left Books, 1974.
Anglo, Sydney. "The Court Festivals of Henry VII: A Study Based upon the Account Books of John Heron, Treasurer of the Chamber." *Bulletin of the John Rylands Library* 43 (1960/61): 12–45.
  "Ill of the Dead: The Posthumous Reputation of Henry VII." *Renaissance Studies* 1 (1987): 27–47.
  Spectacle, Pageantry, and Early Tudor Policy. Oxford: Clarendon Press, 1969.
Archbold, W. E. J. "Sir William Stanley and Perkin Warbeck." *EHR* 14 (1899): 529–34.
Archer, John Michael. *Sovereignty and Intelligence: Spying and Court Culture in the English Renaissance*. Stanford University Press, 1993.
Arthurson, Ian. "Espionage and Intelligence from the Wars of the Roses to the Reformation." *Nottingham Medieval Studies* 35 (1991): 134–54.
Baillie, Hugh Murray. "Etiquette and the Planning of the State Apartments in Baroque Palaces." *Archaeologia* 101 (1967): 169–99.
Barnes, A. W. "Constructing the Sexual Subject of John Skelton." *ELH* 71 (2004): 29–51.
Barrington, Candace. "Misframed Fables: Barclay's Gower and the Wantonness of Performance." *Medievalia* 24 (2003): 195–225.
Barthes, Roland. *Mythologies*. Trans. Annette Lavers. New York: Hill & Wang, 1972.
  "The Death of the Author." *Image/Music/Text*. Trans. Stephen Heath. Glasgow: William Collins, 1977. 142–48.
  "Textual Analysis of Poe's 'Valdemar.'" Trans. Geoff Bennington. *Untying the Text: A Post-Structuralist Reader*. Ed. Robert Young. London: Routledge & Kegan Paul, 1981. 133–61.
Baswell, Christopher. *Virgil in Medieval England*. Cambridge University Press, 1995.

Baudrillard, Jean. *Selected Writings*. Ed. Mark Poster. Cambridge, MA: Polity Press, 1988.
Baumgartner, Emmanuèle. "Trouvères et 'Losengiers.'" *Cahiers de Civilisation Médiévale* 25 (1982): 171–78.
Dunbar the Makar. Oxford: Clarendon Press, 1992.
Gavin Douglas: A Critical Study. Edinburgh University Press, 1976.
Bawcutt, Priscilla. "The Art of Flyting." *Scottish Literary Journal* 10 (1983): 5–24.
"Dunbar's Christmas Carol." *Scottish Language and Literature, Medieval and Renaissance: Fourth International Conference 1984, Proceediings*. Ed. Dietrich Strauss and Horst W. Drescher. Frankfurt-on-Main: P. Lang, 1986. 381–92.
"Dunbar's Use of the Symbolic Lion and Thistle." *Cosmos* 2 (1986): 83–97.
"The Earliest Texts of Dunbar." *Regionalism in Medieval Manuscripts and Texts*. Ed. Felicity Riddy. Cambridge: D. S. Brewer, 1991. 183–98.
"Henryson's 'Poeit of the Auld Fassoun.'" *Review of English Studies* n.s. 32 (1981): 429–34.
Baxter, J. W. *William Dunbar: A Biographical Study*. Edinburgh: Oliver & Boyd, 1952.
Bellamy, Elizabeth J. *Translations of Power: Narcissism and the Unconscious in Epic History*. Ithaca, NY: Cornell University Press, 1992.
Benjamin, Walter. *The Origin of German Tragic Drama*. Trans. John Osborne. London: Verso, 1998.
"Theses on the Philosophy of History." *Illuminations*. Ed. and intro. Hannah Arendt. Trans. Harry Zohn. New York: Fontana Press, 1992. 245–55.
"The Work of Art in the Age of Mechanical Reproduction." *Illuminations*. 211–44.
Bennett, H. S. *English Books and Readers, 1475–1557: Being a Study in the History of the Book Trade from Caxton to the Incorporation of the Stationers' Company*. 2nd edn. Cambridge University Press, 1969.
Bennett, J. A. W. "*Nosce te ipsum*: Some Medieval and Modern Interpretations." *The Humane Medievalist, and Other Essays in English Literature and Learning, from Chaucer to Eliot*. Ed. Pietro Boitani. Rome: Edizioni di storia e letteratura, 1982. 135–72.
Berger Jnr., Harry. "Bodies and Texts." *Representations* 17 (1987): 144–66. Reprinted in *Situated Utterances: Texts, Bodies, and Cultural Representations*, New York, 2005, 99–128.
Betten, Anne. "Lateinische Bettellyrik: Literarische Topik oder Ausdruck existentieller Not? Eine vergleichende Skizze über Martial und den Archipoeta." *Mittellateinisches Jahrbuch* 11 (1976): 143–50.
Blackwell, C. W. T. "Humanism and Politics in English Royal Biography: The use of Cicero, Plutarch and Sallust in the *Vita Henrici Quinti* (1438) by Titus Livius de Frulovisi and the *Vita Henrici Septimi* (1500–03) by Bernard André." *Acta Conventus Neo-Latini Sanctandreani*. Ed. I. D. McFarlane. Binghamton, NY: Medieval and Renaissance Texts and Studies, 1986. 431–40.
Blake, N. F. "Wynkyn de Worde: The Later Years." *Gutenberg Jahrbuch* (1972): 128–38.

Blanchard, W. Scott. "Skelton: The Voice of the Mob in Sanctuary." *Rethinking the Henrician Era: Essays on Early Tudor Texts and Contexts*. Ed. Peter C. Herman. Urbana: University of Illinois Press, 1994. 123–44.

Bloch, Marc. *The Royal Touch: Sacred Monarchy and Scrofula in England and France*. Trans. J. E. Anderson. London: Routledge & Kegan Paul, 1973.

Bloch, R. Howard. *Etymologies and Genealogies: A Literary Anthropology of the French Middle Ages*. University of Chicago Press, 1983.

   Medieval Misogyny and the Invention of Western Romantic Love. University of Chicago Press, 1991.

   "Silence and Holes: The *Roman de silence* and the Art of the Trouvère." *Yale French Studies* 70 (1986): 81–99.

Blumenfeld-Kosinski, Renate. "The Scandal of Pasiphae: Narration and Interpretation in the *Ovide moralisé*." *Modern Philology* 93 (1996): 307–26.

Boehrer, Bruce Thomas. *Parrot Culture: Our 2,500-Year-Long Fascination with the World's Most Talkative Bird*. Philadelphia: University of Pennsylvania Press, 2004.

Boffey, Julia. *Manuscripts of Courtly Love Lyrics in the Later Middle Ages*. Cambridge: D. S. Brewer, 1985.

   "The Maitland Folio Manuscript as a Verse Anthology." *William Dunbar. "The Nobill Poyet": Essays in Honour of Priscilla Bawcutt*. Ed. Sally Mapstone. East Linton: Tuckwell Press, 2001. 40–50.

   "'Withdraw your hande': The Lyrics of The Garland of Laurel from Manuscript to Print." *John Skelton and Early Modern Culture*. Medieval and Renaissance Texts and Studies 300. Ed. David Carlson. Tempe, AZ: Arizona Center for Medieval and Renaissance Studies, 2008. 135–46.

Borch-Jacobsen, Mikkel. *The Freudian Subject*. Trans. Catherine Porter. Stanford University Press, 1988.

Bordman, Gerald. *Motif-Index of the English Metrical Romances*. Helsinki: Suomalainen Tiedeakatemia, 1963.

Bossy, John. *Christianity in the West 1400–1700*. Oxford University Press, 1985.

Bourdieu, Pierre. *Language and Symbolic Power*. Ed. and intro. John B. Thompson. Trans. Gino Raymond and Matthew Adamson. Cambridge, MA: Harvard University Press, 1991.

   The Logic of Practice. Trans. Richard Nice. Cambridge: Polity Press, 1990.

Brooks, Peter. *Reading for the Plot: Design and Intention in Narrative*. Oxford: Clarendon Press, 1984.

Brownlow, F. W. "The Book Compiled by Maister Skelton, Poet Laureate, Called *Speake, Parrot*." *English Literary Renaissance* 1 (1971): 3–26.

   "The Date of *The Bowge of Courte* and Skelton's Authorship of 'A Lamentable of Kyng Edward the IIII.'" *English Language Notes* 22 (1984): 12–20.

   "*Speke Parrot*: Skelton's Allegorical Denunciation of Cardinal Wolsey." *Studies in Philology* 65 (1968): 124–39.

Bryan, Jennifer. *Looking Inward: Devotional Reading and the Private Self in Late Medieval England*. Philadelphia: University of Pennsylvania Press, 2008.

Bühler, Curt F. *The Fifteenth-Century Book: The Scribes, the Printers, the Decorators*. Philadelphia: University of Pennsylvania Press, 1960.

"The *Liber de dictis philosophorum antiquorum* and Common Proverbs in George Ashby's Poems." *PMLA* 65 (1950): 282–89.

Burrow, Colin. "The Experience of Exclusion: Literature and Politics in the Reigns of Henry VII and Henry VIII." Ed. Wallace, *Cambridge History*. 793–820.

"Tudor Sanctuaries." Review of Fox, *Politics and Literature in the Reigns of Henry VII and Henry VIII*. *Essays in Criticism* 41 (1991): 51–61.

Burrow, J. A. *Medieval Writers and their Work*. Oxford University Press, 1982.

"The Poet as Petitioner." *SAC* 3 (1981): 61–75.

"The Portrayal of Amans in *Confessio Amantis*." *Gower's Confessio Amantis: Responses and Reassessments*. Ed. A. J. Minnis. Cambridge: D. S. Brewer, 1983. 5–24.

Calin, William. *The French Tradition and the Literature of Medieval England*. University of Toronto Press, 1994.

Canitz, A. E. Christa. "A Benefice for the Prophet: William Dunbar's Petitionary Poems." *SSL* 33–34 (2004): 42–61.

Carlson, David R. *English Humanist Books: Writers and Patrons, Manuscript and Print, 1475–1525*. University of Toronto Press, 1993.

"Alexander Barclay and Richard Pynson: A Tudor Printer and His Writer." *Anglia* 113 (1995): 283–302.

"The 'Grammarians' War' 1519–21, Humanist Careerism in Early Tudor England, and Printing." *Medievalia et Humanistica* 18 (1992): 157–81.

"King Arthur and Court Poems for the Birth of Arthur Tudor in 1486." *Humanistica Lovaniensa* 36 (1987): 147–83.

"The 'Opicius' Poems (British Library, Cotton Vespasian B.iv) and the Humanist Anti-Literature in Early Tudor England." *Renaissance Quarterly* 55 (2002): 869–903.

"Politicizing Tudor Court Literature: Gaguin's Embassy and Henry VII's Humanists' Response." *Studies in Philology* 85 (1988): 279–304.

"The Writings of Bernard André (c. 1450–c. 1522)." *Renaissance Studies* 12 (1998): 229–50.

Carpenter, Christine. "Henry VII and the English Polity." *The Reign of Henry VII: Proceedings of the 1993 Harlaxton Symposium*. Ed. Benjamin Thompson. Stamford, Lincs.: Paul Watkins, 1995. 11–30.

Cerquiglini, Jacqueline. *"Un engin si soutil": Guillaume de Machaut et l'écriture au XIVe siècle*. Geneva: Slatkine, 1985.

"'Le Clerc et le louche': Sociology of an Esthetic." *Poetics Today* 5 (1984): 479–91.

Chew, Samuel C. *The Pilgrimage of Life*. 1962, rpt. Port Washington, NY: Kennikat Press, 1973.

Chrimes, S. B. *Henry VII*. 2nd edn. Intro. by G. W. Bernard. 1972; New Haven: Yale University Press, 1999.

Coiner, Nancy. "Galathea and the Interplay of Voices in Skelton's *Speke, Parrot*." *Subjects on the World's Stage: Essays on British Literature of the Middle Ages and the Renaissance*. Ed. David G. Allen and Robert A. White. Newark, NJ: University of Delaware Press, 1995. 88–99.

Condon, M. M. "Ruling Elites in the Reign of Henry VII." *Patronage, Pedigree and Power*. Ed. Charles Ross. Phoenix Mill, Gloucs.: Alan Sutton, 1979. 109–42.

Connolly, Margaret. *John Shirley: Book Production and the Noble Household in Fifteenth-Century England*. Aldershot: Ashgate, 1998.
Constans, Léopold. *La Légende d'Oedipe étudiée dans l'antiquité, au moyen âge et dans les temps modernes*. Paris: Maisonneuve, 1881.
Conway, W. M. *The Woodcutters of the Netherlands in the Fifteenth Century*. Cambridge University Press, 1884.
Cook, A. S. "Skelton's *Garlande of Laurell* and Chaucer's *House of Fame*." *MLR* 11 (1916): 9–14.
Cooney, Helen. "Skelton's *Bowge of Court* and the Crisis of Allegory in Late-Medieval England." *Nation, Court and Culture: New Essays on Fifteenth-Century English Poetry*. Ed. Helen Cooney. Dublin: Four Courts Press, 2001. 153–67.
Coote, Lesley A. *Prophecy and Public Affairs in Later Medieval England*. Woodbridge: York Medieval Press, 2000.
Copeland, Rita. "Lydgate, Hawes and the Science of Rhetoric in the Late Middle Ages." *MLQ* 53 (1992): 57–82.
   "The Pardoner's Body and the Disciplining of Rhetoric." *Framing Medieval Bodies*. Ed. Sarah Kay and Miri Rubin. Manchester University Press, 1994. 138–59.
Copjec, Joan, *Read my Desire: Lacan against the Historicists*. Cambridge, MA: MIT Press, 1994.
Cuddy, Neil. "The Revival of the Entourage: The Bedchamber of James I, 1603–1625." Starkey et al., *The English Court*. 173–225.
Currin, John M. "Persuasions to Peace: The Luxembourg-Marigny-Gaguin Embassy and the State of Anglo-French Relations." *EHR* 113 (1998): 882–904.
De Certeau, Michel. *The Practice of Everyday Life*. Trans. Steven Rendall. Berkeley: University of California Press, 1984.
De Man, Paul. "The Rhetoric of Temporality." *Blindness and Insight: Essays in the Rhetoric of Contemporary Criticism*, 2nd edn. Theory and History of Literature 7. Minneapolis: University of Minnesota Press, 1983. 187–228.
Delany, Sheila. "Run Silent, Run Deep: Heresy and Alchemy as Medieval Versions of Utopia." *Medieval Literary Politics: Shapes of Ideology*. Manchester University Press, 1990. 1–18.
Derrida, Jacques. *Archive Fever: A Freudian Impression*. Trans. Eric Prenowitz. University of Chicago Press, 1995.
   Dissemination. Trans. Barbara Johnson. University of Chicago Press, 1981.
Dickey, Stephen. "Seven come Eleven: Gambling for the Laurel in *The Bowge of Courte*." *Yearbook of English Studies* 22 (1992): 238–54.
Dinshaw, Carolyn. *Chaucer's Sexual Poetics*. Madison, WI: University of Wisconsin Press, 1989.
Dolar, Mladen. *A Voice and Nothing More*. Cambridge, MA: MIT Press, 2006.
Dorsch, T. S. "Of Discretioun in Asking: Dunbar's Petitionary Poems." *Chaucer und seine Zeit: Symposium für Walter F. Schirmer*. Ed. Arno Esch. Tübingen: Martin Niemeyer Verlag, 1968. 285–92.

Doyle, A. I. "English Books in and out of Court from Edward III to Henry VII." Scattergood and Sherborne, *English Court Culture*. 163–81.
Dunnigan, Sarah M. *Eros and Poetry at the Courts of Mary Queen of Scots and James VI*. Basingstoke: Palgrave Macmillan, 2002.
Ebin, Lois A. *Illuminator, Makar, Vates: Visions of Poetry in the Fifteenth Century*. Lincoln, NE: University of Nebraska Press, 1988.
 "Lydgate's Views on Poetry." *Annuale Medievale* 18 (1977): 76–105.
Échard, Sian. "Pre-Texts: Tables of Contents and the Reading of John Gower's *Confessio Amantis*." *Medium Ævum* 66 (1997): 270–87.
Edington, Carol. *Court and Culture in Renaissance Scotland: Sir David Lindsay of the Mount*. Amherst, MA: University of Massachusetts Press, 1994.
Edmunds, Lowell. "Oedipus in the Middle Ages." *Antike und Abendland* 22 (1976): 140–55.
 John Skelton: The Critical Heritage. London: Routledge & Kegan Paul, 1981.
 Stephen Hawes. Boston: Twayne, 1985.
Edwards, A. S. G. "An Allusion to Stephen Hawes, c. 1530." *Notes and Queries* 224 n.s. 26 (1979): 397.
 "Deconstructing Skelton: The Texts of the English Poems." *Leeds Studies in English* 36 (2005): 335–53.
 "Dunbar, Skelton and the Nature of Court Culture in the Early Sixteenth Century." *Vernacular Literature and Current Affairs in the Early Sixteenth Century: France, England and Scotland*. Studies in European Cultural Transition 6. Ed. Jennifer Britnell and Richard Britnell. Aldershot: Ashgate, 2000. 120–34.
 "From Manuscript to Print: Wynkyn de Worde and the Printing of Contemporary Poetry." *Gutenberg Jahrbuch* (1991): 143–48.
 "Poet and Printer in Sixteenth-Century England: Stephen Hawes and Wynkyn de Worde." *Gutenberg Jahrbuch* (1980): 82–88.
Edwards, H. L. R. *Skelton: The Life and Times of an Early Tudor Poet*. London: Jonathan Cape, 1949.
Elias, Norbert. *The History of Manners*. Trans. Edmund Jephcott. Vol. I of *The Civilizing Process*. Oxford: Basil Blackwell, 1982.
 Power and Civility. Trans. Edmund Jephcott. Vol. II of *The Civilizing Process*. Oxford: Basil Blackwell, 1982.
Elton, G. R. *The Tudor Revolution in Government: Administrative Changes in the Reign of Henry VIII*. Cambridge University Press, 1953.
 "Tudor Government: The Points of Contact III. The Court." *Transactions of the Royal Historical Society* 5th series. 26 (1976): 211–28.
Enders, Jody. *The Medieval Theater of Cruelty: Rhetoric, Memory, Violence*. Ithaca, NY: Cornell University Press, 1999.
 Rhetoric and the Origins of Medieval Drama. Ithaca, NY: Cornell University Press, 1992.
Enterline, Lynn. *The Rhetoric of the Body from Ovid to Shakespeare*. Cambridge University Press, 2000.

"Embodied Voices: Petrarch Reading (Himself Reading) Ovid." *Desire in the Renaissance: Psychoanalysis and Literature*. Ed. Valeria Finucci and Regina Schwartz. Princeton University Press, 1994. 120–45.
Evans, Deanna Delmar. "Ambivalent Artifice in Dunbar's *The Thrissill and the Rois*." *SSL* 22 (1987): 95–105.
Fechner, G. T. *Elemente der Psychophysik*. 2nd edn. 2 vols. Leipzig: *s.n.*, 1889.
Ferguson, Margaret W. "Saint Augustine's Region of Unlikeness: The Crossing of Exile and Language." *Georgia Review* 29 (1975): 842–64.
Ferster, Judith. *Fictions of Advice: The Literature and Politics of Counsel in Late Medieval England*. Philadelphia: University of Pennsylvania Press, 1996.
Fideler, Paul A. and T. F. Mayer, ed. *Political Thought and the Tudor Commonwealth: Deep Structure, Discourse and Disguise*. London: Routledge, 1992.
Fink, Bruce. *The Lacanian Subject: Between Language and Jouissance*. Princeton University Press, 1995.
Finkelstein, Richard. "Amplification in William Dunbar's Aureate Poetry." *Scottish Literary Journal* 13 (1986): 5–15.
Fish, Stanley. *John Skelton's Poetry*. New Haven, CT: Yale University Press, 1965.
  "Authors-Readers: Jonson's Community of the Same." *Representations* 7 (1984): 26–58.
Fisher, John H. *The Emergence of Standard English*. Lexington, KY: University Press of Kentucky, 1996.
Foucault, Michel. *The Archaeology of Knowledge*. Trans. A. M. Sheridan-Smith. London: Tavistock, 1972.
  Discipline and Punish: The Birth of the Prison. Trans. Alan Sheridan. London: Allen Lane, 1977.
  The History of Sexuality, vol. I, *An Introduction*. Trans. Robert Hurley. New York: Pantheon, 1978.
Fowler, Elizabeth. *Literary Character: The Human Figure in Early English Writing*. Ithaca, NY: Cornell University Press, 2003.
Fox, Alistair. *Politics and Literature in the Reigns of Henry VII and Henry VIII*. Oxford: Basil Blackwell, 1989.
  "Prophecies and Politics in the Reign of Henry VIII." *Reassessing the Henrician Reformation: Humanism, Politics and Reform 1500–1550*. Ed. Alistair Fox and John Guy. Oxford: Basil Blackwell, 1986. 77–94.
  "Stephen Hawes and the Political Allegory of *The Comfort of Lovers*." *English Literary Renaissance* 17 (1987): 3–21.
Fox, Denton. "Middle Scots Poets and Patrons." Scattergood and Sherborne, *English Court Culture*. 109–27.
Fradenburg, Louise Olga. *City, Marriage, Tournament: Arts of Rule in Late Medieval Scotland*. Madison, WI: University of Wisconsin Press, 1991.
  "The Manciple's Servant Tongue: Politics and Poetry in the *Canterbury Tales*." *ELH* 52 (1985): 85–118.
  "Spectacular Fictions: The Body Politic in Chaucer and Dunbar." *Poetics Today* 5 (1984): 493–517.

Franceschini, Ezio. "Il 'Liber philosophorum moralium antiquorum.'" *Atti della Reale Academia Nazionale dei Lincei*, anno CCCXXVII, 6th series. Memorie della Classe di Scienze Morali Storiche e Filologiche 3 (1930): 354–99.
Freud, Sigmund. *The Standard Edition of the Complete Psychological Works*. Ed. and trans. James Strachey et al. 24 vols. London: Hogarth Press and the Institute of Psycho-Analysis, 1953–73.
Frost, Ulrich. *Das "Commonplace Book" von John Colyns: Untersuchung und Teiledition der Handschrift Harley 2252 der British Library in London*. Europäische Hochschulschriften Reihe 14. Angelsächsische Sprache und Literatur. Frankfurt-on-Main: Peter Lang, 1988.
Fuss, Diana. *Identification Papers*. New York: Routledge, 1995.
Fyler, John. *Language and the Declining World in Chaucer, Dante and Jean de Meun*. Cambridge University Press, 2007.
Gillespie, Vincent. "Justification by Faith: Skelton's *Replycacion*." *The Long Fifteenth Century: Essays for Douglas Gray*. Ed. Helen Cooper and Sally Mapstone. Oxford: Clarendon Press, 1997. 273–312.
Gingerich, Owen and Melvin J. Tucker. "The Astronomical Dating of Skelton's *Garlande of Laurell*." *Huntington Library Quarterly* 32 (1969): 207–20.
Girard, René. *To Double Business Bound: Essays on Literature, Mimesis and Anthropology*. Baltimore, MD: Johns Hopkins University Press, 1988.
Goldberg, Jonathan. *Sodometries: Renaissance Texts, Modern Sexualities*. Stanford University Press, 1993.
   Voice Terminal Echo: Postmodernism and English Renaissance Texts. London: Methuen, 1986.
Goldstein, R. James. *The Matter of Scotland: Historical Narrative in Medieval Scotland*. Lincoln, NE: University of Nebraska Press, 1993.
   "Normative Heterosexuality in History and Theory: The Case of Sir David Lindsay of the Mount." *Becoming Male in the Middle Ages*. Ed. Jeffrey Jerome Cohen and Bonnie Wheeler. New York: Garland, 2000. 349–65.
Goodman, Anthony. "Henry VII and Christian Renewal." *Studies in Church History* 17 (1981): 115–25.
Grady, Frank. "Gower's Boat, Richard's Barge, and the True Story of the *Confessio Amantis*: Text and Gloss." *Texas Studies in Literature and Language* 44 (2002): 1–15.
Gray, Douglas. *Themes and Images in the Medieval English Religious Lyric*. London: Routledge & Kegan Paul, 1972.
   "Rough Music: Some Early Invectives and Flytings." *English Satire and the Satiric Tradition*. Ed. Claude Rawson and Jenny Mezciems. Oxford: Basil Blackwell, 1984. 21–43.
Green, Richard Firth. *Poets and Princepleasers: Literature and the English Court in the Later Middle Ages*. University of Toronto Press, 1980.
   "The *Craft of Lovers* and the Rhetoric of Seduction." *Acta* 12 (1985): 105–25.
Greenblatt, Stephen J. *Renaissance Self-Fashioning from More to Shakespeare*. University of Chicago Press, 1980.
Greene, Roland. "Calling Colin Clout." *Spenser Studies* 10 (1992): 229–44.

Greene, Thomas M. *The Light in Troy: Imitation and Discovery in Renaissance Poetry*. New Haven, CT: Yale University Press, 1982.
Griffiths, Jane. *John Skelton and Poetic Authority: Defining the Liberty to Speak*. Oxford: Clarendon Press, 2006.
Griffiths, Jeremy and Derek Pearsall, ed. *Book Production and Publishing in Britain 1375–1475*. Cambridge University Press, 1989.
Grignaschi, Mario. "La Diffusion du *Secretum secretorum* ('*Sirr-al-'asrâr*') dans l'Europe occidentale." *Archives d'Histoire Doctrinale et Littéraire du Moyen Âge* 47 (1980): 7–70.
　"L'Origine et les métamorphoses du '*Sirr-al-'asrâr*'." *Archives d'Histoire Doctrinale et Littéraire du Moyen Âge* 43 (1976): 7–112.
Grummitt, David. "Henry VII, Chamber Finance and the 'New Monarchy': Some New Evidence." *Historical Research* 72 (1999): 229–43.
　"Household, Politics and Political Morality in the Reign of Henry VII." *Historical Research* 82 (2009): 393–411.
Gunn, Steven J. "The Court of Henry VII." *The Court as a Stage: England and the Low Countries in the Later Middle Ages*. Ed. Steven Gunn and Antheun Janse. Woodbridge: Boydell Press, 2006. 132–44.
　"The Courtiers of Henry VII." *EHR* 108 (1993): 23–49.
　"Literature and Politics in Early Tudor England." *Journal of British Studies* 30 (1991): 216–21.
Guy-Bray, Stephen. *Homoerotic Space: The Poetics of Loss in Renaissance Literature*. University of Toronto Press, 2002.
Hadfield, Andrew. *Literature, Politics and National Identity: Reformation to Renaissance*. Cambridge University Press, 1994.
Halpern, Richard. *The Poetics of Primitive Accumulation: English Renaissance Culture and the Genealogy of Capital*. Ithaca, NY: Cornell University Press, 1991.
Hardie, Philip. *Ovid's Poetics of Illusion*. Cambridge University Press, 2002.
Harris, Kate. "Patrons, Buyers and Owners: The Evidence for Ownership and the Rôle of Book Owners in Book Production and the Book Trade." Griffiths and Pearsall, *Book Production and Publishing in Britain*. 163–99.
Hasler, Antony J. "Allegories of Authority in the Poems of John Skelton, Stephen Hames and William Dunbar." Ph. D. dissertation, Cambridge University, 1996.
　"Cultural Intersections: Skelton, Barclay, Hawes, André." *John Skelton and Early Modern Culture. Medieval and Renaissance Texts and Studies 300*. Ed. David Carlson. Tempe, AZ: Arizona Center for Medieval and Renaissance Studies, 2008. 63–84.
　"Hoccleve's Unregimented Body." *Paragraph* 13 (1990): 164–83.
　"William Dunbar: The Elusive Subject." *Bryght Lanternis: Essays on the Language and Literature of Medieval and Renaissance Scotland*. Ed. J. Derrick McClure and Michael R. J. Spiller. Aberdeen University Press, 1989. 194–208.
Hay, Bryan S. "William Dunbar's Flying Abbot: Apocalypse Made to Order." *SSL* 11 (1973/74): 217–25.
Heiserman, A. R. *Skelton and Satire*. University of Chicago Press, 1961.

Hellinga, Lotte and Wytze Hellinga. *The Fifteenth-Century Printing Types of the Low Countries*. Amsterdam: Menno Hertzberger, 1966.
Herrmann, Erwin. "Spätmittelalterliche englische Pseudoprophetien." *Archiv für Kulturgeschichte* 57 (1975): 87–116.
Hobbins, Daniel. "Arsenal MS 360 as a Witness to the Career and Writings of Bernard André." *Humanistica Lovaniensa* 50 (2001): 161–98.
  "The Poet Laureate as Stabilizer: Bernard André and the *Vita Regis Henrici Septimi*." *Proceedings of the Medieval Association of the Midwest* 4 (1997): 61–79.
Hodnett, Edward. *English Woodcuts, 1450–1535*. Oxford University Press, 1935.
Holub, Robert C. *Reception Theory: A Critical Introduction*. London: Methuen, 1984.
Hult, David F. *Self-Fulfilling Prophecies: Readership and Authority in the First Roman de la Rose*. Cambridge University Press, 1986.
Hyde, Isabel. "Primary Sources and Associations of Dunbar's Aureate Imagery." *MLR* 51 (1956): 481–92.
Ingham, Patricia Clare. "Losing French: Vernacularity, Nation, and Caxton's English Statutes." Kuskin, *Caxton's Trace*. 275–98.
Ives, Eric W. *The Common Lawyers of Pre-Reformation England: Thomas Kebell, A Case Study*. Cambridge University Press, 1983.
Jaeger, C. Stephen *The Origins of Courtliness: Civilizing Trends and the Formation of Courtly Ideals 939–1210*. Philadelphia: University of Pennsylvania Press, 1985.
  "The Barons' Intrigue in Gottfried's *Tristan*: Notes Toward a Sociology of Fear in Court Society." *JEGP* 83 (1984): 46–66.
James, Mervyn. "English Politics and the Concept of Honour, 1485–1642." *Society, Politics and Culture: Studies in Early Modern England*. Cambridge University Press, 1986. 308–415.
Jameson, Frederic R. "Beyond the Cave: Modernism and Modes of Production." *The Horizon of Literature*. Ed. Paul Hernadi. Lincoln, NE: University of Nebraska Press, 1982. 157–82.
Jansen, Sharon L. *Political Protest and Prophecy under Henry VIII*. Woodbridge: Boydell Press, 1991.
Johnson, Ian R. "Walton's Sapient Orpheus." *The Medieval Boethius: Studies in the Vernacular Translations of "De consolatione philosophiae."* Ed. A. J. Minnis. Cambridge: D. S. Brewer, 1987. 139–68.
Jones, Richard Foster. *The Triumph of the English Language: A Survey of Opinions Concerning the Vernacular from the Introduction of Printing to the Restoration*. Stanford University Press, 1953.
Joukofsky, Françoise. *La Gloire dans la poésie française et néolatine du XVIe siècle, des Rhétoriqueurs à Agrippa d'Aubigné*. Geneva: Droz, 1969.
Kallet-Marx, Lisa. *Money, Expense and Power in Thucydides' History 1.5–24*. Berkeley: University of California Press, 1993.
Kantorowicz, Ernst H. *The King's Two Bodies: A Study in Medieval Political Theology*. Princeton University Press, 1957.
  Courtly Contradictions: The Emergence of the Literary Object in the Twelfth Century. Stanford University Press, 2001.

The Place of Thought: The Complexity of One in Late Medieval French Didactic Poetry. Philadelphia: University of Pennsylvania Press, 2007.

Kay, Sarah. "The Contradictions of Courtly Love and Origins of Courtly Poetry: The Evidence of the *Lauzengiers*." *JMEMS* 26 (1996): 209–53.

Keightley, G. R. "The *Cronyques of Spaygne* in Caxton's Version of the Trojan History of Raoul Le Fèvre." *Medium Aevum* 49 (1980): 73–89.

King, Pamela M. "Dunbar's *The Golden Targe*: A Chaucerian Masque." *SSL* 19 (1984): 115–31.

Kipling, Gordon. "Henry VII and the Origins of Tudor Patronage." *Patronage in the Renaissance*. Ed. Guy Fitch Lytle and Stephen Orgel. Princeton University Press, 1981. 117–64.

The Triumph of Honour: Burgundian Origins of the Elizabethan Renaissance. The Hague: Leiden University Press, 1977.

"The Queen of May's Joust at Kennington and the *Justes of the Moneths of May and June*." *Notes and Queries* 229 n.s. 31 (1984): 158–62.

Kleineke, Wilhelm. *Englische Fürstenspiegel vom Policraticus Johanns von Salisbury bis zum Basilikon Doron König Jakobs I*. Halle: Martin Niemeyer Verlag, 1937.

Knapp, Ethan. *The Bureaucratic Muse: Thomas Hoccleve and the Literature of Late Medieval England*. University Park, PA: Pennsylvania State University Press, 2001.

Kratzmann, Gregory. *Anglo-Scottish Literary Relations 1430–1550*. Cambridge University Press, 1980.

Kuskin, William. *Symbolic Caxton: Literary Culture and Print Capitalism*. Notre Dame, IN: University of Notre Dame Press, 2008.

Kuskin, William, ed. *Caxton's Trace: Studies in the History of English Printing*. Notre Dame, IN: University of Notre Dame Press, 2006.

Lacan, Jacques. *Écrits: The First Complete Edition in English*. Trans. Bruce Fink with Héloïse Fink and Russell Grigg. New York: W. W. Norton, 2006.

The Four Fundamental Concepts of Psycho-Analysis. Ed. Jacques-Alain Miller. Trans. Alan Sheridan. London: Hogarth Press and the Institute of Psycho-Analysis, 1977.

The Seminar of Jacques Lacan. Book II. The Ego in Freud's Theory and in the Technique of Psychoanalysis 1954–55. Trans. Sylvana Tomaselli. Notes by John Forrester. New York: W. W. Norton, 1988.

The Seminar of Jacques Lacan Book VII. The Ethics of Psychoanalysis 1959–1960. Ed. Jacques-Alain Miller. Trans. and notes by Dennis Porter. New York: W. W. Norton, 1992.

Lander, J. R. *Government and Community: England 1450–1509*. London: Edward Arnold, 1980.

"Bonds, Coercion and Fear: Henry VII and the Peerage." *Crown and Nobility, 1450–1509*. London: Edward Arnold, 1976. 267–300.

Lanham, Richard. *The Motives of Eloquence: Literary Rhetoric in the Renaissance*. New Haven, CT: Yale University Press, 1976.

Laplanche, J. and J.-B. Pontalis. *The Language of Psycho-Analysis*. Trans. D. Nicholson-Smith. London: Karnac Books and the Institute of Psycho-Analysis, 1988.
Lavezzo, Kathy. *Angels on the Edge of the World: Geography, Literature and English Community, 1000–1534*. Ithaca, NY: Cornell University Press, 2006.
Lawton, David. *Chaucer's Narrators*. Woodbridge: D. S. Brewer, 1985.
"Dullness and the Fifteenth Century." *ELH* 54 (1987): 761–99.
Lawton, Lesley. "The Illustration of Late Medieval Secular Texts, with Special Reference to Lydgate's *Troy Book*." *Manuscripts and Readers in Fifteenth-Century England: The Literary Implications of Manuscript Study, Essays from the 1981 Conference at the University of York*. Ed. Derek Pearsall. Cambridge: D. S. Brewer, 1983. 41–69.
Lerer, Seth. *Chaucer and his Readers: Imagining the Author in Late-Medieval England*. Princeton University Press, 1993.
Courtly Letters in the Age of Henry VIII: Literary Culture and the Arts of Deceit. Cambridge University Press, 1997.
"The Rhetoric of Fame: Stephen Hawes's Aureate Diction." *Spenser Studies* 5 (1985): 169–84.
Leupin, Alexandre. "The Powerlessness of Writing: Guillaume de Machaut, the Gorgon and *Ordenance*." *Yale French Studies* 70 (1986): 127–49.
Lewis, C. S. *The Allegory of Love: A Study in Medieval Tradition*. Oxford: Clarendon Press, 1936.
Leyerle, John. "The Two Voices of William Dunbar." *University of Toronto Quarterly* 31 (1961/62): 316–38.
Lochrie, Karma. *Covert Operations: The Medieval Uses of Secrecy*. Philadelphia: University of Pennsylvania Press, 1999.
Lucas, Peter J. "The Growth and Development of English Literary Patronage in the Late Middle Ages and Early Renaissance." *The Library* 6th series 4 (1982): 219–48.
Lukacher, Ned. *Primal Scenes: Literature, Philosophy, Psychoanalysis*. Ithaca, NY: Cornell University Press, 1986.
Lyall, Roderick J. *Alexander Montgomerie: Poetry, Politics and Cultural Change in Jacobean Scotland*. Medieval and Renaissance Texts and Studies 298. Tempe, AZ: Arizona Center for Medieval and Renaissance Studies, 2005.
"Alexander Barclay and the Edwardian Reformation, 1548–52." *Review of English Studies* 20 (1969): 455–61.
"The Stylistic Relationship between Dunbar and Douglas." *William Dunbar, "The Nobill Poyet": Essays in Honour of Priscilla Bawcutt*. Ed. Sally Mapstone. East Linton: Tuckwell Press, 2001. 69–84.
"Tradition and Innovation in Alexander Barclay's 'Towre of Vertue and Honoure'." *Review of English Studies* n.s. 23 (1972): 1–18.
Macdougall, Norman. *James III: A Political Study*. Edinburgh: John Donald, 1982.
James IV. Edinburgh: John Donald, 1989.
"'The Greatest Scheip that ewer Saillit in Ingland or France': James IV's 'Great Michael.'" *Scotland and War, AD 79–1918*. Ed. Norman Macdougall. Edinburgh: John Donald, 1991. 36–60.

MacFarlane, Leslie J. *William Elphinstone and the Kingdom of Scotland, 1431–1514: The Struggle for Order*. Aberdeen University Press, 1985.
Mackie, R. L. *King James IV of Scotland: A Brief Survey of his Life and Times*. Edinburgh: Oliver & Boyd, 1958.
Manley, Lawrence. *Literature and Culture in Early Modern London*. Cambridge University Press, 1995.
Mann, Jill. "Satiric Subject and Satiric Object in Goliardic Literature." *Mittellateinisches Jahrbuch* 15 (1980): 63–86.
Manzalaoui, Mahmoud. "The *Secreta secretorum*: The Medieval European Version of 'Kitab Sirr-ul-Asrar.'" *Bulletin of the Faculty of Arts, University of Alexandria* 15 (1961): 83–107.
Mapstone, Sally. "The Advice to Princes Tradition in Scottish Literature, 1450–1500." PhD dissertation, Oxford University, 1986.
  "Older Scots Literature and the Court." *The Edinburgh History of Scottish Literature*. Vol. 1 of 3. Edinburgh University Press, 2007. 273–85.
  "Was there a Court Literature in Fifteenth-Century Scotland?" *Studies in Scottish Literature* 26 (1991): 410–22.
Mapstone, Sally, ed. *William Dunbar, "The Nobill Poyet": Essays in Honour of Priscilla Bawcutt*. East Linton: Tuckwell Press, 2001.
Martin, Joanna. *Kingship and Love in Scottish Poetry, 1424–1540*. Aldershot: Ashgate, 2008.
Marx, Karl. *Capital: A Critique of Political Economy*. Trans. Samuel Moore and Edward Aveling. 4 vols. London: Lawrence & Wishart, 1954.
Mayer, T. F. "Tournai and Tyranny: Imperial Kingship and Critical Humanism." *Historical Journal* 34 (1991): 257–77.
Meale, Carol M. "The Compiler at Work: John Colyns and BL MS Harley 2252." *Manuscripts and Readers in Fifteenth-Century England*. Ed. Derek Pearsall. Cambridge: D. S. Brewer, 1983. 82–103.
  "Patrons, Buyers and Owners: Book Production and Social Status." Griffiths and Pearsall, *Book Production and Publishing in Britain*. 201–38.
Medvedev, P. N. and M. M. Bakhtin. *The Formal Method in Literary Scholarship: A Critical Introduction to Sociological Poetics*. Trans. Albert J. Wehrle. Baltimore, MD: Johns Hopkins University Press, 1978.
Mendenhall, John Cooper. *Aureate Terms: A Study in the Literary Diction of the Fifteenth Century*. Lancaster, PA: Wickersham Print Co., 1919.
Meyer-Lee, Robert J. *Poets and Power from Chaucer to Wyatt*. Cambridge University Press, 2007.
Middleton, Anne. "Chaucer's 'New Men' and the Good of Literature in the *Canterbury Tales*." *Literature and Society. Papers from the English Institute, 1978*. Ed. Edward Said. Baltimore, MD: Johns Hopkins University Press, 1980. 15–56.
Miller, D. A. *The Novel and the Police*. Berkeley: University of California Press, 1988.
Miller, Jacqueline T. *Poetic License: Authority and Authorship in Medieval and Renaissance Contexts*. Oxford University Press, 1986.

Minnis, A. J. *Medieval Theory of Authorship: Scholastic Literary Attitudes in the Later Middle Ages*. 2nd edn. Philadelphia: University of Pennsylvania Press, 1988.
Morgan, D. A. L. "The House of Policy: The Political Role of the Late Plantagenet Household, 1422–1485." Starkey et al., *The English Court*. 25–70.
Mortimer, Nigel. *John Lydgate's Fall of Princes: Narrative Tragedy in its Literary and Political Contexts*. Oxford: Clarendon Press, 2005.
Nelson, William. *John Skelton, Laureate*. New York: Columbia University Press, 1939.
Nicholson, Ranald. *Scotland: The Later Middle Ages*. Edinburgh: Oliver & Boyd, 1974.
Nitecki, Alicia K. "Gavin Douglas's Yelling Fish: *The Palice of Honour*, Lines 146–8." *Notes and Queries* 226 (1981): 118–19.
Nolan, Maura. *John Lydgate and the Making of Public Culture*. Cambridge University Press, 2005.
  "'Now wo, now gladnesse': Ovidianism in *The Fall of Princes*." *ELH* 71 (2004): 531–58.
Norman, Joanne. "William Dunbar: Grand Rhétoriqueur." *Bryght Lanternis: Essays on the Language and Literature of Medieval and Renaissance Scotland*. Ed. J. Derrick McClure and Michael R. G. Spiller. Aberdeen University Press, 1989. 179–93.
Norton-Smith, John. "Ekphrasis as a Stylistic Element in Douglas's *Palis of Honoure*." *Medium Aevum* 48 (1979): 240–53.
  "The Origins of 'Skeltonics.'" *Essays in Criticism* 23 (1973): 57–62.
Olson, Glending. "Making and Poetry in the Age of Chaucer." *Comparative Literature* 31 (1979): 272–90.
Owst, G. R. *Literature and Pulpit in Medieval England: A Neglected Chapter in the History of English Letters and of the English People*. Rev. edn. Oxford: Basil Blackwell, 1961.
Paleit, Edward. "Lucan in the Renaissance, Pre-1625: An Introduction." *Literature Compass* 1 (2005). 19 January 2010.
Parker, David R. *The Commonplace Book in Tudor London. An Examination of BL MSS Egerton 1995, Harley 2252, Lansdowne 762, and Oxford Balliol College MS 354*. Lanham, MD: University Press of America, 1998.
Parker, P. "Stephen Hawes." *Times Literary Supplement*. 21 June 1928. 468.
Parker, Patricia A. *Inescapable Romance: Studies in the Poetics of a Mode*. Princeton University Press, 1979.
  Literary Fat Ladies: Rhetoric, Gender, Property. London: Methuen, 1987.
  "Deferral, Dilation, Différance: Shakespeare, Cervantes, Jonson." *Literary Theory/Renaissance Texts*. Ed. Patricia Parker and David Quint. Baltimore, MD: Johns Hopkins University Press, 1986. 183–209.
  "Virile Style." *Premodern Sexualities*. Ed. Louise Fradenburg and Carla Freccero. New York: Routledge, 1996. 201–22.
Parkinson, David. "The Farce of Modesty in Gavin Douglas's *The Palis of Honour*." *Philological Quarterly* 70 (1990): 13–25.
  "Mobbing Scenes in Middle Scots Verse: Holland, Douglas, Dunbar." *JEGP* 85 (1986): 494–509.

Patterson, Lee. *Chaucer and the Subject of History*. London: Routledge, 1991.
"Court Politics and the Invention of Literature: The Case of Sir John Clanvowe." *Culture and History, 1350–1600: Essays on English Communities, Identities and Writing*. Ed. David Aers. Detroit: Wayne State University Press, 1992. 7–42.
"Making Identities in Fifteenth-Century England: Henry V and John Lydgate." *New Historical Literary Study: Essays on Reproducing Texts, Representing History*. Ed. Jeffrey N. Cox and Larry J. Reynolds. Princeton University Press, 1993. 69–107.
"On the Margin: Postmodernism, Ironic History, and Medieval Studies." *Speculum* 65 (1990): 87–108.
"Perpetual Motion: Alchemy and the Technology of the Self." *SAC* 15 (1993): 25–57.
"'What is me?': Self and Society in the Poetry of Thomas Hoccleve." *Studies in the Age of Chaucer* 23 (2001): 437–70.
Pearsall, Derek. *John Lydgate*. London: Routledge & Kegan Paul, 1970.
Old English and Middle English Poetry. London: Routledge & Kegan Paul, 1977.
"Hoccleve's *Regement of Princes*: The Poetics of Royal Self-Representation." *Speculum* 69 (1994): 386–410.
Perkins, Nicholas. *Hoccleve's "Regiment of Princes": Counsel and Constraint*. Cambridge: D. S. Brewer, 2001.
Pinkernell, Gerd. "Lefèvre." *Dizionario critico della letteratura francese*. 2 vols. Turin: Unione tipografica-editrice torinese, 1972. 654–55.
Poirion, Daniel. *Le Poète et le prince: l'évolution du lyrisme courtois de Guillaume de Machaut à Charles d'Orléans*. Paris: Presses Universitaires de France, 1965.
Psilos, Paul D. "'Dulle' Drede and the Limits of Prudential Knowledge in Skelton's Bowge of Court." *Journal of Medieval and Renaissance Studies* 6 (1976): 297–317.
Putter, Ad. "Animating Medieval Court Satire." *The Court and Cultural Diversity*. Ed. E. Mullally and J. Thompson. Cambridge: D. S. Brewer. 1997. 67–76.
Pye, Christopher. *The Regal Phantasm: Shakespeare and the Politics of Spectacle*. New York: Routledge, 1990.
Rambuss, Richard. "'Processe of tyme': History, Consolation and Apocalypse in the *Book of the Duchess*." *Exemplaria* 2 (1990): 659–83.
Reiss, Edmund. *William Dunbar*. Boston: Twayne, 1979.
Reiss, Timothy J. *Mirages of the Self: Patterns of Personhood in Ancient and Early Modern Europe*. Stanford University Press, 2003.
"Montaigne and the Subject of Polity." *Literary Theory/Renaissance Texts*. Ed. Patricia Parker and David Quint. Baltimore, MD: Johns Hopkins University Press, 1986. 115–49.
Rhodenizer, Vernon Blair. "Studies in Stephen Hawes's Pastime of Pleasure." PhD dissertation, Harvard University, 1918.
Ribémont, Bernard. "Histoires de perroquets: petit itinéraire zoologique et poétique." *Reinardus* 3 (1990): 155–71.
Richardson, Malcolm. "Henry V, the English Chancery, and Chancery English." *Speculum* 55 (1980): 726–50.

Russell, J. Stephen. "Skelton's *Bouge of Court*: A Nominalist Allegory." *Renaissance Papers* 2 (1980): 1–9.

Sale, Helen Stearns. "The Date of Skelton's *Bowge of Court*." *MLN* 52 (1937): 572–74.

Scala, Elizabeth. *Absent Narratives, Manuscript Textuality and Literary Structure in Late Medieval England*. New York: Palgrave Macmillan, 2002.

Scanlon, Larry *Narrative, Authority, and Power: The Medieval Exemplum and the Chaucerian Tradition*. Cambridge University Press, 1994.

——— "The King's Two Voices: Narrative and Power in Hoccleve's *The Regement of Princes*." *Literary Practice and Social Change in Britain, 1380–1530*. Ed. Lee Patterson. Berkeley: University of California Press, 1990. 210–47.

Scase, Wendy. *Literature and Complaint in England 1272–1553*. Oxford University Press, 2007.

Scattergood, V. J. "Fashion and Morality in the Late Middle Ages." *England in the Fifteenth Century: Proceedings of the 1986 Harlaxton Symposium*. Ed. Daniel Williams. Woodbridge: Boydell Press, 1987. 255–72.

——— "Insecurity in Skelton's *Bowge of Courte*." *Genres, Themes and Images in English Literature from the Fourteenth to the Fifteenth Century. The J. A. W. Bennett Memorial Lectures, Perugia. 1986*. Ed. Piero Boitani and Anna Torti. Tübingen: Gunter Narr Verlag, 1988. 186–209.

——— "Literary Culture at the Court of Richard II." Scattergood and Sherborne, *English Court Culture*. 29–43.

——— "Skelton's *Garlande of Laurell* and the Chaucerian Tradition." *Chaucer Traditions: Studies in Honour of Derek Brewer*. Ed. Ruth Morse and Barry Windeatt. Cambridge University Press, 1990. 122–38.

——— "Skelton's 'Ryotte': 'A Rusty Gallande'?" *Notes and Queries* 219 n.s. 21 (1974): 83–85.

Scattergood, V. J. and J. W. Sherborne, ed. *English Court Culture in the Later Middle Ages*. London: Duckworth, 1983.

Schor, Naomi. "Blindness as Metaphor." *differences* 11 (1999): 76–105.

Scollen-Jimack, Christine. "Marot and Deschamps: The Rhetoric of Misfortune." *French Studies* 42 (1988): 21–32.

Scott, Tom. *Dunbar: A Critical Exposition of the Poems*. Edinburgh: Oliver & Boyd, 1966.

Sedgwick, Eve Kosofsky. *Between Men: English Literature and Male Homosocial Desire*. New York: Columbia University Press, 1985.

Shell, Marc. *The Economy of Literature*. Baltimore, MD: Johns Hopkins University Press, 1978.

Shuffleton, Frank. "An Imperial Flower: Dunbar's *The Goldyn Targe* and the Court Life of James IV of Scotland." *Studies in Philology* 72 (1975): 193–207.

Simpson, James, and Larry Scanlon, ed. *John Lydgate: Poetry, Culture and Lancastrian England*. Notre Dame, IN: University of Notre Dame Press, 2006.

Simpson, James. *"Piers Plowman": An Introduction to the B-Text*. London: Longman, 1990.

Reform and Cultural Revolution. Vol. 11 of *The Oxford English Literary History, 1350–1547.* Oxford University Press, 2002.

"The Death of the Author?: Skelton's *Bouge of Court.*" *The Timeless and the Temporal: Writings in Honour of John Chalker by Friends and Colleagues.* Ed. Elizabeth Maslen. London: Queen Mary and Westfield College, Department of English, 1993. 58–77.

Smith, Julie A., "An Image of a Preaching Bishop in Late Medieval England: The 1498 Woodcut Portrait of Bishop John Alcock." *Viator* 21 (1990): 301–22.

"The Poet Laureate as University Master: John Skelton's Woodcut Portrait." *Renaissance Rereadings: Intertext and Context.* Ed. Maryanne Cline Horowitz, Anne J. Cruz and Wendy A. Furman. Urbana: University of Illinois Press, 1988. 159–83.

Smith, D. Vance. *Arts of Possession: The Middle English Household Imaginary.* Minneapolis: University of Minnesota Press, 2003.

"Body Doubles: Producing the Masculine *Corpus.*" *Becoming Male in the Middle Ages.* Ed. Jeffrey Jerome Cohen and Bonnie Wheeler. New York: Garland, 2000. 5–19.

Spearing, A. C. *Medieval Dream-Poetry.* Cambridge University Press, 1976.

The Medieval Poet as Voyeur: Looking and Listening in Medieval Love-Narratives. Cambridge University Press, 1993.

Medieval to Renaissance in English Poetry. Cambridge University Press, 1985.

Spiegel, Gabrielle. *Romancing the Past: The Rise of Vernacular Prose Historiography in Thirteenth-Century France.* Berkeley: University of California Press, 1993.

Starkey, David, *The Reign of Henry VIII: Personalities and Politics.* 2nd edn. London: Collins & Brown, 1991.

"The Age of the Household: Politics, Society and the Arts *c.*1350–*c.*1550." *The Later Middle Ages.* Ed. Stephen Medcalf. New York: Methuen, 1981. 225–90.

"Henry VI's Old Blue Gown: The English Court Under the Lancastrians and Yorkists." *Court Historian* 4 (1999): 1–28.

"Intimacy and Innovation: The Rise of the Privy Chamber, 1485–1547." Starkey et al., *The English Court.* 71–118.

"The King's Privy Chamber." PhD dissertation, Cambridge University, 1973.

Starkey, David, et al., ed. *The English Court: From the Wars of the Roses to the Civil War.* London: Longman, 1987.

Stevens, John. *Music and Poetry in the Early Tudor Court.* Cambridge University Press, 1961.

Straker, Scott-Morgan. "Rivalry and Reciprocity in Lydgate's *Troy Book.*" *New Medieval Literatures* 3 (1999): 119–47.

Strohm, Paul. *England's Empty Throne: Usurpation and the Language of Legitimation 1399–1422.* New Haven, CT: Yale University Press, 1998.

Politique: Languages of Statecraft between Chaucer and Shakespeare. Notre Dame, IN: University of Notre Dame Press, 2005.

Social Chaucer. Cambridge, MA: Harvard University Press, 1989.

Theory and the Premodern Text. Minneapolis: University of Minnesota Press, 2000.

"Hoccleve, Lydgate and the Lancastrian Court." *Cambridge History of Medieval English Literature*. Ed. David Wallace. Cambridge University Press, 1999. 640–61.

"Saving the Appearances: Chaucer's 'Purse' and the Fabrication of the Lancastrian Claim." *Hochon's Arrow: The Social Imagination of Fourteenth-Century Texts*. Princeton University Press, 1992. 75–94.

Summit, Jennifer. *Lost Property: The Woman Writer and English Literary History, 1380–1589*. University of Chicago Press, 2000.

Sunderland, Luke. "*Le Cycle de Renart*: From the *Enfances* to the *Jugement* in a Cyclical *Roman de Renart* Manuscript." *French Studies* 62 (2008): 1–12.

Sutch, Susie Speakman and Anne Lake Prescott. "Translation as Transformation: Olivier de la Marche's *Chevalier délibéré* and its Hapsburg and Elizabethan Permutations." *Comparative Literature Studies* 25 (1988): 281–317.

Tarnoff, Maura. "Sewing Authorship in John Skelton's *Garlande or Chapelet of Laurell*." *ELH* 75 (2008): 415–38.

Taylor, Rupert. *The Political Prophecy in England*. New York: Columbia University Press, 1911.

Teskey, Gordon. *Allegory and Violence*. Ithaca, NY: Cornell University Press, 1996.

Thomas, Keith. *Religion and the Decline of Magic*. London: Weidenfeld & Nicolson, 1971.

Thompson, Benjamin, ed. *The Reign of Henry VII: Proceedings of the 1993 Harlaxton Symposium*. Stamford, Lincs.: Paul Watkins, 1995.

Todorov, Tzvetan. "Language and Literature." *The Languages of Criticism and the Sciences of Man: The Structuralist Controversy*. Ed. Richard Macksey and Eugenio Donato. Baltimore, MD: Johns Hopkins University Press, 1970. 125–33.

Tolmie, Sarah. "Kingmaking: The Historiography of Bruce and Lancaster in Royal Biography, Ceremonial and Document." PhD dissertation, Cambridge University 1998.

"The *Prive Scilence* of Thomas Hoccleve." *SAC* 22 (2000): 281–309.

Trapp, J. B. "The Owl's Ivy and the Poet's Bays." *Journal of the Warburg and Courtauld Institutes* 21 (1958): 227–55.

"The Poet Laureate: Rome, *Renovatio* and *Translatio imperii*." *Rome in the Renaissance: The City and the Myth*. Ed. P. A. Ramsey. Binghamton, NY: Medieval and Renaissance Texts and Studies, 1982. 93–130.

Travis, Peter W. "Chaucer's Heliotropes and the Poetics of Metaphor." *Speculum* 72 (1997): 399–427.

Tucker, Melvin J. "The Ladies in Skelton's 'Garlande of Laurell.'" *Renaissance Quarterly* 22 (1969): 333–45.

"Setting in Skelton's *Bowge of Courte*: A Speculation." *English Language Notes* 7 (1970): 168–75.

"Skelton and Sheriff Hutton." *English Language Notes* 4 (1967): 254–59.

Turner, Victor. *The Ritual Process: Structure and Anti-Structure*. 1969; Ithaca, NY: Cornell University Press, 1977.

Tuve, Rosamond. *Allegorical Imagery: Some Medieval Books and their Posterity*. Princeton University Press, 1966.

Uebel, Michael. *Ecstatic Transformation: On the Uses of Alterity in the Middle Ages.* New York: Palgrave Macmillan, 2005.
Uhlig, Klaus. *Hofkritik im England des Mittelalters und der Renaissance: Studien zu einem Gemeinplatz der europäischen Moralistik.* Berlin: Walter de Gruyter, 1973.
Varty, Kenneth. *Reynard, Renat, Reinaert and Other Foxes in Medieval England.* Amsterdam: Amsterdam University Press, 1999.
Vitz, Evelyn Birge. "The *I* of the *Roman de la Rose*." *Genre* 6 (1973): 49–75.
Wakelin, Daniel. *Humanism, Reading and English Literature 1430–1530.* Oxford University Press, 2007.
Walker, Greg. *John Skelton and the Politics of the 1520s.* Cambridge University Press, 1988.
  Writing under Tyranny: English Literature and the Henrician Reformation. Oxford University Press, 2005.
  "The Expulsion of the Minions Reconsidered." *Historical Journal* 32 (1989): 1–16.
  "John Skelton and the Royal Court." *Vernacular Literature and Current Affairs in the Early Sixteenth Century: France, England and Scotland.* Ed. Jennifer Britnell, and Richard Britnell. Studies in European Cultural Transition 6. Aldershot: Ashgate, 2000. 1–15.
Wallace, David. "'Whan she translated was': A Chaucerian Critique of the Petrarchan Academy." *Literary Practice and Social Change in Britain, 1380–1530.* Ed. Lee Patterson. Berkeley: University of California Press, 1990. 156–215.
Wallace, David, ed. *The Cambridge History of Medieval English Literature.* Cambridge University Press, 1999.
Wallace, Nathaniel Owen. "The Responsibilities of Madness: John Skelton, 'Speak, Parrot,' and Homeopathic Satire." *Studies in Philology* 82 (1985): 60–80.
Waller, Gary. *English Poetry of the Sixteenth Century.* London: Longman, 1986.
Watts, John. "'A new ffundacion of is crowne': Monarchy in the Age of Henry VII." *The Reign of Henry VII: Proceedings of the 1993 Harlaxton Symposium.* Ed. Benjamin Thompson. Stamford, Lincs.: Paul Watkins, 1995. 31–53.
  "Was there a Lancastrian Court?" *The Lancastrian Court: Proceedings of the 2001 Harlaxton Symposium.* Ed. Jenny Stratford. Donington: Shaun Tyas, 2003. 253–71.
Weiss, Roberto. *Humanism in England During the Fifteenth Century.* 3rd edn. 1941; Oxford: Basil Blackwell, 1967.
Wenzel, Siegfried. "The Pilgrimage of Life as a Late Medieval Genre." *Mediaeval Studies* 35 (1973): 370–88.
  'Unrecorded Middle English Verses.' *Anglia* 92 (1974): 55–78.
Whigham, Frank. *Ambition and Privilege: The Social Tropes of Elizabethan Courtesy Theory.* Berkeley: University of California Press, 1984.
Williams, Deanne. *The French Fetish from Chaucer to Shakespeare.* Cambridge University Press, 2004.

Wilson, Edward. "Local Habitations and Names in MS Rawlinson C 813 in the Bodleian Library, Oxford." *Review of English Studies* n.s. 41 (1990): 12–44.
Winser, Leigh. "*The Bowge of Courte*: Drama Doubling as Dream." *English Literary Renaissance* 6 (1976): 3–39.
Wolffe, Bertram. *The Crown Lands, 1461 to 1536: An Aspect of Yorkist and Early Tudor Government*. London: Allen & Unwin, 1970.
Woolf, Rosemary. *The English Religious Lyric in the Middle Ages*. Oxford: Clarendon Press, 1968.
Yeager, R. F. *John Gower's Poetic: The Search for a New Arion*. Cambridge: D. S. Brewer, 1990.
Zeeman, Nicolette. "The Idol of the Text." *Images, Idolatry, and Iconoclasm in Late Medieval England: Textuality and the Visual Image*. Ed. Jeremy Dimmick, James Simpson and Nicolette Zeeman. Oxford University Press, 2002. 43–62.
  "The Verse of Courtly Love in the Framing Narrative of the *Confessio Amantis*." *Medium Aevum* 60 (1991): 222–40.
Zettersten, Arne. "On the Aureate Diction of William Dunbar." *Essays Presented to Knud Schibsbye*. Ed. M. Chesnutt et al. Copenhagen: Akademisk Forlag, 1979. 51–68.
Zink, Michel. *The Invention of Literary Subjectivity*. Trans. David Sices. Baltimore, MD: Johns Hopkins University Press, 1999.
  The Plague of Fantasies. London: Verso, 1997.
Zumthor, Paul. *Le Masque et la lumière: la poétique des grands rhétoriqueurs*. Paris: Editions du Seuil, 1978.
  "The Great Game of Rhetoric." Trans. Annette and Edward Tomarken. *New Literary History* 12 (1981): 493–508.

MANUSCRIPTS

BL MS Harley 69
BL MS Harley 336
BL MS Harley 2252
BL MS Royal 19.A.viii
BL MS Royal 19.B.iv
Bodleian MS Rawlinson C. 813
Cambridge University Library, MS Ll. 5. 10
Cambridge University Library, MS Mm.4.42
Cambridge, Magdalene College, Pepys Library, MS 2553
London, College of Arms MS R.36
London, National Archives, PRO E 36/214

Index

Abraham, Nicolas and Maria Torok 152, 214n24
absolutism
    and rhetoric 210n53
    and Scotland 17
    Tudor 17, 166, 183n84
L'Abuzé en Cour 47, 49, 53, 191n25
Aers, David 182n70
Aeschbach, Marc 209n49
Alan of Lille 134
Alberic of Monte Cassino 55
alchemy 66, 196n20
Alcock, John, bishop of Ely 92–93, 94, 97
Alington, Sir Giles 89
allegory 2, 3, 37, 50–51, 60, 81, 82, 94, 110, 111, 113, 116, 122, 124, 127, 149, 158, 177n23
    and love 50–51, 112, 115, 116, 168, 169
    and lyric 117
    and narrative 117
    and romance 122
    and self-presentation 3–4, 5, 169
    and violence 169, 214n28
    as "courtly figure," 4
    as *integumentum* 49–50, 51, 52, 55, 58, 122
    heraldic 32
amplification 147, 180n51
anamorphosis 110, 120
Anderson, David Rollin 202n12
Anderson, Perry 184n84
André, Bernard 1, 20–22, 25–31, 32, 128, 145, 185n18, 186n23, 186n24
    as historiographer royal 21
    Vita Henrici Septimi 3, 19, 20, 23, 32, 39, 41, 43, 186n20
Anglicus, Bartholomaeus, *De proprietatibus rerum* 103
Anglo, Sydney 190n15, 205n4, 205n8
apocalypse 134, 135, 138, 143, 147, 154, 211n73, 212n88
Archbold, W. E. J. 190n16
Archer, John Michael 57
Archpoet 71, 73, 78

artes dictaminis 10
artes poeticae 54
artes rhetoricae 35
Arthur, Thomas 170
Arthurson, Ian 190n16, 191n22
Ashby, George
    Dicta Philosophorum 12, 13, 136, 180n58–181n58, 181n63
Augustine, St., of Hippo 2
    De doctrina christiana 49
aureate diction 10, 34, 35, 48, 66, 100, 103, 187n36
author
    and *accessus ad auctores* 88
    as *auctor* 9, 88, 126, 128, 147
    as female 160
    as male courtier 57–58
    of printed book 61, 112–13
    self-authorship 160, 161, 164
authority 2, 3, 7, 17, 19, 47, 48, 50, 60, 90, 92, 107, 114, 120, 124, 128, 140, 142, 143–44, 145, 158
    and poetic genealogy 17, 21, 47, 128
    as *auctoritas* 43, 107, 174n6
    Bourdieu and 174n2
    of literary precursor 5, 7–11, 14, 37–38, 51
    poetic 143, 159, 168, 172
    royal 110, 171
    translation and 89, 100
    vernacular and 44, 128
    (*see also* poet, monarch, translation, vernacular)
auxesis 147, 155

Bacon, Sir Francis 45, 194n73
Baillie, Hugh Murray 201n85
Bale, John 108
Barbour, John, *Bruce* 11
Barclay, Alexander 1, 88, 145, 161, 169
    and masculinity 91
    and monastic identity 88, 89, 90, 91, 92–94, 98
    and nation 94, 98
    and place 92–94
    dedications 89–90

Barclay, Alexander (cont.)
  Eclogues 3, 88
  The Life of St. George 89–90 (*see* Mantuan)
  The Mirror of Good Manners 89
    (*see* Mancini)
  The Ship of Fools 89, 91, 92
Barlowe, Jerome 98
Barnes, A. W. 44
Barrington, Candace 202n8
Barthes, Roland 40, 120, 128
Baswell, Christopher 202n2
Baudrillard, Jean 85
Baumgartner, Emmanuèle 211n80
Bawcutt, Priscilla 64, 75, 76, 79, 82, 103, 105, 187n36, 188n44, 188n50, 189n2, 196n14, 197n37, 200n75, 201n88, 202n3, 204n34, 204n43
beast fable 77
Beaufort, Humphrey, Duke of Gloucester 7–8
Bellamy, Elizabeth J. 202n5
Benjamin, Walter 31, 169
Bennett, H. S. 206n18
Bennett, J. A. W. 119
Benoît de Ste-Maure, *Le Roman de Troie* 127, 209n50
Berger, Harry, Jnr. 17–18
Berkeley, Countess of 8
Bernard of Chartres 179n44
Betten, Anne 195n8
Bilney, Thomas 170
Blackwell, C. W. T. 186n20
Blake, N. F. 206n18
blindness 19, 22, 25–29, 30, 42, 68, 185n16
Bloch, Marc 200n67
Bloch, R. Howard 50, 95, 193n53
Blumenfeld-Kosinski, Renate 216n58
Boccaccio, Giovanni 8, 99
  Genealogie deorum gentilium libri 125, 126, 209n49
body
  and disease 78
  and growth 74
  and integrity 98
  and language 99
  and petition 71–76, 84
  and purse 74–76
  and rhetoric 55
  as constraint 73, 84
  courtier's 95, 99
  impotent 75–76, 172
  in pain 73, 84
  in pieces 96 (*see* ego, Lacan)
  maternal 24–25
  monstrous 65, 67, 102
  patron's 5, 7, 12
  poet's 5, 9, 11, 26
  royal 6, 13–14, 23, 25, 39, 45, 47, 60–61, 83, 84, 85, 132, 172, 182n68
  subject's 7
  (*see* monarch, poet)
Boehrer, Bruce Thomas 213n19
Boethius, *De consolatione philosophiae* 8, 116
Boffey, Julia 168, 175n12, 195n5, 215n46
book 121, 127, 133, 135, 147, 156
  printed 112–13 (*see* print)
Borch-Jacobsen, Mikkel 15
Bosch, Hieronymus 151
Bossy, John 198n40
Bosworth Field, battle of 22, 26–28
Bourdieu, Pierre, 22, 185n11
  on symbolic capital 10–11, 179n50, 180n51
  (*see* authority)
Bower, Walter, *Scotichronicon* 11
Bracciolini, Giovanni Poggio 43, 107
Brant, Sebastian 89
Brooks, Peter 206n14
Brownlow, F. W. 190n12, 213n12, 213n22, 214n30
Bruce, Robert (Robert I, king of Scotland) 11
Bryan, Jennifer 182n71
Bühler, Curt F. 181n63
Burgh, Benet 9–10, 179n44 (*see* Lydgate, *Secrees*)
Burrow, Colin 169, 210n67
Burrow, J. A. 71, 85, 178n35, 197n32, 198n41

Calais conference 155–56
Calin, William 212n87
Canitz, A. E. Christa 196n23
Carlson, David R. 22–23, 26, 31, 89, 128, 145, 184n1, 184n2, 185n10, 185n12, 185n13, 202n7, 214n31, 215n42
Carmeliano, Pietro 20, 22, 128, 184n4
  Suasoria Laeticiae 24
carnival 54, 72, 95, 97, 150, 151, 154, 155, 158, 166
Carpenter, Christine 184n84
catalogue 101, 161, 162
Cato, *Distichs* 136
Cawood, John 90
Caxton, William
  Curial 48, 108, 193n58
  Eneydos 43–44
  Historye of Reynart the Foxe 1, 174n3
  Recuyell of the Historyes of Troye 125–26, 127, 209n48
Cerquiglini, Jacqueline 68, 76, 198n56
chamber finance, Tudor 46
Chartier, Alain
  La Belle Dame Sans Merci 140
  Curial 47, 48, 49, 50, 56 (*see also* Caxton)

Dialogus Familiaris Amici et Sodalis 15
Le Livre de l'espérance 16
Chaucer, Geoffrey 47, 100, 106, 109, 140, 161
  and audience 12
  as precursor 5, 7–8, 10, 37, 128, 133, 135, 159, 160, 172, 179n42, 179n47
  The Book of the Duchess 139
  Clerk's Tale 10, 48
  The House of Fame 103, 106, 159, 168
  Knight's Tale 99
  The Legend of Good Women 100, 133, 163, 164
  Pardoner's Tale 97
  The Parliament of Fowls 32, 39, 195n77, 205n6
  Parson's Tale 73
  Squire's Tale 167
  Tale of Sir Thopas 102
  Troilus and Criseyde 8
Chew, Samuel C. 208n41
Chrétien de Troyes, *Lancelot, ou le chevalier de la charrette* 36
Cicero, Marcus Tullius
  De officiis 207n23
  Pro Caelio 96
city 146, 147, 154
clothing 108, 110
Coiner, Nancy 214n34
Columnis, Guido de, *Historia Destructionis Troiae* 209n50
Colyns, John 146, 151, 152
commodity 45, 91, 152
  courtier as 54
  Latin as 21, 22
  poem as 7, 31
  poet as 8
commonplace book 146
complaint 39, 64, 65, 158
  and love 110, 117–18, 129, 130, 135, 141, 143, 145, 146
Condon, M. M. 46
Connolly, Margaret 178n40
Constans, Léopold 210n58
Conway, W. M. 208n43
Cook, A. S. 214n37
Coote, Lesley A. 211n72
Copeland, Rita 55, 210n53
Copjec, Joan 189n55
Copland, Robert 99, 105, 204n49, 205n6
correctio 115
counsel 5, 9, 13–14, 136, 142, 145, 172, 182n67
court 1–3, 41, 45, 49, 53–55, 56, 65, 69, 76, 94, 146
  and ambition 65, 68, 149, 208n45
  and bureaucracy 72
  and city 175n9
  and competition 67
  and print 3, 176n15

Burgundian 111, 122, 123, 124
clerisy at 57–58
culture 19, 111, 175n12
defining 2, 175n10
English 19, 21, 47, 89, 111, 168, 176n13
imagined 98, 146
infernal 97
itinerant 96
revels 36, 37, 192n40
Ricardian 177n31
Scottish 12, 17, 66, 80, 83, 87, 176n13, 189n58, 204n34
Tudor 110, 134, 141, 142, 143, 175n10, 175n12
Yorkist 175n11
(*see* monarch, poet)
Court of Sapience, The 134
courtiership 48–49, 56, 175n11
  and duplicity 1, 4
  and prince 95–97
"courtly" poetry 175n12
  and "game of love" 132
Craft of Lovers, The 140
Crétin, Guillaume 71, 74, 86
Cuddy, Neil 83
curial satire 45, 46, 47, 49, 54, 56, 60, 68, 94, 97, 193n52
Currin, John M. 184n2

Damian, John 66
Dante Alighieri 133
De Certeau, Michel 153–54
  strategy and tactic in 153
De Man, Paul 177n23
death 97–98, 119, 121, 123, 124–25
  author and 98, 128
Deguileville, *Pèlerinage de la vie humaine* 111
  narrator of 111–12, 118, 122
Delany, Sheila, 196n20
Derrida, Jacques 186n23
  and archive 100, 101, 102, 105, 106
Deschamps, Eustache 71, 74, 75, 77, 85, 197n37, 197n38, 198n41, 198n59, 199n60, 199n65, 199n66
desire 17, 18, 34, 36, 38, 39, 49, 53, 79, 80, 88, 95, 111–14, 117, 130, 138, 141, 146, 152, 168
  and romance 121
  and will 82
  and writing 168
  mimetic 66
  royal 32
dialogue, love poetry and 117, 143
Dickey, Stephen 47, 192n38, 194n65
dilatio 134, 162, 166
Dinshaw, Carolyn 163
discourse 176n14

Dolar, Mladen 204n41
Donatus 111
Dorsch, T. S. 79
Douglas, Gavin 1, 3, 12, 87, 107, 145
    as cleric 104, 204n34
    Eneados 87–88, 101, 106, 107
    The Palice of Honoure 3, 34, 87, 98–107; 1553 edn (Robert Copland) 99, 105, 204n49; 1579 edn (Henry Charteris) 99, 204n49
Doyle, A. I. 175n12
dream-poetry 32, 33–34, 35, 45, 50, 52, 56, 58, 59, 61, 69, 161, 167, 169, 192n38
Dunbar, William 1, 3, 12, 63–86, 100, 145, 172, 187n36
    and benefices 63, 66, 67, 77, 80, 81, 82
    and duplicity 67–70
    and female voice 67, 79
    and pension 63, 64, 80
    and punishment 66–67, 80
    and style 34, 35, 103 (*see* aureate diction)
    and writing 66, 67–70, 78
    "Apon the Midsummer Ewin, mirriest of nichtis" (*The Tretis of the Tua Mariit Wemen and the Wedo*, B3) 59, 68, 76, 79
    "Be diuers wyis and operatiounes" (B5) 68, 78
    "Complane I wald, wist I quhome till" (B9) 64, 67, 69, 79
    "Gladethe, thoue queyne of Scottis regioun" (B15) 79
    "In secreit place this hyndir nycht" (B25) 68
    "Lucina schyning in silence of the nycht" (B29) 66
    "Madam, your men said thai wald ryd" (B30) 188n53
    "My heid did yak yester nicht" (B35) 73, 76
    "My lordis of chalker, pleis yow to heir" (36) 72
    "O gracious princes guid and fair" (B73) 67, 80
    "Off benefice, sir, at everie feist" (B43) 67, 68, 77
    "Off every asking followis nocht" (B44) 79
    "Quhen Merche wes with variand windis past" (*The Thrissill and the Rois*, B52) 3, 19, 32–35, 65, 79, 100, 104
    "Richt arely one Ask Wedinsday" (B57) 79
    "Ryght as the stern of day begouth to schyne" (*The Goldyn Targe*, B59) 3, 32–33, 34, 35–38, 39, 41, 101
    "Sanct saluatour, send siluer sorrow" (B61) 73, 75, 76, 78
    "Schir, for your grace, bayth nicht and day" (B63) 79
    "Schir, I complane off iniuris" (B64) 66, 80
    "Schir, lat it neuer in toune be tald" (B66) 76
    "Schir, ye haue mony seruitouris" (B67) 66, 67, 69, 78

"Schir, yit remember as befoir" (B68) 65, 67, 70, 72, 77, 78
"The wardraipper of Wenus boure" (B72) 67
"This hinder nycht, halff sleiping as I lay" (B75) 67, 69, 76, 77, 80
"This hindir nycht in Dumfermeling" 188n53
"This waverand warldis wretchidnes" (B79) 71, 72
Dunnigan, Sarah M. 186n25

Ebin, Lois 187n36, 188n40, 191n28, 206n11, 207n23
Êchard, Sian 178n37
Eco, Umberto 147
economy 147
    exchange 164
    gift 152
Edington, Carol 189n58
Edmunds, Lowell 210n58
Edward IV, king of England 20, 25, 46
Edwards, A. S. G. 122, 176n15, 189n7, 205n6, 206n20, 208n43, 209n48, 212n5, 213n6, 215n46
Edwards, H. L. R. 214n39
ego
    ego-ideal 142
    Lacan and 16
    mimetic 15
    (*see* body, Freud)
ekphrasis 32, 35, 36, 38
Elias, Norbert 193n52, 193n58, 203n25
Elizabeth I, queen of England 173
Elizabeth of York, queen of Henry VII 23, 32, 185n15
Elton, G. R. 175n10, 183n84, 184n85
encyclopaedic tradition 104, 111, 112, 113
Enders, Jody 155
Enterline, Lynn 162, 189n8, 204n45
epic 87, 88, 99
espionage, Tudor 45, 57, 190n16, 191n22
euhemerism 125
Eusebius, *Chronicle* 126
Evans, Deanna Delmar 187n32
exegesis 48, 91, 110, 114, 152, 154, 158

Fall, 148
    and language 148, 150
    and metaphor 188n47
fame
    and name 161, 163, 165, 167
    and poetry 67, 69, 70, 113, 121, 122, 124, 147, 163, 164, 167
    as *gloire* 111
Faques, Richard 160–62
Ferguson, Margaret W. 188n47

Index

Ferster, Judith 182n66
fetish 150 (*see* Freud)
Feylde, Thomas, *A Controversy Between a Lover and a Jaye* 109
figuration 114–16, 122, 125, 145, 152–53, 159
Finkelstein, Richard 188n40
Fish, Stanley 56, 190n14, 194n74, 197n23
Fisher, John H. 178n38
The Floure and the Leafe 206n19
flyting 65, 70, 106, 145, 171
food 152–53
Fortescue, Sir John 182n68
Foucault, Michel 83, 176n14, 201n86
Fowler, Elizabeth 166
Fox, Alistair 168, 190n14, 203n22, 203n29, 210n59, 211n72, 211n75, 212n90
Fox, Denton 175n12, 176n15
Fradenburg, Louise O. 13, 16, 27, 33, 38, 39, 41, 99, 181n62, 183n77, 185n14, 186n25, 187n30, 189n58, 196n22, 197n23, 200n76, 200n77, 201n81, 203n25, 204n34, 204n43
Franc, Martin le, *Le Champion des Dames* 68
Freud, Sigmund 16, 94, 142, 186n23
  and dirty joke 80, 166
  and displacement 4
  and ego-ideal 12, 181n60
  and fetish 51, 192n36
  and primal scene 27
  and uncanny 194n67
  The Ego and the Id 12
  Mourning and Melancholia 142
  (*see too* ego, Lacan, fetish, uncanny)
Froissart, Jean, *Dit dou Florin* 197n29
Frost, Ulrich 146
Fuss, Diana 177n27
Fyler, John M. 213n10

Gaguin, Robert 19, 22, 184n2
Gairdner, James 28, 185n18, 186n24
garden 33–34, 35, 37, 40, 100, 101
genre 2, 3–4, 10, 11, 18, 33, 44, 100, 101, 110, 113, 118, 119, 121, 124, 126, 127, 135, 141, 142, 146, 147, 161, 168, 176n14
Geoffrey of Vinsauf, *Poetria Nova* 54, 188n40, 192n47
Gigli, Giovanni 20, 22, 23, 184n4
  Epigramma in natalem principis 23, 24
  Genethliacon 23, 24–25
Gillespie, Vincent 216n7
Gingerich, Owen 215n42
Girard, René 196n18
Glasgow, Peace of 32
Glossa Ordinaria 148
glossing 114, 116, 121, 137, 154
Goldberg, Jonathan 124, 165, 213n20

Goldstein, R. James 11, 171
Goodman, Anthony 183n84
gossip 79, 80, 115
Gower, John 8, 10, 106, 109, 128, 140, 159, 168
  Confessio Amantis 6–7, 139, 202n8
Grady, Frank 178n37
Grammarians' War 155
Gray, Douglas 196n14, 198n44, 207n29, 207n32
Green, Richard Firth 15, 128, 175n12, 178n38, 179n46, 184n6, 189n2, 212n85
Greenblatt, Stephen 3, 196n23, 210n67
Greene, Roland 44, 166
Greene, Thomas M. 179n46
Griffiths, Jane 148, 189n2, 213n15, 216n7
Grignaschi, Mario 181n66
Grummitt, David 190n17, 191n21, 191n24
Gunn, Steven 176n13, 190n17, 205n5
Guy-Bray, Stephen 93

Hadfield, Andrew 215n44
Halpern, Richard 149, 166, 212n4, 214n26
Harris, Kate 162
Hary, *Wallace* 11–12
Hawes, Stephen 1, 21, 91, 108–44, 145, 169, 176n15
  as groom to chamber 108–09
  The Comfort of Lovers 21, 109, 110, 117, 129–44; "truth" in 130–34
  The Example of Virtue 108, 114, 208n43, 208n45
  The Pastime of Pleasure 108, 129, 143
Hay, Bryan Scott 196n20
Hay, Sir Gilbert, *Buik of King Alexander* 13–14, 84
Heiserman, A. R. 190n13
Hellinga, Lotte 208n43
Henry IV, king of England 6, 7
Henry V, king of England (as Prince of Wales) 7, 179n47, 205n9
Henry VI, king of England 9, 25
Henry VII, king of England 1, 17, 19, 20, 21, 22, 26, 27–30, 31–32, 41, 45, 98, 108, 109, 128, 131, 132, 175n10, 183n84, 194n73
  court style of 191n24
  library of 210n54
  propagandist use of Lancastrian lineage 205n8
Henry VIII, king of England 17, 109, 129, 156, 161, 183n84–184n84
heraldry 32, 35, 39–40, 41, 134, 138, 189n58
Heron, John, Treasurer of the Chamber 108
Herrmann, Erwin 211n72
historicism 169
historiography 11, 19 (see André), 25, 26–30
history
  sacred 150, 154, 155
  universal 105
Hobbins, Daniel 185n18, 186n23

Hoccleve, Thomas 5–6, 85
  La Male Regle 74, 198n45
  The Regement of Princes 7, 8, 14, 66, 75, 192n38
Holbein, Hans, *The Ambassadors* 120
Holub, Robert C. 199n61
Holyrood Palace 83, 200n81
household
  royal 45–46, 53, 106
  Tudor 210n59
Howard, Sir Edward 97
Howard, Elizabeth Tylney, Countess of Surrey 160, 161, 162
Howard, Thomas, Duke of Norfolk 90
Hult, David F. 33, 50
humanism 19–31, 43, 128, 161, 184n1
Hyde, Isabel 188n40
hysteron proteron 136, 162

identification, 5, 8, 9–11, 12–15, 16–17, 18, 21, 23, 25, 52–53, 79, 85, 86, 140, 141, 142, 143, 149, 161, 177n27
  and rivalry 66–67
  gendered 80
imitatio 179n46
  and obedience 16
imperium 23, 31, 32
  and *translatio imperii* 26
Ingham, Patricia Clare 195n76
The Isle of Ladies 136

Jaeger, C. Stephen 175n11, 193n57, 194n64, 194n70
James I, king of Scotland, *The Kingis Quair* 33
James III, king of Scotland 12, 19, 32, 201n83
James IV, king of Scotland 12, 17, 19, 31–32, 39–40, 63–86, 87, 106, 171, 200n76, 200n77
  and architecture 83
  and tournaments 200n81–201n81
  as *roi inconnu* 83
  marriage to Margaret Tudor 31–32
James V, king of Scotland 1, 171–72, 201n85
James VI of Scotland (I of England) 173
James, Mervyn 127
Jameson, Fredric 201n87
Jansen, Sharon L. 211n72
Jerome, St. 126
John of Salisbury 193n52
Johnson, Ian R. 179n42
Jones, Richard Foster 185n8
Joukofsky, Françoise 206n13
Juvenal, satire and 161

Kallet-Marx, Lisa 213n9
Kantorowicz, Ernst H. 83, 181n61
Kay, Sarah 52, 206n17, 211n80
Kebell, Thomas 191n25

Keightley, G. R. 209n48
King, Pamela M. 35
Kinsman, Robert S. 151
Kipling, Gordon 122, 124, 132, 185n7, 206n12, 206n13
Kleineke, Wilhelm 181n66
Knapp, Ethan 177n30
Kratzmann, Gregory 174n5
Kuskin, William 17, 43–44

La Marche, Olivier de, *Le chevalier délibéré* 122–24, 208n43
La Mote, Jehan de, *Li regret Guillaume Comte de Hainaut* 68
Lacan, Jacques 41, 53, 102, 203n28
  and anamorphosis 120
  and *das Ding* 52–53, 59
  and ego, 16
  and gaze 189n55
  and *Vorstellungen* 53
Lancastrians 5–6, 7, 21, 109
Lander, J. R. 46, 191n19
Lanham, Richard 59
Laplanche, Jean and Jean-Bertrand Pontalis, *The Language of Psycho-Analysis* 10, 181n60
Latin 21–31, 34, 90, 100, 106, 168, 187n36
  and diction 35
  and metre 21, 22, 27, 28
laureation 21, 22, 44, 98, 159–62, 164, 167, 189n2
  and authority 43
  and mediation 162
  and Skelton 43, 44, 91, 98, 145, 146, 160
  (*see* authority, Skelton)
Lavezzo, Kathy 148, 155, 214n26
Lawton, David 5, 188n41
Lawton, Lesley 205n9
Lefèvre, Raoul 126, 209n48
Lemaire de Belges, Jean
  Les Epîtres de l'amant vert 149
  Le Temple de Vertu et d'Honneur 91
Leomarte, *Sumas de historia troyana* 209n48
Lerer, Seth 106, 175n12, 189n2, 205n5, 207n24, 207n26, 210n67, 213n8, 213n20, 215n45
letter and literalization 52, 58–61, 155
Leupin, Alexandre 183n78
Lewis, C. S. 119, 120, 124
Leyerle, John 196n11
Liber philosophorum moralium antiquorum 180n58, 181n63
Liddale, Sir James, of Halkerton 11–12
Lindsay, Robert, of Pitscottie 83
Linlithgow Palace 83, 201n85
Locher, John 89
Lochrie, Karma 194n62, 200n73
London 91, 151, 152

look 19, 35–37, 38, 41–42, 48, 55, 56, 57, 59, 180n58
  and eye 74
  and indirection 68
  and voyeurism 68, 165
  royal 78, 86
Lorris, Guillaume de, and Jean de Meun, *Le Roman de la Rose* 4, 33, 34, 40, 50, 105, 111
  "I" in 111
losengiers 136, 211n80
loss 97, 110, 138, 139, 141, 142, 154, 162
  Edenic 148
love 2, 8, 24, 40, 49–52, 98, 116, 127
  and *dit* 32, 36, 110, 163, 168
  and poetry 18, 110, 163, 168, 174n7, 175n12
  and rhetoric 114
  game of 132
Lucan, *Pharsalia* 29–30
Lucas, Peter J. 175n12
Lucian of Samosata, *Lexiphanes* 192n48
Lukacher, Ned 27
Lyall, R. J. 34, 173, 202n6, 202n7, 202n14, 203n31, 204n33
Lydgate, John 5–6, 10, 21, 44, 47–48, 59, 88, 90, 99, 106, 109, 112, 115, 128, 135, 140, 143, 159, 168, 178n32, 180n51, 187n36, 203n30
  Balade in Commendation of Our Lady 187n36
  The Fall of Princes 7–8, 48, 202n6, 210n58
  Isopes Fabules 183n77, 191n28
  Letter to Gloucester 75
  Secrees of Old Filisoffres 9, 191n28
  The Siege of Thebes 203n30
  The Temple of Glas 135, 140
  Troy Book 109, 179n47, 205n9, 209n50
Lyndsay, Sir David 12, 31, 82, 171
  Answer to the Kingis Flyting 171
  The Complaynt of Schir David Lindesay 171
  Ane Dreme 171
lyric 26, 124, 161
  and love 125, 168
  and narrative 119
  penitential 119

MacDougall, Norman 32, 83, 186n30, 200n80, 200n81, 201n83
MacFarlane, Leslie J. 183n82
Machaut, Guillaume de 74, 76, 161
  Le Dit dou Lyon 206n19
  Remède de Fortune 114, 207n21
Mackie, R. L. 200n79
Macrobius 49, 52
Maitland, Sir Richard, of Lethington 64
Mancini, Domenico 89, 90
  De quattuor virtutibus 89
Manley, Lawrence 203n16
Mann, Jill 195n9

Mannyng, Robert, of Brunne 135
Mantuan (Baptista Spagnuoli) 89, 90, 91, 94
  Adulescentia (Eclogues) 91, 92, 93, 96, 203n18
manuscripts 31, 162, 175n12
  BL MS Domitian A18 26, 185n18, 186n23
  BL MS Harley 69 210n60
  BL MS Harley 336 24
  BL MS Harley 2252 146–47, 148
  BL Royal MS 19 A VIII 181n58
  BL Royal MS 19 B IV 181n58
  Bodleian MS Rawlinson C 813 117–18, 129
  Cambridge, Pepys Library, 2553, Magdalene College (Maitland Folio) 63–64, 77
  College of Arms MS R36 210n61, 210n63, 210n64
  MS Camb. Univ. Ll. 5. 10 (Reidpeth Manuscript) 63, 82
  MS Camb. Univ. Mm.4.42 181n58
  National Archives PRO E 36/214 205n4
  National Library of Scotland Adv. MS 1.1.6 (Bannatyne Manuscript) 187n31
manuscripts and graphic culture 17–18
Manzalaoui, Mahmoud 181n66
Map, Walter 2
Mapstone, Sally 12, 176n13, 182n67
Marot, Clément 198n59
Martin, Joanna 188n53
marvels 146, 148, 152, 155
Marx, Karl 152
masochism 48, 80
Matthew of Vendôme 188n42, 194n72
Mayer, Thomas F. 183n84
Meale, Carol M. 175n12, 212n6
Medvedev, P. N. and M. M. Bakhtin, *The Formal Method in Literary Scholarship* 3, 4
  and refraction 3
memory 32, 41, 93, 130, 141, 142
Mendenhall, John Cooper 187n36
metamorphosis 67, 98, 103, 156, 158, 159
metaphor 35, 36, 103
  and loss 143
  as *translatio* 34, 158, 188n42
  illumination as 48 (see metaphor)
  paternal 40
Meyer-Lee, Robert 6, 168, 169, 184n6, 187n36, 189n2, 191n28, 202n6, 202n13, 206n9, 210n67, 214n26
Middleton, Anne 215n52
Miller, D. A. 76
Miller, Jacqueline T. 179n44
minion, Henrician 149, 213n20
Minnis, A. J. 174n6, 202n4
misogyny, medieval 95–96, 116

modesty *topos*, 5, 8–11, 41, 44, 48, 109, 172
  and stance of "dullness," 5, 48, 136, 194n64
Molinet, Jean 74, 75, 82
monarch 3, 21, 64, 141
  and *communitas* 171, 181n62
  and documents 1, 174n3
  and grace 78
  as knight of romance 79
  as lady of courtly love 79, 80
  and love 29, 86
  as model 15, 16
  as patron 1, 20, 25
  as physician 200n67
  as poet 28, 29
  male, 25
  (*see* authority, body)
money 46, 47, 55, 61, 75, 193n53
monstrosity
  and landscape 101
  and vision 70
  (*see* body)
Montaigne, Michel de 177n26
Morgan, D. A. L. 175n11
Mortimer, Nigel 177n30
Morton, John, Archbishop of Canterbury 92, 94, 97
mourning 108, 123, 131, 142
Mustard, Wilfred P. 93, 94, 203n18

name 164, 165
narcissism 142, 164
narrative, 111, 118, 121, 122, 123, 139, 142
  and death 121, 124
  and lyric
  and voice 110, 119, 121, 124, 125, 143
  narrators 122
nation 7, 11, 21, 88, 98, 151, 159
  Scotland and England, comparative study of 173
Nelson, William A. 89, 154, 189n1, 214n30
Nicholson, Ranald 186n30
Nitecki, Alicia K. 204n42
Nolan, Maura 178n32
nominalism 49, 192n43
Norman, Joanne 196n11
Norton-Smith, John 165, 187n36, 205n51

Oedipus 130, 143
Olson, Glending 215n52
oratio 116
origins 19, 34, 41, 107, 138, 141, 142, 167
  and dynasty 21, 26–28, 39
  of state 125
  paradisal 146
Orme, Nicholas 202n6, 202n7

Ovid 44, 99, 102, 106, 135, 149, 156, 159, 160, 162, 164
  Heroides 164
  Metamorphoses 106, 156
Owst, G. R. 200n70

pageantry 35, 38, 110
Paleit, Edward 186n26
paradise 148–49, 155
paranoia 45, 47, 52, 57, 58, 61
Parker, David R. 213n6
Parker, P. 211n68
Parker, Patricia A. 27, 162, 211n73
Parkinson, David 102, 104, 105, 196n21
parrot, 151
  as "green lover" 149, 152, 157
  as Psittacus 158
pastoral 92–94, 169
  and homosociality 93
  and mourning 93–94
patronage 70, 88, 89, 91, 97, 123, 149, 154, 161, 172, 197n23
  erotics of 23, 28–29, 79, 80
  female 8, 132, 133, 134, 140, 141, 160, 162, 163, 165
  representations of 1, 4–5, 7–9, 8–12, 14, 16, 164
  Scottish 12
  Tudor 17, 46, 61, 133
  (*see* monarch, poet)
Patterson, Lee 177n31, 182n70, 182n71, 196n20, 210n58
Pearsall, Derek 9, 119, 175n12, 177n32, 191n27
pedagogy 111, 113, 155
  and discipline 111
  and *disputationes* 155
  and exposition 112–13
penitence 71, 72, 73, 120
  charity and 73
Perkins, Nicholas 177n31, 182n66
personification (prosopopeia) 3, 33, 36, 50, 52, 61, 69, 80, 110, 111, 114–18, 121, 122, 125, 169
petitionary poetry 54, 63–86, 141, 143
  languor and 73
  love petitions 117
  melancholy and 80
Petrarch, Francesco 9, 44, 48, 55, 161, 162
Piccolomini, Eneo Silvio
  De miseriis curialium epistola 91, 94, 95, 96–97, 203n15
Piepho, Lee 203n17, 203n18
pilgrimage as genre 113, 118, 119, 123, 124
Pinkernell, Gerd 209n48
poet 1–2, 34, 48
  and age 5, 6–9, 14, 71, 76, 80, 85
  and court 15–16, 41, 43, 110, 149, 176n13
  and identity 2, 171

and monarch 1, 29, 172
and poverty 7–8, 73–76, 84
and signature 6, 7, 34, 73, 123, 139, 168, 208n45
as cleric 68, 75–76, 99, 145, 154, 168
as dreamer 34
as petitioner 63–86
as prophet 141, 143
as sign of monarch 108
self-imagining 21
poetry
  and inspiration 169
  and making 163
Poirion, Daniel 13, 15, 183n78, 196n17
Premierfait, Laurent de 7–8
Prescott, Anne Lake 123
print 17–18, 43–44, 47, 61, 89, 90, 91, 108–09, 162
  and court 3, 176n15
Privy Chamber 17, 45, 46, 60, 83, 205n5
prophecy 110, 130, 139–40, 141, 142, 143, 145, 146, 154–55, 161
  political 110, 134, 141, 147, 163
  prophecies of Merlin 134, 135
Pseudo-Oppian, *Cynegetica* 214n27
Psilos, Paul D. 51
purgatory 120, 125
purse, petitionary poem and 72
  (*see* body)
Puttenham, George 4, 168, 173
Putter, Ad 57, 197n28
Pye, Christopher 37
Pynson, Richard 88–89

queen 23, 25
Quintilian, *Institutio Oratoria* 55, 213n9

Rambuss, Richard 212n88
Ramsay, Allan 187n31
ratio 116
reader, imagined 43–44, 76, 112–13, 147, 157
  gender and 149, 163
The Receyt of the Lady Kateryne 206n12
Reiss, Edmund 196n16, 198n51
Reiss, Timothy J. 177n26
renovatio 21
rhetoric 54, 59
  and discipline 55, 115
  and figuration 114–16
  and love 114
  and state 115, 128, 210n53
  as *dispositio* 125
  as *elocutio* 116
  as *inventio* 113, 114, 128
Rhetorica ad Herennium 55, 207n22
rhétoriqueurs, grands 16, 108, 111, 123
Rhodenizer, Vernon Blair 209n46

Ribémont, Bernard 213n19
Richard II, king of England 6–7
Richard III, king of England 20, 22, 185n15
Richardson, Malcolm 178n38
rivalry 20, 65–66, 70, 82, 83, 140, 156, 172
Roman de Renart 1, 174n3
  Gherard Leeu, *Reinaert* 1, 174n3
  tradition of 1, 174n3
  (*see also* Caxton)
romance 111, 113, 121, 122, 124, 125, 130, 138, 142
Roy, William 98
Russell, J. Stephen 192n43
Rutebeuf 196n15
  De Brichemer 198n39
  La Complainte Rutebeuf 196n15
  La Griesche d'Yver 196n16, 198n40
  La Pauvreté de Rutebeuf 78
  La Repentance Rutebeuf 71, 197n31
  Le Mariage Rutebeuf 196n15

Sale, Helen Stearns 190n12
Sallust 27, 30, 90, 186n20
  Bellum Iugurthinum 89
sanctuary 155
Sauchieburn, battle of (1488), 19
Scala, Elizabeth 167
Scanlon, Larry 177n32, 178n38
Scase, Wendy 196n12
Scattergood, John 175n12, 181n59, 190n13, 193n51, 214n37, 215n51
Schor, Naomi 185n16
Scollen-Jimack, Christine 64
Scots 106
Scott, Tom 196n22, 198n51
secrecy 3, 13, 18, 47, 48, 52, 110, 127, 128, 151, 168
Secretum Secretorum 13–14
Sedgwick, Eve Kosofsky 79
Shakespeare, William, *Hamlet* 182n68
Shell, Marc 191n24
Sheriff Hutton Castle 159, 161, 163, 164
Shirley, John 8, 178n40
Shuffleton, Frank 187n38
sickness 73–76
Siculus, Diodorus
  Bibliotheca Historia 43, 165
signs, 50
  and carnality 49, 51
Simpson, James 176n14, 194n69, 202n2
Skelton, John 1, 30, 43–62, 88, 91, 140, 145–67, 168, 169, 176n15
  as *orator regius* 145
  court career 145
Skeltonics 165, 166
  Agaynst a Comely Coystrowne 44, 51

Skelton, John (cont.)
  The Bowge of Courte 1, 3, 42, 44, 45, 47–62, 91, 109, 136
  Calliope 145, 146
  Collyn Cloute 145
  Dyvers Ballettys and Dyties Solacyous 44
  The Garlande of Laurell 3, 44, 106, 146, 159–67
  genesis 160
  Magnyfycence 56, 145, 165
  Manerly Margery Milk and Ale 44, 165
  Phyllyp Sparowe 140, 146, 166
  A Replycacion Agaynst Certayne Yonge Scolers Abjured of Late 169–70
  Speculum Principis 165
  Speke Parott 3, 145, 146–59, 169
  The Tunnynge of Elynour Rummynge 166
  Upon the Dolorous Dethe of the Erle of Northumberlande 29, 43, 44
  Ware the Hauke 146
  Why Come Ye Nat to Courte? 145, 214n27
  "Womanhod, wanton, ye want!" 51
Smith, D. Vance 39, 41, 198n48
Smith, Julie A. 93, 189n2
sound 103, 170
  as material 23, 25
Spearing, A. C. 5, 32, 35, 70, 99, 116, 191n30, 192n39, 195n75, 195n77, 197n30, 204n34, 207n25, 212n84, 214n33, 214n38, 214n39, 215n43
spectacle 36, 42, 47, 70, 102
speculum principis 14, 80
  petitioner and 80–81, 84
  monarch and 83
speech 37, 152–53, 155
  plain 67–70, 169
Spiegel, Gabrielle 186n26
Spreit of Gy, The 120
Stanley conspiracy 45
Starkey, David 45, 83, 176n13, 180n51, 183n84–184n84, 191n23, 194n73, 205n5
Statius, *Thebaid* 99
Stevens, John 214n35
Stewart, Alexander, duke of Albany 12
Stirling Castle 201n85
  chapel royal at 83
  "kingis hous" at 83
Straker, Scott-Morgan 177n31
Strohm, Paul 6, 27, 176n13, 176n17, 178n38, 180n57, 191n24
style, high 10–11, 44, 47–48
  and Dunbar 34, 35 (*see* aureate diction)
subject 10, 64
  and insufficiency 70
  and mutability 5
  and secrecy 18

as lover 33, 36–37, 104, 110–18, 130
courtly 57
of devotional writing 182n71
of *énoncé* and *énonciation* 119, 207n33
poetic 12–15, 47, 48, 49
political 61, 177n26
speaking 119
(*see* poet, patron)
Summit, Jennifer 174n7
Sunderland, Luke 174n4
Surrey, Henry Howard, Earl of 168
Sutch, Susie Speakman 123
syntax 10, 47–48, 51

Taillevent, Michault 197n36
Tarnoff, Maura 215n50
Taylor, Rupert 211n72
temporality and time 112, 122, 125, 146, 151
  and petition 142
  and prophecy 143
  narrative 125
  of reading 125
  of writing 125
Teskey, Gordon 169
testament 72
Theocritus 93
Thomas, Keith 200n67
Tignonville, Guillaume de 180n58–181n58
Todorov, Tzvetan 207n33
Tolmie, Sarah 177n31, 188n49
Torti, Anna 58
tournaments 138
  Greenwich (1506) 132
  "Juste of the Moneth of May" (1507) 132
translatio 99, 158, 188n42, 202n2 (*see* metaphor)
translation 7, 8, 87–107
  and authorial identity 90
  and mediation 94
Trapp, J. B. 184n4, 189n2
Travis, Peter 100
Treaty of Perpetual Peace 19
Tucker, Melvin J. 160
Tudor, Arthur, son of Henry VII 22–25, 29, 32, 186n23
Tudor iconography 134, 138
Tudor, Margaret, daughter of Henry VII, 31–32, 33
  in Dunbar's poetry 79, 80
  marriage to James IV, 17, 19, 31–32, 83
Tudor, Mary, daughter of Henry VII 131–32, 133, 205n5
Tudor, Mary, queen of England 98
Tudor polity 17, 183n84
Turner, Victor 181n62
Tuve, Rosemond 206n17

"Twelve Letters Save England" 135
Tyndale, William 98
typology 151, 152

Uebel, Michael 148
Uhlig, Klaus 192n40, 193n57, 194n70, 194n71
uncanny 58–59, 98, 128, 157, 163, 194n67

vates, poet as 19, 22, 26, 28, 189n2
vernacular 7, 44, 48, 51, 66, 99, 100, 114, 125, 128, 136, 141, 151, 155, 159, 166
   and poetic genealogy 17, 21, 47, 128
   as patrilineal 159–60, 163, 165
   dialect 116
   English 21–22
Veysey, John, bishop of Exeter 90
Virgil 88, 135, 159, 172
   Aeneid 99, 105, 106, 107
   Eclogues 93, 106
   Georgics 93
Vitelli, Cornelio 20, 22, 184n4
Vitz, Evelyn Birge 206n15, 207n28
voice 28, 29, 38, 64, 100–01, 103, 159, 187n36
   as maternal object 101

Wakelin, Daniel 43, 184n1
Walker, Greg 145, 168, 175n9, 190n12, 210n55, 213n20
Wallace, Nathaniel Owen 213n11
Wallace, Sir William, of Craigie 11–12
Waller, Gary 196n22
Walter of Chatillon 74, 199n63

Walton, John 8, 179n42
Warbeck, Perkin 26, 32, 200n81
Watts, John 176n13, 184n84
Weiss, Roberto 184n3
Wenzel, Siegfried 206n16
West, Nicholas, bishop of Ely 90
Westminster, Roger, prior of Ely 92, 93, 97
"When cuckoo time cometh oft so soon" 135
Whigham, Frank 193n60
White, Beatrice 90, 93, 203n18, 203n21, 203n26, 204n33
Williams, Deanne 206n14, 207n24
Williams, Janet Hadley 172
Wilson, Edward 207n26
Winser, Leigh 192n40, 194n65
Wolffe, B. P. 191n20
Wolsey, Thomas, Cardinal 98, 145–46, 149, 150, 151, 152, 153, 154–56, 158, 161; as Antichrist 154, 155
woodcuts 1, 113, 208n43
Woolf, Rosemary 198n44, 200n72, 207n32
Worde, Wynkyn de 1, 44, 61, 108, 111, 132, 176n15, 206n20, 208n43
Wyatt, Sir Thomas 3, 133, 168, 210n67

Yeager, R. F. 178n35
Younge, John, *Fyancells of Margaret* 40, 186n30

Zeeman, Nicolette 118, 174n7, 178n35, 188n48
Zettersten, Arne 187n36
Zink, Michel 196n16
Zumthor, Paul 16, 108, 182n76, 183n78

CAMBRIDGE STUDIES IN MEDIEVAL LITERATURE

1 Robin Kirkpatrick *Dante's Inferno: Difficulty and Dead Poetry*
2 Jeremy Tambling *Dante and Difference: Writing in the "Commedia"*
3 Simon Gaunt *Troubadours and Irony*
4 Wendy Scase *"Piers Plowman" and the New Anticlericalism*
5 Joseph Duggan *The "Cantar De Mio Cid": Poetic Creation in its Economic and Social Contexts*
6 Roderick Beaton *The Medieval Greek Romance*
7 Kathryn Kerby-Fulton *Reformist Apocalypticism and "Piers Plowman"*
8 Alison Morgan *Dante and the Medieval Other World*
9 Eckehard Simon (ed.) *The Theatre of Medieval Europe: New Research in Early Drama*
10 Mary Carruthers *The Book of Memory: A Study of Memory in Medieval Culture*
11 Rita Copeland *Rhetoric, Hermeneutics and Translation in the Middle Ages: Academic Traditions and Vernacular Texts*
12 Donald Maddox *The Arthurian Romances of Chrétien de Troyes: Once and Future Fictions*
13 Nicholas Watson *Richard Rolle and the Invention of Authority*
14 Steven F. Kruger *Dreaming in the Middle Ages*
15 Barbara Nolan *Chaucer and the Tradition of the "Roman Antique"*
16 Sylvia Huot *The "Romance of the Rose" and its Medieval Readers: Interpretations, Reception, Manuscript Transmission*
17 Carol M. Meale (ed.) *Women and Literature in Britain, 1150–1500*
18 Henry Ansgar Kelly *Ideas and Forms of Tragedy from Aristotle to the Middle Ages*
19 Martin Irvine *The Making of Textual Culture: Grammatical and Literary Theory, 350–1100*
20 Larry Scanlon *Narrative, Authority and Power: The Medieval Exemplum and the Chaucerian Tradition*
21 Erik Kooper *Medieval Dutch Literature in its European Context*
22 Steven Botterill *Dante and the Mystical Tradition: Bernard of Clairvaux in the "Commedia"*
23 Peter Biller and Anne Hudson (eds.) *Heresy and Literacy, 1000–1530*
24 Christopher Baswell *Virgil in Medieval England: Figuring the "Aeneid" from the Twelfth Century to Chaucer*

25 James Simpson *Sciences and Self in Medieval Poetry: Alan of Lille's "Anticlaudianus" and John Gower's "Confessio Amantis"*
26 Joyce Coleman *Public Reading and the Reading Public in Late Medieval England and France*
27 Suzanne Reynolds *Medieval Reading: Grammar, Rhetoric and the Classical Text*
28 Charlotte Brewer *Editing "Piers Plowman": the Evolution of the Text*
29 Walter Haug *Vernacular Literary Theory in the Middle Ages: The German Tradition in its European Context*
30 Sarah Spence *Texts and the Self in the Twelfth Century*
31 Edwin Craun *Lies, Slander and Obscenity in Medieval English Literature: Pastoral Rhetoric and the Deviant Speaker*
32 Patricia E. Grieve *"Floire and Blancheflor" and the European Romance*
33 Huw Pryce (ed.) *Literacy in Medieval Celtic Societies*
34 Mary Carruthers *The Craft of Thought: Meditation, Rhetoric, and the Making of Images, 400–1200*
35 Beate Schmolke-Hasselman *The Evolution of Arthurian Romance: The Verse Tradition from Chrétien to Froissart*
36 Siân Echard *Arthurian Narrative in the Latin Tradition*
37 Fiona Somerset *Clerical Discourse and Lay Audience in Late Medieval England*
38 Florence Percival *Chaucer's Legendary Good Women*
39 Christopher Cannon *The Making of Chaucer's English: A Study of Words*
40 Rosalind Brown-Grant *Christine de Pizan and the Moral Defence of Women: Reading Beyond Gender*
41 Richard Newhauser *The Early History of Greed: the Sin of Avarice in Early Medieval Thought and Literature*
42 Margaret Clunies Ross *Old Icelandic Literature and Society*
43 Donald Maddox *Fictions of Identity in Medieval France*
44 Rita Copeland *Pedagogy, Intellectuals, and Dissent in the Later Middle Ages: Lollardy and Ideas of Learning*
45 Kantik Ghosh *The Wycliffite Heresy: Authority and the Interpretation of Texts*
46 Mary C. Erler *Women, Reading, and Piety in Late Medieval England*
47 D. H. Green *The Beginnings of Medieval Romance: Fact and Fiction, 1150–1220*
48 J. A. Burrow *Gestures and Looks in Medieval Narrative*
49 Ardis Butterfield *Poetry and Music in Medieval France: From Jean Renart to Guillaume de Machaut*
50 Emily Steiner *Documentary Culture and the Making of Medieval English Literature*
51 William E. Burgwinkle *Sodomy, Masculinity, and Law in Medieval Literature*

52 Nick Havely *Dante and the Franciscans: Poverty and the Papacy in the "Commedia"*
53 Siegfried Wenzel *Latin Sermon Collections from Later Medieval England*
54 Ananya Jahanara Kabir and Deanne Williams (eds.) *Postcolonial Approaches to the European Middle Ages: Translating Cultures*
55 Mark Miller *Philosophical Chaucer: Love, Sex, and Agency in the "Canterbury Tales"*
56 Simon Gilson *Dante and Renaissance Florence*
57 Ralph Hanna *London Literature, 1300–1380*
58 Maura Nolan *John Lydgate and the Making of Public Culture*
59 Nicolette Zeeman *"Piers Plowman" and the Medieval Discourse of Desire*
60 Anthony Bale *The Jew in the Medieval Book: English Antisemitisms, 1350–1500*
61 Robert J. Meyer-Lee *Poets and Power from Chaucer to Wyatt*
62 Isabel Davis *Writing Masculinity in the Later Middle Ages*
63 John M. Fyler *Language and the Declining World in Chaucer, Dante and Jean de Meun*
64 Matthew Giancarlo *Parliament and Literature in Late Medieval England*
65 D. H. Green *Women Readers in the Middle Ages*
66 Mary Dove *The First English Bible: The Text and Context of the Wycliffite Versions*
67 Jenni Nuttall *The Creation of Lancastrian Kingship: Literature, Language and Politics in Late Medieval England*
68 Laura Ashe *Fiction and History in England, 1066–1200*
69 J. A. Burrow *The Poetry of Praise*
70 Mary Carruthers *The Book of Memory: A Study of Memory in Medieval Culture*
71 Andrew Cole *Literature and Heresy in the Age of Chaucer*
72 Suzanne M. Yeager *Jerusalem in Medieval Narrative*
73 Nicole R. Rice *Lay Piety and Religious Discipline in Middle English Literature*
74 D. H. Green *Women and Marriage in German Medieval Romance*
75 Peter Godman *Paradoxes of Conscience in the High Middle Ages: Abelard, Heloise and the Archpoet*
76 Edwin D. Craun *Ethics and Power in Medieval English Reformist Writing*
77 David Matthews *Writing to the King: Nation, Kingship, and Literature in England, 1250–1350*
78 Mary Carruthers (ed.) *Rhetoric Beyond Words: Delight and Persuasion in the Arts of the Middle Ages*
79 Katharine Breen *Imagining an English Reading Public, 1150–1400*
80 Antony J. Hasler *Court Poetry in Late Medieval England and Scotland: Allegories of Authority*

81 Shannon Gayk *Image, Text, and Religious Reform in Fifteenth-Century England*
82 Lisa H. Cooper *Artisans and Narrative Craft in Late Medieval England*
83 Alison Cornish *Vernacular Translation in Dante's Italy: Illiterate Literature*
84 Jane Gilbert *Living Death in Medieval French and English Literature*
85 Jessica Rosenfeld *Ethics and Enjoyment in Late Medieval Poetry: Love after Aristotle*

OHIO UNIVERSITY LIBRARY
Please return thi